T0272187

Eighteenth-century Scottish theologians reflected on the legacy received from their predecessors of the long Reformation era, the subject of Professor Donald Macleod's authoritative earlier study, *Therefore the Truth I Speak: Scottish Theology 1500-1700*. This successor volume begins with chapters on Thomas Boston, the influential author of Human Nature in its Fourfold State, covers the *Marrow* controversy about the relationship of repentance and faith, examines the doctrinal views of the Seceders, analyses the branch of Reformed theology known as Hypothetical Universalism and discusses the rise of the Moderate opinions that challenged Evangelical convictions. Professor Macleod is careful to provide an account of the authors of the day as well as of their doctrinal positions. He also has a practical purpose, to expound the teaching of the eighteenth century about the experience of grace so as to give insight into the same experience in the twenty-first century.

DAVID BEBBINGTON
Emeritus Professor of History, University of Stirling, Scotland

From the Marrow Men to the Moderates continues the story of the Scottish church begun in *Therefore the Truth I Speak*. This second volume traces it from the days of Thomas Boston through the *Marrow* Controversy, the Secession, and the remarkable James Fraser of Brea, to the rise of Moderatism. This is Scottish Church history and theology as only the late Donald Macleod could tell it. In these to-be-treasured pages his unmatched knowledge of Scotland's pastor-theologians combines with an obvious love for both them and their theology. And all this is expressed with the vibrancy and at times sheer exhilaration of his writing. We are grateful that although writing through days of personal weakness Professor Macleod managed to sustain his own interest to the end in order to attract our attention to men and issues that were great because the gospel itself is so great. In this he wonderfully succeeded. His own shrewd analysis of the twists and turns of the Scottish Church, coupled with cameo portraits of men whose Christian ministries were marked by equal measures of spirituality and struggle, simply add to the enjoyment of these pages. This is a thrilling book, and sympathetic readers will almost certainly feel that its one major disappointment is that it comes to an end.

SINCLAIR B. FERGUSON
Chancellor's Professor of Systematic Theology, Reformed Theological Seminary

Donald Macleod has added to an illustrious writing career this tremendous volume on Scottish theology during the eighteenth century. Anyone interested in the rich and consequential history of the Scottish church will benefit immensely from this well-written, deeply learned, carefully judicious, and engrossing work. It is superb from start to finish. Surely, this series of volumes is destined to become a standard work in the field of Scottish ecclesiastical history and theology.

KEVIN DEYOUNG
Senior Pastor, Christ Covenant Church (PCA), Matthews, North Carolina;
Associate Professor of Systematic Theology, Reformed Theological Seminary,
Charlotte, North Carolina

From *the* Marrow Men *to the* Moderates

Scottish Theology 1700-1800

Donald Macleod

MENTOR

Copyright © Donald Macleod 2023

Paperback ISBN 978-1-5271-1048-9

Ebook ISBN 978-1-5271-1107-3

Published in 2023

by

Christian Focus Publications Ltd,
Geanies House, Fearn, Ross-shire,
IV20 1TW, Scotland.

www.christianfocus.com

CIP catalogue record for this book is available from the British Library.

Cover design by Daniel Van Straaten

Printed by Bell & Bain, Glasgow

CONTENTS

Foreword

I CAN HEAR his voice when I read him.

In the autumn of 1987, I began my studies at the University of Edinburgh. Fresh out of seminary in the U.S., I was excited to learn more of the riches of Scottish theology. Though my doctoral work would be spent in the world of the early church, I had been interested in the theologians of Scotland since my childhood (I am a Duncan after all). Here I was in Scotland, on the Mound in Edinburgh, near so much history, near the graves of so many heroes, near so many resources for the study of Scottish church history and theology, surrounded by so much expertise on the subject, it could not help but become something far more than an avocation.

Like many who are picking up this book, I had been helped by works like John Macleod's *Scottish Theology in relation to Church History* (which has been kept in print off and on by various publishers over the last eighty years), and James Walker's *The Theology and Theologians of Scotland, 1560–1750* (given as the Cunningham Lectures at New College in 1870-71). My interest had been stimulated by hearing the preaching of well-known Scottish ministers and theologians like Eric Alexander and Sinclair Ferguson. In seminary, I had been inspired and instructed in the subject by an able historical theologian, David B. Calhoun, who spent a good bit of time on Scottish theology in his 'History of the Reformed Tradition' course, as well as in his 'Reformation and Modern Church History' overview. But now I was at New College. Its library beckoning me. And next door: The Free Church of Scotland College (now known as Edinburgh Theological Seminary).

I asked and received permission to audit Donald Macleod's Systematic Theology lectures, which I did for the next two years. I also went to numerous public lectures that he offered. I heard him expound Dickson, Durham, Rutherford, Gillespie, Traill, Bruce, Boston, Guthrie,

Cunningham, Chalmers and others in the course of his teaching, often engaging with their thought, and explaining the debates of their times. I visited him in his office, seeking to learn more, peppering him with questions, gleaning every crumb of insight I could catch. But it was in church under his ministry of the Word that I especially learned the heartbeat of his theology.

The first time I heard Donald Macleod preach was a communion sermon in Edinburgh in October of 1987. I will never forget it, though it was half a lifetime ago. For many years I could recite the whole thing almost verbatim. Even now, four decades later, I can give you most of it. I have never heard a more powerful exposition of the love of God. The truths that I had heard him carefully formulate and explain in the classroom, were proclaimed with melting intensity in the pulpit: the perfect fusion of heat and light.

The things that I learned from him, in pulpit and classroom, were not only informative but formative. He not only shaped my thinking in terms of theological assessment and discernment, but had a profound effect on me experientially in terms of my understanding of God and the Christian life, of Christ and the Gospel.

Since that time I have had the joy of republishing a number of his shorter works, including *The Humiliated and Exalted Lord* (from lectures that he gave at a Theological Studies Fellowship conference in Swanwick, Derbyshire, England in the mid-1970s, that had been previously appeared under the title *Philippians 2 and Christology*) and *Shared Life: The Trinity and the Fellowship of God's People*, a wonderful, brief, popular treatment of the doctrine of the Trinity (now happily kept in print by Christian Focus Publications). I have also commended (and sometimes required!) dozens of his articles to my students at Reformed Theological Seminary over the years.

For instance, no student has escaped my Covenant Theology course without reading Donald's seminal *Banner of Truth* articles on 'Covenant' (*Banner of Truth*, 141:22-28), 'Federal Theology – An Oppressive Legalism?' (125:21-28), 'The Lord's Supper as a Means of Grace' (64:16-22), 'Qualifications for Communion' (65:14-20) and 'The Real Presence' (66:13-16) or his superb entry on 'Covenant Theology' in the *Dictionary of Scottish Church History and Theology*, 214-218. And I myself have re-listened to hundreds of his sermons and lectures. His unique tone of voice and Lewis accent is imprinted upon the ear of my mind and heart.

So, when I read these pages, I can still hear him. Even as I read I remember hearing bits and pieces of the thoughts of this book coming out in his lectures, and wishing I had more. Then, I read the first volume *Therefore the Truth I Speak: Scottish Theology 1500–1700*, and I wished I had more. I subsequently had the privilege of interviewing Donald (along with Sinclair Ferguson and Doug Kelly) on Scottish Theology in 2020, and even then I wished I had more. Indeed, I urged him to keep writing, to give us more. Now, as I read this book, I wish I had more. But for that, I will have to wait. On May 21 of this year, his pilgrim days were ended, and his faith became sight.

What you are thus holding is not only the mature assessment of a crucial era in Scottish church history and theology by one of Scotland's most important contemporary theologians but his last word. As Macleod himself tells you in the preface, he does not write as a disinterested observer, but with the aim of helping us to conserve 'what is best in our theological past,' and to provide 'a resource and stimulus as a new generation seeks to re-form the church: not to match the tastes of a new age, but to meet its needs.'

As he wrote, he knew the end was near. The sands of time were sinking. His moment of opportunity was fleeting. He wanted to have a last word with us, and to think with us (in the words of his hero Thomas Chalmers) of 'the littleness of time' and of 'the greatness of eternity.'

I will now read him, and hear him, again. And wish I had more.

LIGON DUNCAN
Reformed Theological Seminary
Jackson, Mississippi, USA
Summer, 2023

Preface

A PREVIOUS VOLUME, *Therefore the Truth I Speak*, sought to trace the thinking of key figures in Scotland's Reformed tradition from its beginnings with Patrick Hamilton and George Wishart in the sixteenth century to the Episcopalian Calvinist, Robert Leighton, at the close of the seventeenth. This volume continues the story, but it is a story of discontinuity as well as continuity. The approach of Thomas Boston and Ebenezer Erskine is of a piece with that of their seventeenth-century predecessors, John Knox, Samuel Rutherford and David Dickson. The thought of Principal William Robertson and the Moderates is not. Not only do the doctrinal emphases change: in the wake of the Enlightenment those who were honoured in the seventeenth century as thinkers, preachers and martyrs, come to be pilloried in the eighteenth as vulgar, semi-literate fanatics; and as the Moderates began to apply the Patronage Act of 1712 with increasing rigour they made it their business to ensure that Scottish pulpits were occupied by men whose primary qualification was not that they were distinguished by piety and evangelistic zeal, but that they were acceptable to the landed gentry and to others reputed to be people of culture and fine taste. The result was a Kirk divided into two parties, the Moderates (favoured by the gentry) and the evangelicals (favoured by the people, and hence commonly referred to as the Popular Party);[1] and although the lines were not always clearly drawn, the division was clear enough in the General Assembly, where the two parties sat opposite one another in the adversarial manner of the modern House of Commons.

---

1.   For a more comprehensive overview of eighteenth-century Scottish evangelicalism, see John R. McIntosh, *Church and Theology in Enlightenment Scotland: The Popular Party, 1740–1800* (East Linton: Tuckwell, 1998).

The century also saw the first major breach in the Church of Scotland, when Ebenezer Erskine's protest against patronage led to the Secession of 1733; and although the original secession involved only four ministers, they drew after them thousands of the rural peasantry and thousands more of the urban artisans. It was a blow from which the Kirk never recovered, not only because the Secession tore the heart out of many congregations, but because it introduced into parish life an inter-denominational rivalry which made it easy for the disaffected to play off the one against the other; and once the first fateful step was taken, it created a precedent which was all too easy to follow. Schism ceased to be unthinkable, other secessions followed, and even the Seceders themselves divided into further groups as suspicious of each other as they were of the Established Church.

As with the previous volume, many deserving names have had to be omitted, most notably John Maclaurin and John Erskine, both of whom remained loyal to the legacy of Reformed Orthodoxy while at the same time adjusting to the changing cultural environment. Both realised that the doctrines of Knox and the Covenanters were no longer accepted unquestioningly by their fellow countrymen. Deism and the Enlightenment had raised serious issues, created a distaste for religious enthusiasm, and bred a new generation of 'cultured despisers' of the historic Protestant creed. Maclaurin and Erskine show a keen awareness of the change in the religious atmosphere and of the doubts, reservations, and difficulties which were now likely to be troubling their hearers. They realised that the pulpit must address the prevailing prejudices against the gospel; and even as they preach on something so central as the cross, you can almost hear them reminding themselves that not everyone now takes for granted the doctrine of redemption by the blood of Christ. The result is a style of delivery better adapted to changes in taste, and a new, more apologetic note, reflecting their belief that they are called not only to proclaim the gospel but to offer a defence of it and to remove prejudices against its reception.

But despite the sterling orthodoxy and apologetical sensitivity of Maclaurin and Erskine, they were not game-changers in the sense that Ebenezer Erskine and William Robertson were; nor did they, like Fraser of Brae, introduce any novelty into Scottish theology or, like John Brown of Broughton Place, set a new course for biblical exegesis. Even so, they deserve a place in Scottish theology's hall of fame, and omitting them leaves me feeling distinctly uneasy.

It is not only historic Reformed theology that today labours under a cloud of suspicion, however. Many question the value of history itself as an academic discipline. Henry Ford famously declared that, 'History is more or less bunk'; the German philosopher, Hegel, asserted that, 'The one thing we learn from history is that we learn nothing from history'; and the distinguished Oxford historian, H. A. L. Fisher, lamented in the Preface to his acclaimed *History of Europe,* 'Men wiser and more learned than I have discovered in history a plot, a rhythm, a predetermined pattern. These harmonies are concealed from me.' There is, he added, only one safe rule for the historian: 'he should acknowledge in the development of human destinies the play of the contingent and the unforeseen.'[2]

But before we dismiss the study of history as of little value to the preacher or theologian, we should pause to remind ourselves of the prominent part it plays in the biblical revelation. God could have chosen to reveal Himself by means of propositions, proverbs, poetry, allegories, epistles, and theological treatises; and He has, of course, made conspicuous use of all of these. For the most part, however, He has chosen to reveal His Name through historical narratives. This is most obvious in the Old Testament, which begins with the story of Abraham, Isaac and Jacob, proceeds to the drama of the Exodus, continues through the history of David and his family, and concludes with an account of Israel once again in captivity and exile. All the rest of the Old Testament, including the Psalms and the Prophets, is clearly set within this unfolding historical narrative, and the New Testament follows the same pattern. The gospels are historical narratives, closely bound up with the contemporary history of Palestine, and only through these narratives can we learn anything of the person and mission of Jesus Christ; Acts tells the story of the infant church, freshly empowered by the Holy Spirit, and yet clearly influenced by both the opportunities and the challenges presented by contemporary world-history; the apostolic epistles are all addressed to specific historical churches, each existing in a fallen world and each reflecting the pressures of their own time and place.

It is through this narrative, with all its fascinating characters, all its high points, and all its low points, that God has built His reputation, and only by studying it carefully can we come to know His Name and then proceed to hallow it.

---

2. H. A. L. Fisher, *A History of Europe* (London: Edward Arnold, 1936), p. v.

The history of the post-apostolic church cannot likewise claim to be the story of an ongoing divine revelation. Its pastors and teachers hold no direct apostolic commission, nor do they describe their writings as holy scriptures breathed out by God (2 Tim. 3:16). Instead, far from providing us with fresh divine revelation, they themselves were, and are, subject to the Canon of Scripture. There the faith had been delivered once and for all, and the mandate of later preachers, theologians, and church councils was not to add to it, but to expound it.

But it is precisely in our role as expositors that historical theology is invaluable because it means that we don't need to start at the beginning all over again. Others have gone before us: many of them, like Augustine, Aquinas, Luther and Calvin, among the most spiritually minded and brilliant intellects of their age. Between them they forged a long tradition of biblical exegesis and exposition: a tradition embodied not only in countless vernacular versions of Scripture, but also in a veritable treasure-trove of creeds, commentaries, homilies, treatises and hymns.

The result is that the modern Christian theologian is in a similar position to the modern scientist, who sees the data of the visible world, not only through their own powers of observation, but also in the light of the 'laws' already discovered by Archimedes, Copernicus, Isaac Newton, Michael Faraday, James Clerk Maxwell, Albert Einstein, and Marie Curie. The discoveries of these giants underlie all the research currently being conducted by physicists, chemists, biologists, and geneticists all over the world; and every twenty-first-century preacher and theologian similarly owes a massive debt to antiquity. Wisdom did not begin with us, and while content to be mere expositors, we bring to that task the witness of past ages. When we begin, we are already in possession of the doctrines which the early Church Fathers and the Reformers enshrined in their creeds, confessions, and voluminous writings: doctrines such as the Trinity, the Deity of Christ, Justification by Faith alone, and the Sovereignty of Divine Grace, to mention but a few. This doesn't mean that such doctrines can never be revisited or reformulated, any more than Einstein was forbidden to question the theories of Newton. But it does mean that until they are falsified, the theological gains of the past remain as paradigms which we bring to the interpretation of every individual biblical text; and it means too that, rather than repeatedly fighting past battles, we are free to address fresh challenges and to explore theological themes which have hitherto lain neglected.

But the task of historical theologians is not finished when they have merely given a faithful account of the theological discussions of the past (including the social, economic, ethnic, and personal factors which have influenced these discussions). They must also venture, in all humility, to subject these discussions, and the conclusions they led to, to a theological evaluation. The authority of great names, or even Ecumenical Councils, is never enough. We have to move on to ask, Were their positions justified in the light of Scripture? And even as we ask that question, we are conscious that our own understanding of Scripture is fallible and subject to review by our peers. But we must still venture.

I am grateful to Christian Focus, and especially to the Reverend Malcolm Maclean, my Editor, for their continuing encouragement and advice. The religious face of Scotland has changed dramatically even while this work has been in progress, but I hope and pray that it may make some small contribution to conserving what is best in our theological past, and to providing a resource and stimulus as a new generation seeks to re-form the church: not to match the tastes of a new age, but to meet its needs. Let them remember, however, how brief is our moment of opportunity:

> Frail as summer flower we flourish;
> Blows the wind and it is gone;
> But while mortals rise and perish,
> God endures unchanging on.

DONALD MACLEOD
April 2023

1

Thomas Boston: the Man and His Ministry

WHEN THOMAS BOSTON was born in 1676 the Stuart policy of violent repression against the popular religion of Scotland was approaching the height of its ferocity; and so, too, was the passion of popular resistance. Ministers who refused to subscribe to prelacy were still being outed from their congregations; those of them who then dared to preach at field-conventicles faced the death penalty (Donald Cargill was executed in 1681, James Renwick in 1688); people who attended such conventicles risked eviction, transportation or imprisonment; peasants who hesitated to swear their wholehearted belief in the royal supremacy when challenged by the dragoons faced summary execution (the Wigtown Martyrs, Margaret Wilson and Margaret Lauchlison were drowned in the waters of the Solway in April 1685; John Brown of Priesthill was shot by Claverhouse's dragoons in the presence of his wife and children that same year).

But the reaction was not confined to defiant field-preaching. The right to bear arms against tyrants had long been an established principle in Scottish theology, and it was reasserted unambiguously by such later Covenanters as John Brown of Wamphray and Alexander Shields.[1] Archbishop Sharp, the arch-advocate of repression, was assassinated in 1679; Richard Cameron's *Sanquhar Declaration* of June 1680 disowned the authority of Charles II and protested against the succession to the throne of his brother, James, Duke of York; after Cameron was killed when he and his small band were

---

1. John Brown, *An Apologetical Relation of the Particular Sufferings of the Faithful Ministers and Professors of the Church of Scotland since August 1660* (Rotterdam, 1665. Reprinted in *The Presbyterian's Armoury*, Edinburgh: Ogle and Oliver and Boyd, 1846, Vol. 3); Alexander Shields, *A Hind Let Loose: an Historical Representation of the Testimonies of the Church of Scotland* (Utrecht: 1687).

overtaken by a detachment of dragoons in July 1680, his mantle fell on James Renwick, whose *Apologetical Declaration* (1684) was a declaration of war against any who actively obstructed them in their pursuit of 'the ends of their covenants'.[2] Renwick himself was executed on 17 February 1688, the last martyr of the Covenant.

These events all took place in Boston's childhood, but by the time he was ordained to his first charge, Simprin in Berwickshire, in 1699, the situation in Scotland had changed dramatically. The last of the Stuarts, James II/VII, had been forced into exile in December 1688, the Glorious Revolution had led to William of Orange being installed as King of the United Kingdom in 1689, and as part of the Revolution settlement prelacy had been abolished, Presbyterianism established, and the Westminster Confession confirmed as 'the public and avowed confession' of the Kirk. From that point onwards, Scotland's religious wars, such as they were, would be fought on paper and in the courts of the church, leaving men like Boston free to shepherd their flocks in comparative peace. In the course of a ministry which lasted from 1699 to 1732 he would publish one of the enduring classics of Scottish theology, *Human Nature in its Fourfold State*; play a key role in the major doctrinal debate of the eighteenth century, the *Marrow* controversy; and earn himself, almost incidentally, a reputation as one of the most influential figures of our theological history.

But he would do so despite having to work in the most unfavourable circumstances. For one thing, he was not a man of outstanding intellectual gifts. This is not to say that he was not able, but he was not in the first rank, compared to, for example, a Thomas Chalmers or a Jonathan Edwards. 'Rabbi' Duncan called him 'a commonplace genius' and Hugh Miller declared that he was by no means superior to such later Moderates as William Robertson and Hugh Blair, and far inferior to them as a writer.[3] Such judgements need not be taken as canonical, though it has to be said that if Scottish theologians were to be judged solely on the quality of their writing few would figure in any Hall of Fame. But as Miller himself points out, however inferior Boston

---

2. For extracts from the *Apologetical Relation*, see William Croft Dickinson and Gordon Donaldson (eds.,), *A Source Book of Scottish History*, Vol. III (2nd. Edition, Edinburgh: Thomas Nelson, 1961), p. 181. Renwick makes plain that their 'war' was not against those who merely differ from them in 'judgement and persuasion', but against the 'cruel and bloodthirsty', particularly the justiciary and the military, and their informers.

3. Hugh Miller, *The Headship of Christ*, p. 229.

might be as a stylist (and that's debatable), he stood in far higher repute among the common people of Scotland than any of the *literati* who ever occupied Scottish pulpits; and the reason for this is clear. It was the common people he addressed, and it was to their piety he gave voice; and this, rather than any inferiority on Boston's part, is the real reason why modern heirs of the Scottish Enlightenment dismiss him with contempt. It is not his style, but his message, that prompted such scholars as David Daiches (clearly writing at second-hand) to portray him as a man obsessed with the fate of the damned.[4] They wanted a 'kindlier' tale, beautifully told, but not the truth.

Another remarkable feature in the background to Boston's ministry was that he never in his lifetime occupied a central or national position. He served two parishes in the Borders, Simprin and Ettrick, both small, both rural, and both peripheral. Simprin was, in his own words, 'remote and inconsiderable': indeed, so inconsiderable that at one point he suggests that no one in the town had to walk more than a few paces to get to church. Some of his colleagues, he wrote, 'thought me happy because I had so few people. Some thought me wretched because I had such a poor stipend.'[5] Even so, he had to wait a long time before even this door opened to him. We are inclined to assume that patronage came into the Kirk only after the Union, when a perfidious United Kingdom parliament passed the infamous Patronage Act of 1712. In reality, it had been established practice before the Reformation, and although condemned by both the First and the Second Books of Discipline it had never been eradicated and would persist in the Established Church until 1874. Boston was one of its victims. Licensed on 15 June 1697 he was clearly not to the taste of heritors, and had to wait more than two years before he was ordained. He was not the sort of man to compromise in order to secure preferment, and he made no attempt to ingratiate himself with those who were in a position to advance his career. Although naturally diffident to an extreme, his diffidence left him when he entered the pulpit, and he himself admitted that he did his cause no good by not bowing to the heritors when he entered the pulpit, preaching on

---

4. David Daiches, *God and the Poets: the Gifford Lectures, 1983* (Oxford: Clarendon Press, 1984), pp. 136-37.

5. *Memoirs of the Life, Times, and Writings of Thomas Boston of Ettrick. Written by Himself* (1776. New edition, Glasgow: John McNeilage, 1899, p. 125). The *Memoirs* also occupy the whole of Volume XII of *The Complete Works of the Late Rev Thomas Boston* (12 vols., 1853. Reprinted Stoke-on-Trent: Tentmaker Publications, 2002).

themes others avoided, speaking out on the sins of the land, and refusing to socialise after the Sabbath's work was done. He felt no bitterness, however: indeed, he thought the patrons were often right. He was not their man, recording on one occasion, 'I do believe that they and I both agreed that, in respect of my temper and way, I was not for the parish of Clackmannan.'[6] In the end, he was grateful for Simprin, having concluded that, 'if I was at all to be admitted to the holy ministry, it should be at Simprin, as unfit for a more considerable post.'[7] Ettrick, to which he was called in 1707, was little better, but he contented himself with the thought that, 'though it was a small charge, yet it was *my* charge,' and it was his duty to minister to those to whom God had called him, whether many or few.[8]

It is notable, too, that in his own day Boston was never a star preacher who drew great crowds. Even in his own parish few saw his worth. 'In the visiting of the parish,' he records in 1712, 'I was much discouraged. The ministry of this church [Ettrick] is like to die unlamented. I have no sympathy from any of my people, or next to none.'[9] Nor was he at all lionised by his clerical colleagues. He was on the losing side in the *Marrow* controversy, and generally found himself swimming against the tide, and forced to dissent from decisions of the General Assembly. He was not alone in feeling alone, of course. Others, too, felt disillusioned and marginalised, and although Boston had died the year before the Secession of 1733 it was his friends that led it; and his own son, Thomas Boston the younger, left the Church of Scotland in 1757, and in 1761 became co-founder (with Thomas Gillespie) of the Relief Church.

But what troubled him the most, especially in the early years, was that he had so few books. He comforted himself with the assurance that though he lacked commentaries, 'a heavenly frame of spirit, and soul-exercise … were two excellent commentators,'[10] but nevertheless he never forgot the day a neighbouring minister looked at his little bookcase and sneered at its contents. Nor did he forget the day when, on his way to preach, he noticed a student of Divinity among those entering the church.

---

6. *Memoirs*, p. 40.
7. ibid., p. 80.
8. ibid., p. 203, italics added.
9. ibid., p. 254.
10. ibid., p. 118.

His heart sank, because he hadn't been able to give his text the detailed attention a commentary would have afforded. The student would not be impressed. However, the library began to build up, albeit slowly. Within a year he possessed a copy of *De oeconomia foederum*, the *magnum opus* of 'the evangelical Witsius'.[11] By 1706 he possessed a four-volume edition of the *Works* of Turretine, and in 1707 he purchased Poole's *Annotations* (a commentary covering the whole Bible), but only ten years after his induction to Simprin did he become the happy possessor of a Hebrew Bible. He notes, too, the purchase of a book of sermons by Thomas Manton: he had bought it because it contained some sermons on Philippians 3:3, on which he was preaching at the time. By the time he came to write his *Notes on the Marrow of Modern Divinity* (1721–22) he had clearly read widely. This would make an interesting study in its own right, but it certainly included Luther, Calvin, Zanchius, Polanus, Peter Martyr, Mastricht, William Ames, John Ball, Ursinus, Downham, Grotius, Reynolds, John Preston, Burroughs, Thomas Goodwin, as well as such Scottish writers as Patrick Hamilton, John Davidson, Robert Rollock, Thomas Halyburton and Knox's *History of the Reformation*.

His pursuit of books had its ups-and-downs, however. On one occasion, he was awaiting a parcel as eagerly as a man expecting to receive a fortune, only to be told that the parcel had been lost. He took it as God's chastisement, and submitted. Eventually, however, the lost treasure was found, and delivered.

Why, then, considering all the disadvantages under which he laboured, is Thomas Boston's one of the best-known names in Scottish theology? The simple answer is that he left behind him a considerable body of literature, little of which was published in his own lifetime, but which, when eventually collected, filled twelve large volumes; and this legacy was of such a quality that it has had both an enduring and an extensive influence.[12]

This corpus, well-nigh the largest in the history of Scottish theology, reflected Boston's untiring diligence. Having the care of only small parishes, it would have been tempting to skimp on his sermon-preparation, to talk down to his rural congregations, and to avoid the profounder themes of the Christian faith. Boston didn't fall into any of these traps. Instead, he regarded

---

11. ibid., p. 115.

12. *The Complete Works of the Late Rev. Thomas Boston, Ettrick*, 12 vols., ed. Samuel M'Millan (Aberdeen: 1848–52. Reprinted Stoke-on-Trent: Tentmaker Publications, 2002).

the smallness of his parishes as a God-given opportunity to engage in earnest study,[13] and in this resolve he never wavered, whatever the inconveniences. One summer, when a new manse was being built (and the old had, presumably, been demolished), he studied in either the stable or the barn. He also decided at an early point in his ministry to write out all his sermons in full; and not only his sermons, but his conclusions on every other subject which captured his attention. He had an active and restless intellect which left him incapable of giving up on any question till he had thought it through to a resolution; and once resolved it was committed to writing. It is to this habit that we owe, for example, his series of studies, *Miscellaneous Questions,* including the influential, 'Who have a right to baptism, and are to be baptised?'[14]

Boston was also given to setting himself goals. In his early days at Simprin he set himself to learn French. Later he turned to Hebrew and, in the opinion of John Macleod, became the most thorough student of the Hebrew Bible that Scotland produced in his day.[15] He certainly achieved such proficiency that the Hebrew Bible became his delight. Later still, some time around 1716, he became fascinated with the Hebrew accents. We now know that these accents are not original but were added by the Masoretes, successive generations of Jewish scholars who, in the years between A.D. 600 and A.D. 1000, sought to establish the definitive text of the Hebrew Bible. In its original form that text consisted only of consonants, but the Masoretes added two additional features: vowel-points, to define pronunciation, and accents to indicate where the stress should be placed in chanting. Boston, however, had assumed that the accents went back close to the original, and he was profoundly disturbed when he discovered that Louis Cappell (1585–1658), Professor of Hebrew at the Protestant Seminary in France, had argued (and in the opinion of many,

---

13.   Smallness is relative, of course. Boston's congregations would not have been small by today's standards.

14.   See Boston, *Works,* Vol. 6, pp. 11-220. Jonathan Edwards was given to the same habit (see his 'Miscellaneous Observations on Important Theological Subjects' in *The Works of Jonathan Edwards,* 2 vols. 1834. Reprinted Edinburgh: Banner of Truth Trust, 1974, Vol. 2, pp. 459-51). Cf. George Gillespie, *A Treatise of Miscellany Questions* (1639. Reprinted in *The Presbyterian's Armoury;* 3 Vols., Edinburgh, 1846; Vol. II [The Treatise runs to 122 pages, but with separate pagination within the volume]).

15.   John Macleod, *Scottish Theology in relation to Church History since the Reformation* (1943. Second edition 1946, reprinted Edinburgh: Banner of Truth Trust, 2015), p. 157. James Walker describes Boston as 'one of the great figures in our theological history' (James Walker, *The Theology and Theologians of Scotland 1560–1750;* Second Edition revised, 1888. Reprinted Edinburgh: Knox Press [Edinburgh], 1982, p. 30).

demonstrated) that the accents were of much more recent origin, having been inserted by the Masoretes only in the fifth century.[16] As always, Boston addressed the question vigorously, and came to the conclusion that, *contra* Cappell, 'the accents are the true key to the genuine version and sense of the Hebrew text, and that they are divine.'[17] As ever, Boston committed his conclusions to writing, and the result was a Latin treatise, *Tractatus Stigmologicus Hebraicus*, published posthumously (1738) in Amsterdam. The *Tractatus* has long been forgotten, but Boston was not entirely wrong. As Bruce Waltke points out, the accents not only help to beautify the chant; by denoting the stress of a word they can also clarify the meaning (Waltke cites the difference between the English 'pre-sént' and present). He also points out that the accents can signalise the connection between words, quoting as an example Isaiah 40:3, which, depending on the position of the stress can read either: *The voice of him that crieth in the wilderness, Prepare ...* or, *A voice of one calling: 'In the desert prepare ...'* (NIV).

The man himself

So then, out of Boston's study, in his small and marginal rural parish, came books which would one day be found in countless ordinary homes all over Scotland. But before we look at his writings, what of the man himself?

Boston was a Borderer, born in Duns in 1676. His father, a native of Ayr, had suffered for refusing to take the Abjuration Oath,[18] and Boston recalled going as a child to visit him in prison to keep him company. His father's piety influenced him profoundly, but he was also influenced by the preaching of Henry Erskine (the father of Ralph and Ebenezer), whom he heard preaching in the area of Duns when he was only twelve years old. Years later, he recalled some of Erskine's texts, and it is probably to this time we should date Boston's conversion. He became a student at Edinburgh University when only thirteen years old, and graduated in both Arts and Divinity, but seems to have owed little to the instruction offered by either department.

Those who seek a psychological profile of Boston will find abundant materials in his *Memoirs*, written in the first instance for his children, and completed in 1730, but first published only in 1776. He describes himself as

---

16. The oldest Masoretic manuscript goes back only to the ninth century.

17. Boston, *Memoirs*, p. 291.

18. Passed in 1664, the Oath required people to disown the policies of the Cameronians, who had renounced the authority of James VII.

diffident and 'little serviceable' in public affairs, and no less backward in conversation, being naturally silent. This bashfulness, he laments, had done him much harm, yet while always timid before he preached, he found that he was fearless once the door of the pulpit closed behind him.

But not only was he diffident and bashful, he was also a depressive, given to fits of melancholy. To some extent this was circumstantial. Boston had a difficult life, beginning with his father's imprisonment, followed by his long wait for a call, and then the challenges he faced in both his parishes. While the Revolution Settlement had put an end to Stuart persecution, not everyone was happy. In the south of Scotland in particular, there were many who were profoundly dissatisfied with the constitution of the church as settled in 1688. One reason for this was that there had been no formal vindication of the faithful Presbyterians who had contended so valiantly during the years of repression; another was that many of the curates who had been parties to the persecutions continued to occupy their pulpits without any profession of repentance. But what caused the deepest resentment was that the Revolution Settlement refused to acknowledge the continuing obligation of the national covenants (the National Covenant of 1638 and the Solemn League and Covenant of 1643). This was no merely academic matter. It meant, in the view of the disaffected, that the principles which had been enshrined in these documents were vulnerable to change; and these included the divine right of Presbytery and the spiritual independence of the church. Later developments, and particularly the passing of the Act of Patronage by the UK Parliament in 1712, would show that these concerns were not without foundation. Nor were the misgivings confined to the church settlement. Some also denied the lawfulness of the constitutional settlement on the two related grounds that the existing civil rulers lacked the qualifications laid down in the Word of God, and that they were not committed to the covenants the nation had sworn in 1638 and 1643.[19]

These dissident views had their roots in the field-preaching of Donald Cargill, Richard Cameron and James Renwick, whose followers, alienated from the church, formed themselves into 'societies' for prayer, fellowship and testimony. These societies later came together in a loose association known as 'the United Societies', and those who adhered to them as the 'Society people' (or, after the Revolution, as 'Cameronians').

---

19. *The Correspondence of the Rev. Robert Wodrow*, Vol. 1, ed. Thomas M'Crie (Edinburgh: Wodrow Society, 1842) p. 51 fn. Hereafter *Wodrow's Correspondence*, Vol. 1.

When Boston came to Ettrick in 1707, he found that several families in the parish were among those who dissented from the Revolution Settlement, dissociated themselves from the Kirk, and adhered instead to the ministry of the Reverend John MacMillan (1669–1753). From his student days, MacMillan had shown a clear sympathy with the 'Society people', but despite these sympathies, he trained for the ministry of the Church of Scotland and was inducted to the parish of Balmaghie in Kirkcudbrightshire in 1701. He remained, however, a persistent and vociferous critic of the Revolution Settlement, highlighting what he regarded as the defections of the church, and was deposed in 1703 for refusing to retract a paper of 'grievances' he had presented to the Presbytery of Kirkcudbright. In 1706 he accepted a call to be the Minister of the Covenanting Societies, and he served as their only minister till he was joined by Thomas Nairn in 1743. Together, they then formed the Reformed Presbytery.[20]

MacMillan had a wide following, scattered throughout the south of Scotland, and he had no conscience about extending that following by alienating people from their parish ministers. It is often the case with such self-appointed prophets, however, that they choose as their special targets, not the openly heretical and ungodly, but those whose soundness and piety present the greatest obstacle to the progress of their own party. This was to be Boston's fate. MacMillan made a point of preaching frequently in his neighbourhood, and sometimes within the bounds of his parish; MacMillan publicly confuted points Boston had made in his sermons; he visited the homes of Boston's people, portraying him as an enemy, and even as a liar. The result was that Boston had to suffer the presence among his hearers of those who were openly disaffected; and then, in 1708, many left him for good after he had observed a Fast appointed, not by the Church, but by the Government. Worst of all, perhaps, it became a distraction. When attendances were low, he concluded it was because people had forsaken him to go and hear MacMillan; when there was a 'throng', 'I really thought some had the [sic] rather come out that day that I might see they were not gone to his meeting.'[21]

On top of all this Boston had domestic sorrows which were severe even by the standards of the eighteenth century. His wife, née Catherine Brown,

---

20. See DSCHT, 'MacMillan, John'. Wodrow 1.51, 67. *Early Letters*, p. 281.
21. *Memoirs*, p. 247.

became ill six weeks into their marriage and never recovered. For the last ten years of his life she was confined to bed, and he lived in constant anxiety that she might be taken from him at any time. They married on 7 July 1700, and he has left a remarkable pen-portrait of her: a portrait of romance tinged with comedy. 'A woman of great worth,' he wrote,

> whom I therefore passionately loved, and inwardly honoured: A stately, beautiful and comely personage, truly pious and fearing the Lord, of an evenly temper, patient in our common tribulations, and under her personal distresses: A woman of bright natural parts, an uncommon stock of prudence; of a quick and lively apprehension, great presence of mind in surprising incidents; sagacious and acute in discerning the qualities of persons.[22]

There is more in the same romantic vein,[23] but the attraction wasn't entirely romantic. To an earlier eulogy he had added, 'and that I reckoned her very fit to see to my health'[24] (her father being a physician and she herself being skilled 'in physic and surgery')[25]. This reflects Boston's life-long concerns with his health, and his tendency towards hypochondria. At one point he even took the step (amusing or drastic, depending on one's point of view) of cutting-off his hair and wearing a wig; but whatever this did for his health, he eventually found it troublesome 'when going abroad' and so, he writes, 'I betook me to my own hair.'[26] In the event, however, it was his wife's health, not his, that filled their married life with anxiety: so much so that when he left home on a preaching engagement he worried that he might find on his return that she had passed away. Latterly, he even feared that he might find her dead when he returned to the manse after taking a service in the church.[27] Despite his fears, however (and, indeed all the signs), she outlived him by five years.

Yet his wife's chronic and often painful illness was not the only sadness Boston had to bear. Of his ten children, he buried all but four of them.

---

22. ibid. p. 149.

23. 'My difficulty,' he wrote early in their relationship, 'was not to get to love her, but rather to bound it' (ibid., p. 39).

24. ibid., p. 42.

25. ibid., p. 162.

26. ibid., p. 52. Despite his fragile health Boston notes in 1731 that he was never prevented from preaching through indisposition.

27. 'Sometimes I have gone with a trembling heart to the pulpit, laying my account with being called out of it to see her expire,' ibid., p. 149.

One infant took ill while he was away on a preaching engagement, and by the time he came back the funeral had already taken place. On another occasion, he was overwhelmed with sorrow when they nailed down the coffin because he had omitted to kiss the dust: a dust which, he believed, was united to Christ.

When we add the pain of his domestic circumstances to the seriousness with which Boston addressed the responsibilities of his office and the pain he felt over what he saw as declensions in the Church he loved, it is hardly surprising that he had moments of profound despondency. 'I found myself in great danger by melancholy,' he records one day in 1712, 'and was more broken that way than ever, and unless God would keep, there was no help from any other quarter.'[28] But he was very realistic about it, and while he knew by bitter experience that Christians are not immune to it, he certainly never saw it as either a product of grace or a friend of grace. On the contrary, 'Melancholy is an enemy to gifts and grace – a greater friend to unbelief, as I have often found in my own experience.'[29]

Boston's theology

So much of the man. But what of his theology? In his own lifetime only two of his works were published: *Human Nature in Its Fourfold State*, first published in 1720; and his edition of *The Marrow of Modern Divinity*, with copious notes, written in 1721–22, but published only in 1726; and although other individual compositions such as his *View of the Covenant of Grace* began to be published after his death, it was only in 1767 that the first relatively complete collection of his *Works* appeared. The definitive twelve-volume edition of the *Complete Works* had to wait, as we have seen, until the mid-nineteenth century (1848–1852).

By any standards, this is a considerable corpus, and it is as impressive in scope as it is in bulk. Critics such as David Daiches peddle the myth that Boston preached obsessively on the wrath of God, hell, and the destiny of the damned, all of it coloured by an uncompromising and constantly reiterated version of the Calvinist doctrine of predestination.[30] It was

28. ibid., p. 254.

29. ibid., p. 252.

30. David Daiches, *God and the Poets: The Gifford Lectures, 1983* (Oxford: Clarendon Press, 1985), pp. 134-35. It is too often overlooked that the doctrine allegedly driving Robert Wringhim, the main character of the novel, was not predestination, but

hardly surprising, Daiches suggests, that this, the staple theological diet of the Scottish peasantry, bred a culture of antinomianism: after all, if you are one of the elect, then whatever crimes you commit, they will not affect your final salvation. Then, for good measure, Daiches latches on to the coincidence between Boston being the Minister of Ettrick and the novelist, James Hogg, being the 'Ettrick Shepherd', to argue that Hogg's work, *Confessions of a Justified Sinner,*[31] reflects reports of Boston's preaching handed down through a hundred years of Ettrick tradition.

This suggests that Hogg's novel was an anti-Calvinist tract, reflecting his alienation from the Covenanting heritage of the Borders.[32] There is no evidence, however, that Hogg harboured anti-Calvinistic sentiments, and in any case the criticism does scant justice to the subtlety of his work. His job as a novelist was to tell a story, and he does so brilliantly; but we should hesitate to define the story as a 'study in' something or as a thinly disguised exercise in theological propaganda; and while his 'justified sinner,' Robert Wringhim, is a totally credible (if elusive) character, Hogg nowhere suggests that he is a typical product of Boston's style of preaching. He comes across as a one-off: a psychotic who has latched on to one particular religious idea, pushed it to what he thinks are its logical conclusions, and then used it to justify his own psychopathic behaviour.

This is not to say that the portrait of Wringhim has no connection with reality. We have all met religionists who have no pleasure but in opposition, just as we have met the malevolence that assures its victims that it has 'no aim but your own good', and the young convert who tells you that there are thirteen kinds of faith. But it is a huge leap from this to the conclusion that the antinomianism represented by Wringhim was a widespread and natural consequence of the Scottish pulpit.

What is really disappointing about Daiches' assessment of Boston's message is its lack of academic rigour. Even the most cursory glance at the Tables of Contents in Boston's twelve volumes should have alerted

---

justification, the key doctrine of the Lutheran Reformation. Calvin gladly appropriated it, but it was not he who 'discovered' it.

31. James Hogg, *The Private Memoirs and Confessions of a Justified Sinner* (1824. Reprinted Edinburgh: Canongate, 1994, with an Introduction and Notes by David Groves).

32. For a slightly fuller assessment of Hogg's novel, see Donald Macleod, 'Scottish Calvinism: A Dark, Repressive Force?' in the *Scottish Bulletin of Evangelical Theology*, Vol. 19, No. 2 (2001), pp. 200-04.

him to the breadth and variety of the Ettrick Preacher's interests. Yes, there are sermons on hell and on divine wrath, but though such subjects are not to our modern taste, they clearly featured in the preaching of both our Lord and His apostles, and in this respect, as in all others, Boston saw himself as no more than his Master's voice. Besides, far from giving the doctrine of hell undue prominence, he fell under censure (with others) for supporting the view (put forward in the *Marrow of Modern Divinity*) that the fear of hell was not a proper motive for Christian obedience.[33]

Of course, Boston's output was not confined to preaching, but even if we limit ourselves to his sermons, it is clear that his pulpit ministry covered the 'whole counsel of God'. There are series of sermons on the Ten Commandments,[34] the Sacraments,[35] and the Lord's Prayer.[36] There are splendid Christological series such as the eight discourses on 'Christ Jesus duly prized' (based on Philippians 3:8),[37] and another seven on 'The Christian Life Delineated'.[38] Many are straightforwardly evangelistic sermons, reflecting Boston's lifelong passion for the free offer of the gospel; but there are one-off sermons on such themes as the pleasures of real religion, the privileges of God's faithful servants, union with Christ, the necessity of self-denial, the evil of schism, governing the tongue, and loving our enemies. And there are some which border on the mystical, such as 'The Soul's Espousal to Christ'[39] and 'Mourning the Absence of Christ'.[40]

In sum, what we find in Boston's sermons is preaching which shows keen pastoral awareness and addresses the spiritual needs of his own time and place, and yet remains of enduring value because it is rooted in minute study of the Scriptures, extensive theological scholarship, and profound personal piety.

---

33. One of the propositions censured in the 1720 Act of the General Assembly condemning the *Marrow* was that, 'The Fear of Punishment, and Hope of Reward, [are] not allowed to be Motives of Believer's Obedience.'

34. Under the heading, 'The Moral Law the Rule of Man's Obedience' (*Works*, Vol. 2, pp. 59-374).

35. ibid., Vol. 2, pp. 460-526.

36. ibid., Vol. 2, pp. 526-645.

37. ibid., Vol. 4, pp. 125-95.

38. ibid., Vol. 10, pp. 489-636.

39. ibid., Vol. 4, pp. 22-31.

40. ibid., Vol. 4, pp. 60-67.

Boston's style

What of the style? Boston would probably have replied, 'Well, *what* of the style?' Hugh Miller compared him unfavourably with Hugh Blair (1718–1800), Minister of St Giles and Professor of Rhetoric and Belles Lettres at Edinburgh University in the heyday of the Enlightenment.[41] But judgements on style are notoriously subjective. Miller, himself well-immersed in Belles Lettres, was judging Boston by the standards of the Augustan period in English literature, and Boston was certainly no Joseph Addison or Jonathan Swift. Neither do his sermons reflect the great rolling periods of Miller's contemporary, Thomas Chalmers, best-selling author of his day; nor, indeed, the tightly-knit, painstaking prose of Miller himself. But then, who today reads Chalmers or, indeed, Miller? The truth is, Boston never saw himself as an artist, and it is hard to imagine him revising his draft and then revising the revision. He had something to say, and he aimed to say it, not elegantly but plainly; and when all is said and done, the reader seldom has to wrestle with a Boston sentence to make it yield its meaning.

A Soliloquy on the Art of Man-Fishing

Boston's first serious composition was his *Soliloquy on the Art of Man-Fishing*. It was written on the eve of his ordination to Simprin in September 1699 but was published only posthumously (1773).[42] As the title suggests, it is very much a discussion with himself as might be expected, and it begins by addressing the question whether he had an 'ordinary' call to preach the gospel, using the word 'ordinary' to distinguish the call to be a pastor (an 'ordinary' office) from the call to be a prophet or apostle ('extraordinary' offices), and it quickly becomes clear that Boston's understanding of the call had little about it of the mystical or of the 'irresistible compulsion'. Instead, he saw it as consisting, first of all, in the possession of the requisite gifts, such as an above-average knowledge of Christian doctrine, allied to 'some dexterity' in communicating that knowledge to others;[43] secondly,

---

41. Hugh Miller, *The Headship of Christ and the Rights of the Christian People* (4th edition, Edinburgh: William P. Nimmo, 1870), p. 229.

42. *Works*, Vol. 5, pp. 5-43. Quotations in this chapter are from an edition of the *Soliloquy* published in 1900 (Paisley and London: Alexander Gardner), with Introductory Note by Rev. D. D. F. Macdonald.

43. Earlier, however, he had cautioned that gifts alone would not do the business: 'A man may preach as an angel, and yet be useless' (*A Soliloquy on the Art of Man-Fishing,* p. 19. Further page-references will be given in brackets in the text).

in a willingness to take up the work, and of this he was in no doubt, remembering that ever since he was a boy at school he had desired to be a preacher of the gospel 'because of all men ministers were most taken up with spiritual things' (p. 61); and thirdly, and indispensably, in the call of the Church, especially when, as in his own case, the call (to Simprin) had come without any initiative on his own part. Boston would not have considered any amount of subjective certainty a call to the ministry. It was the call of the people that 'made my darkness as noon day' (p. 62).

Boston has little to say on such matters as sermon-preparation: he was after all, a comparative novice at this point, though he had been preaching regularly since being licensed two years previously. We do know, however, that he often struggled to settle on a text, that he made diligent use of commentaries (when he had them), and that early in his ministry he adopted the practice of writing out his sermons in full (though he does not appear to have delivered them by reading). He leaves us in no doubt, however, as to the high ideals he brought to his calling, stressing that as it is the business of a fisherman to catch fish, so it is the business of a preacher to catch souls. He hints, too, at the difference between a fisherman and an angler. To an angler, fishing is a fair-weather pursuit, but to the fisherman it is his livelihood, and 'a storm that will affright others they will venture on, that they may not lose their fish' (p. 28). In the years to come, Boston would often have to venture out when his mood and his circumstances made it hard to go and face the people. Yet go out he must: 'O my soul, refuse not any occasion of preaching when Christ calls thee to it' (p. 107). This is reminiscent of St Paul's injunction to Timothy, 'Preach the word; be ready in season and out of season' (2 Tim. 4:2).

The preacher, then, must never forget his errand, which is to labour to win souls to Christ. Even when not actively engaged in it, he is thinking about it, reflecting on what he is doing, pondering the reasons for failure and wondering what he could do better. Nor is this to be a matter of casual, undisciplined thought. The fisherman must *study* the species he hopes to catch, and in the same way the preacher must study the different species of sinners, where they lurk (hiding from the gospel), and the best means of catching them. For this, like the fisherman, he has his own special net, God's Word of peace and reconciliation; and here, at the very outset of his ministry, we find Boston's stress on what became the hallmark of his life and struggles: the free and universal offer of the gospel. The net is to be spread out ready to catch all that will come into it; or, as he expands it a few moments later, 'God excludes none from the benefits of the gospel that will not exclude themselves; it is free to all' (p. 29).

But the preacher knows, too, that every fish caught in the net struggles to get free. Some will just touch the net, raising your hopes, but they slip away never to be seen again. Others who seem to be well enmeshed, and even securely held, are too often lost. Why? the preacher asks. Is he using the wrong mesh: perhaps too wide, the warnings and invitations too vague and general, leaving the conscience untouched; or so narrow and intricate that the fish quickly turn away? Yet the true gospel preacher will persevere in the face of all such discouragements. Confident that the Holy Spirit can drive even the most profligate sinner into his net, he despairs of the conversion of none.

The *Soliloquy*, even though so inspirational and so laden with spiritual common sense, is, we must remember, the work of a young man and it reflects the natural assumption of youth that the main concern even of the pastor of a settled congregation must be to catch new converts. That will always be a high priority, not least in securing the allegiance to Christ of the children and young people of the congregation. But as St Paul made plain to the Ephesian elders (Acts 20:28), the pastor has a flock to feed, and this is where Boston's future strength would lie. He was no Whitefield or Spurgeon, though he had his own modicum of converts; and he would make a significant contribution to evangelism by the way that, particularly in the course of the *Marrow* controversy, he clarified the unconditional nature of the gospel and the freeness of gospel invitations. But the main charge laid on him as a preacher would be the same as the one the Lord laid on St Peter: 'Feed my lambs. Feed my sheep' (John 21:15-17).

The Crook in the Lot

There is a fine example of Boston's pastoral ministry in one of his last compositions, *The Crook in the Lot*, first published in 1737.[44] His starting point is that, under the providence of God, a certain course of events falls

---

44. *Works*, Vol. III, pp. 495-590. The full title is *The Sovereignty and Wisdom of God Displayed in the Afflictions of Men, Together with a Christian Deportment Under Them*. The treatise is the substance of three sermons based respectively on Ecclesiastes 7:13, Proverbs 16:19 and 1 Peter 5:6. 'The Crook in the Lot' was the title of the first sermon, based on the words, 'Consider the work of God: for who can make that straight which he hath made crooked?' Further page references are given in brackets in the text.

to every human being, and in that course there are always, to one degree or another, 'crooks': disagreeable, humiliating or frustrating adversities that cut across the grain of our natural expectations or our individual temperaments. Our will goes one way, the dispensation another; and no one, saint or sinner, is exempt. Our neighbour's lot, seen from a distance, may seem perfectly adjusted to their wishes, 'but that is a false verdict; there is no perfection here, no lot out of heaven, without a crook' (p. 499); and what is true of men and women in general is particularly true of God's children: 'His darling ones ordinarily have the greatest crooks made in their lot' (p. 526), and the reason for this is clear: there is no coming to the promised land but through the wilderness. Nor can we at any point escape from that wilderness: 'We may indeed have our station changed; but the remove will be out of one wilderness station to another' (p. 501). Yet nobody's lot in this world is wholly crooked: even in the wilderness Israel 'in the midst of many mourning times, had some singing ones' (p. 570).[45]

Boston knows from his pastoral experience that the Crook can vary widely from temperament to temperament. What might be a Crook to one might not be a Crook to another. But he also knows that the Crook can come in a wide variety of forms, and he cites some curious instances. He raises our eyebrows when he suggests that one of these might be our personal appearance, but he restores equilibrium when he illustrates this from the example of the Apostle Paul, who thought his appearance made him contemptible (2 Cor. 10:10); Isaiah's Crook was that no one believed his message (Isa. 53:1); for many, like Boston himself, the Crook was 'relational', especially his domestic and family circumstances; for others it would be a matter of their honour, their reputations compromised by slander or misunderstanding; for yet others the Crook would occur in their vocational or professional lives. But sometimes the nature of the Crook is less obvious. It may be the result of some sinful action on our own part, or it may come where we expected the greatest comfort. It may even come from God giving us what we want.

Boston warns, too, that the Crook in the Lot may sometimes be permanent. Indeed, that was part of the message of his text. If every Crook is 'the doing of God' (p. 3), 'who can make straight what He hath made crooked?' (Eccles. 7:13). This, of course, was his own experience: his wife

---

45. He instances Exodus 15:1, Numbers 21:17.

never recovered from her illness. It reflected, too, Paul's experience of the thorn in his flesh (2 Cor. 12:1-10). The Lord made plain to him that he had to live with it. And it is true, too, of countless others who have had to come to terms with some form of mental illness, physical disability, or some other life-limiting factor. Sometimes our lives may be irreparably damaged by the actions of others; and what is even more distressing, they may be damaged by actions of our own: 'The thing may fall out in a moment, under which the party may go halting to the grave' (p. 500).

Yet, at the risk of appearing inconsistent, Boston also writes, 'There is no crook but what may be remedied by him, and made perfectly straight' (p. 525). What can he mean? He is certainly not saying that we are bound to submit impassively to every Crook in our Lot. Though we cannot 'even' them, we should apply to God and ask Him to remove any Crook 'that in the settled order of things may be removed' (p. 525). The qualification is important. There are some situations that in 'the settled order of things' cannot be removed: some forms of congenital conditions, for example. But there are others within the 'settled order of things' that God can remedy, and since 'he loves to be employed in settling Crooks', He calls us to employ Him in that way even when, humanly speaking, there is no hope. It is His prerogative, after all, to work wonders. The surest and shortest way is to go straight to God with the Crook.

This will not, however, comfort every sufferer. Some, as Boston recalls, will say, 'Yes, I know this Crook could be mended, but it never will, because it is plainly God's will that it should remain, and prayer for its removal is hopeless.' But this, the Ettrick Pastor replies, is the language of unbelieving haste. Abraham and Sarah faced what they thought was a hopeless situation, yet it was remedied. Nothing can make it needless in such a case to apply to God.

Or another may object, 'But I've applied to him again and again for it, yet it is never mended:' to which Boston replies, 'Delays are not denials,' and we shouldn't let the application drop from our prayers out of despondency. If God has a mind to even it, He will ensure we keep on praying. He acknowledges that sometimes the prayers are not answered, the trouble continues, and so we are apt to conclude that our prayers have not been accepted. But this, he writes, is a mistake. They are accepted immediately, but not answered: 'The Lord does with them as a father with the letters coming thick from his son abroad, reads them one by one with pleasure, and carefully lays them up to be answered at his convenience. And when the answer comes, the son will know how acceptable they were to his father' (p. 581).

What we want, of course, is a Christian life without crooks, but this, says Boston, is impossible. The 'unmixt' dispensation is reserved for the other world. This one will be a wilderness to the end.

What then? There are Crooks that cannot be straightened, and Crooks that God could straighten, but doesn't. Boston's answer is both uncompromising and unoriginal: we must recognise that the Crook is the work of God and, having done so, we must submit to it as His will. His sovereignty should silence us, and His wisdom should satisfy us, even though we cannot see. This is not some asylum of ignorance forced upon us by a problem of our own making, such as the Reformed doctrine of predestination. It is the same sort of submission as we hear from the lips of our Lord Himself on at least two occasions: first, when He contemplates the mystery that His gospel is hid from the wise and learned, and revealed to babes, and exclaims, 'Even so, Father: for so it seemed good in thy sight' (Matt. 11:26); and, secondly, in the Garden of Gethsemane, where, well-nigh overwhelmed by the suffering that is now so near, He cries, 'Not my will, but thine, be done' (Luke 22:42). We find it, too, in the suppressed anguish of Job (Job 1:21): 'The Lord gave, and the Lord hath taken away; blessed be the name of the Lord.' And we find it in the assurance that sustained the Apostle Paul in his life of service and suffering. 'We know,' he declares, 'that all things work together for good to them that love God' (Rom. 8:28).

The greatest Crook in the Lot, writes Boston, conforms to God's will, and that will never deviate from its central preoccupation: God's love for His people and His determination to conform them to the image of His glorious Son (Rom. 8:29). Sometimes we can see how the Crooks work for our good, perhaps by drawing our attention to some false step we have taken or some dangerous course we are pursuing. But sometimes we have no option but to betake ourselves to the words of Jesus, 'What I do thou knowest not now; but thou shalt know hereafter' (John 13:7); or to the words of William Cowper:

> Deep in unfathomable mines
>   of never-failing skill,
> He treasures up His bright designs
>   and works His sovereign will.

Yet we note, once again, that Boston never romanticises suffering as if it always tends to our moral and spiritual good. 'There is nothing,' he writes, 'that gives temptation more easy access than the crook in the lot' (p. 502); and again, 'Satan's work is by the crook in the lot either to bend or break people's spirit, and oftentimes by bending to break them' (p. 529). The danger of sinking under discouragement and immoderate grief is ever-present, leaving us unfit for both the common affairs of life and the duties of religion. There, one suspects, is the voice of experience.

Baptism

In August 1704 Boston began to keep a book which he called *The Miscellany Manuscript*,[46] in which he recorded, for his own satisfaction, his thoughts on several subjects which had troubled him since the beginning of his ministry. The resulting 'Miscellany Questions' now occupies over two hundred pages of the sixth volume of Boston's *Complete Works,* and it contains some of Boston's most valuable contributions to Scottish theology, but it must surely be one of the few books in the world which came to be written only because the author himself lacked books. Having no access to other authors, he was forced to think through the questions for himself, resulting, he says, in greater distinctness than he might otherwise have attained, 'and thus my scarcity of books proved a kind disposal of Providence towards me.'[47]

Among the questions addressed in the *Miscellany* are, 'Whether all sins, past, present, and to come, are pardoned together and at once,' 'Why the Lord suffereth sin to remain in the regenerate,' and 'Whether repentance be necessary in order to the obtaining of the forgiveness of sins.' This last, in particular, anticipates issues that would later arise in connection with the *Marrow* controversy. He is already, for example, showing his impatience with 'debates about the conditionality of the covenant of grace' and laying down that 'gospel repentance doth not go before, but comes after the remission of sin, in the order of nature.'

But the most significant contribution from Boston's *Miscellany Manuscript* (which he never intended for publication) was his treatment of the question, 'Who have a right to baptism, and to be baptised?' It arose directly out of his early experience in Simprin, where he found that many of those applying

---

46. *Memoirs*, p. 163.
47. ibid., p. 159.

for the baptism of their infant children were not only grossly ignorant but well-nigh unteachable. He was particularly affected by one case where he refused the application for some time, and then, when he eventually yielded, was troubled by doubts as to whether either the man or his wife had given a satisfactory account of the fundamental principles of Christianity. This brought him, as he says, 'closely to consider that point,'[48] leading to the conclusion that the prevailing practice of virtually indiscriminate baptism was indefensible. A neighbouring minister, anxious to 'clear' him of such a disturbing view, then gave him a copy of *A Discourse of the Visible Church* by an English clergyman, Mr Fulwood, who argued that baptism should be given without respect to saving grace. This didn't shake Boston from his position, but it did have one unintended consequence: 'From that time I had little fondness for national churches strictly and properly so-called, as of equal latitude with the nations.' It would be too much to read into this a disavowal of the Establishment Principle (the obligation on the state to recognise, support and protect Christianity as the national religion). What Boston did disavow, and emphatically, was the idea that the church was co-extensive with the parish, that every resident must be presumed to be a Christian, and that as such each had a right to Christian baptism (and Christian marriage and burial). The issue, as Boston saw it, was what was meant by church membership, and from that day to this, confusion between church and parish has been a virus at the heart of Western Christianity.

When Boston transcribed his earlier jottings into the finished essays of *The Miscellany Manuscript* he quoted extensively from Fulwood's work. He also quoted extensively from others such as Zanchius and Richard Baxter who shared Fulwood's point of view.

But one man he doesn't quote, even though he was the principal architect of the view of church membership which had so long prevailed in Scotland: Samuel Rutherford. Rutherford had set forth his views in *A Peaceable and Temperate Plea for Paul's Presbyterie in Scotland* (London, 1642),[49] and although Boston never refers to it he clearly had it very much in mind.[50]

---

48. ibid., p. 163.

49. *A Peaceable and Temperate Plea for Paul's Presbyterie in Scotland* (London, 1642). Chapter XII, pp. 164-87.

50. See further the Chapter, 'The Idea of the Church and Membership In It' in John Macpherson, *The Doctrine of the Church in Scottish Theology* (Edinburgh; Macniven and Wallace, 1903), especially pp. 82-90.

The specific question Rutherford addresses is whether baptism should be administered only to infants born of parents one of whom, at least, is known to be a believer.[51] His answer is uncompromising: '*All* the infants borne within the visible church, *whatever be the wickedness of their nearest Parents*, are to be received within the Church by Baptism' (italics added). Few Presbyterians would challenge the principle that infants born within the visible church are to be baptised. The problem is whether wicked parents can still be regarded as belonging to the visible church. Rutherford assumes that they can, and that on that basis their children should be baptised.

Some of the arguments he uses to support his position are predictable. For example, under the Old Testament every male was circumcised no matter how wicked his parents; in the ministry of John the Baptist everyone who came to hear was baptised without further examination or scrutiny, even though John described the Jews of his day as 'a brood of vipers'; and when Peter addressed the thousands of Jews gathered in Jerusalem on the Day of Pentecost he urged them all to be baptised on the ground, 'the promise is to you and to your children' (Acts 2:38-39). None of these, however, is without its difficulties. Jews who flagrantly violated the Law were cut off from the people; John made plain that his baptism was a baptism of repentance; and in the event, only those Jews who openly received the apostolic word were baptised on the Day of Pentecost. It is true, however, that in none of these instances was there any close scrutiny to ensure that only those who were 'Israelites indeed' received the sacrament.

But some of Rutherford's arguments are less obvious. He argues, for instance, that while the child of impious parents can derive no right to baptism from his immediate parents he can derive such a right from his more remote ancestry. In support of this he refers to such a passage as Exodus 20:6-7, where God speaks of visiting the iniquity of the fathers on the children to the third and fourth [generation] of those who hate Him, 'but showing mercy unto thousands [of generations] of them that love me, and keep my commandments.' If that is the case, he claims, then the wickedness of the immediate parents cannot remove the mercy of the covenant from their children because the faithfulness of God continues through the blood-line to the thousandth generation, and thus the ungodliness of the child's father and mother cannot exclude it from the seals of the covenant. More

---

51. *A Peaceable and Temperate Plea for Paul's Presbyterie in Scotland*, p. 164.

explicitly he writes, 'The sins of no one, or two, or four persons do interrupt the course of God's immutable covenant.'[52] In other words, if you belong to a 'race of covenanters' you have a right to the blessings of the covenant.

Rutherford draws a similar conclusion from the 'infallible promise of the covenant' as given in Genesis 17:7, where God promises Abraham, 'I will establish my covenant between me and thee, and thy seed after thee, in their generations, for an everlasting covenant, to be God unto thee and to thy seed after thee.' This, he says, makes a difference between the seed of Christians and the seed of Turks and pagans (even though, presumably, the seed of Christians may be as wicked as the seed of Turks and pagans). It appears unthinkable to Rutherford that the grandchildren and great-great-grandchildren of those who were in covenant with God should be in no better case than the descendants of pagans. The sins and wickedness of nearest parents cannot cut off their children from the infallible promise of the covenant.

Rutherford puts to the same use the words of Romans 11:16, 'if the root be holy, so are the branches.' This holiness, he insists, cannot be meant of personal and inherent holiness. Absalom, for example, was born of holy David, and yet was completely lacking in personal holiness. The reference must therefore be to 'federal holiness', derived from their being descended from the Patriarchs and the Prophets, and from 'the holy seed of the Jews'.[53] A fortiori, argues Rutherford, since 'God has become a God to us and to our seed, the seed must be holy with the holiness of the chosen Nation, and holiness external of the covenant, notwithstanding the fathers and mothers were as wicked as the Jews who slew the Lord of glory.'[54]

Boston's reply

Boston's treatment of this question in his *Miscellany* extends to almost a hundred pages and is clearly the product of careful and rigorous thought. It also reflects his familiarity not only with Rutherford's *Peaceable Plea* (though he doesn't quote it), but also, as we have seen, with the writings of others who shared Rutherford's position. It is a mistake, however, to view Boston's study as an exercise in polemics. It was an attempt, very

---

52. ibid., p. 168.
53. ibid., p. 170.
54. ibid., p. 170.

early in his ministry, to clarify his own thinking on an important pastoral issue, it was for his own private use and, like the other five chapters of the *Miscellany*, was first published only in 1753, twenty-one years after Boston's death. But even though he had no thought of publishing, and expected no eye to see it but his own, he still crafted it carefully and with an obvious determination to be fair to those from whom he differed. For example, he allows Zanchius ('that judicious divine') to express his view in an extended quote (pp. 139-44) which he reproduces without interruption or comment in the body of his own text, and the unwary reader might easily conclude that the sentiments expressed in these pages are Boston's own, until he suddenly announces that, regretfully, he cannot agree with them.[55]

Boston's conclusion, in distinction from Rutherford's, is that 'none but the children of visible believers, or *such as can make a credible profession*, have right before the church, or a visible right, to the sacrament of baptism.'[56] This clearly implies that Boston rejects Rutherford's arguments, and especially his plea that children who cannot derive a right to baptism from their immediate parents may, nevertheless, derive it from remote forebears who lived a godly life: a position which, in Boston's view, leads to absurd consequences.

For example, many infants, even in covenanted Scotland, were descended from families which had been openly godless for as many generations as anyone could remember, and if they were to receive baptism it would have to be in the name of a God whom, quite literally, neither they nor their fathers knew. Further, if it were appropriate to baptise an infant on the grounds that it had godly ancestors, then the children of pagans and Muslims (descendants of the Seven Churches of Asia) had a right to baptism, even though having nothing in common with the church of God.[57] Indeed, on Rutherford's premises baptism would have to be given to every infant in the world, since there is not a family under heaven which does not have godly ancestors in

---

55. Cf. Macpherson's comment that Boston's discussion of this topic might serve as an example to modern controversialists: 'Without note or comment or even a single interjected critical remark he presents the arguments of the ablest defenders of this [Rutherford's] thesis with all possible fulness and force as if he were stating his own position' (*The Doctrine of the Church in Scottish Theology*, p. 86).

56. *Works*, Vol. 6, p. 162 (italics added). Further page-references from this source will be in brackets in the body of the text.

57. For example, the descendants of John of Damascus (born in Damascus to a wealthy Arab-Christian family about A.D. 675), the last of the recognised Church Fathers, and one of the first Christian theologians to challenge the claims of Islam, are almost inevitably Muslims. He died in Syria, *circa* 749.

its blood-line, 'which will hold true, so long as it remains undoubted that all the world is come of Noah and of Adam' (p. 147). Nor is Boston impressed with the argument derived from God's promise that His mercy extends to thousands of generations of those who love Him (Exod. 20:5-6). At one level, he comments that it would be hard to find anyone in the world distanced from godly parents by more than a thousand generations, but he also points out that the number of generations from Abraham to Christ was only 'thrice fourteen' (forty-two),[58] and yet within that time-scale 'the Jews are broken off, and unchurched, and had no right to the seals of the covenant' (p. 151). It would be absurd, then, to argue that because someone had a godly ancestor four (or forty) generations ago this constitutes them a member of the visible church and thus entitled to have their child baptised.

Boston is equally dismissive of the idea of a right to baptism based on the holiness of an infant's place of birth (p. 164). How, he asks, is a place made holy, especially so holy that the mere fact of being born in it gives it a title to the holy ordinance of baptism? The proposed answer was that a place is holy because a holy people lives in it, but this merely provokes further questions: What holiness does a holy people communicate to the spot of ground on which they live; and supposing a spot of ground to be holy, should we bar pagans from coming in lest they defile a holy place with their unclean feet? Conversely, were the lands of Egypt and Babylon made holy places seeing they were places where God's holy people lived for many years; and would Egyptian and Babylonian infants have had a right to circumcision since their lands were once sanctified by the presence of the holy people?

But still he is not done. Was an infant unchurched simply because it was born in a pagan country? Take, for example, a godly woman with child who was cast out of her country before she gave birth: 'Is the poor infant therefore a stranger to the covenant, and no church member, because born [sic] in a pagan country? No, sure: the place of a child's birth can never prejudice the right it has to the promise and covenant of God' (p. 146). Only by the unchurched state of the parents can we know these infants to be unchurched; and only by the faith of one or both parents is an infant made 'holy' (1 Cor. 7:14).[59] And then, recurring to the image of the refugee

---

58. Based on the genealogy in Matthew 1:1-17.

59. According to Rutherford, the 'unbelieving' husband is not someone who is unconverted, but a Turk or a pagan. This conforms to his view that unless they had explicitly repudiated the Christian faith the default position was that everyone in Scotland was a Christian and thus had a right to baptism.

woman with child, he asks: supposing she were cast up on the Scottish coast and brought forth a child, would that child *ipso facto* have a right to baptism? Even Rutherford would have been hard-pressed to answer that in the affirmative.

All this may seem remote from life in modern Scotland: a secular country where, to put it in crude commercial terms, demand for baptism has fallen away sharply. Still, while the church no longer has the social position she once had, she is still a visible presence, and the idea that everyone born 'in the parish' has a right to baptism is by no means dead; and while the sacrament is no longer revered for its spiritual significance it is still valued as a social occasion.[60]

Yet 'probable' surely means more than an ability to recite the Apostles' Creed or even the Shorter Catechism. The faith professed should be able to give an account of itself and (even more important) should find visible expression in an external Christian lifestyle. Even so, however, the church has to be aware that since she can look only at the outward appearance she may often find herself giving baptism to people who have no right to it *coram Deo*; and by the same token she may also on occasion deny baptism to those who do have a right to it *coram Deo*. Only the Great Day will declare whether her judgements were right or wrong.

What emerges from Boston's reflections is a picture of a pastor who took his responsibilities with regard to the sacraments extremely seriously, and who, probably, was too much given to fear of erring on either the right hand or the left. But of one thing he was sure: when a profession was visibly contradicted by habitual profanity, gross ignorance, and regular contempt for the preaching of the Word, parents had no right to the baptism of their child, no matter how godly his great-grandfather.

The Lord's Supper

It followed from Boston's definition of a credible profession that anyone who had a right to baptism also had a right to the Lord's Supper. The underlying truth here was that both sacraments signified and sealed the same blessings, a point encapsulated in the generic definition of a sacrament offered in the Shorter Catechism (92).[61] This makes no distinction between

---

60. See further, the disturbing study by David F. Wright, *What has Infant Baptism done to Baptism? An Enquiry at the End of Christendom* (Milton Keynes: Paternoster, 2005).

61. 'A sacrament is an holy ordinance instituted by Christ; wherein, by sensible signs, Christ, and the benefits of the new covenant, are represented, sealed, and applied to believers' (*Shorter Catechism,* Answer 92).

baptism and the Lord's Supper but lays down that in each sacrament, equally, 'Christ and the benefits of the new covenant are represented, sealed, and applied to believers.' The judgement the church has to make, therefore, is whether the applicant can sincerely and credibly claim to have experienced these blessings. This was no easy judgement, and Boston is careful to allow for such facts as that someone may be a *living* member of the body of Christ without being a *lively* one. It remained however that, before the church, no one but visible believers had a right to either sacrament. Equally, however, it was inconsistent to bar from the Lord's Table those who were unhesitatingly admitted to baptism. Both sacraments were for believers, for believers only, and for all believers. On the face of things, this is certainly the pattern we find in the New Testament, where we find no instance of anyone baptised being told to wait back from the Supper. It is clear, for example, that those baptised at Pentecost partook immediately of the Breaking of Bread (Acts 2:42).

This, as Boston was fully aware, was a radical divergence from the views of Rutherford, but the exact point of divergence must be noted carefully. Boston fully agreed with Rutherford's insistence that only those should be admitted to Communion whom the church, in the judgement of charity, can recognise as having exercised the self-examination stipulated by the Apostle (1 Cor. 11:28), give evidence of understanding the nature and purpose of the sacrament, and are capable of maintaining a witness to the death of Christ (1 Cor. 11:26). This meant, for both Boston and Rutherford, that children (deemed incapable of examining themselves) were not to be admitted to the Table.[62]

Where the two men differed was over Rutherford's insistence that a much lower standard of profession was to be looked for with regard to admission to baptism. Parents who were ignorant or even 'scandalously flagitious' might have a right to baptism, but not to the Supper; and the basis of Rutherford's position was that the Supper presupposes 'faith, and the begun life of God, and the new birth.'[63]

---

62. This should have meant in practice that the theological definition of a child should be someone who is incapable of examining himself or herself in relation to the Lord's Supper. Conversely, a young person who *was* capable of such self-examination should not be treated as a child. We must be careful, however, of making cognition the only criterion. An adult with learning difficulties may still have faith in Christ and show love for Him. Conversely, a child may have the same degree of faith and love as an adult with learning difficulties. In both cases blessing may be conveyed through the 'sensible signs'.

63. Rutherford, *A Peaceable and Temperate Plea for Paul's Presbyterie in Scotland*, p. 185.

But then, the same presupposition lies behind the sacrament of baptism as administered by the apostles, who baptised only where faith, repentance and a willingness to profess the name of Christ, whatever the risks, gave good evidence of 'the begun life of God'. There are indeed instances where the event showed that some of those baptised were not genuine disciples, and this may suggest that the apostles were not infallible judges of those who responded to the call to be baptised. Alternatively it may suggest that they didn't think it necessary to subject new converts to careful scrutiny: after all, in an age when there was a real cost to Christian discipleship they had a right to assume that the willingness to face persecution was itself a mark of spiritual sincerity. What we cannot find, however, is an instance of the apostles baptising someone who was 'scandalously flagitious'. Nor, as we have seen, is there an instance of people who have been baptised being excluded from the Table. The presumption was that someone who had confessed the name of Christ and thereupon been baptised with water had also put on Christ and been baptised in His Spirit.

There is another interesting dimension to this discussion: what do we mean by church membership? According to Rutherford, it is 'most false' to argue that only those admitted to the Lord's Supper should be regarded as 'Church-members of Christ's visible body'.[64] Nor would he have been content with merely extending the concept to include all who had been baptised. At his most extreme he would have regarded everyone born in Scotland, a nation covenanted to God, as a member of the visible church, but when pressed to a narrower definition he would have based it not on either sacrament but on the Word: 'We think multitudes are members of the visible Church,' he writes, 'who must be hearers, as knowne unbelievers, who are not to be admitted to the Sacrament.'[65]

All this is a far cry from the modern practice of defining church membership by means of a Roll of Communicants. From one point of view (Rutherford's), the visible church includes all those who, because they live in a Christian country, exist within the sound of the gospel and are duty-bound to attend the preaching of it; from another it includes those who are

---

64. ibid., p. 184.

65. ibid., p. 187. By 'must be hearers' he means that as members of the visible church it is their duty to be hearers of the Word. A few pages earlier (p. 184) he had spoken of those who are admitted into Christ's visible body 'as ordinary hearers of the word, such as are ignorants, and many unconverted professors.'

regular hearers but are unconverted; and from yet another it includes the excommunicated who, although not in the meantime to be admitted to the Lord's Supper, are to be admitted to the preaching of the Word since this is the means of bringing men to repentance.[66]

New England

Scotland was not, however, the only country where such discussions were taking place. In the Congregational churches of New England there emerged in the mid-seventeenth century what came to be labelled (by its opponents) the 'Half-Way Covenant'. Originally, these churches, like those they had left behind in England, restricted admission to the sacraments to those who were converted, and in the quest for proof of such conversion the practice arose of requiring all those who sought admission to give a conversion-narrative, detailing what had first led them to an interest in spiritual things, and how they had come to know the Lord. One result of this practice was that more and more parents were denied baptism for their children, and this in turn led to more and more families becoming unchurched, creating a real risk of the colonial counties losing their Christian character.

It was in response to this that more and more churches began to adopt the Half-Way Covenant, according to which parents were allowed to present their children for baptism on condition that they publicly confessed their agreement with Christian doctrine. They were not, however, admitted to the Lord's Supper; nor were they granted other privileges such as the right to vote in church meetings.

The similarities between this and the practice advocated by Rutherford are obvious. But the similarities with what came to be the general practice in Scotland's Highland churches are no less so. Here, too, parents were granted baptism for their children without being required to profess any real allegiance to the Lord; indeed, while readily acknowledging that in

---

66. According to Boston (*Works*, Vol. V, p. 185), the children of such a person are to be baptised, 'because the church still looks on such a person as a living, though not a lively member of Christ, as one savingly in covenant with God, evidenced by their former walk, before the hour of temptation.' The excommunicated (whatever form such excommunication may take) are still to be regarded as in 'church communion', in the hope that the church's pastoral care will lead to their restoration. It is important to note that despite their different approaches, Rutherford and Boston were both motivated by an evangelistic concern, as Macpherson notes: 'Rutherford and Boston were led to their respective and conflicting theories of the Church and membership in it by their evangelical sympathies and their longings for the salvation of sinners' (ibid., p. 89).

their own view they were not Christians at all. All that was required was more or less regular church attendance, along with a profession of belief in some basic Christian doctrines (or, minimally, some knowledge of the Shorter Catechism). Few were ever turned away. But as with Rutherford and the New England Congregationalists, a far higher standard was required for admission to the Lord's Supper. The result was a radical, and sometimes acrimonious, divergence between the Christianity of the north of Scotland and the Christianity of the south, the south being scandalised that non-communicants could receive baptism, and the north being scandalised that 'everyone' was admitted to Communion.[67] The situation became particularly fraught when churches in the south denied baptism to parents of Highland background on the ground that they weren't communicants, without enquiring into the reasons why they weren't. In many such cases it arose not out of contempt for the sacrament, but out of a feeling of personal unworthiness allied it has to be said to a deeply ingrained fear of eating and drinking 'damnation' to oneself.[68] Overall, argued Highland spokesmen, such an attitude was more creditable than that of those who took Communion without the least self-examination; and more creditable, too, than the practice of those churches that allowed indiscriminate admission to both sacraments. The reality is that both the north and the south were in error: the south in condoning indiscriminate admission to both sacraments; the north in fencing the Lord's Supper with too many discouragements. Neither practice could have claimed Boston's support. For him there could be no admission to either sacrament without a credible profession of faith; and, conversely, a credible profession warranted admission to both sacraments.

In mid-eighteenth-century North America, a further development took place with regard to the sacraments. Towards the end of his ministry, Solomon Stoddart (1643–1729), the grandfather of Jonathan Edwards and

---

67. See the discussion in John Kennedy, *The Days of the Fathers in Ross-shire* (1861. Reprinted Inverness: Christian Focus Publications, 1979), pp. 110-25.

68. The word 'damnation' occurs in the AV translation of 1 Corinthians 11:19, 'For he that eateth and drinketh unworthily, eateth and drinketh damnation to himself.' In the Shorter Catechism (Answer 97), 'damnation' is quite rightly replaced by 'judgement'. The context makes plain that what the apostle has in mind is a temporal judgement on the congregation as a whole: 'This is why many of you are weak and ill, and some have died' (esv). The problem at Corinth was not 'unworthy communicants' but blatant irreverence and, with it, contempt for the poor. The rich humiliated those who had nothing (1 Cor. 11:22).

his predecessor as Minister of Northampton (Massachusetts), adopted the view that the Lord's Supper was a converting ordinance, and that unconverted people should not only be freely admitted to the Lord's Table, but told that it was their duty to come. This threw the sacrament open not only to those who could make no credible profession of real piety, but to many who openly admitted, or even boasted, that they had no love for Jesus Christ and absolutely no interest in the Covenant; and their lifestyle was entirely in accordance with such a profession.

Jonathan Edwards, to his dismay, found himself in profound disagreement with his revered grandfather on this question, and reluctantly made his disagreement public in his *Qualifications for Communion*.[69] Though its focus is the Lord's Supper, we hear once again the same basic concerns as we hear in Boston,[70] including the distinction between *coram Deo* and *coram ecclesiae* and the distinction between 'Who has a right to ask?' and 'Who has a right to be granted?' There is a helpful clarification, too, of the distinction between the 'internal' covenant and the 'external' covenant. The point, says Edwards, is not that there are two covenants, but that there are two sorts of people who profess the covenant. On the one hand, there are those who are in the covenant internally and sincerely as real believers (or, in the words of Jesus, 'in spirit and in truth', John 4:23); on the other hand, there are those who are in it only externally, by mere profession and outward appearance.

But the key point in Edwards' *Inquiry* is that none should be admitted to Communion or to the privileges of the church but such as in the church's judgement are godly or gracious persons. He is careful, as are the Scottish theologians, to point out that inward grace and purity are not as such the condition on which the church admits people to the sacraments: no one, we hear once again, can know the state of another man's mind.[71] The

---

69. Full title, *An Humble Inquiry into the Rules of the Word of God Concerning the Qualifications Requisite to a Complete Standing and Full Communion in the Visible Church* (Boston, 1749. Republished in *The Works of Jonathan Edwards*, revised and corrected by Edward Hickman, 2 Vols., 1834. Reprinted Edinburgh: Banner of Truth Trust, 1979). For the *Inquiry into Qualifications for Communion*, see Vol. One, pp. 431-84. Yale edition. This *Inquiry* has been inexplicably neglected by subsequent writers on church and sacraments.

70. Bearing in mind that Boston's *Treatise of Miscellany Questions* was first published only in 1753, four years after Edwards' *Qualifications*. It had been written, however, sometime around 1704.

71. Cf. Duncan's comment in *Macbeth*, Act 1, Scene 4: 'There's no art, To find the mind's contrivance in the face.'

church's business is with the profession only, but (and this is an important caveat) what is professed, and what must be visible, is real discipleship and real godliness: not a mere absence of scandal, or a knowledge of Christian doctrines, or (as on Stoddart's understanding) a professed willingness to be converted, but a proper visibility of godliness in the eye of the public. 'The thing which must be visible and probable, in order to visible saintship,' writes Edwards, 'must be saintship itself, or real grace and true holiness';[72] and in illustration of this he quotes the example of a person baptised in infancy who then, in adulthood, 'properly own their baptismal covenant' by taking their first Communion: 'The meaning is, that they now, being capable to act for themselves, do professedly and explicitly make their parents' act, in giving them up to God, their own, by expressly giving themselves up to God.'[73]

But to return to Scotland: Did Rutherford have a point when he suggested that we should not limit the concept of 'membership of the visible church' to 'communicant members' but should widen it to include (at least) those who are more or less regular hearers? Does this indicate that they wish to identify with Christ, albeit at a distance; and if so, what rights should such 'members' have? Should they, for example, have a right to vote in the election of office-bearers, and particularly in the election of ministers?

These are clearly questions of administration rather than of theology, but they do have a bearing on the need to ensure that the church remains fit for purpose. The prevailing view in the presbyterian tradition has been that only members in full communion have a right to vote in such an election and to add their signatures to a call. However, the practice has also arisen of using a separate Form of Concurrence in a call to be signed by those who are not communicants but are 'ordinary hearers'. Technically, such signatures do not carry decisive weight: what matters is whether the call has been signed by a majority of the communicants. In practice, however, a presbytery would have serious reservations about sustaining a call if a high proportion of 'ordinary hearers' were opposed to it.

Behind this lies a shared concern for evangelism which, paradoxically, drove the attitude to baptism of both Boston and Rutherford, though it led to opposite conclusions. Rutherford (like Dickson, and

---

72. *Works*, Vol. 1, p. 437.
73. ibid., pp. 443-44.

indeed Solomon Stoddart and John Kennedy) cherished the idea of the external covenant, and feared that denial of baptism would alienate many who would otherwise remain under the sound of the gospel and thus give ground to hope that one day they might experience its saving power. From this point of view, 'ordinary hearers' (or 'adherents' as they came to be called) were seen as the pool out of which the 'fisher of men' drew His converts; or, as John Macpherson puts it, reflecting on Rutherford's view that the membership of the church consists not of those admitted to the Lord's Table but of the 'called', 'It is out of the church membership that communicants are drawn.'[74]

Boston, on the other hand, feared that indiscriminate baptism hindered, rather than promoted, the gospel. The judgement of the church had to be regulated by the judgement of God, and when that judgement was violated (as it was by indiscriminate baptism) there could be no expectation of divine blessing. Instead, the church, the gospel and the sacrament were brought into disrepute, while at the same time the 'scandalously flagitious' were confirmed in the illusion that since they had the church's seal of approval all was well with their souls; and so spiritual things didn't need to be taken seriously.

It is not easy to adjudicate on this. On the one hand, it is certainly important to bear in mind the principle of 'the bruised reed and the smoking flax' (Isa. 42:3) and, rather than crush and extinguish it, exercise patience in the hope of fanning it into flame; and it is important, too, that when baptism is denied, the reasons for denying it should be carefully explained. On the other hand, we have to make clear that baptism is not (any more than Communion) a civil right acquired by mere residence in the parish.

But when all is said and done, we must avoid the temptation to make the fear of losing people our guiding principle in the governance of the church. Where would we draw the line? Indiscriminate baptism leads to indiscriminate Communion, and indiscriminate Communion leads, in quick time, to indiscriminate admission to Scotland's pulpits. The only way to prevent such outcomes is to insist that the sacraments are for those who can sincerely profess to love God and His Christ, and our pulpits for those who can sincerely promise to dedicate their lives to preaching 'Jesus Christ and him crucified' (1 Cor. 2:2).

---

74. Macpherson, *The Doctrine of the Church in Scottish Theology*, p. 77.

2

Thomas Boston and The Fourfold State

IN SEPTEMBER 1699, shortly before his induction to Simprin, Boston resolved to begin a series of sermons on 'the doctrine of man's natural state; judging the sight and sense thereof to be the foundation of all real religion. And minding to take it in parcels, for the more clear discovery thereof, both in the sinfulness and misery of it, I began my study of it, for that Sabbath, on the guilt of Adam's first sin, or original sin imputed.'[1] This series never progressed beyond this first natural 'state', but it contained the seed of Boston's best-known work, *Human Nature in its Fourfold State.*[2] When he moved to Ettrick in June 1707, he resolved to lay the same foundation for his ministry as he had laid at Simprin, his great concern being 'to impress the people with a sense of their need of Christ, and to bring them to consider the foundations of practical religion.'[3] Initially, he engaged in 'direct preaching of Christ', basing his sermons on the parable of the wise and foolish builders, but in May 1708, he resolved on a different approach, and decided to 'begin an ordinary, the same for substance, as in the first years of my ministry in Simprin, but prosecuted after another manner.'[4] Part of that ordinary 'contained the doctrine of man's fourfold state' and this occupied him till October 1709. As the phrase, 'after another manner' indicates, however, this was to be no mere repetition of the Simprin series: instead of being confined to the 'natural' state of fallen human nature, it

---

1. *Memoirs, Works* Vol. 12, p. 91.
2. Philip Graham Ryken, *Thomas Boston as Preacher of the Fourfold State* (Edinburgh: Rutherford House, 1999), pp. 57-85.
3. Boston, *Memoirs*, p. 217.
4. ibid., p. 217.

would deal with man's fourfold state, including the state of innocence, the state of grace, and the eternal state.

At the time, Boston had no intention of publishing, and when he looked back later at the reception given to *Human Nature in its Fourfold State* he regarded it as a remarkable providence that he was led to make a second attempt on the subject. Providence, he concluded, had had its own design, but that design was 'unknown to and unlooked for by me, till the event discovered itself years after.' But many years would pass before the 'event' discovered itself, making plain that the preaching of these sermons was 'not in vain'.[5]

It was a friend in Duns, Dr Trotter, who first suggested to Boston (in 1711) that he should print some of his sermons. Boston initially rejected the idea, but eventually conceded that if anything of this nature were to be done, his sermons on the Fourfold State would be the most suitable. Having seen the notes, the doctor 'sent pressing letters to put me on to that work',[6] and in January 1712 Boston began to write out the sermons; but he had scarcely begun when he was overtaken by a 'disabling fit of melancholy', and the following months and years would see many such fits. Sometimes what he had written seemed so bare and empty that he laid the project aside; at other times he felt his heart swell with vanity, and at others he found it difficult to settle on a way of arranging his material. But he persevered, even taking encouragement from the fact that, 'Satan has made a strange bustle against the work.' He completed his first revision of the material in March 1713, but this revision never made it to the press. Instead, he reworked the material, though introducing only minor changes,[7] and completed the process in the autumn of 1719. He still had his doubts, however, seeing it as 'but a mean piece'; and to make matters worse, he had a dispute with his financial backer, who not only thought Boston's style would be 'nauseous to the polite world',[8] but approached the printer without his permission and introduced his own 'corrections'. Even after Boston corrected the corrections, the backer still 'smoothed' some expressions, and Boston was so unhappy that when the first edition appeared in 1720 it was published anonymously. There followed a further seven years' labour, dealing with the

---

5. ibid., p. 217.
6. ibid., p. 242.
7. ibid., p. 287.
8. ibid., p. 322.

unwanted corrections, and by the time the final recension was published in 1729 the unwanted corrections had been removed, and the *Fourfold State* was now entirely Boston's own work. He received his personal copy from the printers in January 1730 and notes, 'I took and spread it before the Lord, praying for a blessing to be entailed on it, for the conviction and conversion of sinners and edification of saints, for the time I am in life, and after I shall be in the dust.'[9] By this time, Boston had little more than two years to live.

In terms of specific doctrines, Boston's theology adheres undeviatingly to traditional Reformed Orthodoxy. What is not so traditional, however, is Boston's use of the fourfold-state framework. Previous theologians had indeed used the concept of 'state' or 'estate' but few if any had used it to deliver what is in effect a systematic theology, or at least a systematic biblical anthropology. Augustine had referred to four states of the human will,[10] but had not extended the concept to the successive phases of the destiny of man; the Westminster Confession (Chapter 9) had done the same, delineating the extent of our freedom of will in the states successively of innocency, sin, grace and glory; and the Shorter Catechism had likewise spoken of an estate of creation (Answer 13), a state of sin and misery (Answer 17) and a state of salvation (Answer 20).[11] None of the Westminster documents, however, had used the idea of a fourfold state as a framework for their doctrine of man. Witsius had spoken of the transition from a state of wrath to a state of grace and of a final transition to a blessed and glorious state;[12] but his key organising principle remained the idea of the threefold covenant.[13] Turretin had posed the question, 'What was the liberty of Adam in the state of innocence?' and had replied, 'Since man can be viewed in a fourfold state – the instituted state of nature, the destitute [state] of sin, the restored [state] of grace and the appointed [state] of glory his liberty ought also to be considered in different ways in reference to them.'[14] We know that Boston

---

9. ibid., p.421.

10. Philip Ryken, *Thomas Boston as Preacher of the Fourfold State*, p.69.

11. Similarly the Larger Catechism, Answers 21, 23 and 30.

12. Herman Witsius, *The Economy of the Covenants between God and Man* (2 Vols., tr. William Crookshank, 1822. Reprinted 1990 with *Introduction* by J. I. Packer; Escondido, California: The den Dulk Christian Foundation), Bk. II, Chap. VII, 16; Bk. III: Chap. XIV, 4.

13. The Covenant of Works, the Covenant of Grace, and the Covenant of Redemption (between the Father and the Son).

14. Francis Turretin, *Institutes of Elenctic Theology*, tr. George Musgrave Giger, ed. James T. Dennison, Jr., (Phillipsburg: P&R Publishing, 3 Vols, 1992–97), Vol. 1, p.569.

was familiar with Turretin,[15] and may well have picked up from him the idea of a fourfold state, but Turretin puts it to a much more limited use than we see in Boston.

Nearer home, Davidson's Catechism had declared that the first part of Christian doctrine was 'our miserable estate by nature', and had then gone on to declare, 'except ye be persuaded of this point, and acknowledge it to be maist true, all our teaching, and all your hearing, is but in vain.'[16] But Davidson stopped there. He did not precede his reference to 'our miserable estate by nature' with some reflection on a prior state of innocence, nor did he go on to speak of a subsequent state of grace or a final state of glory. What is notable, however, is that he not only speaks of the misery of our natural state, but that he stresses the importance of our being sure on this point: unless we are persuaded on this point all subsequent teaching will be in vain. This was exactly Boston's perspective. 'I was determined,' he wrote in 1699, 'to begin with preaching to them the doctrine of man's natural state, judging the sight and sense thereof to be the foundation of all real religion';[17] and although he had not gone on to preach on the other 'states' while at Simprin, his early preaching in his first parish was the germ of the series to which his exposition of the remaining states was added during his ministry at Ettrick. He never lost sight of the fact that experientially, if not logically, Christian faith begins with a clear grasp of the desperate spiritual plight of humanity. The same conviction lay behind Dr Martyn Lloyd-Jones 1944 lectures, *The Plight of Man and the Power of God*.[18] It was also the order followed by Thomas Chalmers in his discussion of the 'Subject-Matter of Christianity' in his *Institutes of Theology*: first, 'The Disease for which the Gospel Remedy is Provided' and then, secondly, 'The Nature of the Gospel Remedy.'[19] More fundamentally, it is the order followed by the Apostle

---

15. Boston, *Memoirs*, p. 239.

16. Horatius Bonar, *Catechisms of the Scottish Reformation* (London: Nisbet, 1866), p. 329. John Davidson (1549–1604) was Minister successively of Liberton, Canongate (Edinburgh) and Prestonpans of Prestonpans. He was an outspoken critic of Episcopacy and of the policy of James VI. The full text of his Catechism, first published in 1602, forms Appendix II in Bonar's *Catechisms of the Scottish Reformation* (pp. 324-57).

17. Boston, *Memoirs*, p. 93.

18. D. Martyn Lloyd-Jones, *The Plight of Man and the Power of God* (London: Hodder and Stoughton, 1942). Four of the five chapters of this book were delivered as Lectures at the Free Church College, Edinburgh, in March 1941.

19. Thomas Chalmers, *Institutes of Theology* (2 Vols., Edinburgh: Thomas Constable, 1856), Vol. 1, pp. 317-444.

Paul in his *Epistle to the Romans*, where the premise of his proclamation of justification *sola gratia* is that 'all have sinned and fall short of the glory of God' (Rom. 3:23).

Another notable feature of Boston's treatment of his subject is that, unlike the treatises of the great doctors of Reformed Orthodoxy, his approach is both directly exegetical and unashamedly homiletical. This doesn't mean that *The Fourfold State* consists of the *ipsissima verba* Boston had used in the pulpits of either Simprin or Ettrick, but despite the many revisions of the text in the years leading up to publication, he can still claim that they are 'the same sermons'.[20] Throughout the long editorial process the doctrinal content remained the same. But so, too, did the basic format. Each chapter begins with a biblical text, and the text is no mere ornament. Boston is careful to note the scope and purpose of the passages he cites, each is allowed to speak its own message, and the reader is left in little doubt that the doctrine being set forth was indeed the core doctrine of the text. There followed, of course, considerable development of that doctrine, but there was also close pastoral application, with careful attention to such objections as might have occurred to his readers, and to such difficulties and misunderstandings as might have occurred to them. Above all, there were constant exhortations to take the doctrines, whether solemn or consolatory, to heart; and, typically, each chapter would conclude on an evangelistic note. In these respects, *The Fourfold State* clearly exemplifies Barth's principle that 'the task of theology and the task of preaching are one'.[21]

As we have seen, Boston anticipated a special difficulty with regard to managing one section of his proposed book. What he had in mind specifically was how best to arrange the material on the state of grace, but the difficulty seems to have been resolved in a special *eureka* moment when it was 'given' to him to cast his thoughts in a shorter and more natural method than before, 'which never came into my head before that day.'[22] We can judge what this 'shorter and more natural method' was from the outcome. He delivered his thoughts on the state of grace under two comprehensive headings: 'Regeneration' and 'The Mystical Union between Christ and Believers.' These, according to Boston, are the 'great and

20. Philip Ryken, *Thomas Boston as Preacher of the Fourfold State*, p. 67.

21. Quoted in Eberhard Busch, *Karl Barth: His life from letters and autobiographical texts*, tr. by John Bowden (Eugene, Oregon; Wipf & Stock, no date), p. 147.

22. *Memoirs*, p. 259.

comprehensive changes on a sinner, bringing him into the state of grace,'[23] and it is safe to say that these two chapters are the finest in the book.

Regeneration

The text for the first of these is 1 Peter 1:23, 'Being born again, not of corruptible seed, but of incorruptible, by the word of God, which liveth and abideth for ever', and the overall structure of the chapter follows the contours of the passage, dealing first of all with the nature of regeneration ('the state of begun recovery'),[24] followed by the means by which the change is brought about. The chapter is also organically linked to the previous one, where Boston has demonstrated man's utter inability to recover himself, and his absolute need of the grace of Christ. Indeed, not only is man not able to redeem himself: by himself he is unable even to accept the divine help offered in the gospel. Only the power of grace can break the chains that bind him.

Boston devotes several pages to reflecting on misconceptions of regeneration: a reflection arising from the observation that, 'Where Christianity is the religion of the country, many are called by the name of Christ, who have no more of him than the name' (p. 204). The premise is much less relevant to the post-Christian society we live in today, but even so we would do well to heed the warning that it is possible to engage in all the outward duties of religion without being born again: 'All the external acts of religion are within the compass of natural abilities. Yea, hypocrites may have the counterfeits of all the graces of the Spirit' (p. 205). Boston then adds the further caution that strictness in religious practices (and, no doubt, the censoriousness which is often partnered to such strictness) is no sign of the new birth. After all, the Pharisees had so much of it 'that they looked on Christ as little better than a mere libertine'.

Leaving such observations behind, Boston presses on to develop the theme that regeneration is a real and thorough change, not in the substance of the soul (it remains the same soul), but in its qualities; and the change is

---

23. *Human Nature in its Fourfold State*, p. 203. Quotations from this work are from the paperback edition published by the Banner of Truth Trust (London, 1964). The full title is *Human Nature in its Fourfold State of Primitive Integrity, Entire Depravity, Begun Recovery, and Consummate Happiness or Misery*. In *The Complete Works of Thomas Boston* it occupies pp. 9-375 of volume eight.

24. *The Fourfold State*, p. 203. Further references will be given in brackets in the text.

universal. Original sin affects the whole man, and renewing grace must go as far as the disease, with the result that the person who is new-born 'gets not only a new head, to know religion, or a new tongue, to talk of it, but a new heart to love and embrace it, in the whole of his conversation' (p. 209). Yet, while every part of the soul is renewed, no part is perfectly renewed. Those who are born again come to the new world of grace imperfectly holy, and need to be nurtured (and tolerated). Nevertheless, the change is a lasting one: 'The seed is incorruptible, says the text; and so is the creature that is formed of it' (p. 209).

Having laid down these general principles, Boston then comes to particulars, and discusses, in turn, the effects of the new birth on the mind, the will, the affections, the conscience, the memory, the body, and the conversation (referring mainly to social relations).[25]

The mind

First of all, the mind is savingly enlightened, particularly in the knowledge of Christ, and such enlightenment 'carries the soul beyond mere opinion to the certain knowledge of Christ and his excellency' (p. 211), enabling it to see the suitableness of his gospel to both the divine perfections and the soul's own personal case: 'Hence the regenerate admire the glorious plan of salvation through Christ crucified, rest their dependence upon it and heartily acquiesce therein' (p. 211). By comparison, all created excellences are darkened, just as the rising of the sun makes the stars to hide their heads.

Underlying such language there is a clear spiritual aesthetic reminiscent of the psalmist's longing to see the beauty of the Lord (Ps. 27:4). The unbeliever, by contrast, sees no beauty in Christ (Isa. 53:2). But besides beauty, the enlightened mind also sees in Christ a fulness sufficient to 'satisfy the boundless desires of an immortal soul' (p. 212). Then, recognising that it is no easy thing to acquiesce in divine revelation, Boston describes the light of grace as 'an overcoming light, determining men to assent to divine truths on the mere testimony of God' and disposing the new-born to receive

---

25. It has to be born in mind, of course, that the mind, the will, the affections, the conscience, and the memory are not component parts of the soul, functioning independently of one another. However, modern psychology still distinguishes between the cognitive, the emotional, the affective and the volitional; and neuro-science relates these functions closely to different parts of the brain.

the kingdom of God as a little child, 'who thinks he has sufficient ground to believe anything if his father do but say it is so' (p. 213).

The will

Secondly, regenerating grace 'gives the will a new turn'. Boston is careful to point out, however, that this does not mean that the will is forced. It is 'sweetly, yet powerfully drawn' by the 'heavenly oratory' of the Mediator's lips. Yet, supernatural though the experience is, it is not irrational. The heavenly oratory *persuades* sinners, and this goes back to the Lord's love for the soul He died for: a love that 'acts so powerfully that it must come off victorious' (p. 214). It is interesting to note here the close interaction between the cognitive and the volitional. Strictly speaking, it is the mind, not the will, that is persuaded, but once the mind is persuaded, the will turns (though we have to remind ourselves, as the Shorter Catechism points out [Answer 31] that in effectual calling God renews as well as persuades). It would be unwise, however, to see these as separate actions. When God's time comes, the one divine word is simultaneously both persuasive and re-creative, and thus grants, through grace, the response it commands.[26]

The effect of this renewal is to bring the human will into conformity to the will of God, but there are, says Boston, two aspects to this. First, we are brought into conformity to God's *preceptive* will, and thus filled with a holy inclination to obey all that God commands (already a robust answer, surely, to the charge that Boston and his *Marrow* brethren were antinomians); and, secondly, our wills are conformed to God's *providential* will. Instead of aspiring to plot their own course, the regenerate sinner is reconciled with things they could never have been reconciled to in their unregenerate state. Here Boston homes in on one detail in particular: the renewed soul is reconciled to the covenant of peace. The unregenerate heart, by contrast, could never be pleased with it: 'Were it put into their hands to frame it according to their minds they would blot many things out of it which God has put in, and put in many things which God has kept out.' But the renewed heart is entirely satisfied with the covenant: 'there is nothing in it which they would have out; nor is anything left out of it, which they would have in' (p. 216). And now

---

26. Cf. Augustine's prayer, 'Grant what you command, and command what you will' (*Confessions* Bk. X.40. See the Oxford World's Classics edition, translated by Henry Chadwick; Oxford University Press, 1998, p. 202).

that the mind is enlightened and the will renewed there is room made for Christ in the innermost parts of the soul, the inner door of the will being now opened to Him as well as the outer door of the understanding: a fascinating distinction between the cognitive and the volitional, but not one which should be understood chronologically. The mind is no sooner persuaded than the will is turned.

The affections

Thirdly, the new birth effects a twofold change in the affections: it rectifies misplaced affections so that the main stream of a person's desire is no longer towards the world, but towards God; and it regulates and sanctifies lawful affections.

What Boston has in mind under the first heading is that there may, for example, be desires after Christ which are rooted not in love for Him, but in self-love; and there may also be an unsanctified sorrow for sin arising only from a fear of divine wrath. Grace sanctifies such affections, making them run in the new channel of love to God, giving Him the chief place in our hearts and lives, and pulling down all rivals. The regenerate person is prepared to give up even lawful enjoyments when they threaten his relationship with Christ. In sum, grace turns the affections upside down: the very truth that Thomas Chalmers would later encapsulate in his sermon, 'The Expulsive Power of a New Affection.'[27]

Boston's survey also includes some reflection on the effect that regeneration has on the conscience[28] and on the body, whose members were once 'instruments of unrighteousness unto sin, but are now servants to righteousness and holiness' (Rom. 6:13, 19). Nor is he content with merely stating the general principle. Drawing on biblical allusions, he sent his congregation home conscious as never before of the use to which they were putting their eyes, their ears and their tongues.

---

27. See Thomas Chalmers, *Discourses on the Application of Christianity to the Commercial and Ordinary Affairs of Life* (Edinburgh: Constable, 1848), pp. 209-33. The key idea of the sermon is that love of the world cannot be expelled by merely exposing its vanity and insignificance. Instead, the mind must be presented with a vision of something more lovely, represented by Chalmers as 'some happy island of the blest', teeming with 'beatific scenes, and beatific society.' In the terminology of Jesus, the love of earthly treasure can be expelled only by the discovery of 'the pearl of great price'.

28. 'The renewed conscience drives the sinner to Jesus Christ, as the only Physician who can draw out the sting of guilt' (*The Fourfold State,* p. 221).

Less predictable was the attention Boston gave to the impact of regeneration on the memory. It had not wanted its share of depravity, but no less certainly would it share in the benefits of renewing grace, and one clear practical result of this would be that the memory is weakened with regard to things that are not worth remembering. In particular, grace teaches men to forget injuries and drop their resentments. On the other hand, the memory is strengthened for spiritual things, storing up the truths and precepts of Scripture; and this may be the case even with those not naturally gifted with a good memory. 'Grace', writes Boston, 'makes a heart-memory, even where there is no good head-memory' (p. 221). Beyond this, the memory is also the storehouse of former experiences of God's goodness, and from it faith and hope may draw comfort in many a dark hour. Conversely, however, it also presents old guilt anew before the conscience, making it 'bleed afresh' even though the sin is already pardoned. Memory can 'bring in a word, which in a moment sets the whole soul astir' (p. 222).

Finally, regeneration leads to a transformed lifestyle. There will, for example, be a change in social preferences. Formerly, the new convert despised the company of converted people; now he delights in it. 'In vain,' writes Boston, 'do men pretend to religion while ungodly company is their choice' (p. 223). Underlying this is the fact that the piety of Protestant Scotland was always a social affair. Believers loved getting together, and this was one factor behind the great Communion gatherings. People were attracted not only by the preaching, but by the calls of friendship and by the pleasures of spiritual comradeship: a comradeship which was frequently justified by appeal to the words of Malachi 3:16, 'they that feared the Lord spake often one to another.'

But it was not only in his attitude to the saints that the new-born person was changed. Grace transforms all our relationships: 'It does not only make good men and good women, but makes good subjects, good husbands, good wives, children, servants, and, in a word, good relations in the church, commonwealth and family' (p. 223). And he continues, 'Real godliness will gain a testimony to a man from the consciences of his nearest relations, though they know more of his sinful infirmities than others do.'

At the same time, the change will show in the way a man conducts his outward business. Christians will indeed apply themselves to it, but it will no longer be their consuming passion: 'It is evident that they are carrying on a trade with heaven as well as a trade with earth' (p. 224). But while the regenerate person lives in comparative detachment from his secular business, he is assiduous in the performance of what Boston calls his religious duties, and particularly in prayer. 'It is as natural for one that is born again to pray, as for the new-born babe to cry' (p. 225). Natural it may be, indeed; but whether it is always as easy as it is for a baby to cry, is another matter entirely. The very fact that it is spoken of as a duty should alert us to the difficulties many experience with regard to prayer. An infant does not regard crying as its duty; and it is certainly not tormented, as many evangelicals are today, by its attainments in prayer or by the quality of its crying-life. Still, none will quarrel with the standard Boston sets for the man or woman who has received the Spirit of grace: 'His heart will be a temple for God, and his house a church. His devotion, which before was superficial and formal, is now spiritual and lively, forasmuch as heart and tongue are touched with a live coal from heaven' (p. 225).

We may take Boston's attitude to business as typical of the attitude which prevailed in seventeenth and early eighteenth-century Scottish Presbyterianism, and it certainly does not sit well with the thesis that Calvinists saw success in business as the way to make their calling and election sure; or that, driven by this motive, they practised frugality, wisely invested the money they saved, rationalised industrial and commercial practices, and regarded the resulting prosperity as a mark of divine favour.[29] It would be hazardous to argue that no Presbyterian was ever driven by the profit-motive and that no Calvinist mill-owner ever put profit before humanity,[30] but if they did, it was not as an outcrop

---

29. This was the widely influential thesis argued in Max Weber, *The Protestant Ethic and the Spirit of Capitalism* (1904–05; English translation by Talcott Parsons, 1930: reprinted New York: Dover Publications, 2003). How durable Weber's theory has proved can be seen in, for example, Edmund S. Morgan, *American Slavery, American Freedom: The Ordeal of Colonial Virginia* (New York: Norton and Company, 1975). According to Morgan (pp. 295-96), the Protestant Ethic 'excited in employers and employees alike a zeal for work that exceeded anything the world had formerly known. Men imbued with a yearning for salvation found in diligent, systematic work at their jobs a sign of their predestined election to the joys of paradise. The extraordinary capacity for work displayed by men addicted to the Protestant Ethic was the by-product of a special religious zeal.' African slavery is made to fit into this overall thesis as a way of compelling men to maximum output without provoking rebellion on the part of Virginia's white colonists.

30. See, for example, the experience of Keir Hardie, first Parliamentary Leader of the Labour Party. As a child aged about nine, his earnings of four shillings and sixpence a week (less than 25 pence in 'today's money') were his family's only income. One winter morning he was late for work, having had to tend to his pregnant mother. On arrival, he was told he had to go upstairs to see the Master. He was then kept waiting outside the dining-room

of their Calvinism, but in defiance of the portrait of a Christian lifestyle drawn for them by such preachers as Thomas Boston. In this portrait, men viewed their employment not as their main priority in life, and certainly not as first and foremost a means of growing money, but as a duty laid on them by God; or, more bluntly, they worked, according to Boston (p. 224), because God had said, 'Thou shalt not steal' (Eph. 6:7).

Knowing we are born again

When he addressed the question, 'How shall we know whether we are born again?' it never occurred to Boston to suggest that successful investments might be a sign of divine election. Indeed, while he was not short of moments of melancholy, it does not appear that he himself was overly troubled by the question of assurance; nor was his assurance a matter of logical inference from the 'marks of grace'. It was much more direct, and already implicit in the nature of faith itself. 'Were you to ask me,' he writes, 'if the sun were risen, and how you should know that it were risen or not, I would bid you look up to the heavens, and see it with your eyes. And would you know if the light be risen in your heart? Look in, and see. Grace is light, and discovers itself' (p. 230).

Having said this, however, he does not altogether dismiss the value of the 'marks', and of one 'mark' in particular. It has nothing to do, however, with the fortunes of a man's financial capital. Instead, Boston focuses on the great apostolic sign, 'love of the brethren' (1 John 3:14), 'an evidence whereby the weakest and most timorous saints have often had comfort, when they could have little or no consolation from other marks proposed to them' (p. 231). He points out, perhaps unnecessarily, that 'brethren' cannot refer to those who are our brothers by a common relation to Adam, because, 'however true it is that universal benevolence, a good will to the whole race of mankind, takes place in the renewed soul, as being a lively lineament [delineation] of the divine image,' yet the whole context speaks

---

while the Master, noted for his religious zeal, said a long grace before breakfast. When at last he was admitted, he saw a room such as he had never seen before, and a table loaded with such food as he had never seen before. He was given a long lecture, and warned that, should he sin again, he would be instantly dismissed. Two days later, he was late again for the same reason; and dismissed he was. Recalling the experience years afterwards, he described it as 'not only a turning-point in my life, but also in my outlook on men and things' (William Stewart, *Keir Hardie: A Biography* [London: Keir Hardie Memorial Committee, 1921], p. 4).

of love for those who are the children of God and who, precisely for that reason, are hated by the world (p. 231). Those who are dead in sin cannot love such people; conversely, such love is a clear sign that we have passed from death to life.

It is often suggested that the arrival of the Enlightenment, and with it the new-style preaching of the Moderates, marked an end to the old Calvinism's preoccupation with theological dogma and its replacement with a new emphasis on 'morality'.[31] Boston's careful exposition of the fruits of regeneration, and especially the stress he lays on the impact of the new birth on all our social relationships, shows the hollowness of such a construction; and even a cursory survey of his *Works* is enough to show that this exposition of the practical effects of the gospel was no isolated moment, but a key part of his message. For example, Volume II contains a 320-page exposition of the Ten Commandments; Volume IV contains discourses on such subjects as 'Privileges and Duties of a Christian Spouse,' 'The Fruit of the Spirit,' and 'Anger not to be sinfully Indulged'; and Volume 5 contains sermons on 'The Citizen of Zion an Upright Walker' and, 'The Citizen of Zion a Worker of Righteousness.' Such preaching followed the precedent set by John Calvin, who had included in his *Institutes* (II:VIII) a lengthy exposition of the Moral Law;[32] and a Scottish precedent had also been set a generation before Boston by James Durham's *Practical Exposition of the Ten Commandments*.[33] Such expositions clearly reflect the Reformed doctrine that, while the Law is not the way *to* life, it is the way *of* life prescribed for Christian believers.

This does not mean, however, that there was no difference between 'morality' as preached by such men as Boston and Durham, and morality as preached by the Moderates (and by those of Boston's own day who accused him and other like-minded preachers of being antinomians). For one thing, they had different criteria. The eighteenth-century pulpit, taking

---

31. See, for example, Professor Stewart J. Brown's comment in his essay, 'Moderate Theology and Preaching,' 'Moderates sought to restore the place of good works in Scotland's Reformed theology' (David Ferguson and Mark W. Elliott, [Eds.], *The History of Scottish Theology, Volume II: The Early Enlightenment to the Late Victorian Era*, p. 74).

32. Both Francis Turretin (*Institutes of Elenctic Theology*, Volume Two, pp 38-137) and Charles Hodge (*Systematic Theology*, Vol. III, pp. 277-465) also include extended expositions of the Ten Commandments in their magisterial summaries of Reformed Theology.

33. This volume was published (with a Commendatory Epistle by John Owen) only in 1675, seventeen years after Durham's death. Later editions bore the title, *The Law Unsealed*.

its terminology from the Classics, began to speak of 'virtue', and equated it with civility, refinement, culture and general benevolence. Boston's concern was with sanctification, by which he meant consecration to God and conformity to the image of Christ; and whereas for the Moderates 'virtue' was well within the compass of the 'natural man' (as represented by Seneca, and even David Hume), for Boston, holiness was impossible without renewal and new birth. Its presupposition was union with Christ and the indwelling of the Holy Spirit. More important still, for Boston and those others who continued the Reformation tradition, morality could never be the way to salvation. After all, it required little self-knowledge to realise that Scripture was quite right to speak of our righteousness as no better than filthy rags. This was a note that Moderatism tended to suppress, just as it suppressed the doctrine of original sin and saw little need to major on either the cross of Christ or justification by faith alone. The paradox, as Thomas Chalmers would discover later, is that the mere preaching of morality can never produce it.[34] Only the proclamation of Christ crucified (1 Cor. 1:23) can produce the life-style delineated in First Corinthians Thirteen.

Union with Christ

Having covered the nature of regeneration, Boston turns to the second feature of the state of grace: our union with Christ. This has always been central to the Reformed doctrine of the experience of salvation, as can be seen already in Calvin's answer to the question, 'How do we become partakers of the Grace of Christ?' 'First,' he replies, 'we must understand that as long as Christ remains outside of us, and we are separated from him, all that he has suffered and done for the salvation of the human race remains useless and of no value for us. Therefore, to share with us what he has received from the Father, he had to become ours and to dwell within us.'[35] All that he possesses, Calvin continues, is nothing to us until we

---

34. In an 'Address to the Inhabitants of the Parish of Kilmany,' published in 1815 (the year of his translation to Glasgow's Tron Church), Chalmers described the early years of his ministry in Kilmany as 'an undesigned experiment' devoted mainly to expatiating on 'the meanness of dishonesty, on the villainy of falsehood, on the despicable arts of calumny.' But the experiment had been a complete failure: 'I am not sensible that all the vehemence with which I urged the virtues and the proprieties of social life, had the weight of a feather on the moral habits of my parishioners' (quoted in William Hanna, *Memoirs of the Life and Writings of Thomas Chalmers*; 4 Vols., Edinburgh: Constable, 1852), Vol. I, pp. 430-31.

35. *Institutes*, ed. John T. McNeill, tr. Ford Lewis Battles, III:I, 1.

grow into one body with Him; and this union can be effected only 'by the secret energy of the Holy Spirit, by which we come to enjoy Christ and all his benefits.'

It is at this same point that Boston begins his discussion. The union is not merely a federal, legal or external one between the Mediator and those He represents. It is a spiritual union such that Christ and true believers become one spirit:[36] 'As one soul or spirit actuates both the head and the members in the natural body, so the one Spirit of God dwells in Christ and the Christian'; and precisely because it is spiritual, the union is both real and 'most intimate' (p. 255). He also describes it as 'mystical' (indeed this is his chapter-heading), but he clearly does not mean by this that it provides an avenue to so-called mystical experiences or to 'sensible' communications between man and the divine, far less to absorption into the divine. He uses it purely in the sense of 'mysterious':

> O what mysteries are here! The Head in heaven, the members on earth, yet really united! Christ in the believer, living in him, walking in him: and the believer dwelling in God, putting on the Lord Jesus, eating his flesh and drinking his blood! This makes the saints a mystery to the world, yea, a mystery to themselves (p. 257).

Boston then moves on to a rich exposition of the benefits that flow from our union with Christ: benefits which become ours the moment we are united to Christ by faith, and which we can never lose.

Justification

The first of these is justification, and here Boston graphically emphasises just how complete is the absolution granted to the believer: 'God the Father takes the pen, dips it in the blood of his Son, crosses the sinner's account, and blots them out of his debt-book' (p. 286). Formerly, his sins could not be hidden: now God casts them all behind his back:

> Yea, he casts them into the depths of the sea (Micah 7:19). What falls into a brook may be got up again, but what is cast into the sea cannot be recovered. But there are some shallow places in the sea? True, but their sins are not cast in there, but into the *depths* of the sea; and the depths of the sea are devouring depths, from whence they shall never come forth again. But what if they do not sink? He will cast them in with force, so that they shall go to the ground, and

---

36. *Human Nature in its Fourfold State*, p. 254.

sink as lead in the mighty waters of the Redeemer's blood. They are not only forgiven, but forgotten (p. 287, italics added).

The basis of this is the soul's communion with Christ, taking the word 'communion' in its literal sense of 'sharing'. Once we are united to Christ, all His unsearchable riches become ours, including His righteousness; and righteousness, Boston declares, is an absolute: 'The very name of it implies perfection, for unless a work is perfectly conformed to the law, it is not right, but wrong, and so cannot make a man righteous before God, whose judgement is according to truth' (p. 288). It is exactly such a perfect righteousness that becomes ours in Christ. His righteousness becomes ours, just as our sin became His (2 Cor. 5:21); and although Boston doesn't quite say it, what he is driving towards is that every member of the body of Christ has the same credit in heaven as Christ Himself.

Peace

Secondly, and through our justification, comes peace: peace with God and peace of conscience (peace with ourselves). Boston notes, inevitably, that unbelievers, too, can get their troubled consciences quieted: 'Many,' he notes, 'bury their guilt in the grave of an ill memory: conscience smarts a little; at length the man forgets his sin, and there is an end of it; but that is only an ease before death' (p. 290). Or perhaps they will find peace by the performance of such duties as praying, confessing their sin and resolving never to repeat it, 'and so they become whole again, without an application of the blood of Christ by faith' (p. 290). But for believers, 'sin leaves a sting behind it, which one time or other will create them no little pain,' and the pain is not easily cured: 'The physician's art cannot prevail here: the disease lies more inward than his medicines can reach.' It is soul trouble that has caused the disorder, and 'the physician for this case must be a spiritual physician; the remedies must be spiritual, a righteousness, a ransom, an atonement' (p. 291). The conscience can be truly quieted only by the blood of sprinkling, which purifies as well as pacifies. Yet, though 'only' the blood cleanses, it avails for *all* sin, as the prophet Isaiah proclaims so eloquently: 'Though your sins be as scarlet, they shall be as white as snow; though they be red like crimson, they shall be as wool' (Isa. 1:18).

Adoption

Thirdly, through our union with Christ, who is the Son of God by nature, we, who by nature were children of the devil, *become* children of God by grace. Here, Boston majors on the subjective consequences of this adoption. Believers are not only given a new status as members of the family of heaven (p. 293): they are given the Spirit of the Son (Gal. 4:6), and with it the confidence to approach God as a Father, pouring out their complaints to Him, and seeking necessary supplies. In all their weakness, they can rely on their Father's compassion and pity; when pursued by enemies He is their place of refuge; at a time of common calamity, He is their protection; what He sees they have need of, they will not lack. They are, after all, heirs of God, and He is not only their Provider, but their provision.

But divine correction and discipline are likewise the privilege of God's children: 'they are not suffered to pass with their faults, like others who are not children but servants of the family' (p. 293). On the other hand, because they are children of the Great King, and heirs of salvation, 'they have angels for their attendants.'

Sanctification

The fourth benefit Boston highlights is sanctification, which he traces directly to the fact that in union with Christ we partake of the fulness of His Spirit, the Spirit of holiness. This fulness, Boston reminds us, is not like the fulness of a vessel, which only retains what is poured into it. It is the fulness of a fountain, which is always sending forth its waters, and yet is always full;[37] and where these waters flow, 'there will be found a confluence of all graces. Holiness is not one grace only, but all the graces of the Spirit; it is a constellation of all graces; it is all the graces in their seed and root' (p. 294). And as he had highlighted in his general comments on regeneration, sanctification affects the whole person. There may be 'top branch' graces which appear more conspicuous than the rest but, 'The truth we are sanctified by is not held in the head, as in a prison, but runs, with its sanctifying influences, through heart and life' (p. 294).

In his analysis of sanctification, Boston focuses on two points: mortification and vivification. His portrayal of the former is governed by his understanding of Paul's image of the crucifixion of the old man (Rom. 6:5). There can be little doubt that in the Apostle's thought the old

---

37. Cf. John 4:14: 'Whoever drinks of the water that I will give him will never be thirsty again. The water that I will give him will become in him a spring of water welling up to eternal life' (ESV).

man (the unregenerate man) is definitively crucified and put to death the moment the believer is united to Christ,[38] but Boston, following a long exegetical tradition, picks up on the fact that crucifixion was 'a lingering death', and as such, an image of the slow process of the mortification of sin: 'Sin in the saint, though not quite dead, yet it is dying. If it were dead, it would be taken down from the cross, and buried out of his sight; but it hangs there as yet, working and struggling under its mortal wounds' (p. 295). This clearly implies that the believer still has a battle on his hands, but sin is no longer, as it was in the past, his trade and business. He is walking now in the way of holiness, even though the wind from hell, that was on his back before, is now blowing full in his face, making his travelling uneasy and often driving him off the highway. This is clearly true to experience, but (like this era of Reformed theology as a whole) it fails to do justice to the doctrine of Definitive Sanctification. The death of the old man is not the goal of mortification, but its starting point; or, as John Murray called it, 'the dynamic of the Christian ethic.'[39] Without this, the old Adam becomes an all too convenient excuse for failure.

When it comes to vivification, Boston gives us a succinct definition: 'the soul, being influenced by the sanctifying Spirit of Christ, is enabled more and more to perform all the actions of the spiritual life' (p. 295). Once again, however, he sounds a discriminatory note. How can true sanctification[40] be distinguished from what he calls the 'shadow' of it to be found among some who, though strict professors of Christianity, are not regenerate and whose sanctification is no different from what has appeared among many sober heathens? This latter sanctification, Boston avers, has no supernatural roots, but is the product of man's own spirit, and it reminds him of common boatmen, 'who serve themselves with their own oars; whereas the ship bound for Immanuel's land sails by the blowing of

---

38. On this, see the chapter, 'The Dynamic of the Biblical Ethic,' in John Murray, *Principles of Conduct* (London: Tyndale Press, 1957).

39. John Murray, *Principles of Conduct* (London: Tyndale Press, 1957), pp. 203-28; and John Murray, *The Epistle to the Romans: The English Text with Introduction, Exposition and Notes*, Vol. 1 (Grand Rapids: Eerdmans, 1959), pp. 217-226.

40. In Boston's *Works* Vol. VIII, p. 213, the word 'satisfaction' is used in the first line of the relevant paragraph where 'sanctification' is clearly intended, and the typo is repeated in the Banner of Truth edition (p. 297). The rest of the paragraph makes plain that 'sanctification' is meant.

the divine Spirit' (p. 298).[41] It is a moot point, however, whether this image does full justice to the overall biblical picture, which clearly emphasises the believer's own role in sanctification, not least in the instruction the Apostle Paul gave to the church in Philippi, 'Work out your own salvation' (Phil. 2:12).[42] Even here, however, it is clear that whatever our own input, it is the consequence of prevenient grace, 'for it is God who works in you both the willing and the doing' (Phil. 2:13). We row with all our might precisely because the wind of the Spirit is blowing behind us.

The fundamental concern remains, however: true spiritual life and activity flow from union with Christ, and here Boston's thought takes a fascinating turn, leading him to emphasise that our union is with 'the man Christ'. In the incarnation, human nature is united to the divine person of the Son, and as a result of this union His humanity lies at the fountainhead 'as the glorious means of conveyance of influences from the fountain of Deity' (p. 296). Probing further, he writes that, since there could not be an immediate communion between the holy God and a sinful creature, the Second Person of the Trinity took into a personal union with Himself a sinless human nature; through this union, His human nature immediately receives a fulness of the Spirit; and from this fulness He communicates the Spirit to the members of His body, 'by his divine power and efficacy'. Grace is thus mediated to us through the humanity of Christ, and here Boston takes up the imagery used by our Lord in John 6:51.[43] Believers feed on the precious body of Christ, applying Him to their souls by faith, and thus they partake more and more of the Spirit who dwells in *Him*, to their spiritual nourishment.

But how can there be such a communion between Christ and His members, considering that He is in heaven and they are on earth? Boston replies (p. 297):

> Suppose there were a tree, with its root in the earth, and its branches reaching to heaven, the vast distance between the root and the branches would not interrupt the communication between the root and the top branch: even so,

---

41. A similar image occurs in Karl Barth, *Church Dogmatics*, II:1, p. 569. In Barth, however, it is used to illustrate the Molinist doctrine of the will, whereby justification depends on the cooperation between the human will and prevenient grace, the two working together like two men pulling a boat.

42. Cf. 1 John 3:3, 'Everyone who thus hopes in him purifies himself as he is pure' (ESV).

43. 'I am the living bread which came down from heaven; if any man eat of this bread, he shall live for ever: and the bread which I will give is my flesh, which I will give for the life of the world.'

the distance between the man Christ, who is in heaven, and his members, who are on earth, cannot hinder the communication between them. What though the parts of mystical Christ, namely the Head and the members, are not contiguous, as joined together in the way of corporal union; the union is not therefore the less real and effective. The members of Christ on earth are united to their Head in heaven, by the invisible bond of the same Spirit dwelling in both.[44]

There can be no true sanctification, then, without partaking of the Spirit of holiness; and there can be no partaking of this Spirit, but through Jesus Christ (p. 298): 'The falling dew shall as soon make its way through the flinty rock, as the influences of grace come from God to sinners any other way than through him whom the Father has appointed the head of influences, Col. 1:19, "For it pleased the Father that in him should all fulness dwell"....'

Following his treatment of sanctification Boston focuses on the believer's spiritual growth, beginning with the observation that, 'If a branch grafted into a stock never grows, it is a plain evidence of its not having knit with the stock' (p. 299). But what about those who, instead of growing, are going back? 'There is a great difference,' he replies, 'between the Christian's growing simply, and his growing at all times. A tree that has life and nourishment grows to its perfection, yet it is not always growing; it grows not in the winter. Christians also have their winters, wherein the influences of grace, necessary for their growth, cease.'

The tree's winter, however, is inevitable: a Christian's is not. It is by faith (the 'pipe,' as Boston calls it) that the believer derives gracious influences from Christ, and if that pipe is stopped (as it is when our faith becomes

---

44. This is reminiscent of the argument Calvin uses (*Institutes* IV:XVII, 10) in support of his doctrine of the presence of Christ in the Lord's Supper: 'Even though it seems unbelievable that Christ's flesh, separated from us by such great distance, penetrates to us, so that it becomes our food, let us remember how far the secret power of the Holy Spirit towers above all our senses, and how foolish it is to measure his immeasurableness by our measure. What, then, our mind does not comprehend, let faith conceive: that the Holy Spirit truly unites things separated in space.' This statement has provoked considerable discussion, and some consternation, but interesting light is shed upon it by a comment Calvin makes in the course of his commentary on Psalm 102:24: 'Now since God links (Lat. *coniungit*) us to himself by means of his word, however great the distance of our frail condition from his heavenly glory, our faith should nevertheless penetrate to that blessed state from which he looks down upon our miseries.' Calvin's point, overall, is that just as God can teach us by His Word despite the immense space that separates us, so He can feed us with the bread of life in the sacrament despite the great distance between us and the body of Christ (See Calvin's *Commentary on the Book of Psalms*, Vol. 4; Edinburgh, 1847, p. 121).

dormant and inactive), 'then all the rest of the graces will become dim, and seem ready to be extinguished' (p. 299). Still, the saint's faith is not like the hypocrite's, a pipe laid short of the fountain. It ever remains the bond of union between Christ and the soul, and when the Lord clears the means of conveyance the influences of grace will resume their flow, 'and the believer's graces look fresh and green again.'

And once again, Boston returns to a favourite theme: growing Christians, ingrafted in Christ, 'grow in all the several ways of growth at once' (p. 301). They grow *inward*, cleaving more firmly to Christ; they grow *outward* in good works; they grow *upward* in heavenly-mindedness; and they grow *downward* in humility and self-loathing. The fruits of holiness will be found in the hearts, lips and lives of all who are united to Christ; and, at the farthest possible remove from the antinomianism with which he and his friends were soon to be charged, he insists that the godly person performs the duties of both the first and the second tables of the law: 'In his conversation he is a good Christian, and a good neighbour too. He carries it towards God as if men's eyes were upon him; and towards men, as believing God's eyes to be upon him. Those things which God hath joined in his law, he dares not put asunder in his practice' (p. 303).

There follows some counsel, illuminated by homely horticultural imagery, as to how spiritual fruitfulness may be promoted. The primary thing, as always, is that the branch must be sound at the heart, and this depends entirely on the strength of the bond between it and the stock: 'the smallest twig that is sound at the heart will draw nourishment from the stock and grow, while the greatest bough that is rotten can never recover, because it receives no nourishment' (p. 304). But it is important, too, that the tree should be firm and steadfast, not blown about by the winds of theological and religious fashion (Eph. 4:14, 15): 'Though a tree be never so sound, yet how can it grow, or be fruitful, if you be still removing it out of one soil into another' (p. 304). And remember, he adds, to cut off the suckers:[45] unmortified lusts which use up the energy and nourishment which the tree needs if it is to flourish. To feed our own cravings is to starve our souls.

But removing the suckers can never be enough. The tree must be fed, and the only place where it can be fed is by 'the waters of the sanctuary'.

---

45. A sucker, the plague of rose-growers, is a shoot which grows from the (wild) root-stock, below the graft. It will never produce the desired flowers, but it will deprive the plant of nourishment, and must be pulled off below the graft (not cut above ground).

'Come to these wells of salvation,' he urges, 'not to look at them only, but to draw water out of them'; and here he singles out the Lord's Supper for special mention: 'The sacrament of the Lord's Supper is in a special manner appointed for these ends. It is not only a solemn public profession, and a seal of our union and communion with Christ, but it is a means of most intimate communion with him, and strengthens our union with him, our faith, love, repentance and other graces' (pp. 304-5).

We may note, finally, one other benefit flowing from union with Christ: 'establishment,' or what we know better as the Perseverance of the Saints. *Moved* they may be, but *removed* they never can be, even though there is always some wind blowing, and the branches are never at rest. But the Christian is improved by trial, he writes, invoking another homely analogy: 'the wind in the bellows, which would blow out the candle, blows up the fire' (p. 308). There is a danger, however, of drawing too simplistic a picture here. Suffering can also discourage and depress the spirit, as the writer to the Hebrews testifies when he highlights the danger of 'fainting' under divine rebukes (Heb. 12:3). But Boston is never blind to the need to discriminate. While those truly grafted into Christ are secure, in a time of peace and prosperity (such as the church in Scotland enjoyed in the years following the Revolution of 1688) 'there are a great many branches taken up and put in the stock, which never knit with it, nor live by it, though they be bound to it by the bonds of external ordinances. Now these may stand a while on the stock, and stand with great ease while the calm lasts; but when once the storms arise, and the winds blow, they will begin to fall off one after another' (p. 308). But no matter how violent the storms of trouble and persecution, none of the truly engrafted branches are found missing: 'The least twig growing in Christ shall stand it out, and subsist, when the tallest cedars growing on their own root shall be laid flat on the ground' (p. 309). However, the reason for this is not any inherent durability in believers themselves. There are temptations, he writes, which a believer can no more throw off than a child can overcome a giant, and then deliverance can come 'only from the root that bears them, from the everlasting arm that is underneath them.' 'The great stay of the believer,' he writes, 'is not the grace of God within him; that is a well whose streams sometimes run dry; but it is the grace of God without [outside] him, the grace that is in Jesus Christ, which is an ever-flowing fountain, to which the believer can never come amiss' (p. 312).

The chapter closes, in Boston's manner, on an evangelistic note addressed to both saints and sinners (the unregenerate). Addressing the latter, he warns them of both the sinfulness and the misery of an unregenerate state. But then he hastens on to assure them that their case is not hopeless. Christ is still standing at the door, knocking:

> Heaven is proposing a union with earth still; the potter is making a suit [appeal] to his own clay; and the gates of the city of refuge are not yet closed. O that we could compel you to come in! (p. 231).

Conclusion

After the vagaries of its journey to publication, *The Fourfold State* quickly went on to become a favourite with Scotland's Christian public, especially with the class portrayed in Robert Burns' classic poem, *The Cottar's Saturday Night*. In the fifty years following its publication, it went through more than fifty editions, and that number has since risen to over eighty (including two Gaelic editions, one in 1811 and one in 1825), making it the most published work in the whole history of Scottish theology.[46] Even in the twentieth century it occupied a conspicuous place beside *The Pilgrim's Progress* on many a Scottish bookshelf. Its style didn't meet the approval of the Edinburgh *literati*, and it certainly never became an international best-seller on the scale of the *Sermons* of Hugh Blair, Professor of Rhetoric at Edinburgh University and model of the cultured Enlightenment preacher.[47] But Blair's *Sermons* seldom stretch the mind, while Boston both stretches it and feeds it; and while Boston is unlikely to be awarded critical acclaim, his prose yields its meaning readily. You seldom need to read one of his sentences twice to grasp its meaning.

The Fourfold State may no longer have the popularity it once did, even among those who share Boston's theology, but it is probably safe to say that it is more widely read today than Blair's *Sermons*. Few may have read it from cover to cover, but not the least of its virtues is that you can open it at any chapter and on any page, and quickly come across something worthwhile.

---

46. Thomas F. Torrance, *Scottish Theology from John Knox to John McLeod Campbell* (Edinburgh: T&T Clark, 1996), p. 220.

47. Blair's *Sermons* were published in five volumes between 1777 and 1801. Within seventeen years the first volume had reached its nineteenth edition.

3

The Affair of 'The Marrow'

ON THE 6TH of November 1720, after his travails with his sponsor and his printer, Boston was finally able to handle his bound copy of *The Fourfold State*. By this time, however, other ominous clouds had gathered. We have already seen that, probably as early as 1700, in the course of a visit to one of his parishioners, Boston had come across a copy of *The Marrow of Modern Divinity.*[1] He had borrowed it, 'relished it greatly,'[2] digested its message and

---

1.   Edward Fisher, *The Marrow of Modern Divinity* (London, 1645. Reprinted with Notes by the Rev. Thomas Boston, 1726). This occupies pp. 146-464 of Boston's *Works,* Vol. 7. Quotations from the *Marrow* in this chapter are from a reprint of Boston's edition published in 1978 (Swengel, PA: Reiner Publications). For an updated version with Boston's notes, see Edward Fisher, *The Marrow of Modern Divinity* (Geanies House, Ross-shire: Christian Focus Publications, 2009).

See further, James Hadow, *The Antinomianism of the Marrow of Modern Divinity Detected* (Edinburgh, 1721); Robert Riccaltoun, *A Sober Enquiry into the Grounds of the Present Differences in the Church of Scotland* (Edinburgh, 1723); John Brown of Whitburn, *Gospel Truth Accurately Stated and Vindicated by the Reverend Messrs James Hog, Thomas Boston, Ebenezer and Ralph Erskine* (Edinburgh, 1817); Thomas M'Crie, *Account of the Controversy respecting the Marrow of Modern Divinity*, Vol XXX, No. VIII (1831) to Vol. I, No. II (New Series, 1832); Donald Beaton, 'The Marrow of Modern Divinity and the Marrow Controversy' (*Records of the Scottish Church History Society*, Vol. 1, 1926, pp. 112-34); James Walker, *The Theology and Theologians of Scotland 1560–1750* (Second edition 1888; reprinted Knox Press [Edinburgh], 1982, pp. 86-94); D. M. McIntyre, 'First Strictures on *The Marrow of Modern Divinity*' (*Evangelical Quarterly*, 10 [1938], pp. 61-70); John Macleod, *Scottish Theology in Relation to Church History Since the Reformation* (1943. Reprinted Edinburgh: Banner of Truth Trust, 2015, pp. 145-73); Thomas F. Torrance, *Scottish Theology from John Knox to John McLeod Campbell* (Edinburgh: T&T Clark, 1996, pp. 204-20); David C. Lachman, *The Marrow Controversy: An Historical and Theological Analysis* (Edinburgh: Rutherford House, 1988); Sinclair B. Ferguson, *The Whole Christ: Legalism Antinomianism and Gospel Assurance – Why the Marrow Controversy Still Matters* (Wheaton: Crossway, 2016).

2.   Boston, *Memoirs*, p. 160.

begun to preach it. He began to recommend it to friends, until it eventually came into the hands of James Hog (1658–1734), Minister of Carnock in the Presbytery of Dunfermline,[3] and in 1718 Hog had the First Part reprinted with a Preface from his own pen. This provoked 'a mighty stir', especially in the Presbytery of Fife, where there had already been serious disagreement over the question of the conditionality of the Covenant of Grace; and in a sermon preached before the Synod of Fife in April 1719, James Hadow, Principal of St Mary's College, St Andrews, attacked the *Marrow*. The sermon was quickly published under the title, 'The Record of God, and duty of faith therein required.' The *Marrow* was then complained of to the General Assembly of 1719; the Assembly, without naming the *Marrow*, directed its Commission to inquire into the publishing and spreading of books and pamphlets promoting opinions inconsistent with the Confession of Faith;[4] the Commission referred the matter to the Assembly's Committee for Preserving Purity of Doctrine (on which Hadow, by virtue of his academic position, was a dominant force); and following the report of the Committee, the Assembly on 9 May 1720 passed an Act which condemned the *Marrow* as containing not only some expressions which are 'exceedingly harsh and offensive' but also certain passages and quotations which are 'contrary to the Holy Scriptures, our Confession of Faith and Catechisms'. The *Marrow* was then declared a prohibited book, and all ministers were strictly forbidden to recommend it either by preaching, writing, printing or discourse. As if this were not enough, they were further forbidden to say anything in favour of it, and strictly instructed to warn their people 'not to read or use the same'.[5]

Boston saw the Act as a grievous blow against the doctrine of free grace, but he was not alone in this, and in the ensuing controversy he would be

---

3. For a brief biographical account of Hog, see John Brown, *Gospel Truth Accurately Stated and Illustrated*, pp. 111-21. Boston (*Memoirs*, p. 331) describes him as 'a man of great learning, and singular piety and tenderness.'

4. The overt intention of the Assembly's Act was to call to account anyone who recommended the alleged antinomianism of the so-called 'Auchterarder Creed', and especially the proposition, 'It is not sound and orthodox to teach that we must forsake sin in order to our coming to Christ.' The Presbytery had required all candidates for Licence to subscribe to this 'Creed', but one student complained of this requirement, and the matter came before the General Assembly in 1717. The Assembly declared their abhorrence of the proposition as 'unsound and detestable' and forbade its use in the licensing of probationers. The 1719 Assembly directed that all recommenders of such opinions be called before them to answer for their conduct.

5. See *Acts of the General Assembly of the Church of Scotland M.DC.XXXVIII–M.DCCC.XLII* (Edinburgh. Church Law Society, 1843), pp. 534-36.

acting in concert with others of similar sentiments. Their first step was to prepare a *Representation and Petition* for submission to the General Assembly. It was signed by twelve ministers, who, not surprisingly, quickly became known as the Twelve Brethren.[6] All were eminent in their day, but apart from Boston, the only names that might strike a chord with modern readers would be those of the brothers Ebenezer and Ralph Erskine. Of the two, it was Ebenezer who would play a prominent role.[7] At the time, he was minister of Portmoak in the Presbytery of Kirkaldy and would later be the central figure in the Secession of 1733.[8] A revered preacher and beloved pastor,[9] he had long deplored what he saw as the prevalence of the Neonomian creed, 'by which the Gospel is represented not as a revelation of free grace, but as a *new law* requiring faith, repentance and sincere obedience as the conditions of salvation.'[10] Over against such a 'dangerous, though specious and palatable scheme,' he firmly believed that the sole ground of justification was the righteousness of Christ, who, along with all His benefits, was to be offered freely and unconditionally to sinners, simply as such. These invaluable truths, he believed, had been deeply compromised by the Assembly's condemnation of the *Marrow*. He would play a conspicuous part in its defence.

The first draft of the *Representation* was prepared by the brethren of Fife, including James Hog and the brothers Erskine, but Boston and his colleagues in the south were not entirely happy with it, and he was asked to prepare another, and after several additions and alterations this was

---

6. See the 'Sketches of the Lives of those Ministers who defended the Doctrine of Grace' in John Brown, *Gospel Truth Accurately Stated and Illustrated*, pp. 38-127.

7. For Ralph's part in the controversy, see Donald Fraser, *The Life and Diary of the Reverend Ralph Erskine of Dunfermline, One of the Founders of the Secession Church* (Edinburgh: William Oliphant, 1834), pp.165-81. Fraser also edited a volume, *Fourteen Sermons on Prayer*, by Ralph Erskine (Glasgow: Fullarton, 1840). A six-volume set of *The Works of Ralph Erskine* was published in 1865 and reprinted in 1991 by Free Presbyterian Publications, Glasgow. See too, A. R MacEwen, *The Erskines* (Edinburgh: Oliphant and Anderson, 1900).

8. See Donald Fraser, *The Life and Diary of the Reverend Ebenezer Erskine of Stirling, Father of the Secession Church: To which is Prefixed a Memoir of his Father, the Rev. Henry Erskine of Chirnside* (Edinburgh: William Oliphant, 1831). Erskine Senior, as we have seen, was an influential figure in Thomas Boston's early spiritual life.

9. See James Fisher (Ed.), *Sermons and Discourses upon the Most Important and Interesting Subjects by the late Reverend Ebenezer Erskine* (4 Vols., Edinburgh: John Gray and Gavin Alston, 1761).

10. *The Life and Diary of the Reverend Ebenezer Erskine*, p. 235.

approved and signed by all the Brethren. It craved the Assembly to repeal the Act condemning the *Marrow*, and should have been dealt with by the General Assembly of May 1721, but the Assembly finished its business early, with the result that it was remitted to its Commission to deal with the *Representation*. The Commission accordingly met the day after the Assembly rose, and the Brethren were called before them, only to find themselves treated not as petitioners seeking redress but as offenders who were required to show contrition. This proved inconclusive, however, and so they were asked to attend on the August Commission of Assembly; which they did, but were not called. Instead, they were asked to meet with the November Commission, where they were told that they were required to answer certain queries which would be put to them in writing.

It is clear from Boston's *Memoirs* that the Brethren had some hesitation about answering these queries, partly because they feared that their answers would serve as the basis for further charges; partly because they feared entrapment; and partly because the wording of the queries was taken from Principal Hadow's recently published pamphlet, *The Antinomianism of the Marrow of Modern Divinity Detected*. They also knew that the August Commission had already agreed to transmit to the Assembly an overture vindicating the 1720 Act and severely censuring the Representers.

By this time, Boston was reconciled to the Brethren being cast out of the Church, yet he was clear in his own mind that they should provide answers. His recollection was that the first draft of the 'Answers to the Queries' was prepared by Ebenezer Erskine, but that it was much improved and extended by Gabriel Wilson.[11] They were signed by all the Representers,[12] presented to the Committee on Purity of Doctrine in March 1722, and tabled before the Commission of Assembly in May. But they were never read by the Assembly itself. Instead, the supreme court focused on the overture transmitted from the August Commission of Assembly; and on the basis of this overture the Assembly on 21 May 1722 passed an Act which not only reaffirmed the 1720 Act condemning the *Marrow*, but deplored the 'foul reproaches' and 'undutiful aspersions' cast by 'these twelve brethren' on the supreme

---

11. Wilson was ordained to the parish of Maxton, near Selkirk, in 1709 and he and Boston became lifelong friends. Boston refers to him (*Memoirs*, p. 348) as one whose 'vast compass of reading, with his great collection of books, were of singular use, and successfully employed.'

12. With the exception of John Bonar who was ill at the time.

judicatory of the Church, and appointed the Moderator to rebuke and admonish them: a censure they received 'with all gravity'.[13]

This did not mean, however, that they were yielding the justice of their cause. Boston, anticipating the outcome, had prepared a Protest; and after the rebuke and admonition he gave it in. It was a statement of defiance: close, indeed, to a rejection of the jurisdiction of the Assembly. It affirmed that the Act of 1720 (and other related Acts) were contrary to both the Word of God and the Standards of the Church; declared that they could not acquiesce in them even by silence; and affirmed their determination to continue to bear witness to the 'injured truths' despite the Acts, and notwithstanding the consequences. The Assembly, however, refused to read it, and quickly closed the sederunt. Had they read it, they would have had to note that it called for further, and even more serious, disciplinary measures (including deposition): an action which would have involved a risk of serious civil unrest. By ignoring it, they brought the formal judicial process against the *Marrow* to a conclusion.[14]

Boston's notes on the *Marrow*

But Boston was not done with it. In July 1721 friends suggested that he should write notes on the *Marrow*, and having, as usual, sought the mind of the Lord, he agreed because 'the gospel has got a root-stroke by the condemning of that book';[15] and so urgent did he judge the matter to be that he laid aside all other business including the preparation of the second edition of *The Fourfold State* and (an even greater sacrifice) 'my great work on accentuation'. The *Notes* were finished by July 1722, but not published (along with the text of the *Marrow*) till 1726. In deference to the authority of the General Assembly they were published under a pseudonym, *Philalethes Irenaeus* ('A Peaceable Lover of Truth'). Principal Hadow's *The Antinomianism of the Marrow of Modern Divinity* had been published five years previously, and Boston certainly had the Principal's strictures in view, but he refrained from naming him (or, indeed, any other opponents of the *Marrow*). Posterity, he remarks, unacquainted with such publications as Hadow's, may think many of

---

13. *Acts of the General Assembly of the Church of Scotland*, pp. 548-56.
14. Boston, *Memoirs*, pp. 348-49.
15. ibid., p. 345.

the notes needless, 'but at that time, many had been at much pains to find knots in a rush.'[16]

But by the time Boston's *Notes* came off the press another party had joined the debate: Robert Riccaltoun, Minister of the parish of Hobkirk, near Jedburgh. Riccaltoun was not one of the Brethren, and when his *Sober Enquiry* appeared (in 1723) the judicial process against the *Marrow* had been concluded.[17] John Brown describes Riccaltoun as one of the friends of the Representers and calls his *Enquiry* 'a most judicious treatise'.[18] Others, however, have suggested that he favoured neither party and would have agreed with William Cunningham's suggestion that Hadow and Boston divided the truth between them.[19] He certainly didn't share the Marrow Men's admiration for the book itself, although when it first appeared he saw no danger in it, as he makes plain in his Preface (p. iv); and, anyway, why should men be concerned with 'the sense and meaning' of an author who had been in the grave for at least threescore years? It wasn't worth the pains bestowed upon it, and those who embraced its sentiments so eagerly could have expressed these sentiments much better themselves. He would have been happy to leave the *Marrow* to lie for ever under the most injurious imputations (p. xii). It seemed to him to be of no concern to the Church of Scotland, and he had been happy to leave whatever controversy it generated to men who had nothing else to do. But while he commends the General Assembly's zeal for purity of doctrine and expresses the view that they had

---

16. ibid., p. 350. Boston is alluding to a proverb stemming from the childish practice of looking for knots in a bulrush, that is, looking for difficulties and obscurities where the meaning is already clear.

17. *A Sober Enquiry* was not Riccaltoun's first contribution to the debate. The previous year he had already published *The Politick Disputant: Choice Instructions for Quashing a Stubborn Adversary*, described by David Lachman as 'a devastating piece of satire combined with a penetrating analysis of James Hadow's method and doctrine in *The Antinomianism of the Marrow of Modern Divinity Detected*.' See the article, 'Riccaltoun, Robert,' in *DSCHT*. In-text citations in this section are from Riccoultoun, *A Sober Enquiry*.

18. John Brown, *Gospel Truth*, p. 27.

19. Paul Helm, for example, has recently suggested that Riccaltoun might have approved of Cunningham's sentiments. See his article, 'Blackwell, Halyburton, and Riccaltoun,' in David Ferguson and Mark W. Elliott (Eds.), *The History of Scottish Theology*, Vol. 2 (Oxford: Oxford University Press, 2019), p. 21. Cunningham, who described Boston and Hadow as 'the heads of two different schools of theology in Scotland', made his comment in the course of an essay, 'Zwingle, and the Doctrine of the Sacraments.' See Cunningham, *The Reformers and the Theology of the Reformation* (Edinburgh: T&T Clark, 1862), p. 282.

no alternative but to condemn the *Marrow* as a book, he qualifies this by adding '*as the matter was presented to them*'; by which he clearly means, 'as the Committee on Purity of Doctrine had introduced it to an Assembly whose members had never seen the book.'

Yet, while he is clearly anxious not to appear disrespectful to the Assembly, he couldn't commend those who had brought the matter before them in the first place and thus involved the whole church in a needless controversy. Before he woke up to the danger, he declares, matters had come to a pitched battle. It was odd, he thought, that the Assembly had condemned a book while the one who had recommended it, Mr Hog, had escaped without even a rebuke. But now it was no longer a disagreement between Mr Hog and Mr Hadow. It was a case of the Church on the one side, and some of her members on the other.

Again, it is clear that Riccaltoun held both sides equally to blame for the 'melancholy consequences' that followed; and it is further clear from his comments that the debate was much more of a national affair, and much more bitter, than we could glean from Boston's low-key comments. 'It is well known,' writes Riccaltoun, 'what Heights Zealots of both sides are carried to;' (vi) adding, 'I cannot tell which Side have carried their uncharitable zeal highest.' This is not to say that the key-players on both sides were uncharitable zealots. It is only to acknowledge that Hadow on the one side and the Representers on the other attracted followers who had little comprehension of the issues, but had partisanship in abundance: 'Instead of Hearers of the Gospel,' he wrote, 'Ministers have got censors of their doctrine to preach to' (p. vi), and wherever a preacher goes it is ten-to-one if he is not dismissed as either a dry Moralist and Legal Preacher, or a conceited antinomian or (which is the same) a Marrow-Man and New-Schemer. The anonymous author of *The Politick Disputant* (we now know it was Riccaltoun himself) had been condemned as a Jesuit for daring to suggest that Principal Hadow had misrepresented the *Marrow*, but by the time the term 'antinomian' reached the grass-roots it had come to mean the Representers: men who opposed morality 'because it was an enemy to their lusts'.[20]

But any idea that Riccaltoun apportioned blame equally between Hadow and the Brethren is quite simply wrong. It was the Principal's Synod Sermon that had ignited the controversy; his action in taking it to the Committee on

---

20. Brown, p. 28.

Purity of Doctrine and from there to the General Assembly had turned the affair into a crisis; and then, not content to leave the final word to the Assembly, he had thought fit to bolster its authority by publishing his own pamphlet, *The Antinomianism of the Marrow of Modern Divinity Detected,* a year after the 1720 Act. His whole design in this publication, declares Riccaltoun, had been to persuade his readers 'that the *Marrow's* Abominations are so flagrant, that no man of any Conscience will venture to speak favourably of them, unless he is tainted with the same error;' and to achieve this aim, Hadow, he alleged, had given a great mass of particulars without any order or connection, and succeeded only in filling people's heads with a 'huddle of notions'. Had he taken a more methodical method, weighing-up the views of the contending parties on the key theological points, he would have seen that the 'errors' which had caused such a stir, were in all points the same as those of the Westminster Assembly, 'unless, perhaps, in some points which they thought not fit to determine, and which the most judicious divines have allowed to pass as problems in the Reformed world, without falling out with their neighbours over them' (p. ix).[21]

Throughout *A Sober Enquiry,* Riccaltoun clearly has Hadow in view, as he himself acknowledges when he writes, 'We must propose to meet with him upon every turn' (x).[22] As we would expect, however, following his criticism of the Principal's lack of method, rather than recounting more or less random details, he begins with an introductory chapter which offers a general view of the differences between the two sides, and follows this up with eleven chapters, each devoted to extensive treatment of one or other of the theological issues raised by the dispute: for example, the Law of Faith, the Covenant of Grace between God and Men by a Mediator, the Nature of Gospel Repentance, and the nature of Gospel Holiness. On all such issues he distinguishes carefully between the views of the *Marrow* on the one hand and the views of the Marrow Men on the other; and between the views of the Marrow Men and the views condemned by the General Assembly.

The polemics are sometimes sharp, but the theology of the *Enquiry* is the same as that of Boston's *Notes* and, taken together,[23] and along with

---

21. Earlier (p. x) he had warned of 'the mischiefs which attend authoritative decisions on small matters.' A few pages later (p. xiii) he speaks of the General Assembly being asked to determine every problem ever disputed in a university.

22. By contrast Boston's *Notes* never mentions Hadow. In his *Memoirs* (p. 341), however, he refers to him as 'the spring of that black act of Assembly'.

23. *A Sober Enquiry* was never reprinted, but it is available as an E-book and via print-on-demand.

the 'Answers to the Queries' and Fisher's Catechism, they give a clear picture of that gospel of unconditional grace that was so precious to the Marrow Men and their friends.

Antinomian?

Why did such a gospel bring down on the *Marrow* the charge of antinomianism? We need to remember the theological atmosphere of the time. When Boston began his ministry, a strain of 'legal preaching' had already infected Scotland's pulpits. Indeed, it was no recent thing. John Brown traces it back to the prelates introduced to the Church by James VI and his son, Charles I. These were men of a very different theological outlook from that of the original Reformers, and their influence quickly percolated to the inferior clergy: so much so that in both 1645 and 1650 the Commission of Assembly lamented that many ministers had moved away from preaching the excellency of Christ, the riches of the New Covenant, and justification by faith alone. Instead, they 'pressed duties in a more legal way', not urging them 'from the love of God and grace of the gospel' but as performances which were within the natural compass of every man, and keeping out of sight both the need for special grace and the importance of union with Christ.

Brown wrote with the benefit of hindsight, but the trend had been observed even before the prelates worked their mischief. James Fraser of Brea, writing around 1665, was already noting the contrast between what he read in such men as Knox, Hamilton, Tyndale, Luther and Calvin, and what he read in contemporary divines: 'I perceived,' he wrote, 'a gospel spirit to be in very few, and that the most part of ministers did woefully compound the two covenants, and were of an Old Testament spirit; and little of the glory of Christ, grace, and gospel, did shine in their preaching.'[24]

Thomas Halyburton, Professor of Divinity at St Andrews from 1710 to 1712 (and a colleague of James Hadow's), noted the same trend: 'I saw the evil of legal preaching, which lies in one of two things, or in both. (1) In laying too much stress upon the works of the law, our duties, and strengths: Or, (2) In pressing evangelical doctrines without an eye to that which is the

---

24. *Memoirs of the Rev. James Fraser of Brea, Written by Himself* (1738. 7th edition, with a Short Sketch of Fraser by Gustavus Aird; Inverness, Edinburgh, Glasgow and London), p. 233.

spring of the church's edification, the Spirit of the Lord.'[25] Riccaltoun made a similar observation, though his comments focused on legalism in its Neonomian form, describing 'the New-Law-Men,' not as those who stress obedience to the Moral Law, but as those who talk of faith and repentance as the ground of our acceptance with God.[26]

It should be stressed, of course, that even in the late seventeenth century legalism did not have a monopoly of the Scottish pulpit. Not only did such Presbyterians as John Brown of Wamphray (1610–79), William Guthrie of Fenwick (1620–65), and Thomas Hog of Kiltearn (1628–92), strike a clear evangelical note: it was struck no less clearly by such Episcopalians as Robert Leighton (1611–84) and Henry Scougal (1650–78). Nevertheless, the influence of legalism was widespread, affecting even men like Thomas Boston himself who, early in his career, began to be convicted of 'legality in my own practice'.[27] He set out, as he tells us, to set fire to the Devil's nest, and accordingly delivered his message in a 'rousing strain', believing like many, before and since, that a Boanerges, a son of thunder, was much more likely than a 'still small voice' to knock holes in the demonic fortresses. And it wasn't only a matter of the style of his delivery. It was also a matter of the texts he chose to preach on: texts such as Psalm 50:22, 'Mark this, then, you who forget God, lest I tear you apart, and there be none to deliver.' But when an older minister remarked to him, 'If you were entered on preaching of Christ, you would find it very pleasant,'[28] he took it very much to heart, and immediately changed his 'strain': a change signalised by the fact that very shortly afterwards he prepared a new sermon on Isaiah 61:1, a text which highlights the fact that the preacher's calling, like that of the Lord Himself (Luke 4:18), is to preach good news and to bind up the broken-hearted.[29]

Not long afterwards, he was given a further prod in the same direction, when he was informed that the Reverend George Mair, colleague to Fraser of Brea at Culross, taught that, 'all members of the visible church have a general right to Christ, and the benefits of the covenant, so that they may

---

25. *The Works of the Rev. Thomas Halyburton, with an Essay on his Life and Writings by the Rev. Robert Burns, Paisley* (Glasgow: Blackie and Son, 1833), p. 765.

26. *A Sober Enquiry*, p. 299. Further quotations will be given in brackets in the text.

27. *Memoirs*, p. 160.

28. ibid., p. 30.

29. 'The Spirit of the Lord is upon me, because he has anointed me to proclaim good news to the poor. He has sent me to proclaim liberty to the captives and recovering of sight to the blind, to set at liberty those who are oppressed' (Luke 4:18).

warrantably take possession thereof by faith.'[30] This was strange to Boston at the time, and it may not do justice to Mair's views, but as he looks back on the incident in his *Memoirs*, it is clear that in Boston's mature opinion Mair's teaching did not go far enough:

> I now believe that *sinners of mankind indefinitely, within or without the visible church*, have a real right to Christ, and the benefits of the covenant, so as they may warrantably take possession thereof by faith; the which right is contained in the holy scriptures as the original charter, and is legally intimated *to all that hear the gospel.*[31]

Despite all this, however, it is clear that Boston was still wrestling with these issues when he came across the *Marrow*. This is why he can refer to it as 'coming close to the points I was in quest of,' but this doesn't mean that it was in the *Marrow* that he first encountered what he calls 'the doctrine of Christ'. For example, he was already clear on the free offer of the gospel when he wrote his *Soliloquy on the Art of Man-Fishing* prior to his ordination to Simprin in 1699.[32] His problem was how to reconcile such a doctrine 'with other things which seemed to be truth too'.[33] He meant, presumably, such doctrines as Particular Redemption.

The *Marrow* helped him resolve these difficulties. But it did more: it emboldened him to preach with a new evangelical freedom. Yet he still remained 'confused, indistinct and hampered' with regard to the free, open and unconditional access of sinners to Christ. By July 1704, however, when he preached on Matthew 11:28[34] at a Communion in Coldinghame, the fetters had been broken, and he gave, he says, 'the true sense of that text, since published in the *Notes* on the *Marrow*.'[35] This sermon does not appear in Boston's *Works*, but he returned to the text in a series of sermons preached in January and February, 1711.[36] The key moment comes when he addresses the question of the persons the Lord is inviting. 'I cannot

---

30. *Memoirs*, p. 97.

31. ibid., p. 97, italics added.

32. *A Soliloquy on the Art of Man-Fishing*, p. 29: 'God excludes none from the benefits of the gospel that will not exclude themselves; it is free to all.'

33. *Memoirs*, p. 160.

34. 'Come unto me, all ye that labour and are heavy laden, and I will give you rest'.

35. For this Note, see Boston's edition of *The Marrow*, p. 154. Further citations will be included in the text of this section.

36. *Works*, Vol. 9, pp. 169-219.

agree,' he writes, 'with those that restrain these expressions to those that are sensible of their sins and misery, without Christ, and are longing to be rid of the same; but I think it includes all that are out of Christ, sensible and insensible; *that is, these that have not had, and those that have had, a law-work upon their consciences.*'

This was a core doctrine of the *Marrow*, which completely rejected the idea that a man must repent before he believes; and, along with it, the doctrine that only the broken, convicted sinner was warranted to come to Christ (pp. 142-150). And it was this position, perhaps more than any other, that Principal Hadow brought forward as evidence of the antinomianism of the *Marrow*. He states his own position clearly:

> The truth which I undertake to prove against the *Marrow* is, 'That the evangelical Grace and Duty of repentance goeth before Pardon of Sin, in God's Method of bestowing them; that Remission of Sin is a Consequent Blessing annexed unto Repentance by Divine Promise; and that therefore Ministers in preaching the Gospel, may, and ought to call Sinners to repent, and forsake their Sins, *in Order unto their obtaining the Pardon of them, as well as to believe in Christ for their Justification.*'[37]

With this he contrasted the allegedly antinomian teaching of the *Marrow*, which argued that to allow repentance to go before pardon would be to bring our own works of righteousness into the case for justification.[38]

The Twelve Brethren unequivocally supported the *Marrow's* position (p. 147) on this question, as Boston made plain in his *Notes* (pp. 141-50). However, the question of the relation between repentance and coming to Christ had already become a matter of public debate when, as we have seen, the General Assembly of 1717 condemned the 'Auchterarder Creed', and especially the proposition, 'It is not sound and orthodox to teach that we must forsake sin in order to our coming to Christ.'[39] Boston, a member of that Assembly, believed the proposition to be 'not

---

37. *The Antinomianism of the Marrow of Modern Divinity Detected* (Edinburgh, 1721), p. 51.

38. ibid., p. 54.

39. As Sinclair Ferguson points out, suspicion of the Auchterarder Creed reflected a subtle movement away from seeing forsaking sin as the fruit of grace to making the forsaking of sin 'the precursor for experiencing that grace. Repentance, which is the fruit of grace, thus becomes a qualification for grace' (Sinclair B. Ferguson, *The Whole Christ: Legalism, Antinomianism, and Gospel Assurance – Why the Marrow Controversy Still Matters;* Wheaton: Crossway, 2016, p. 43).

well-worded',[40] but to contain nevertheless a fundamentally important truth. Diffidence prevented him, however, from speaking in its defence, with the result, as he records, that 'my conscience smote me grievously' (he did, however, dissent from the finding).

The wording may indeed not be the most judicious, but the 'Creed' conveyed a priceless truth: Christ welcomes sinners unconditionally. This doesn't mean that sinners aren't required to renounce sin. What the 'Creed' was saying is that it is not necessary to renounce sin *in order to come to Christ*. To Boston and his friends, the idea that we must save ourselves from the love, power and practice of sin *before* we may come to the Saviour was not only a serious deterrent to the poor sinner, but an instance of the conditional grace that they so deplored; and the forces ranged against the 'Creed', and the arguments deployed by its opponents, were the very same as would be marshalled three years later against *The Marrow of Modern Divinity*.

The *Marrow's* discussion of the relation between faith and repentance begins when Nomista, the resident legalist, puts it to Evangelista that, 'Christ requires a thirsting, before a man come unto him, the which, I conceive, cannot be without true repentance (p. 142).' The proposition reflects a long and troubled spiritual journey on Nomista's part. When his conscience had first began to trouble him, he was directed to find relief in improved performance of such duties as Sabbath observance and church attendance, and in giving up his habits of lying and swearing. When these improvements brought no peace, he set himself to fulfilling the law in strict earnest (p. 89) and forced his soul to every duty. He took notice of the inward corruptions of his heart, and resolved to govern his thoughts, moderate his passions, suppress lusts and banish pride: 'then I thought myself not only an outside Christian, but also an inside Christian, and therefore a true Christian indeed.' This worked for a while, till he realised that law-keeping had to be passive as well as active, and so he began to be troubled by his impatience under God's correcting hand, and his murmurings and discontent whenever a calamity befell him. This led to his practising abstinences and fastings, and to lacing his prayers with 'pitiful lamentations'. But not only were there 'pitiful lamentations': by this stage there were also tears, 'the which I was persuaded the Lord did take notice of, and would reward me for it.'

---

40. *Memoirs*, p. 303.

And so on, until at last he was confronted by Evangelista, who shocked him by announcing that 'the vilest sinner in the world ought not to be discouraged from coming unto Christ, and believing in him, by reason of his sins.'[41]

All Nomista can do now is raise objections: 'But, sir, suppose he has not as yet truly repented for his many and great sins, hath he any warrant to come unto Christ, by believing, till he has done so?' Then, when Evangelista speaks of a 'general proclamation' made by Christ, and backs this up by referring to Isaiah's call to 'everyone that thirsteth' (Isa. 55:1), Nomista immediately pounces on the word, 'thirsteth,' and exclaims, 'You see, sir, that Christ requires a thirsting.'

At this point (p. 143) Boston appends a note on Isaiah 55:1, describing it as the most solemn gospel-offer to be found in all the Old Testament and the source of Jesus' parting offer, 'Let him that is athirst come: and whosoever will, let him take the water of life freely' (Rev. 22:17). 'I can see no ground,' writes Boston, 'to think that the thirsting therein mentioned does any way restrict the offer; or that the thirsty there invited, are convinced, sensible sinners, who are thirsting after Christ and his righteousness; the which would leave without [outside] the compass of this solemn invitation, not only the far greater part of mankind, but even of the visible church.' The context, he argues, is decisive on this point, because the thirsting ones to whom the invitation is extended, are not convicted sinners thirsting for Christ, but people who are 'spending money for that which is not bread, and their labour for that which satisfieth not' (in other words, the prophet is addressing, not penitents, but those who are turning to the 'broken cisterns' in the hope of finding the happiness we naturally crave).

But, back to Evangelista. Picking up on Nomista's belief that a man must repent before he believes, he asks him, 'I pray tell me what you do conceive repentance to be, or wherein it does consist?' (p. 143). Nomista replies decisively: 'Why, I conceive that repentance consists in a man's humbling himself before God, and sorrowing and grieving for offending him by his sins, and turning them all to the Lord.' 'And would you,' asks Evangelista, his expression giving no hint of the trap he is setting, 'would you have a man do all this truly before he comes to Christ by believing?' 'Yes,' replies Nomista, confidently, only to be met with the crushing response, 'Why then, I tell you truly, you would have him to do what is impossible' (p. 144).

---

41. ibid., p. 140. The *Marrow's* treatment of this topic occupies pp. 140-50.

Boston's note on this is, once again, an emphatic endorsement: 'I think it nothing strange to find the author so peremptory on this point.' He picks up on Nomista's reference to turning to God and, taking his stand on the fact that no one comes to God but through Christ (John 14:6), argues that since the only way to Christ is through faith, there can therefore be no repentance (turning to God) before there is faith. He follows this up by quoting Acts 5:31, which speaks of Christ as the One who gives repentance, and adds that, if this is so, then sinners should go to Him *for* repentance, 'and not stand off from him until they get it.' In other words, repentance, like remission of sins, is itself a part of salvation, not a qualification for it. Christ gives it, from Him sinners receive it, and to Him they should pray for it.

Here Evangelista injects another crucially important point: Sorrow and grief for displeasing God by sin, necessarily argue love for God (p. 144). In this again, Boston heartily concurs. Repentance is a turning to God in love, but if a convicted sinner lacks even the least assurance that God loves him and sees him, instead, as an enemy angry with his sins, this cannot fail to fill his whole soul with slavish fear of God: 'love utterly unknown to the party beloved can never be an inducement to him to love in return' (p. 145). This was exactly the line taken by the *Marrow*: 'first of all God's favour is apprehended, and remission of sins believed; then upon that cometh alteration of life and conversation' (p. 146).

The most striking thing about Boston's discussion of the relation between faith and repentance, however, is the way it highlights his evangelistic orientation, and particularly his concern for a biblically correct statement of the gospel-offer: one that would leave the way to Christ completely uncluttered, free of the obstacles of preparationism. Here he draws a clear distinction between a sinner's *duty* and a sinner's *warrant*. It is a sinner's duty to repent, but it is not his repentance that gives him a warrant to come to Christ. The warrant is the general call of the gospel, and this gives every sinner the *right* to come. Boston recognises, of course, that, psychologically, no one will seek a Saviour until they feel their need, and this is why the law must be preached. Only in this way can the sinner be made to despair of self-salvation and driven to seek for righteousness in Christ. But Boston is no less aware that we can experience such an awakening, and feel the storms of conscience, and yet never come to Christ. Cain and Judas experienced remorse: a legal repentance evoked not by the good news of the gospel, but by a deep sense of guilt unrelieved by any grasp of divine mercy and love, and leading only to despair.

The great danger, Boston argues, is that unrelieved legal preaching can produce not only a sense of spiritual need: it can convey the impression that we have no warrant to come to Christ until we have plumbed the depths of contrition and soul-sickness; or, which is the same thing, that we must delay our coming to the Saviour till we have qualified for admission by a profound experience of 'the terrors of law and of God'. Boston is deeply disturbed by the damage done by such preaching. It traps distressed consciences in a spiritual maze, convincing them that they dare not believe in Christ till they are sure that they have *truly* repented, and thus condemning them to endless disputations with themselves 'as to the being, kind, measure, and degree of their qualifications for coming to Christ' (p. 142). How can they be sure that their repentance is any better than that of Judas? The time spent in such introspective disputations would be better spent by going forward immediately to Christ, by believing.

The same problem arises when people are taught that they must know that their *faith* is genuine before they can come to Christ. Boston counters robustly: faith is not a qualification for coming to Christ. It is the coming itself, and it will have its saving effects on the sinner, whether he has 'assurance' of it or not (p. 142).[42]

But if our warrant for coming to Christ is neither that we are repentant sinners nor that we are believing sinners, what is it? Again, Boston's reply is unequivocal: it is the general offer of the gospel, which warrants everyone who hears it to come to the Saviour; and as the *Marrow* lays down, 'Jesus Christ requires no portion [dowry] with his spouse' (p. 138). We bring nothing with us but our poverty, and our repentance and faith are as poor as everything else we bring.

Yet, despite the bitterness of the controversy, on this particular point Boston and Hadow were ultimately at one. It is clear from the Preface to *The Antinomianism of the Marrow Detected* that Hadow and others of his circle resented the insinuation that the Brethren were the only Ministers

---

42. Walter Marshall had made the same point in *The Gospel Mystery of Sanctification* (1692. Reprinted Welwyn: Evangelical Press, 1981), p. 51: 'The efficiency or operation of faith, in order to the enjoyment of Christ and his fulness, cannot be the procurement of a bare right or title to this enjoyment; but rather it must be an entrance to it, and taking possession of it.'

in the Church of Scotland who preached the Gospel of Free Grace, and by way of rebuttal he presents a series of *Assertions* in which, he says, he had the concurrence of other prominent figures in the Kirk. One of these *Assertions* was to the effect that while faith and repentance, with their accompanying graces, are both necessary to receiving Christ on His own terms, yet sinners 'are not to bring them unto God, or offer them to Christ, as a Satisfaction for Sin and Cause of Pardon, or as Qualities to Make them Worthy, or to recommend them to the divine Favour, or as any Price in their Hand to purchase and procure Mercy from God, or an Interest in Christ'.[43]

This should serve as a warning against the simplistic view of the *Marrow* controversy as a conflict between evangelicals and legalists. Hadow, no less than Boston, would have endorsed the lines from the hymn, 'Rock of Ages,'

> *Nothing in my hands I bring;*
> *Simply to thy cross I cling.*

The point at issue was who had the right to cling: the truly penitent sinner, or the sinner simply such.

The law of works *versus* the law of Christ

But if the *Marrow* fell foul of its Scottish critics because of its teaching on the relation between repentance and justification, these critics objected no less strongly to the distinction it drew between the Law of Works and the Law of Faith. Hadow addressed this 'antinomian tenet' in Chapter X (pp. 120-30) of *The Antinomianism of the Marrow Detected* and, following the precedent set by the General Assembly's Act of 1720, subjected the language of the *Marrow* to the worst possible construction, attributing to it such sentiments as that a believer is not under the Law, but altogether delivered from it; that the believer does not commit sin; that the Lord is not angry with believers for their sins and does not chastise them for them; and that believers have no cause to confess their sins, or to crave pardon for them (p. 120).

What the *Marrow* had laid down, however, was not that believers were delivered from the Law, but that they were delivered from the Law *as the*

---

43. James Hadow, *The Antinomianism of the Marrow Detected*, pp. x-xi.

covenant of works (p. 158), and the Brethren defended this position robustly, as well they might, since the offending proposition had the full sanction of the Confession of Faith, which had categorically declared (Chapter 19:6) that true believers are 'not under the law, as a covenant of works, to be thereby justified and condemned.'[44] But the Brethren didn't regard this as just an important theological truth. The very first point they made in their *Representation and Petition* of May 1721 was that they regarded their freedom from the covenant of works as the chief branch of 'that precious liberty wherewith Christ hath made us free, and in which the eternal salvation of our souls is wrapt up.'[45]

But what did it mean? The crucial phrase here is 'as a covenant of works'. Believers are not free from the law as such, but from the Ten Commandments in the form of a covenant which promised life on the basis of obedience and eternal death as the punishment of disobedience. The law could no longer say to the believer, 'Do this, and live;' nor could it say, 'Disobey this and you die.' And the reason for this was clear. Christ had fulfilled the law for them and made satisfaction for all their sins; through faith in Him they have escaped eternal death and obtained eternal life; and this, declared Boston, 'is a proof of the whole matter. For how can the law of the Ten Commandments promise eternal life, or threaten eternal death, upon condition of obedience or disobedience, to those who have already escaped eternal death, and received eternal life by faith in Christ?'[46]

Riccaltoun made exactly the same point. Having declared his unswerving adherence to the idea that the believer is free from the law as a Covenant of Works he writes, 'the Believer, once justified freely by grace, is not allowed to be again set to the Bar to be judged by the Law and the Measures of Justice.'[47] He can never be threatened with eternal death, or have any good reason to fear hell.

---

44. The Larger Catechism, A. 97, had taken the same position, declaring those who believe in Christ to be 'delivered from the moral law as a covenant of works, so as thereby they are neither justified nor condemned.' Hadow had overlooked this when he described the position of the *Marrow* as 'a Soporifick for the Antinomian, to encourage him in Licentiousness.' Riccaltoun was happy to point out (p. 390) to the Principal that what he now condemned as an encouragement to licentiousness, he had already subscribed to as the doctrine of the Church of Scotland.

45. Brown *Gospel Truth*, p. 134. The full text of the 'Representation and Petition' is given on pp. 133-43.

46. *The Marrow, with Notes by Thomas Boston*, p.114.

47. *A Sober Enquiry*, p. 391.

This is indeed the marrow of the gospel: in the matter of justification and pardon, the believer is altogether done with the law; and in accord with this, the person who is a complete moral and spiritual failure, condemned not only by the law, but by his own conscience, must not lose hope. Instead, he must cast himself on the One who justifies the ungodly (Rom. 4:5).

But then, in line with the whole Reformed tradition going back to John Calvin, the Marrow Men insisted that though believers are free from the law as a Covenant of Works we are still under the law as the rule for our Christian lives.[48] We may be secure from its condemning power, but we are not secured from its commanding power; nor indeed is it even conceivable that we could be, because the law binds all men, including believers, simply as men.[49] The Brethren had made the same point in their answer to the second of the *Queries*. Asked whether the believer is now bound, by the authority of the Creator, to personal obedience to the Moral Law, they had replied with an emphatic affirmative: 'The believer, since he ceases not to be a creature by being made a new creature, is, and must ever be bound to personal obedience to the law of the ten commands, by the authority of Father, Son and Holy Spirit.'[50] The underlying truth here is that our relation to God as our Father in no way abolishes our relation to Him as the Judge of all the earth and the moral governor of the universe: after all, it was precisely to Israel as the adopted people of God that the law was originally

---

48. This is what Calvin called the Third Use of the Law. The distinction between three uses of the Law had been introduced by Melanchthon in later editions of his *Loci Communes*. First came the civil or political use, the law as enforced by the magistrate; secondly, the law as instituted to convict of sin; thirdly, the law's use among the regenerate (Philip Melanchthon, *The Chief Theological Topics: Loci Praecipui Theologici 1559*, tr. J. A. O. Preus; Saint Louis: Concordia Publishing House, 2011; pp. 120-24). Calvin changes the order, dealing first with the law as the mirror which brings home to us our own sinfulness, secondly with the political use of the law, and thirdly with the place of the law in the lives of the regenerate (see Calvin, *Institutes*, II:VII, 6-12). He refers to the third as 'the principal use' and describes the law (II:VII,13) from this point of view as pointing out the goal toward which we are to strive. But at the same time he insists that the law has been abrogated in the sense that we have been released from 'the bonds of harsh and dangerous requirements, which remit nothing of the extreme penalty of the law, and suffer no transgression to go unpunished' (*Calvin: Institutes of the Christian Religion*; ed. John T. McNeill, trans. Ford Lewis Battles; Philadelphia: Westminster Press, 1960, p. 363).

49. Riccaltoun, ibid., p. 377.

50. See the corresponding language of the Westminster Confession, 19:5: 'The moral law doth for ever bind all, as well justified persons as others, to the obedience thereof; and that not only in regard of the matter contained in it, but also in respect of the authority of God the Creator who gave it: neither doth Christ, in the gospel, any way dissolve, but much strengthen this obligation.'

given; and, conversely, the believer's obedience to the law is prompted both by a love for God as our Father and by a reverence for Him as Creator, Legislator and Judge. Lawlessness is what we have been redeemed from, not what we have been redeemed to.

Yet justification does bring with it a radical change in our relation to the law. It is no longer the Law of Works but the Law of Christ. Hadow deplored this distinction, pronouncing it an 'Antinomian Mystery'. Riccaltoun countered that the expression, 'the law of Christ,' shouldn't offend 'the most delicate ears', but at the same time he noted (p. 380) that Hadow's aversion to it was 'the Pith and Marrow of that learned Man's Book, and the Charge which he pursues with most eagerness.'

What did the *Marrow* and its recommenders mean by this distinction between the Law of Works on the one hand and the Law of Faith or the Law of Christ on the other? They were certainly not thinking of two separate laws. Time and again they insist that the 'matter' of the Covenant of Works and the 'matter' of the Law of Faith are one and the same, namely, the Ten Commandments. The difference is that to the legalist these commands represent the things he must do to earn eternal life, while to the believer they represent the rule by which he must live as one who already enjoys eternal life, but only as a debtor to unconditional grace.[51]

Nor again does the distinction mean that as 'the law of Christ' the law is less extensive and less rigorous. On the contrary, Jesus makes plain that His expectations of His disciples are far more demanding than those of the most rigorous legalist: 'Except your righteousness shall exceed that of the righteousness of the scribes and Pharisees, ye shall in no case enter into the kingdom of heaven' (Matt. 5:20). He isn't presenting Himself here as a new lawmaker carrying more than the two tablets that sufficed for Moses:[52] He

---

51. Cf. Sinclair Ferguson's comment, 'legalism begins to manifest itself when we view God's law as a contract with conditions to be fulfilled and not as the implications of a covenant graciously given to us' (*The Whole Christ,* p. 115).

52. The first question put to the *Queries* was, 'Whether there are any precepts in the gospel, that were not actually given before the gospel was revealed?' (Brown, *Gospel Truth,* p. 146). In reply, the Brethren declare that in the gospel, strictly understood (as good news from heaven), there are no precepts. All precepts, including the command to believe and repent, flow from the law. For example, the gospel is a new object for faith, but faith does not then become a duty for the first time. Adam in Paradise was bound to believe (and to repent, should he sin): 'There never was, nor can be, an instance of a duty owing by the creature to God, not commanded in the moral law, if not directly and expressly, yet indirectly and by consequence' (ibid., p.148).

is opening up the unexpected depth, rigour and inwardness of the Mosaic Law itself. Hatred, as well as homicide, is murder; lust is already adultery; the enemy is to be loved as well as the friend; retaliation is to be replaced by turning the other cheek; judgement of others to be silenced by remembering the beam in our own eye.

These are standards no legalist can reach. The Sermon on the Mount is death to any idea of salvation by works.

Nor did the fact that believers were under the law of Christ, not the law of works, mean that their sins were not real sins. The 1720 Act of Assembly had accused the *Marrow* of teaching that a believer doesn't commit sin, that the Lord can see no sin in a believer, that He is not angry with a believer for his sins, that He doesn't chastise them for them, and that a believer has no cause either to confess his sins or to crave pardon for them. Each of these insinuations the Brethren emphatically rejected. The *Marrow* had indeed insisted that Christ had satisfied for all the sins of believers, but when believers transgress any of the Ten Commandments these transgressions are real sins; and the only reason that these sins do not bring upon us the avenging wrath of God is that Christ bore the guilt of the sins we commit after we are united to Him as well as the guilt of the sins we committed before. And although believers are no longer under the Law of Works, they are under law to Christ, their sins are transgressions of His law, He may be angry with them, and He may chastise them.[53]

There can be no mistaking the *Marrow's* position on this question. When a believer transgresses the law of Christ, 'then hath he cause to confess his sins unto the Lord, and to crave pardon for them, yea and to fast, and to mourn, and humble himself for them, as conceiving them to be a transgression of the law of Christ.'[54] And this single paragraph, declares Boston's note, is not only a rejection of the antinomian error that a believer ought not to mourn for his sins: it is a refutation of all the antinomian constructions put on the statements of the *Marrow*.

One more cautionary word. The fact that the believer is now under a new law, the Law of Christ, means that, when he sins, he is no longer liable to the penalty denounced by the old law, namely, eternal death. But God's anger may still express itself in fatherly chastisement. We must beware, however,

---

53. Boston's *Notes*, p. 156.
54. The *Marrow*, p. 221.

of inferring that in that case we have nothing to worry about. The *Marrow* (p. 227) spells out uncompromisingly what we should fear if we transgress the law, namely, 'the want of near and sweet communion with God in Christ, even in this life, *and a liableness to all temporal afflictions, as fruits and effects of the transgressing that law*' (italics added). Boston adds a sombre comment: 'An awful penalty, if rightly understood, as comprehending all manner of strokes and afflictions on the outward and inner man. His sins lay him open to the whole train of maladies, pains, torments, sores, diseases and plagues incident to sinful flesh; by which he may become a burden to himself and others.' Or, as the writer to the Hebrews put it, 'It is a fearful thing to fall into the hands of the living God' (Heb. 10:31).

But though the Ten Commandments retained all their preceptive force for believers there were, as Riccaltoun puts it, 'alterations', particularly in the way the law is conveyed to believers.[55] When the law was first announced to man, God and he were friends. Now, so long as we remain out of Christ, and still under the law as a Covenant of Works, we receive it at the hands of an angry God before whom we stand as condemned sinners. Here the law is an instrument of justice, announcing to the sinner what he deserves.

The believer, by contrast, receives the law at the hands of a Mediator 'who, by answering the Law's demands, satisfies Justice, and procures peaceable access for the Sinner, both unto God and the Law.'[56] The law can now have no dealings with the Christian except through this Mediator, and only in the light of the reconciliation with God which he has secured. We now receive the law from the hand of a friend; or, in other words, under the terms of the Covenant of Grace. We no longer have to earn our admission to the Kingdom. By God's unconditional grace, we are already 'in', citizens of the kingdom of heaven, and we receive the law not as the instrument by which God restrains His foes but as the instrument by which Christ governs His beloved and willing subjects.

But further, as Riccaltoun again points out, the Mediator always acts in the Father's name, and when he delivers the law to believers it is as the will of one who is already our loving heavenly Father. It is exactly in this light that Jesus describes the rigorous ethic he prescribed for His disciples in the Sermon on the Mount. He called it 'the will of my Father which is in

---

55. *A Sober Enquiry,* p. 378.
56. ibid., p. 379.

heaven' (Matt. 7:21); and at the same time He made it plain that we are to take it with absolute seriousness. Yet the law no longer has the appearance of an awesome judicial system. Instead, we receive it as the house-rules by which God governs His own family.[57] He has loved them from eternity, He has adopted them as His children despite their sin, and He will never give up on them.

Neither, however, will He indulge them. There is always an element of conditionality in relations between God and His creatures, and even between God and His children, as we see in such a passage as Psalm 103:17-18, where we read that God's love for His children is from everlasting to everlasting to 'such as keep his covenant, *and to those that remember his commandments to do them*' (italics added). This clearly implies that there are blessings linked to obedience. For example, the merciful obtain mercy (Matt. 5:7), those who do the Father's will enter the kingdom of heaven (Matt. 7:21), and those who love the law enjoy great peace (Ps. 119:165). But these blessings, though annexed to the law, are conveyed only within the Covenant of Grace, where our salvation is already secure and where God by His sovereign grace enables and prompts His children to the performance of His will.[58]

But not only does the law come to us from a loving heavenly Father and an all-prevailing Mediator: God also writes it on our hearts. This, of course, was one of the terms of the New Covenant announced by Jeremiah (Jer. 31:33), and it is not a demand but a promise: the Spirit erects a new sovereignty over us, through Him God rules His people, and our obedience is accepted through Christ the Mediator.[59]

Riccaltoun offers no reflections as to *how* the Spirit writes the law on our hearts, but the truth may well be that He does it simply by indwelling us. The Law within is the Spirit within. He is the one who, within us, cries out, 'Abba, Father!' (Gal. 4:6); the one who leads us; the one whose fruit we bear; the Marker with whom we keep in step on the King's great parade-ground (Gal. 5:25). And what is written on our hearts is more than bare knowledge. It is an impulse to obey our Father out of love and respect; and, according to the Marrow Men, it stems from the assurance of forgiveness and pardon.

---

57. 'The ongoing function of God's law is not to serve as a standard to be met for justification but as a guide to Christian living' (Sinclair B. Ferguson, *The Whole Christ*, p. 114).

58. ibid., p. 393.

59. ibid., pp. 379-81.

Hadow and his associates viewed this link between assurance and pardon with severe disapproval. They wanted to give a much more prominent role to the fear of hell and the hope of heaven as motives to obedience, and they expressed horror at the suggestion that no one could perform any right and acceptable obedience unless they were sure that they were justified, adopted and in favour with God.[60] From this it would follow, they claimed, that no one was under the law as the law of Christ except those who had assurance that they were reconciled to God and had no reason to fear His wrath and curse.[61]

But this was not what the *Marrow* or the Marrow Men intended. They were not saying that the doubting believer could do nothing right. They had too much pastoral experience (and too much personal experience of doubting) to believe any such thing; and we, three centuries later, have the historical examples of what was achieved by men like Martin Luther, John Bunyan, William Cowper and C. H. Spurgeon, despite their propensity to spiritual depression. But such examples should not be taken as norms, and we should certainly not encourage the idea that doubt is the spur to spiritual diligence. The true norm is stated by the Apostle John: we love Him because He first loved us (1 John 4:19). It is in this sense that the law is the 'law of faith': it promotes an obedience based on what we believe about God, and this includes the assurance that through faith in Christ we are heirs to all the promises of the New Covenant. This, surely, is the point the Apostle Paul was making when he pressed home the duties that follow from the depth and riches of the gospel. 'I beseech you,' he writes, 'by the mercies of God' (Rom. 12:1). Our willingness to present our bodies as living sacrifices and to offer our minds in intelligent service is rooted, not in fear, but in our assurance of the love of a merciful God.

Yet love is not only the spring of obedience: it is the very essence of obedience. Far from being a divinely sanctioned alternative to obeying the Ten Commandments, it is itself the fulfilling of the Ten Commandments; and though this love is deeply inward, and a true affair of the heart, it is also intensely practical, just like the love of God Himself. It feeds the hungry, clothes the naked and takes in the stranger (Matt. 25:33-40). Above all, it is practical in the love it shows for God Himself. 'I love the Lord,' cried the psalmist, 'because he hath heard my voice' (Ps. 116:1).

---

60. Hadow, *The Antinomianism of the Marrow Detected*, p. 72.

61. ibid., p. 119.

4

The Marrow *and the Covenant of Grace*

THE *MARROW*, PUBLISHED in 1646, was a contemporary of the
Scottish divines, David Dickson and Samuel Rutherford, and like them it
espoused the newly emerging Covenant theology. There was, however, one
clear difference. Dickson and Rutherford had both adopted a three-covenant
framework: a Covenant of Works between God and Adam, a Covenant of
Redemption between God the Father and God the Son, and a Covenant of
Grace between God and the believer. The *Marrow*, however, adopted a two-
covenant framework: the Covenant of Works, which Adam breached when 'at
one clap he broke all the ten commandments';[1] and the Covenant of Redemption, a mutual agreement between God and Christ, in which Christ agreed to
assume human nature and to 'yield in man's flesh the price of the satisfaction
of the just judgement of God, and, in the same flesh, to suffer the punishment
that man had deserved' (p. 42).

But for the *Marrow* there was no distinct Covenant of Grace between
God and the believer. 'The covenant of grace,' it declares, 'terminates only
on Christ and his righteousness' (p. 93); or, later, 'all the covenant that
believers are to have regard to, for life and salvation, is the free and gracious
covenant that is betwixt Christ (or God in Christ) and them' (p. 116). The
Marrow Men were even more explicit. In his *View of the Covenant of Grace
from the Sacred Records*,[2] Boston, for example, states categorically, 'The
covenant of redemption and the covenant of grace are not two distinct
covenants, but one and the same covenant' (p. 396). *Fisher's Catechism*, in

---

1. *The Marrow of Modern Divinity*, p. 35. All further references in-text are to this source.

2. *Works*, Vol. 8, pp. 379-604. This was published posthumously (1734), but it was
written around 1728 (*Memoirs*, p. 389).

its explanation of Answer 20 of the Shorter Catechism, and representing at this point the view of Boston's fellow Marrow Man, Ebenezer Erskine, expressed the same sentiment, claiming the support not only of Holy Scripture but of the Westminster Standards, which, argued Fisher, make no distinction between a Covenant of Redemption and a Covenant of Grace.[3] More important, the Scriptures speak of only two covenants, the Covenant of Works and the Covenant of Grace; ascribe the salvation of sinners to the blood of the covenant, but never to the blood of *covenants* (plural); and describe the promises as being made not to many seeds, but to 'one seed, which is Christ' (Gal. 3:16).

We need to take careful note of what exactly Boston and Erskine are saying at this point. They are not denying the reality of what Rollock, Dickson, Rutherford and Witsius called the Covenant of Redemption, that 'eternal counsel of the adorable Trinity, in which the Son of God was constituted by the Father, with the approbation of the Holy Spirit, the Saviour of mankind.'[4] Far from denying such a covenant, Boston and Erskine affirm it wholeheartedly. The problem is that they habitually call it the 'Covenant of Grace', while at the same time denying the reality of the covenant which earlier Scottish theologians called by that name, namely, the covenant between God and the believer. Instead, in the one covenant between God the Father and God the Son, the elect are represented by Christ, their sponsor and representative, but there is no distinct covenant between God and any member of the human race.

It is clear, however, that what really underlies the emphatic rejection of a distinct covenant between God and the believing sinner is a deep-seated

---

3. The strength of Fisher's argument lies in the language of the Larger Catechism (Answer 31), 'The covenant of grace was made with Christ as the second Adam, and in him with all the elect as his seed.' However, the catechisms are not 'standards': Presbyterian ordinands subscribe only to the Confession of Faith, which declares (7:6) simply that, man having made himself incapable of life on the basis of the Covenant of Works, 'the Lord was pleased to make a second, commonly called the Covenant of Grace, whereby he freely offereth unto sinners life and salvation by Jesus Christ.' The offer of this covenant is made to 'sinners', it is of sinners that faith is required, and it is to sinners that the promises are extended. The Shorter Catechism is equally non-specific with regard to 'the party-contractor on man's side', saying no more than that, 'God having out of his mere good pleasure from all eternity elected some to everlasting life, did enter into a covenant of grace.' Like the Confession, it does not say with whom. This probably reflects the fact that at this stage Covenant theology was in its infancy, and it is very doubtful that the question whether there was but one covenant or two was ever before the Westminster Assembly.

4. Witsius, *The Economy of the Covenants between God and Man*, Vol. I, p. 177.

fear of the merest hint of conditional grace. Riccaltoun, who himself was sympathetic to the position of Boston and Erskine on this as on other questions, saw this clearly, even suggesting that the conditionality of the covenant was at the heart of the whole Marrow controversy.[5] Any idea of a covenant to which man was a partner immediately introduced legalism whereas, on the one-covenant view, Christ had done it all, leaving nothing for the believer to do; and the gospel was thus a message of absolute grace, pure gift, and unconditional promise.

We have already noted the wider theological background to the controversy, and particularly the New Legalism (Neonomianism) which had been promoted in England by Richard Baxter, who argued that faith and repentance were gospel statutes, that compliance with them constituted a new 'evangelical obedience', and that this obedience constituted the basis of justification. Underlying this was Baxter's doctrine of Universal Redemption, according to which Christ on the cross had borne the sins of all men and thus made it possible for God to offer salvation to all men on easier 'gospel' terms. Whereas the original Covenant of Works had required perfect obedience to the Moral Law, God had now introduced a New Law or evangelical covenant 'suited to man's present State of Misery'.[6]

It is by no means clear, however, that this New Law offered easier terms. Its tenor, as Baxter spelt it out, was that 'whoever will Repent, Thankfully and Heartily accept Jesus Christ to be his Saviour, Teacher, King and Head, believing him to be the Redeemer, and will Love him (and God in him) above all, and obey him sincerely, to the Death, shall upon his first acceptance be justified and adopted.'[7]

This not only introduced an element of human merit into the gospel; it also created a pastoral problem. If people's justification was based to the slightest degree on some obedience of their own, then the quality of this obedience became a matter of deep personal anxiety. No longer were people looking to Christ alone, the object of their faith: they were looking at their faith itself, and what they found could be deeply disturbing, especially when they looked at the adverbs, 'thankfully,' 'heartily,' and 'sincerely.' Faith, they would quickly realise, was no rock to stand on, yet, according to Baxter,

---

5. Riccaltoun, *A Sober Enquiry*, p. 158.

6. Baxter, *Universal Redemption of Mankind, by the Lord Jesus Christ* (London: 1694), p. 53.

7. ibid., p. 53.

faith, not the sacrifice of Christ, was a believer's imputed righteousness.[8] Many looked at their faith, and doubted if it could take the strain.

One early result of the New Legalism was that Scottish theologians such as Robert Traill and John Brown of Wamphray spoke out strongly against any use of the word 'condition' in connection with justification,[9] and by the time of the *Marrow* controversy this had clearly become the standard evangelical practice in Scotland, as Riccaltoun indicates, when he tells us that no one who called faith a condition would be counted an orthodox divine in Scotland. But however true this may have been of Riccaltoun's contemporaries, earlier divines such as Samuel Rutherford, while openly critical of Baxter's teaching, had no reservations about speaking of faith as a condition of justification.[10]

It would be a pity, however, if a dispute about words led to *sōlā gratiā* and *sōlā fidē* being set up as antitheses to each other. Dickson and Rutherford, while happy to speak of faith as a condition of justification, would have agreed fully with Riccaltoun that it was not a 'federal condition': that is, it was not a condition in the same sense as perfect obedience was a condition in the Adamic covenant. They would have been among the first to insist that faith had no intrinsic merit and was not in any sense a 'qualification' for acceptance with God; they would have insisted that faith itself repudiates the idea of faith in faith, and puts its whole trust in the grace of God and in the sacrifice of Christ; and they would have totally rejected the idea, had it been put to them, of a *mediate* righteousness, as if Christ's righteousness were imputed only to those who already had some sort of personal righteousness through their own evangelical obedience. It is as sinners that we receive God's executive pardon.

---

8. Richard Baxter, *Catholic Theologie: Plain, Pure, Peaceable, for Pacification of the Dogmatical Word-Warriors* (London: 1675), p. 253.

9. John Brown of Wamphray, *The Life of Justification Opened* (1695); Robert Traill, *A Vindication of the Protestant Doctrine of Justification from the Unjust Charge of Antinomianism* (1730).

10. Rutherford states categorically, 'The condition of the covenant is faith,' and then quickly adds, '*This do,* was the condition of the covenant of works. *This believe* is the condition of this covenant [the Covenant of Grace]; because faith sendeth a person out of himself, and taketh off his own bottom, that in Christ he may have his righteousness' (*The Trial and Triumph of Faith*, 1645. Reprinted Edinburgh: Free Church of Scotland, 1845; p. 87). Rutherford saw the doctrine that the Covenant of Grace 'had no condition at all' as a distinctive tenet of antinomians and libertines, and closely linked to the doctrine of eternal justification, according to which the elect were justified before they were born.

It was with good reason that the Protestant doctrine of justification was flagged up as 'justification by faith alone', yet at no point was this regarded as a way of letting works in by the back-door. For proof of this we need only look at Luther's famous translation of Romans 3:28, where, to make the meaning unmistakeably clear, he adds a gloss, and gives the rendering, 'a man is justified by faith *alone* without works of law.' We are justified by faith *alone*, without any works that might be associated with faith or arise from faith or be required to supplement faith. Here, faith and works are presented as sharp antitheses, mutually exclusive of each other, leaving no room for any tension between *sōlā fidē* (by faith alone) and *sola gratiā* (by grace alone). Justification by faith *is* justification by grace.

But not only was this a clear antithesis in the teaching of the Reformers; it was an equally clear antithesis in the New Testament itself, which consistently contrasts justification by faith with justification by works, while at the same time equating justification by faith with justification by grace. For example, boasting is excluded not by the law of works, but by the law of faith (Rom. 3:27); the justified are those who do not work but believe (Rom. 4:4); and the reason why justification depends on faith is so that it may be entirely a matter of grace (Rom. 4:16).[11]

Faith, then, is not a work. It is the renunciation of any pretence to being able to claim salvation as a debt that God owes us as a reward for the quality of our own lives: a recognition that we have no right in law to divine pardon, and that our only hope lies in sovereign divine clemency.

Some twenty years after the *Marrow* controversy. Jonathan Edwards published a discourse on 'Justification by Faith Alone',[12] in which he emphasises strongly that we receive this blessing 'without any manner of goodness of our own'. Yet he also speaks of faith as 'the only condition of justification', and as a grace which has 'a unique office' in relation to this blessing. All other graces are precious, he writes, but we are never said to be justified by love or justified by repentance or justified by hope. That honour belongs to faith alone.

---

11. There is a similar sharp antithesis between justification by faith and justification by works of law in Galatians 2:16, where Paul writes, 'We know that a person is not justified by works of the law, but through faith in Jesus Christ', Cf. Philippians 3:9, where Paul speaks of his desire to be found in Christ, 'not having a righteousness of my own that comes from the law, *but* that which comes through faith in Christ' (italics added).

12. *The Works of Jonathan Edwards*, revised and corrected by Edward Hickman (2 Vols, 1834. Reprinted Edinburgh: Banner of Truth, 1974), Vol. 1, pp. 620-54.

But what gives it this unique influence? The fact, said Edwards, that faith is the 'uniting grace'. Faith receives Christ, faith comes to Him, faith believes into Him. By faith we come to be legally one with Christ, co-heirs of His inheritance, filled with His Spirit. But at the same time Edwards is at pains to point out that union with Christ is not a reward for believing. Faith itself unites us to the Saviour: 'God does not give those that believe a union with or an interest in the Saviour as a *reward* for faith, but only because faith is the soul's *active* uniting with Christ, or is itself the very act of unition *on their part*'.[13]

This is the heart of the matter. We have a title to eternal life because by faith we 'have' the Son of God (1 John 5:12); and, conversely, the fact that faith, and faith alone, is the 'uniting grace' means that without it we can never experience the blessing of justification. The danger was that in the climate created by the New Legalism, fear of the word 'condition' would breed a reluctance to press home the duty of faith. Yet even when they disowned the specific word, 'condition,' orthodox theologians clearly recognised that pardon and faith were intimately connected.

How are justification and faith connected?

But what was the nature of that connection? All accepted that faith was a 'requirement', all freely spoke of it as a necessity, all pressed it on sinners as a duty,[14] and all deemed it to be of such importance that they constantly warned of the danger of counterfeits. The *Marrow* itself described it as the grace that 'coupleth the soul with Christ, even as the spouse with her husband' (p. 133). Many, less romantically, contented themselves with defining faith as the instrumental cause of justification (though it is not clear how one event can be the cause of another without also being a condition of its occurring). Riccaltoun observed that giving and receiving were correlates: the one couldn't be without the other, and, in line with this, faith was seen as the hand that receives Christ and the gift of righteousness.[15]

---

13. Jonathan Edwards, *The Gospel Mystery*, p. 626. Cf. p. 628, 'faith includes the whole act of unition to Christ as Saviour … and however things may be no less excellent than faith, yet it is not the nature of any other graces or virtues directly to close with Christ as a mediator.' Earlier, Walter Marshall had declared that faith is not a bare right or title to the enjoyment of Christ 'but rather it must be an entrance into it, and taking possession of it'.

14. Even in warning of the danger of trumping up faith as the substance of evangelical righteousness, Riccaltoun (*A Sober Enquiry*, p. 142) also admits that, while faith is bestowed in the Covenant of Grace, it is also a duty.

15. Riccaltoun, *A Sober Enquiry*, p. 144.

It was this last view of faith that led to its often being compared to the action of a beggar holding out his hand to receive alms, and the illustration certainly has the merit of highlighting the disproportion between the divine action and the human response: a disproportion we see clearly in John 3:16. God gave His Son: He asks of us only that we believe; and while the gift evokes wonder, love and praise, the action of the beggar evokes no praise at all. He is debtor: a debtor to mercy alone.

Yet the illustration has serious limits. The beggar confronted by a benefactor has entire discretion over whether he holds out his hand or not. It is not his duty to accept the offer. For the hearer of the gospel, however, faith is a duty; and irrespective of whether or not we define it as a condition, it is something God commands,[16] and failure to comply with His command is an act of defiance which carries the gravest consequences. The Lord Himself made this abundantly clear when He declared that whoever doesn't believe is condemned already (John 3:18); and He repeated the point in John 3:36: 'He that believeth on the Son hath everlasting life; and he that believeth not the Son shall not see life; but the wrath of God abideth on him.' No beggar offered even the most generous gift is faced with a challenge of such existential moment.

Is any of this of any practical consequence? Yes! It has a close bearing on our presentation of the gospel. It is a precious truth that Christ paid the whole price of our redemption and that, as a consequence, for us salvation is a free gift. But, as we have noted, giving and receiving are correlates, the one implying the other; and as the Gospel of John makes plain, only those who 'receive' Christ have the right to become children of God (John 1:12). Sadly, humans by nature have little appreciation of the gift, and this is why evangelism can never be merely proclamation. It must also be persuasion (2 Cor. 5:11) because, while the *offer* of salvation is to be made to one and all, the *promise* of salvation is made only to faith; and whether we press it home as a condition, a *conditio sine qua non,* a requirement, a duty, a uniting grace, or a beggar's hand, press it home we must.

Is there a covenant between God and the believer?

But once we shield ourselves against all suspicion of conditional grace, can we then dare to differ from Boston and his friends and go on to believe

---

16. 'It may not be denied that Faith is a Duty, founded upon, and necessarily flowing from the very Frame and Constitution of this Covenant. The Declarations there made, and the promises given forth by the God of Truth, command belief in the most powerful manner' (Riccaltoun, *A Sober Enquiry,* p. 143).

that there is not only an eternal covenant between God the Father and God the Son, but also another covenant, made in time, between God and the believer? Or is any idea of a divine-human covenant unthinkable because of the gulf, metaphysical and moral, between the parties?

The answer depends largely on how we view the covenant between God and Abraham. That there was such a covenant is clear. We see it explicitly in Genesis 17:1-14, especially in verse 7: 'And I will establish my covenant between me and you and your offspring after you throughout their generations for an everlasting covenant, to be God to you and to your offspring after you.'

It is immediately clear that this covenant is entirely a matter of divine initiative and sovereign grace. Abraham did not ask for it, nor was he consulted about its terms. They were simply announced. It was also a matter of pure promise. Nothing in it was a reward for Abraham's past performance; nor was it, like the ancient Near-Eastern treaties imposed by victorious kings on their conquered vassals, a promise of favour and protection on condition of the regular payment of tribute and punitive reparations. The Promised Land was a royal gift, and not even Abraham's lapses and failings could lead to the gift being withdrawn. God had confirmed it with an oath, swearing by Himself (Heb. 6:16-17). Come what may, God would be his God, and the God of his seed.

But was the covenant bilateral? Yes, clearly, otherwise it would be a decree, not a covenant. First and foremost, Abraham had to take God at His word, and it wasn't always easy, especially when God deferred to Sarah's extreme old age the birth of the child who would carry the covenant blood-line. But Abraham believed God, and far from counting this a small thing, God imputed it to him as righteousness. Nor was faith the only stipulation. In response to the promise, Abraham was enjoined to walk before God and be blameless (Gen. 17:2). The covenant-initiator and promise-giver would not be indifferent to the conduct of the covenant beneficiary. Then there was the matter of circumcision: so significant that failure to circumcise was an irremediable breach of the covenant (Gen. 17:14).

In the first instance the covenant with the patriarch was a personal covenant between God and Abraham, but it was also a commitment on God's part to Abraham's seed. They, unlike Abraham, would actually possess the Promised Land, but over and above that, they were to be a blessing to the whole world. As Paul highlights in Galatians 3:16, that promise focused specifically on 'one seed, which is Christ,' through whom salvation would come to all the nations of the earth. Yet, although Paul naturally singles out Christ, he does not limit the seed of Abraham to the promised Messiah, nor does he limit it to the patriarch's physical descendants. Instead, he declares that all who share Abraham's faith, whether Jews or Gentiles, are children of Abraham (Gal. 3:7). All who are in Christ are Abraham's offspring and heirs to the promises God made to him. This is why, in Galatians 3:14, Paul can describe Gentile believers' experience of the Holy Spirit as the fulfilment of God's promise to Abraham.

In line with this, Paul portrays the New Testament church (what Jesus called 'my church', Matt. 16:18) not as a separate, *de novo* planting, but as an engrafting of wild Gentile shoots onto the age-old Abrahamic stock (Rom. 11:17). Once engrafted, the new shoots and the natural branches draw their nourishment from one and the same root, and every branch is heir to the same great promises. God will be their God, and every believer, Jew and Gentile alike, can look forward to the Promised Land as it was understood by Abraham himself: 'a city which hath foundations, whose builder and maker is God' (Heb. 11:10). This is why the psalmist can repeatedly refer to God as 'my God'. In Psalm 43:4, for example, he cries, 'I will praise you with the lyre, O God, my God;' we find it again in Psalm 63:1, 'O God, you are my God; earnestly I seek you;' and again in Psalm 145:1, 'I will extol you, my God and King.' It is the language of both commitment and possession. God was pledged to him with a love that would never let go. There was a bond, the bond of the divine *hesed*, that priceless Hebrew word that spoke of a steadfast love that endures from everlasting to everlasting (Ps. 103:17).

It is this same covenant language we find in Paul when he, too, speaks of God as 'my God', as in the great reassurance he offers to the church at Philippi when he writes, 'My God will supply every need of yours' (Phil. 4:19). Every Christian believer has a right to speak of God in these same terms. Not only is He *involved* in our lives: He is *committed* to us, and the hope we have built on His promises will never put us to shame.

The Covenant of Grace and the Covenant of Redemption

What is the relationship between this Covenant of Grace between God and the believer, and the Covenant of Redemption between God the Father and God the Son?

First and foremost, the covenant between God and the believer, like the Covenant of Redemption, is a covenant to which all three persons of the Blessed Trinity are parties. God is pledged to the believer as the Father, the Son, and the Holy Spirit. At the same time, however, the Son has a special place in the Covenant of Grace, as He has in the Covenant of Redemption. He is the Mediator through whom the estranged parties, God and man, were brought together in friendship; and the way we were brought together was that He, as agreed with the Father and the Holy Spirit, stood surety for us and paid our debts. His blood, and His blood alone, secured the blessings of the New Covenant (Jer. 31:33-34), in which God pledges to forgive His people's sins, to write His law on their hearts and to put His Spirit within them. This is precisely what is signified and sealed to us in the Lord's Supper, especially in the Cup: 'This cup that is poured out for you is the new covenant in my blood' (Luke 22:20, ESV). It is this cup, filled with all the promises of God, that the Saviour offers to us, with the words, 'Drink of it, all of you' (Matt. 26:27); and underlying it is the mighty truth that the Covenant of Grace, with all its free gifts, rests on the Mediator's perfect fulfilment of the Covenant of Redemption.

Christ's last will and testament

There remains, however, a fascinating variant on the covenant theme: the reference in Hebrews 9:16-17 to Christ's last will and testament. Here the writer describes believers as heirs to an eternal inheritance and then relates their possession of the inheritance to the death of the testator: 'For where a will is involved, the death of the one who made it must be established. For a will takes effect only at death, since it is not in force as long as the one who made it is alive.'

The initial challenge here is that English versions of this passage commonly use two different translations of the one Greek word *diathēkē* within the compass of three verses. In verse 15 it is translated 'covenant' ('he is the mediator of a new covenant'); in verses 16-17 it is translated 'will' ('for where a will is involved'). Which is correct?

The answer is that each is correct in its own context. The translation 'will' captures the standard meaning of the word *diathēkē* in secular Greek, whereas the usual word for a covenant was *sunthēkē*. However, when the translators of the Septuagint came to render the Hebrew word *berith* (covenant) they avoided the word *sunthēkē*, and they did so for the very good reason that it suggested the idea of a contract between equals. No *berith* between God and man could ever be a contract between equals.

The word *diathēkē*, on the other hand, eliminated all idea of a negotiated bargain, and the New Testament writers followed the precedent set by the Septuagint, consistently avoiding the word *suntheke* and regularly using *diathēkē* in the sense of covenant. The one exception is here in Hebrews 9:16-17, where the context (and especially the reference to a 'testator,' *diathemenos*), clearly requires the translation 'will' in the sense of last will and testament.

But fascinating as the linguistic interchange may be, the key point here is the portrayal of Christ as one who has bequeathed an inheritance; and, linked to this, the portrayal of believers as the people who were named in His will and who, now that He has died, are in full possession of His estate.

Like all analogies, this one has its limits. For one thing, though the testator has died, He is not dead, but still lives to administer His estate; and furthermore, He Himself is the estate, our priceless inheritance. But the one point that matters for the present is that, when it comes to making a will, the person making it has absolute discretion.[17] He can dispose of his estate as he pleases. In the context of Covenant theology this means that Christ has sovereign authority over the estate He purchased with His blood, and within this framework *He bequeaths the whole of it to each one of His children.*

The Marrow Men took up the idea of Christ as testator with enthusiasm. Boston, for example, speaks of the righteousness of Christ as 'a testamentary gift, made over to you in Christ's testament, wherein sinners of mankind, without exception are the legatees';[18] Riccaltoun describes Christ as 'a testator disponing all the Benefits of his Purchase and ratifying his Testament with his own Blood';[19] *Fisher's Catechism* refers to Him as not only the 'administrator' of the covenant but its appointed 'trustee', who disposes of the estate by way of a testament that conveys all the blessings of the Covenant of Grace to poor sinners.[20]

This portrayal of salvation as a testamentary gift clearly highlights the unconditional nature of grace. A legacy is neither earned, paid for, nor

---

17. Subject in modern law to the rights of spouses and children.
18. Boston, *Works*, Vol. VIII, p. 593.
19. Riccaltoun, ibid., p. 130.
20. *Fisher's Catechism*, 20:99.

negotiated. Instead, it is entirely optional, rooted in the goodwill of the testator, and reflecting his unchallengeable right to dispose of his estate as he pleases. From this point of view the preaching of the gospel can be described as the reading of the Redeemer's will, and this is equally, if not more, true of the sacrament, where the legacy is dramatically symbolised and conveyed to us in terms of the bread of life and the cup of blessing.

But who are the legatees? The Marrow Men answered unequivocally, 'Sinners of mankind without exception.' The will is made out in favour of humanity simply as such. It is, quite literally, good news for every man, and every human being may claim the estate as his by right. Does this mean, then, that all are already *de facto* possessors of eternal life, no action being required from the human side? The answer has to be twofold.

First, if the legatees are sinners of mankind lost, then every human being must be informed of the contents of the will. Otherwise, they can never claim their rights. This is the impulse that drives, or should drive, the Church's missionary effort. Every man, woman and child is from this point of view an heir of salvation. They must be found, and they must be told.

Secondly, if the legatees are to benefit from the bequest, they must accept it. Even in the case of a human will, the will itself does not put the heir in possession of the legacy. It gives a right, but the heir must consent to taking possession, and it is not unknown for the intended beneficiary to decline. An heir may blanch at the responsibility of running a great estate; and many a gospel-hearer may blanch at the cost of discipleship. It is not, after all, a matter of an immediate translation to bliss, but a matter of taking up the cross, and multitudes of human beings decide the estate isn't worth the trouble.

The reason the Marrow Men found the idea of the covenant as testament so attractive was, as we have seen, that it threw the idea of unconditionality into high relief. In contrast to a federal disposition, it was 'a conveyance of grace and bounty, without all conditions properly so called';[21] and this brings us back to the question of the place of faith in the plan of salvation. The friends of the *Marrow* may have scrupled about calling it a condition, but if they were sure that grace was, as they said, 'absolutely unconditional,' they were no less sure that faith was absolutely necessary. Yes, it was a gift, secured by Christ for His people by His covenanted death on the cross. But it was also a duty,

---

21.   Fisher, ibid., 20:100.

and at its heart lay entire satisfaction with, and acquiescence in, the terms of the will. But they were also aware that far from being antitheses, faith and unconditional grace were coordinates, each implying the other. 'Why,' asks *Fisher's Catechism*, 'is believing on Christ the appointed means of instating sinners in the covenant, and legacies thereof?'[22] It answers unequivocally: 'Because hereby the grace of the covenant is preserved entire.' When we trust a Saviour, all the credit goes to the Saviour, not to our trusting. But if we don't trust Him, we shall never be saved.

'Tell every man there is good news for him'

Before taking our leave of the *Marrow*, we must note some of those expressions, allegedly 'contrary to the holy scriptures, our Confession of Faith and Catechisms' which drew down upon it the wrath of Principal Hadow and the General Assembly.

One of these was John Preston's gloss on the form of the Great Commission as recorded in the longer ending of the Gospel of Mark (Mark 16:15): 'Go and tell every man without exception, that there is good news for him; Christ is dead for him; and if he will take him, and accept of his righteousness, he shall have him.'[23] This was one of the expressions on which the Assembly based its charge that the *Marrow* taught universal redemption as to purchase.[24]

Boston, himself a wholehearted believer in the doctrine of particular redemption, insists that Preston's statement has nothing to do with the scope of redemption, and declares categorically that the doctrine of universal redemption is not taught either by Preston or by the *Marrow*. Instead, he argues, the point of Preston's statement as incorporated in the *Marrow*, is the same as that of Revelation 22:17, 'Whosoever will, let him come, and take of

---

22. ibid., 20:109.

23. See Boston's *Notes* on the *Marrow*, pp. 127-30.

24. This may well have been true of Preston, an Anglican divine who, with others such as Edmund Calamy (a member of the Westminster Assembly), stood in the tradition of John Davenant, Bishop of Salisbury, who had advocated a form of Hypothetical Universalism at the Synod of Dort. On Preston, see Jonathan D. Moore, *English Hypothetical Universalism: John Preston and the Softening of Reformed Theology* (Grand Rapids: Eerdmans, 20087). Moore makes a good case for the inclusion of Preston in this school. However, though Boston unreservedly embraced the doctrine of particular redemption, he detected not a whiff of universal redemption in Preston, whom he quotes repeatedly. In any case, whatever Preston's overall position, the expression quoted in the *Marrow* at this point is no more inconsistent with an 'orthodox' Reformed interpretation than is the Apostle John's declaration that Christ is the expiation for the sins of the whole world (1 John 2:2).

the water of life freely.' 'There is,' writes Boston, 'a *quicunque vult*, whosoever will come (none excepted) may have life, and it will cost him nothing.'[25] The offer is universal. God's 'deed of gift and grant' is to every man.

Here Boston highlights two Old Testament analogies, the cities of refuge and the brazen serpent. The cities were for every man who was being pursued by an avenger of blood; the serpent for all who had been bitten by the fiery serpents (Exod. 21:8). In the same way, the preacher may tell every human being that there is a Saviour provided for him: a crucified Christ for *him*, and if he makes use of Him he will be saved. This is not to tell every man that he is already redeemed or already pardoned or already saved; but it is to promise everyone, without exception, and no matter how gross their sins, that if they trust in Christ they will be saved. In this respect, the human race is in a quite different position from the angels. For the fallen angels, no Saviour is provided; for the human race, there is; and the gospel call gives every fallen human being a warrant to come to Him.

In conjunction with this, Boston also emphasises, once again, that our being persuaded that Christ died for us, is part of the definition of saving faith. This immediately smacks of Arminianism: after all, if you believe that Christ died equally 'for all men and for every man', then you instantly assure yourself that 'Christ died for me'. But the two cases, Boston insists, are quite different. When the Arminian says that he believes that Christ died for him, he is simply making a general statement about the human race: the same sort of statement as, 'I was created.' He is not saying that he is sure that Christ loves him in particular or that He is calling him personally. Nor is the Arminian saying that he sees the gospel-call as a personal offer to him of the divine gift of salvation, including the promise that if he accepts the gift (God's 'free offer') he will receive eternal life, and never lose it. But precisely this persuasion, Boston believes, lies at the heart of saving faith. It means trusting in the love of God, in the promises that flow from that love, and in the unshakeable steadfastness of that love as a love from which nothing can ever separate us (Rom. 8:38-39). Every hearer of the gospel has a right to believe that this gift of life more abundant is offered to herself.

---

25. Boston, *Notes*, p. 127. Cf. Riccaltoun, *A Sober Enquiry*, p. 122: '*Christ is dead for him*, but how? Was it to purchase Salvation for him whether he Believes or not? No such Thing; but so far as no Man shall ever Perish for want of a Saviour to Die for them. *If he will take Him,* dead as he is, *and accept of his Righteousness,* which by his Death he has wrought out, he shall have him.' (Italics original, representing direct quotes from the *Marrow*.)

Be verily persuaded that Jesus Christ is yours

Another contentious statement on which Boston offers an extended note is the counsel offered by Evangelista when, having dealt with Nomista (the legalist), he turns to Neophytus, the young Christian, and tells him, 'Be verily persuaded in your heart that Jesus Christ is yours, and that you shall have life and salvation by him; that whatsoever Christ did for the redemption of mankind, he did it for you.'[26]

It was this and similar statements that led to the charge that, according to the *Marrow*, assurance was of the essence of faith. Much of Boston's note is taken up with citations designed to show that the doctrine of the *Marrow* on this question is identical with what was preached by Protestant divines from the beginning 'and sealed with the blood of martyrs'. Faith, in general, he argues, is a real persuasion: someone who believes is persuaded. The special nature of saving faith, however, is that it is an *appropriating* persuasion, where we take Christ for ourselves. This is more than simply assenting to the gospel as true. It is to 'relish' the gospel as good.

In what sense is Christ ours? By the 'deed of gift and grant' made by God to 'mankind lost': in other words, He is ours in the offer of free and unconditional grace. 'Deed of gift and grant' is a legal term. In conveyancing, for example, it might mean being presented with the title-deeds and keys to a property, asking no more of the beneficiary than that he accepts. In evangelistic terms it means that in the gospel God sets Christ before us as a free gift and says, 'He is yours. Take him.' By this offer, Boston insists, Christ is ours before we believe, not in the sense that we already have a saving interest in Him, or are already in a state of grace, but in the sense that in common with the whole human race we have a title to Him and a right to take Him as our very own Saviour; and here he, too, draws on the familiar analogy of a piece of gold being offered to a poor man. The offer makes the piece of gold really his: 'Take it. It's yours.' But if the poor man doesn't take it, the gold never becomes his in possession, and he has no benefit from it.[27] Similarly, the 'giving' mentioned by the *Marrow* is not a giving in possession, but a giving by way of grant, *whereupon we may take*

---

26. Boston, *Notes*, pp. 118-26.

27.   Another less familiar analogy would be the refusing of an executive pardon offered by, for example, the President of the United States or the Sovereign of the United Kingdom. Someone convinced of his innocence might refuse such a pardon because it implies an admission of guilt.

possession; and the party to whom the grant is made is not the elect only, but mankind lost. The title-deeds to Christ are already made out in the name of sinners; we are sinners; and we have an immediate right to take possession. Boston even goes so far as to say that the great sin of unbelief lies, not in refusing to believe that God gives eternal life to the elect, but in refusing to believe that God has made a grant of eternal life to ourselves personally, 'so that we as well as others are warranted and welcome to take possession of it.'[28]

He is also at pains, however, to clarify what is meant by the promise, 'You shall have life and salvation by him.' Salvation, he declares, signifies 'a life of holiness as well as happiness: salvation from sin, as well as from wrath: not in heaven only, but begun here and completed hereafter.'[29] Far from being antinomian, then, this 'appropriating assurance' is utterly inconsistent with an unwillingness to part with sin, and with any purpose of heart to continue in it. On the contrary, it is always accompanied by a turning from sin to God 'with full purpose of, and endeavour after, new obedience' (*Shorter Catechism,* Answer 87).

'Whatever Christ did, he did for you'

Another element in the persuasion referred to by the *Marrow* was, 'Whatsoever Christ did for the redemption of mankind, he did it for you'; and, like the previous citation, this too was used as proof that, in contradiction of the Westminster Confession (18:3), it made assurance to be of the essence of faith.

Boston's first reaction to the charge is, 'Be it so! Assurance *is* of the essence of faith.' To believe and to be assured (or persuaded) are synonymous; and this brings us back once again to Hebrews 11:1. Faith is convinced of the reality of things unseen.

The problem is that the Marrow Men and their opponents were at cross-purposes. Hadow understood the assurance in question to be the same as the one pronounced on in Chapter 18 of the Westminster Confession,

---

28. Here again Riccaltoun's sentiments correspond with those of Boston. The deed of gift and grant holds forth the Covenant of Grace 'without either universal Redemption to support the Truth of the general Offer, or conditional Offers to confine the Grant to particular Persons ... and makes it reasonable for everyone to believe in an all-sufficient Saviour there held forth; and to make use of all the Means which God has appointed to convey his Spirit unto his People, for bringing them into the Bond of the Covenant' (*A Sober Enquiry,* p. 122).

29. Boston's *Notes,* p. 120.

namely, the assurance that one is in a state of grace and salvation, and acquitted of all sin; and, building on this misconception, he went on to charge the *Marrow* with teaching that it is by this faith (the faith that we are already justified) that we are justified; and as if this were not enough, he also accused the *Marrow* of teaching, firstly, that no one is a true believer 'who doth not know himself to be justified, adopted, and in Favour with God through Christ' and, secondly, that there is no need to confirm this assurance by self-examination and the marks of grace.[30]

Boston immediately points out that the author of the *Marrow* is not referring here to assurance as defined in Chapter 18 of the Confession, that is, the assurance whereby believers are sure that they are in the state of grace.[31] That is an assurance *deduced* from faith, whereas what the *Marrow* has in mind is an assurance which is *in* faith:[32] a direct act in which we are assured (or, indeed, know) that Christ is offered to us personally, and that we have a right to take Him as our Saviour. Boston also points out, however, that the *Marrow* does not speak of our being *fully* persuaded, but only of our being really persuaded, and this is not at all inconsistent with doubting. Indeed, a person may have this persuasion, and have total trust in Christ as a Saviour, and yet not be sure that he has the right trust and the right persuasion. A believer can doubt his faith without doubting the Saviour, 'than which nothing is more ordinary among serious Christians.'[33]

It is the possibility of believers having such doubts that provides the background to the Westminster Confession's treatment of assurance. However, when it comes to speak of Saving Faith (Chapter 14) it emphasises precisely the same direct act of faith to which the *Marrow* was pointing: the faith by which we believe to be true whatever God reveals in His Word, and then proceed to embrace His promises and to rest upon Christ for salvation (14:2). This, though in different terminology, is exactly the 'appropriating persuasion' of Boston and the *Marrow*; and, like Boston, the Confession acknowledges that this persuasion varies in

---

30. Hadow, *The Antinomianism of the Marrow of Modern Divinity Detected*, pp. 18-27.

31. Boston, *Notes*, p. 118.

32. Boston, *Notes*, p. 121.

33. This last expression cuts two ways. Taken one way, it undercuts the idea that if you have doubts, you are not a Christian; taken in the other it suggests that if you don't have doubts, you are not a 'serious' Christian. Unfortunately, the latter idea took a firm hold in some strands of Scottish piety, leading to the very un-Protestant idea that unshaken assurance should be viewed with suspicion.

degree, sometimes weak, sometimes strong. But whatever the believer's ups-and-downs, faith itself is certain that the Bible is the Word of God, that Christ is the only Saviour, and that He is ours to come to. Nor is this a bare certainty: it is an *appropriating* certainty, which no sooner exists than it trusts in Christ for justification, sanctification and eternal life.

It is faith so defined, this combination of assurance and appropriation, of conviction and trust, that is of the essence of faith. In plain English, it *is* faith.

But dare we affirm without qualification that the other form of assurance, the believer's assurance that he is in state of grace, is not of the essence of faith? At first sight, this appears to be the confessional position: but only at first sight. What it does say (18.3) is that this assurance 'doth not *so* belong to the essence of faith, but that a true believer may wait long, and conflict with many difficulties, before he be partaker of it.' The 'so' is crucial. It is indeed true that all believers do not get this assurance immediately or enjoy it unbrokenly,[34] but this is no warrant for the idea that lack of assurance is the normal Christian experience. The 'so' implies that in some sense the assurance that we belong to God's family *is* of the essence of faith; or, in other words, just as it would be abnormal for a child to doubt whether her parents love her, so it is abnormal for a Christian to doubt the love that will never let her go. 'The certainty of truth is not enough for the Christian,' wrote Herman Bavinck. 'He also needs the certainty of salvation.'[35]

In line with this, the quest for such certainty was one of the great driving forces behind the Reformation.[36] But not only was it a driving force. It was a core element in the teaching of the Reformers. Calvin, for example, placed it at the heart of his definition of faith: 'We shall have a full definition of faith,' he wrote, 'if we say that it is a firm and sure knowledge of the divine favour toward us, founded on the truth of a free promise in

---

34. Note, however, the experience of Andrew Bonar who, at the age of seventy-nine, records in his diary, 'The Lord has enabled me to lean upon Christ day by day, for sixty years, or rather fifty-nine. He took hold of me that year [1830] and has never left me in darkness as to my interest in Him all that time' (*Andrew A. Bonar: Diary and Life,* edited by Marjory Bonar; London: Banner of Truth, 1960, pp. 363-64).

35. Herman Bavinck, *The Certainty of Faith* (1901. English translation, Potchefstroom: Institute for Reformational Studies, 1998), p. 39.

36. 'This powerful movement was born out of a deeply felt need for the assurance of salvation' (Bavinck, ibid., p. 16). So long as the doctrine of salvation by works cast its shadow over Christianity such assurance was impossible.

Christ, and revealed to our minds, and sealed on our hearts, by the Holy Spirit.'[37] We see this view reflected again in his comment on the opening words of the Lord's Prayer: 'It would be foolish, nay crazy, presumption to invoke God as Father, except as far as we know ourselves to be ingrafted into the body of Christ as sons.'[38] Even more forthright is his comment on Galatians 4:6:[39] 'where the pledge of the divine love towards us is wanting, there is assuredly no faith … none is a Christian save he who has been taught by the teaching of the Holy Spirit to call God his Father.'[40]

Scottish Reformers spoke with the same voice. John Davidson's *Catechism* (1602) asks, for example, 'What is Faith?' and replies boldly, 'It is ane heartlie assurance, that our sins are freely forgiven us in Christ.'[41]

By Boston's time, the two forms of assurance, one, the assurance that trusts Christ as Saviour, the other, the assurance that one has indeed exercised that trust, had long been distinguished as the *direct* act of faith and the *reflex* act of faith.[42] By the eighteenth century however, another distinction was gaining currency, that between the assurance of faith and the assurance of sense, and though Boston makes no use of it in his *Notes*, it does occur in the Brethren's *Answers to the Queries*,[43] in Ebenezer Erskine's *Sermons*, and in *Fisher's Catechism*. Fisher notes that believers do not at all times enjoy an assurance of God's love, and then, referring to Answer 36 of the Shorter Catechism, asks whether it is the assurance of faith or the assurance of sense that is mentioned in this answer. 'It is the assurance of sense,' he replies, 'or the sensible *assurance of God's love*' (italics his). Then, turning to the difference between them, he writes that the object of the

---

37. Calvin, *Institutes* III:II, 8.

38. Calvin, *A Harmony of the Gospels Matthew, Mark and Luke*, 2 Vols., tr. A. W. Morrison (Grand Rapids: Eerdmans, 1994), Vol. 1, p. 206.

39. 'And because ye are sons, God sent forth the Spirit of his Son into your hearts, crying, Abba, Father.'

40. *Calvin's Commentaries: Galatians, Ephesians, Philippians and Colossians*, tr. T. H. L. Parker (Grand Rapids: Eerdmans, 1996), p. 75.

41. See Horatius Bonar, *Catechisms of the Scottish Reformation* (London: James Nisbet, 1866), p. 340.

42. Boston, *Notes*, pp. 132, 235. The *reflex* act of faith is well described by Evangelista in his reply to a query put by Neophytus, who is sure that Christ is the true foundation, but wants to be sure that he is truly building on it: 'Well, now I understand what you mean; it seems you do not want a ground for your believing, but for believing that you have believed' (*The Marrow of Modern Divinity*, p. 235).

43. See Brown, *Gospel Truth*, p. 176.

assurance of faith is Christ in the promise, but the object of the assurance of sense is Christ formed in the soul; or, alternatively, the assurance of faith is founded on the infallible Word of God, 'but the assurance of sense upon the person's present experience of God's love.'[44]

Erskine's views on the distinction between the assurance of faith and the assurance of sense appear clearly in an excellent series of six sermons under the heading, 'The assurance of faith opened and applied,' based on Hebrews 10:19-22.[45] His main concern, as the title suggests, is with the assurance of faith, but in the third sermon he lays down the proposition, 'That there is a great difference betwixt the assurance of *faith*, and the assurance of *sense*, which follows upon faith.'[46] Here Erskine, like Boston, uses the traditional terminology: 'The assurance of faith is a *direct*, but the assurance of sense is a *reflex* act of the soul.'[47] The foundation of the one is objective, looking to Christ *without*, the foundation of the other is subjective, looking *within*. Erskine then illustrates the difference by citing the experience of Abraham: 'By the assurance of faith Abraham believed that he should have a son in his old age, because God who cannot lie had promised; but by the assurance of sense, he believed it when he got Isaac in his arms.'[48]

But is our assurance that God loves us, and is at peace with us, really a matter of 'sense'? The word is irritatingly ambiguous. For example, we perceive things with our senses, particularly with our sense of sight. This was Abraham's experience in the case cited by Erskine. He believed he had a son when he saw Isaac in his arms. This was a totally sensory experience, but we cannot hold Christ in our arms, and neither can we hold assurance

---

44. Essentially the same statement of the distinction is given in Answer VIII of the *Answers to the Queries*, Brown, p, 178. The assurance of faith looks to Christ, the promise and covenant of God; but the assurance of sense looks inward at the works of God, such as the person's own graces, attainments, and experiences: 'The one says, I take him for mine; the other says, I feel he is mine.' In accordance with this distinction, 'God may be a forgetting and withdrawing God to my feeling, and yet to my faith, my God and my Lord still.'

45. Ebenezer Erskine, *Sermons and Discourses upon the Most Important and Interesting Subjects* (4 Vols; Edinburgh: 1761), Vol. 1, pp. 287-380.

46. ibid., p. 312.

47. This was the terminology of Turretin, who commented that in the *reflex* act of faith the soul not only believes, but knows that it believes (just as in the natural life, the soul not only understands, but is also conscious of its own operation and knows that it understands – which is the peculiar privilege of the rational soul' (Turretin, *Institutes of Elenctic Theology*, Vol. 2, p. 620).

48. Erskine, ibid., p. 312.

in our arms. On the other hand, the word 'sense' can also be used in such a statement as, 'I sense it;' and this is indistinguishable from, 'I feel it,' which in the present context means, 'I feel that I have accepted Christ,' or, 'I feel that God loves me,' and 'I feel it because he smiles and shines on me.'[49]

But what are these smiles and shinings? Are they merely the times when we feel good about ourselves and our spiritual lives? Turretin speaks of 'the sweetness of spiritual consolation',[50] and this is indeed a reality in the life of believers, but can we speak of it as the ground of our assurance and not, rather, as the result of our assurance; especially when that assurance has been enhanced and deepened by specially gracious providences and thrilling answers to prayer? Yet this, too, needs balance. The sweetness of spiritual consolation can also be enjoyed in times of adversity, even times of extreme adversity. Paul and Silas could sing in prison (Acts 16:25).

The *Marrow* spoke of our believing that we have believed. But can we really see our own faith? Can we be aware of our love for Christ and our trust in His saving work? More fundamentally, is it possible for us to know what's in our own consciousness, and even to be as sure of what we see in there as we are of what we see with our eyes and hear with our ears?

There is good reason to believe that we can: indeed, Paul presupposes as much when he urges us to examine ourselves to see whether we are in the faith (2 Cor. 13:5).[51] Just as surely as we know whether we believe something or want something or support some cause or love someone or trust someone, so we can know that we believe the gospel, look to the cross of Christ as our only hope, and are daily aware of the flesh lusting against the Spirit. These facts do not belong to the realm of sense, but they are facts nonetheless, and we are aware of them.[52] 'We know that we know him,' writes the Apostle John (1 John 2:3); the disciples collectively protest, 'We

---

49. Brown, ibid., p. 176.

50. Turretin, *Institutes of Elenctic Theology*, p. 620.

51. This ability to know what's in our own consciousness would later become a key element in Scottish Common-Sense Realism, a movement associated with such philosophers as Thomas Reid (1710–96) and extending to such thinkers as Thomas Chalmers. According to this school, the workings of the mind could be subjected to the same type of scientific observation as Sir Isaac Newton applied to sensible/physical objects.

52. The Latin term, *sensus,* can be used to refer to 'sense-perception' but it is not limited to this. It denotes perception or awareness in general. It is in this sense that Calvin, for example, used it when he spoke of the *sensus divinitatis* implanted in every human heart (*Institutes* I:III, 1). There can be no sensory awareness of God, who is pure spirit.

have believed, and have come to know, that you are the Holy One of God'
(John 6:69); Paul can declare, 'I know whom I have believed' (2 Tim. 1:12);
and Peter assumes that his readers know that they love Jesus even though
they have never seen Him, and therefore rejoice with inexpressible joy in
the hope of glory (1 Pet. 1:8).

We can be as sure of these things as we are of any other item stored in
our minds. But is this best described as a sense, placed beyond the reach of
enquiry, and cherished only as something that's 'better felt than telt'? In the
case of the direct act of faith, the mind is sure of Christ. In the case of the
reflex act of faith, the mind is sure that it believes.

Yet, that having been said, assurance, and the joy that goes along with
it, do not rest mainly, or even normally, on a second-order process of
observation and inference. It is the assurance that Christ loves us, and longs
to embrace and forgive us, that makes us turn to Him in the first place. He
does not come to love us because we believe in Him. We believe in Him
because He loves us and calls us, 'Come unto me, and I will give you rest'
(Matt. 11:28). When we come to Him, His Spirit fills us, bearing His own
precious fruit of 'love, joy and peace' (Gal. 5:22). It is 'fruit', however: not
something we struggle to produce, but something He produces in us when
we keep in step with Him (Gal. 5:25).

Why did the *Marrow* command so little support?

One of the most remarkable features of the *Marrow* controversy is how little
support the book and its friends could muster within the Church. Wodrow,
writing home from the General Assembly on 19 May 1720, reported that
the propositions extracted from *The Marrow of Modern Divinity* were
'very unanimously condemned', and it was clearly a condemnation in
which he heartily concurred. 'The propositions,' he writes, 'were so gross,
that here was no reasoning of any force against them.'[53] He was even more
scathing about the Brethren's 'Representation' against the 1720 Act: 'I like
the representation, as to the doctrine of it, fully as ill as the Marrow, yea,
much worse';[54] and his parting-shot after the end of formal proceedings in
1722 was, 'I hope, through the divine goodness, Antinomianism shall never

---

53. *The Correspondence of the Rev. Robert Wodrow*, ed. Rev. Thomas McCrie, Vol.
2 (Edinburgh: Wodrow Society, 1843), p. 529. Just in case we wouldn't get the point,
Wodrow's editor 'explains' in a footnote, 'Wodrow belonged to the Anti-Marrow men.'

54. ibid., p. 559.

take hold in this land.'[55] He had clearly been fully persuaded by Hadow's statement of the case.

Yet, although Wodrow did not share the profound antipathy to patronage which came to be the defining characteristic of what came to be known as the popular or evangelical party, he was a man of evangelical sympathies, who spoke warmly of Boston as 'a faithful servant of no small solidity and sufficiency',[56] and at the same time put on record the pleasure with which he had read *The Fourfold State*. His biographies did much to safeguard the legacy of such giants as Robert Bruce, David Dickson and William Guthrie of Fenwick, and he admired such evangelical stalwarts as Thomas Halyburton (1674–1712) and John MacLaurin (1693–1754).[57]

Wodrow should serve as a warning, then, against taking men's attitude to the *Marrow* as the criterion of whether they were evangelicals or not. As John Brown pointed out, the Marrow Men themselves recognised that many pious ministers scrupled at expressions in the Marrow;[58] and even among the 'violent anti-Marrow men' there were those who were blameless in their doctrine and zealous in their ministry. Among these were such as John M'Laren, whose ministry at Edinburgh's Tolbooth Kirk 'met with much acceptance among judicious Christians' and whom Brown describes as 'eminently holy in his practice'; Professor William Hamilton of Edinburgh University, 'an able divine,' who several years after the controversy declared to Boston his satisfaction 'with what we called the deed of gift, and his conviction that the gospel could not be preached without it';[59] and, most intriguingly of all, John Willison of Dundee.

Willison is the biggest enigma in the opposition to the *Marrow*. John Macleod describes him as one of those who were 'quite alive to the working of a legal and unevangelical leaven in the pulpit teaching of many in the ministry';[60] he was a fervent and active opponent of patronage, a robust apologist for the Cambuslang and Kilsyth revivals, and sympathetic to

---

55. ibid., p. 664.

56. ibid., p. 554.

57. Halyburton was one of those who noted (and lamented) the growing prevalence of 'legal preaching' (*Works*, 765).

58. John Brown, *Gospel Truth*, p. 17.

59. Brown, ibid., p. 17.

60. John Macleod, *Scottish Theology*, p. 177.

Ebenezer Erskine and the brethren who seceded to form the Associate Presbytery in 1733. He was also the author of a clutch of widely read devotional works such as *The Afflicted Man's Companion, A Sacramental Directory*, and *The Mother's Catechism* (1731).[61] Yet he went along with the majority in condemning the *Marrow*.

The primary reason for this, in Willison's case, as in Wodrow's, was that he thought many of the *Marrow*'s statements lent themselves to an antinomian interpretation. He was also ill at ease, as David Lachman points out, with the tendency of the Marrow Men to introduce 'new modes of speaking' into the pulpit, and to censure the old ones.[62] Yet his own phraseology was sometimes fully in line with that of the Brethren. For example, he uses the phrase, 'an appropriating persuasion'; declares, 'I believe and admire his [God's] love to the elect in general, and to me in particular'; and writes, 'I will apply his blood and righteousness to myself in particular, and rest on him as one that "loved me and gave himself for me."' Such an 'appropriating faith,' he insists, 'is necessary to my justification.' He also believed wholeheartedly that, 'A crucified Christ, with all his purchase, is offered to all the hearers of the gospel; yea, Christ in his word speaks to every sinner, man, and woman, in particular, as though he called them by name and surname.'[63]

How can we explain this determination of even their evangelical colleagues to distance themselves from the Marrow Men? One factor, certainly, is that in 1720 the affair had been rushed through the Assembly, affording members little opportunity to scrutinise it before the fateful Act of condemnation was passed. The Committee for Purity of Doctrine presented their report on Monday 16 May, highlighting by means of selected extracts what they regarded as objectionable propositions and offensive expressions in the *Marrow*. The matter was debated on Thursday and, considering the

---

61. Like *Fisher's Catechism*, the *Mother's Catechism* sought to explain the Shorter Catechism, though Willison's was aimed more specifically at very young children, for whom the Assembly's Catechism was deemed too difficult. It was translated into Gaelic in 1752 as *Leabhar Cheist na Màthair do'n Leanabh Og*.

62. David C. Lachman, *The Marrow Controversy* (Edinburgh: Rutherford House, 1988), p. 194.

63. See *Mediation XXV* in John Willison, *Sacramental Meditations and Advices, for the Use of Communicants*, 1747. The dividing line between evangelicals and legalists is further blurred by the fact that when James Hadow died, there were found among his papers 'a solemn personal covenant' and other indications of 'the exercise of a truly pious mind' (Brown, *Gospel Truth*, p. 17).

pressures of a busy Assembly, we can be sure that few members did more than read the report and the small number of extracts. The report, backed by Hadow's standing as the Professor of Divinity at Scotland's premier university, steered the Assembly towards the conclusion he wanted, and the Act condemning the *Marrow* was then passed on Friday.[64]

This leads to a second factor: respect for the General Assembly as the supreme court of the Church. From the moment the 1720 Act was passed, any defence of the *Marrow* was contumacy. Today, we are used to disagreeing with decisions of a General Assembly, and even to dissenting from them, but in the eighteenth century that was not the mood. Besides, the Assembly had not only expressed disagreement with the *Marrow:* it had passed an executive order forbidding any minister of the Church to speak well of it, and men naturally shrank from openly defying such a clear instruction. Even Boston, as we have seen, fully expected the Brethren's 'Dissent and Protest' to lead to their exclusion from the Church; and when Riccaltoun dared to lock horns with Hadow (and by implication with the 1720 Act) he did so under the cloak of anonymity (it is to his son, writing after his father's death, that we owe the information that he was the author of both the *Sober Enquiry* and *The Politick Disputant*). Then there is the oft-repeated story of the Reverend John Colquhoun of Leith (1748–1827) reminding his congregation that while he was forbidden to recommend the *Marrow*, he was not forbidden to recommend Boston's *Notes*.[65]

Thirdly, we have to recognise that there was indeed a widespread and longstanding fear of antinomianism. The generation of Henderson, Gillespie and Rutherford had entertained these same fears, and Rutherford had even devoted a whole treatise to the subject.[66] But it wasn't a merely theoretical antinomianism that had been on their mind. During their time in London as Commissioners to the Westminster Assembly they had seen the practical influence of antinomianism among the countless sects then active in the city, emphasising the primacy of 'inner light' over the authority of Scripture, opposing the idea of any settled church order, and

---

64. See the account in Wodrow's *Correspondence*, Vol. 2, footnote pp. 527-28.

65. See John Macleod, *Scottish Theology*, pp. 229-30.

66. Samuel Rutherford, *A Survey of the Spiritual AntiChrist* (London 1648). Yet, although all three were in London when the *Marrow* was published in 1645, there is no hint that either they, or any other contemporary, charged it with antinomianism.

encouraging forms of political action that threatened to lead to anarchy. It was easy to relate the *Marrow* to this background, and Hadow had explicitly done so, linking the *Marrow* to English independency and then linking independency to the sectaries.[67] It is hardly surprising in the circumstances that the Establishment, civil and ecclesiastical, had its antennae tuned to give early warning of any such trends in Scotland, and malicious critics could certainly dig out of the *Marrow* statements which could be deployed to suit their case.

But long after the dust of controversy had settled, the *Marrow* continued to be viewed with suspicion by distinguished evangelical theologians. One such was James Buchanan, Thomas Chalmers' successor as Professor of Systematic Theology at New College, Edinburgh, who, referring to the *Marrow*, gave it as his judgement that 'a book which is held even by its admirers to require explanatory or apologetic notes, may be fairly presumed to contain some unguarded expressions, which might be understood in a sense dangerous to some part of the scheme of divine truth.'[68]

As already noted, admirers of the *Marrow* readily admitted that it contained some unguarded expressions. But were these few expressions of sufficient gravity to warrant a solemn Act of the General Assembly which fell just short of condemning it to be burned, like *Lex Rex,* by the public hangman? Besides, the *Marrow* was not condemned because of its few unguarded expressions. It was condemned for its alleged antinomianism, a serious charge by any standard; and although the Marrow Men were never personally accused of it, they were inevitably associated with it. They had every right, then, to point out that the alleged antinomian expressions could not bear the weight put upon them. They might also have pointed out that

---

67. Hadow, *The Antinomianism of the Marrow Detected,* p. 9: 'Edward Fisher, the Author of the *Marrow,* was a Tool, whom the Independents sought to encourage at that Juncture. He was as to employment a Barber in London, who took upon himself to be a Minister of a separate or Independent Congregation, as may be gathered from the Book itself, and so set up for the Independent Way, in Opposition to Presbyterian Government.' Hadow is here exploiting the fact that the ministers who commended the *Marrow,* most notably Joseph Caryl and Jeremiah Burroughs, were part of the vocal group of Independents who had frustrated the implementation of the Solemn League and Covenant (1643) at the Westminster Assembly. These were effective debating-points, but the reference to Fisher as a barber is reminiscent of the jibe, 'Is not this the carpenter?' (Mark 6:3).

68. James Buchanan, *The Doctrine of Justification: An Outline of its History in the Church and of its Exposition in Scripture* (1867. Reprinted London: Banner of Truth, 1961), p. 197.

even the Scriptures themselves required explanatory and apologetic notes: a fact to which the ceaseless flow of Bible commentaries bears clear witness, as does, indeed, the on-going need for expository preaching.

More worrying are the sentiments of William Cunningham, who gave it as his opinion that, 'Principal Hadow and Thomas Boston may be regarded as the heads of two different schools of theology in Scotland in the early part of last century, and, as happens not unfrequently in theological discussions, they divided, we think, the truth between them in the points controverted.'[69]

This, surely, is a case of Homer nodding. Hadow was certainly not speaking the truth when he levelled his charges against the *Marrow*. It did not, for example, teach universal redemption as to purchase, or that holiness is not essential to salvation; nor did it teach that a believer doesn't commit sin, or that the Lord does not chastise a believer for his sin, or that a believer has no cause to crave pardon for his sin.[70] More important, where they differ on substantive theological issues it is simply not the case that Hadow was as close to the truth as Boston. Hadow was wrong to argue that repentance comes before faith, wrong to argue that the fear of hell should still be a motive for a believer's obedience, and wrong to deny that assurance (as the *Marrow* understood it) is of the essence of faith.

It was their position on this last point that served as the spur to Cunningham's damning Boston and his colleagues with faint praise. The *Marrow's* position on assurance was identical, as Boston pointed out, with that of the Reformers and particularly with that of John Calvin; and behind Cunningham's judgement on the *Marrow* lies the fact that he seriously disagreed with Calvin's doctrine of assurance. This was partly because (dare it be said?) he misunderstood it, taking it to mean 'a belief that our own sins have been forgiven, and that we have been brought into a state of grace.'[71] Cunningham points out, quite correctly, that as a definition of saving faith this would be absurd: the belief that we are already justified cannot itself be the faith that justifies. He then goes on to focus on Calvin's famous definition of faith in Book III of the *Institutes*:

> We shall have a right definition of faith if we call it a firm and certain knowledge of God's benevolence toward us, founded upon the truth of the freely given

---

69. William Cunningham, *The Reformers and the Theology of the Reformation* (Edinburgh: T. and T. Clark, 1862), pp. 281-82.

70. For these charges, see *The Antinomianism of the Marrow Detected*, p. 120.

71. Cunningham, *The Reformers and the Theology of the Reformation*, p. 118.

promise in Christ, both revealed to our minds and sealed upon our hearts through the Holy Spirit.[72]

Cunningham is remarkably critical of this statement. It wouldn't be surprising, he suggests, to find Luther making such a rash and exaggerated statement, 'But it is certainly strange that a man of such wonderful soundness and penetration of judgement as Calvin' should have made it.[73]

At this point Cunningham is at cross-purposes with Calvin because the passage quoted from the Reformer does not bear out the definition of faith that Cunningham attributes to him, namely, that saving faith is the assurance of being in a state of grace. This, had it been true, would have been no more than a statement about ourselves, but Calvin's 'right definition' does not describe faith as an assurance about ourselves, but as an assurance about God: not an assurance about our own new birth or any other point of our spiritual experience, but a belief about God's goodwill and benevolence as manifested in Christ; and it is through such faith that we are justified. The assurance which, according to the Marrow Men, comes before justification is not the assurance that we are in a state of grace, but that God is a loving God: the assurance that when He says, 'Come unto me,' He means it; the assurance that if we do come we will not be turned away; the assurance, to express it in the terms of the *Marrow,* that in God's deed of gift and grant, His salvation is freely offered to ourselves personally, giving us an unconditional right to take it, and an equally unconditional right to press it on the acceptance of others.

Long-term significance of the controversy

What was the long-term significance of the *Marrow* controversy? It certainly did not mark the emergence of two parties in the Church. For one thing, the Marrow Men were too few in number to form a party in any meaningful sense. For another, there had long been two parties: those who had been prepared to acquiesce in the impositions of secular government (prelacy in the seventeenth century, patronage in the eighteenth), and those opposed to such impositions; and, more or less involving the same personnel, those whose ministry had a legalistic and moralistic tone, and those who put Christ crucified and unconditional grace at the heart

---

72. Calvin, *Institutes,* III:II, 7.
73. Cunningham, ibid., p.119.

of their message. These lines had been drawn long before the *Marrow* controversy, and they would remain in evidence long afterwards.

Nor is there any direct link between the *Marrow* controversy and the Secession of 1733. True, the catalyst for the secession was the suspension and ultimate deposition of a key Marrow Man, Ebenezer Erskine, and he was followed into secession by his brother Ralph, another Marrow Man. Boston, however, had died in 1732, and although James Hog lived till December 1734 he didn't join Erskine and his three colleagues to form the Associate Presbytery at Gairney Bridge in December 1733. Apart from Ralph Erskine, then, who was present as an observer at Gairney Bridge, and would join them later, none of the surviving Marrow Men countenanced the secession; and one of them, John Williamson, opposed it strongly. In any case, what led to Erskine's suspension and the secession that followed, had nothing to do with the issues raised by the *Marrow,* and everything to do with patronage.

What can be said, however, is that the Secession, in its various branches, cherished the *Marrow* legacy and became its custodian, as the Associate Presbytery, the main Secession body, made plain in its judicial testimony of 1740, when it listed among the 'injuries' done to the Doctrine of Grace the 1720 Act of Assembly condemning the *Marrow.*[74] While declaring in no uncertain terms that nothing in the *Marrow* 'in the least countenances universal redemption as to purchase', the testimony hastens on to endorse the concept of a 'deed of gift or grant' made by God in favour of all mankind. This deed, declares the Presbytery, is the preacher's warrant to make a 'full, free and unhampered offer of Christ, his grace, righteousness and salvation' to every human being; and, conversely, it is the warrant which every sinful man and woman has to receive Christ as their own Saviour.[75]

This is the real legacy of the *Marrow* controversy. It clarified the fulness, freeness and universality of the gospel-offer, and strengthened the resolve of generations of Scottish preachers and missionaries who, while fully aware of the powerlessness of the human word without the touch of the eternal Spirit, took with deadly seriousness the divine charge to tell the Good News to every man. The praise of a few such men is in all the churches; most worked and died in obscurity, but Thomas Chalmers spoke for them all when he

---

74. See Adam Gib, *A Display of the Secession Testimony*, 2 Vols, Edinburgh 1774; Vol. 1, p. 178.

75. ibid., p. 179.

recorded in his journal, 'I am reading *The Marrow of Modern Divinity*, and derive from it much light and satisfaction on the nature of faith. It is a masterly performance, and I feel a greater nearness to God, convincing me that Christ is the way to Him, and an unconditional surrender of ourselves to Christ the first and most essential step of our recovery.'[76]

---

76. William Hanna, *Memoirs of the Life and Writings of Thomas Chalmers;* 4 Vols., Edinburgh: Thomas Constable, 1851–52; Vol. 1, p. 298.

5

Ebenezer Erskine and the Secession of 1733

WHEN THOMAS BOSTON died in May 1732 Scotland was on the threshold of one of the most brilliant periods in her intellectual and cultural history, the Scottish Enlightenment. This was the era when Edinburgh could be described as 'the Athens of the north' and as 'a hotbed of genius', and the plaudits were fully deserved. The city was home to a remarkable cluster of brilliant thinkers and scientists who not only won worldwide fame at the time but profoundly influenced key areas of life down to the present day: men such as David Hume the philosopher; Adam Smith the economist; James Hutton the geologist; Joseph Black the chemist; James Watt the engineer; and the architects, Robert and James Adam. The legacy of their genius is all around us still.

Sadly, however, there was to be no comparable flowering of theological genius. Instead, the years between 1732 and 1832 were so close to being a theological wasteland that it is tempting to leap from Thomas Boston to Thomas Chalmers, omitting all that lies between. Far from being a golden age for Scottish Christianity the eighteenth century would see its influence irreparably diminished.

Patronage

The first blow, and completely unrelated to the Enlightenment, was the Secession of 1733, when Ebenezer Erskine and three colleagues formed the Associate Synod, the first significant split within Scottish Protestantism since the Reformation. The issue, almost inevitably, was patronage: the very same as had led the parishioners of Leuchars to lock the doors of their church to prevent the induction of the unwanted presentee, Alexander

Henderson, as far back as 1612. The grievance continued to fester, but the Glorious Revolution seemed to have brought relief when the 1690 *Act establishing Presbyterian Government* declared null and void the power hitherto exercised by patrons. This looked promising in that it took away the right of a single patron to have his own nominee installed in a vacant charge. It fell short, however, of giving parishioners the right to choose their own minister. Instead, the right to nominate was vested in the heritor, along with local elders; and considering that the heritor was the local laird on whose land the church was built (and that the elders were often his tenants) his wishes would almost always be decisive.

It was clearly no easy matter to rid the church of the evil of patronage. But things were about to get worse. Scarcely was the ink dry on the Treaties of Union in 1707 when the United Kingdom Parliament, no longer under a Whig administration, but led by a Tory government dominated by High Church Anglicans, dedicated to the landed interest and the advancement of episcopacy, and paranoid about people-power, passed the Church Patronage Act which restored to the lairds the rights of patronage of which they had been deprived in 1690.[1]

This was a blatant betrayal of the terms of the Union, which had stipulated that the worship, discipline and government of the Church of Scotland (as defined in 1690) was to continue unaltered 'in all succeeding generations'.[2] Even before the Bill became law, the General Assembly, in a Humble Address to the Queen, was clearly warning Her Majesty and her ministers that the restoration of patronage would 'disoblige' the vast majority of her good subjects (including, it has to be said, the majority of the ministers of the Kirk).[3] The Assembly pointed out that ever since the Reformation patronage had been seen as a great yoke and burden by the people of Scotland; that the Act was a contravention of the constitution of the Church of Scotland as guaranteed by the treaty of union, and solemnly ratified by the Acts of Parliament of both kingdoms; that the Act would inevitably obstruct the

---

1. The Act came into force on 1 May 1712. Only a late amendment ensured that the presentee must be a Presbyterian (Wodrow 1.277). Many of the patrons, however, were episcopalians; and Scottish representation in parliament was minimal: the same number of MPs as Cornwall.

2. *A Source Book of Scottish History*, 3 Vols., edited by William Croft Dickinson and Gordon Donaldson (Edinburgh: Nelson, 1954), Vol. 3, p. 490.

3. *Acts of the General Assembly of the Church of Scotland*, pp. 470-71.

work of the gospel; and, not least that it would create disorder and disquiet throughout church and nation. Once the Bill became law a similar protest was entered by the General Assembly every year for the next ninety years.

But a Humble Address was as far as the Church was prepared to go. Leading churchmen such as William Carstares, conscious of widespread resentment among the English of what they saw as a second (Presbyterian) establishment alongside the Anglican one, were governed by the need to keep parliament on-side. But parliament also needed to keep the Church on-side because it was the main bulwark against the Jacobitism which was being actively promoted by France and which commanded wide support among disaffected episcopalians. Carstares lobbied quietly against the Act, but his opposition was a measured one. 'In the way of protest,' wrote A. R. McEwan, 'he went as far as was deemed possible and safe. His policy was to object, to contend, to resist, and when resistance failed, to concede as though the point conceded had not been vital.'[4] But the point had been vital, and Kenneth Ross is absolutely right when he describes this 1712 Act as 'productive of more mischief in Scottish ecclesiastical life than any other single piece of legislation.'[5]

The Assembly, too, was correct when it warned that the restoration of patronage would lead to disquiet and disorder. In some instances, the Act was simply ignored, and vacancies continued to be filled as before. In others, the patron refrained from exercising his right. In yet others, presbyteries refused to proceed with the induction of the presentee. In still others the people refused to attend the induction of a presentee they didn't want. There were disputes between heritors and presbyteries, between heritors and people, and between presbyteries and people; and sometimes there was serious disturbance.

The overall pattern was one of confusion, and so it continued till the Act of Queen Anne bore its ultimate fruit in the Disruption of 1843. A century before that crisis, however, in an attempt to establish some sort of order, the General Assembly of 1732 passed an *Act anent the Method of Planting Vacant Charges*.[6] The Act clearly envisaged itself as a purely interim measure pending the repeal of the 1712 Parliamentary Act. In the meantime, there

---

4. A. R. MacEwen, *The Erskines* (Edinburgh: Oliphant, Anderson and Ferrier, 1900), p. 14.
5. Article 'Patron, Patronage, Patronage Acts' in *DSCHT*.
6. *Acts of the General Assembly of the Church of Scotland,* p. 620.

had to be an established rule focused specifically on the role of presbyteries in settling vacant charges. It had been a long-established practice that if, after a lapse of six months, no steps had been taken to fill the vacancy, the right to fill it fell to the presbytery, but up to this point no uniform procedure had been laid down for such cases, and this left presbyteries a fair degree of discretion. In particular it left them free to consult the people and even to give them a decisive say.

The 1732 Act deprived them of this discretion. There was now a clear rule: consultation was to be limited to heritors and elders, in whom was vested the whole right to select a minister to fill the vacancy. The people had no say beyond being allowed to express disapproval, but any such expression had to be accompanied by reasons, these were then to be weighed by the presbytery, and their decision was final; and while the form of a call was to be retained, it was to be signed only by the heritor and the elders.

Ebenezer Erskine quickly saw that this was an attempt not only to limit the rights of presbyteries, but also to limit, and even eliminate, the rights of the people; and at the same time to enhance the rights and powers of heritors. He dissented when the measure was adopted by the Assembly on 16 May 1732, asking, 'What difference does a piece of land make between man and man in the affairs of Christ's kingdom, which is not of this world?'[7] Shortly afterwards he made his disapproval plain in a Sunday evening sermon to his own congregation in Stirling, but the critical moment came a few months later, on 10 October 1732, when it fell to him as moderator to preach the opening sermon at the Synod of Perth and Stirling.[8] His text was Psalm 118, verse 22,[9] and, as his biographer remarks, 'he expressed himself with great freedom against the growing defections in doctrine and government; and, in particular, against the rigorous execution of the law of patronage, and the act of the previous assembly [May 1732] respecting the settlement of vacant churches.'[10]

The text was carefully chosen. Patronage was a rejection of the rights of the people, and in the rejection of the people, Christ Himself, the chief

---

7. Donald Fraser, *The Life and Diary of the Reverend Ebenezer Erskine of Stirling, Father of the Secession Church* (Edinburgh: William Oliphant, 1831), p. 359.

8. For the full text of the sermon, see Ebenezer Erskine, *Sermons and Discourses upon the Most Important and Interesting Subjects* (4 Vols. Edinburgh, 1761), Vol. 3, pp, 92-125.

9. 'The stone which the builders rejected, the same is made the head-stone of the corner.'

10. *The Life and Diary of the Reverend Ebenezer Erskine*, p. 36.

cornerstone, is rejected. Yet the passage is not used as a mere peg for the preacher's own personal sentiments. The sermon follows the contours of the text, moving from the idea of the church as a building, to the relation of Christ to the building, and then focusing on the workmen employed as builders – the ministers of the gospel working under the oversight of Christ Himself, the principal builder. Warming to this theme he quickly moves on to declare that no one can warrantably lay a stone in this building unless he is regularly called; central to this is not only the call of God, but also the call of the church; and the call of the church, he proclaims unequivocally, 'lies in the free choice of the Christian people.'[11] It is to them, the church, and not to patrons, heritors, or any particular set of men, that the wisdom to make such a choice is given, just as it is the natural privilege of a household or any human society to choose its own servants and officers.

> What a miserable bondage would it be reckoned for any family to have stewards or servants imposed on them by strangers or enemies, who might give the children poison instead of medicine! And shall we suppose that ever God granted to any set of men, patrons, heritors, elders, or whatever they be, a power to impose servants on his family, without their consent, being the freest society in the world.[12]

Having asserted the rights of the people, the sermon then moves to the even more explosive topic of the 'fatal errors' of the builders spoken of in the text. In the first instance, of course, Erskine saw these as the Jewish leaders who had rejected the Messiah, but it was no difficult matter to align with them those contemporary builders who would not allow Christ a room in His own house. For some moments we hear echoes of the *Marrow* controversy in pointed references to the legal preaching which pared off the spiritual meaning of the law, flattered men that it was in their own human power to keep it, and set before them the prospect of justification by their own personal obedience. But he quickly returns to his main object: the fatal error of patronage. There were clear parallels between its defenders and the ancient Jewish builders: like the Jewish builders they were continually dabbling in politics; like the Jewish builders they were bringing the church near to ruin by conducting its affairs according to 'the rotten pomp' of carnal wisdom and policy; like the Jewish rulers

11. Erskine, *Sermons and Discourses*, Vol. 3, p. 102.
12. ibid., p. 102.

they greatly valued their connections with the great folk, and treated the common folk (especially those among them who 'owned' Christ) as 'an unhallowed mob'; like the Jewish rulers who got the ascendancy in the Sanhedrin, once they got it they took care to keep it 'by bringing in none but men of their own stamp and spirit'; and if any man dared raise his voice against them, combinations were formed against him and the edge of the church's discipline turned against him as a turbulent person who was an enemy to the law and to the people.

Then, having lost the people, the 'rulers' gave themselves up to all manner of sloth and indolence, 'taking care to feed their own bellies, and enrich themselves with the good of this world, while in the meantime they entirely neglected the flock and heritage of God' (108).[13] Compared to the least of Christ's babes, whom they despised as 'the accursed mob', they were spiritually as blind as moles.

Before he finishes, Erskine makes plain his views on the two Acts which lay at the heart of the mischief: the 1712 Act of the United Kingdom parliament and the 1732 Act of the General Assembly. By the former, power was given to a 'malignant' lord or laird to present a man to the charge of precious souls who had no more concern about their salvation than 'the great Turk'.[14] Of the latter he declares that it was a rejection of the authority of Christ who had given no warrant to confer the spiritual privileges of His house upon the rich beyond the poor. To Erskine, patronage was a blatant form of elitism, and to reinforce the point he invokes the Apostle James' memorable warning against partiality:[15]

> For if there come unto your assembly a man with a gold ring, in goodly apparel, and there come in also a poor man in vile raiment; and you have respect to him that weareth the gay clothing, and say unto him, Sit thou here in a good place; and say to the poor, Stand thou there, or sit here under my footstool; are ye not then partial in yourselves, and are become judges of evil thoughts? (James 2:2-4).

---

13. ibid., p. 108.

14. ibid., p. 119. The word, 'malignant,' echoes the dispute between protestors and resolutioners. Erskine (and the Secession) clearly saw themselves as continuing the protestor tradition of such men as Samuel Rutherford and the martyred James Guthrie, who described the resolutioners as 'the Malignant Party'. See David Lachman's article, 'Protesters' in DSCHT.

15. ibid., p. 120.

But not only was patronage elitist (a fact underlined for decades to come by the presence of 'the Laird's loft' in parish churches), but it also meant that the power of electing ministers was lodged in the hands of men who were 'generally disaffected to the power of godliness, to the doctrine, discipline, worship and government of this church, as well as to the government of our gracious Sovereign, King George, and the Protestant succession in his family.'[16] Not only, in other words, were the patrons spiritually clueless; many of them were episcopalians, still pining for the House of Stuart, and hostile to the new Hanoverian dynasty.

The sermon is a *tour de force*. Well argued, passionate and courageous, it might well serve as a definitive presentation of the case against patronage. But it was not the way to gain friends and influence people, and it is hardly surprising that many in this audience of ministers and elders felt they were being got at, because, indeed, they were. And not only were the members of this local synod being got at. In Erskine's view the malaise was widespread, and a 'corrupt, erroneous and ignorant ministry' was running counter to 'the great plot of Heaven', and spoiling, marring and destroying the whole building.[17] It was in such terms that those who followed Erskine would describe the ministers of the Established Church for generations to come.

Complaints were quickly raised by members of synod, a committee was appointed to confer with Erskine, and after three days of keen debate it was resolved that he be censured for some 'indecorous' expressions (shades, again, of the *Marrow* controversy) 'tending to disquiet the peace of the Church, and impugning several acts of Assembly and proceedings of church judicatories.'[18] Various procedures, some regular and some irregular, followed, but Erskine could not be persuaded to express regret, and the case came before the General Assembly of 1733. The Assembly was of the same mind, and ordered that Erskine be rebuked and admonished 'at their own bar'. Out of a dutiful regard to the judicatories of the Church, Erskine submitted to being rebuked and admonished, as he had done with his fellow Marrow Brethren in 1723, but he also lodged a protest against the censure on the ground that it implied that he had contravened the Word of

---

16. ibid..
17. ibid., p. 116.
18. *Life and Diary of Ebenezer Erskine,* p. 362.

God and the Standards of the Church.[19] At the same time he claimed the liberty 'to preach the same truths of God, and to testify against the same or like defections in the Church upon all proper occasions.' Three other ministers, William Wilson of Perth, Alexander Moncrieff of Abernethy, and James Fisher of Kinclaven (Erskine's son-in-law), had given their written adherence to the protest. At this point, none had any intention of seceding from the Church.

But then providence took a remarkable turn. Erskine did not read out his protest; he merely placed it on the clerk's table, and since the submission of a protest was not a recognised Assembly procedure, the officials simply ignored it. And there the 'paper' (as it is described in the official records of the Assembly) would have remained, unread and unrecorded, while the Assembly moved quickly to the next item of business. It happened, however, to fall off the table; and as it fell it happened to catch the eye of a member of the Assembly who picked it up, read it and was so overwhelmed with horror that he immediately drew it to the attention of the moderator; and he, equally horrified, urgently solicited the attention of the Fathers and Brethren to 'an insufferable insult' done to the authority of the Assembly:[20] the premise being that while one might dissent from a decision of the Assembly, a protest, claiming the liberty to repeat the offence, was an act of defiance and a rejection, in effect, of the jurisdiction of the Assembly.

Once again, attempts were made to persuade Erskine and his colleagues to withdraw their protest and to express sorrow for their misbehaviour; but all attempts failed, and on 8 August 1733 the Commission of Assembly suspended the protestors from the exercise of their ministry, with the ominous warning that, should they defy the suspension and continue to exercise a ministry, they would face a higher censure: deposition. They ignored the warning, continued to minister to their loyal congregations, and in November 1733 they were loosed from their charges, their congregations were declared vacant, and all ministers of the Church of Scotland prohibited from employing any of them in any ministerial capacity.

A few weeks later, on 5 December 1733, Erskine, Wilson, Moncrieff and Fisher held a historic meeting at Cairney Bridge near Kinross to form the Associate Presbytery. Two others who were present as observers, Ralph

---

19. For the terms of the protest, see *The Life and Diary of Ebenezer Erskine,* pp. 365-66.
20. Erskine's *Life and Diary,* p. 367.

Erskine (Ebenezer's brother) and Thomas Mair, joined them later. At this point, however, they were careful not to set themselves up as a separate formal judiciary, and limited their Presbytery meetings to prayer and conference. There was no recognition of new candidates for the ministry, no licensing of those who had completed their studies, and no induction to vacant charges.

Conversely, in the years immediately after 1733, the General Assembly, influenced by men such as John Willison of Dundee (and conscious of the continuing Jacobite threat) also acted in a conciliatory spirit, even to the extent that in 1734 it repealed the offending Act of 1732 on the grounds that its passing had not been in accordance with the Barrier Act, and had been found 'hurtful to this church' (a reference to the fact that it had led to expressions of grievance throughout the country). In 1736 the Assembly went even further, passing an *Act against Intrusion of Ministers into Vacant Congregations* which recognised that ever since the Reformation it had been a settled principle of the Church that no minister should be intruded into a parish contrary to the will of the congregation, and recommending that Presbyteries pay serious regard to this principle whenever settling vacant congregations.

Nothing, however, could heal the breach. The Brethren refused to return to the jurisdiction of the Church, and in 1735 they decided to set up their own jurisdiction. As was to be expected, they explicitly disavowed patronage, enacting that all ministers and all office-bearers should be appointed by the call and consent of a majority of communicants, and declaring (in line with Erskine's Synod sermon) that no preference should be given to some voices over others 'upon the account of secular considerations'. In 1736, in pursuance of the liberty claimed by Erskine in his protest, they adopted the *Judicial Testimony*, tracing the defections of the Church back to 1650.[21] Then, finally summoned before the Assembly of 1739, they responded, as James Guthrie had done in 1651 when summoned to appear before the King to answer for his preaching, with a *Declinature*, declaring the judicatories of the National Church unlawful. The situation was now beyond remedy, and in 1740 (by which time the original four seceding ministers had become eight) they were deposed from the ministry of the Establishment by a well-nigh unanimous vote of the General Assembly. Far from being overawed or dismayed, however, they simply continued their work.

---

21. Thus identifying with James Guthrie and his fellow protesters.

The 'Breach'

But all too soon, the Secession suffered its own secession when in 1747 there occurred 'the Breach' between Burghers and Antiburghers; and, as so often in the case of breaches, it had little to do with the gospel. The occasion was the Burgess Oath enacted in 1744 to be sworn by all burghers of the cities of Glasgow, Edinburgh and Perth. At a civic level, it was no small matter, since only burghers could engage in trade or commerce, and only burghers could vote. The problem was that the Oath contained a religious clause in the following terms: 'I profess and allow with my heart, the true religion presently professed within this realm, and authorised by the laws thereof.' To scrupulous Seceders this seemed to imply an endorsement of the National Church they had felt bound to leave, but they weren't content with simply deciding that they couldn't personally take the Oath. They decided they couldn't hold communion with any Seceder who did.

This group was led by Adam Gib. Born in the Perthshire parish of Muckhart in 1714, Gib was awakened to spiritual concern by the sight of a public execution while a student in Edinburgh. Then, following the intrusion of an unwanted patron's nominee into his native parish, he joined the Secession (Associate Presbytery) in 1735; and having abandoned his original intention of a career in medicine he entered on the study of divinity under William Wilson, one of the original fathers of the Secession. Having completed his studies he was ordained in 1745 as the first Secession minister in Edinburgh, where he served a large congregation on Bristo Street till his death in 1788. This instantly put him in a powerful position within the Secession. The year of his ordination was, of course, the year when the Young Pretender, having gained control of the city of Edinburgh, declared his father the rightful King of Scotland. Most of the clergy fled the city as the rebel army approached, but Gib remained; and not only did he remain but, despite the city being occupied by Jacobite soldiers, he publicly prayed for the Hanoverian King, George II.

Gib is a figure whom it is hard to like, but impossible to ignore. He was not inclined to do (or say) things by halves, and the so-called 'religious clause' of the Burgess Oath offended him deeply. But other Seceders, and most notably Ebenezer Erskine, saw no inconsistency between being a Seceder and taking the Oath, taking it to mean no more than a commitment to 'the true Protestant religion' and its associate, the Protestant succession. Gib, however, looked at such issues through a microscope, and what he saw at the heart of the Oath was the religion of the Revolution Settlement of 1688: a settlement which in his view betrayed the nationally covenanted religion of 1638. In his own mind, then, he was perfectly entitled to argue against taking the Oath: after all, interpreted narrowly, the 'religion presently professed' was still blighted by such evils as patronage. As such, 'the present religion' could easily be construed as a longstanding defection against which the Secession, collectively and individually, was bound to testify; and, conversely, acquiescence in the Burgess Oath could be construed as betrayal of that testimony.

It would have counted nothing with Gib that Ebenezer Erskine, now aged sixty-seven, had forty-four years of ministry and suffering behind him, compared with Gib's own two; nor would it have influenced him in the least that William Wilson had been his tutor in Divinity. He could never live with those who disagreed with him, nor might it ever have occurred to him to leave such questions to the individual conscience, and so in 1747 he and his followers separated from the Associate Synod to form a new Antiburgher body, the General Associate Synod. The first meeting took place in Gib's own house, and he would dominate the synod for the rest of his life. Not for nothing was he dubbed 'Pope' Gib, and not for the last time did a presbyterian body come to be the fiefdom of one dominating personality.

Gib was a prolific author and pamphleteer, but the work for which he is best remembered is his *Display of the Secession Testimony,* published in two volumes in 1774. It covers successively the Rise, State and Maintenance of the Testimony, and under the last of these it gives a detailed account, from an Antiburgher point of view, of the events leading up to 'the Breach' (or, as Gib calls it, 'the rupture').[22] Not content with merely leaving the Associate Synod and setting up yet another separate jurisdiction, they proceeded (on the assumption that they were the one true Church of Scotland) to depose and excommunicate Erskine, Wilson and the others who had refused to agree with them. Their action shows an appalling lack of a sense of proportion. Fully aware of the gravity of delivering former colleagues up to Satan (1 Cor. 5:5), they painted them in the darkest possible colours as obstinate heretics, troublers of the peace of the church, scandalous and incorrigible professors, contumacious and rebellious. Then, although it was

---

22. Gib, *The Present Truth: A Display of the Secession Testimony*, Vol. 2, p. 49.

they, the Antiburghers, who had dissociated themselves from the Associate Synod and set up a rival jurisdiction, they described Erskine and his colleagues as 'the separating brethren', thus laying on them the guilt for the schism, and proceeded to condemn their refusal to condemn the Burgess Oath as subversive of the faith, destructive of the power of godliness, and as undermining the peace, order and unity of the church. Most remarkably of all, Erskine and his colleagues, they allege, had overturned the Secession Testimony, 'which the Lord had graciously brought forth among us, in this day of grievous backsliding' and thus threatened to wreck 'the whole frame of a witnessing Church body through Britain and Ireland'.[23] The synod, Gib concluded, now had the honour of having restored due vigour and discipline to the ordinances of the Church, and displaying Christ's royal banner in opposition to the present woeful apostasy.

Yet, however indefensible the act of excommunication in this instance, Gib has left a clear view of both the nature and limits of such discipline.[24] The excommunicated must continue to be regarded as brothers and as members of the body of Christ; the excommunication is not perpetual, but only for a time, until the brother or sister repents; and it does not interrupt ordinary civil relationships. The rights and duties of husbands and wives, parents and children, masters and servants, rulers and subjects, remain as before, 'for excommunication cannot break these bonds of nature and morality, whereby men are mutually bound together.'[25] What it did break was the bonds of ecclesiastical fellowship, and for Gib and those who followed him this meant that no Antiburgher, lay or clerical, could have any communion in holy things with their former colleagues and friends. They could not pray with Burghers, partake of the Lord's Supper with them, or engage in public worship with them. Carried to its logical extreme (and it was), it prohibited Antiburghers from worshipping with any Christian not of their own denomination.

It would be a mistake to see the tone set here by Gib, writing in 1774, as characteristic of the whole Secession tradition, or even of its Antiburgher stream. But the pain of such breaches reaches far beyond the corridors of ecclesiastical politics, as we see in the case of Ebenezer Erskine. Not

---

23. ibid., p. 110.

24. ibid., pp. 100-11.

25. ibid., p.103

only did it mean that he was now distanced from former friends and colleagues,[26] it also involved, as do all church disputes, pain within his own family. While he himself thought it perfectly consistent with the Secession testimony to take the Oath, his son-in-law, James Scott, did not, and became a committed Antiburgher. The tension this caused appears in a letter Erskine wrote in May 1750 to his daughter, Alison (Mrs. Scott):

> I would be glad to see you here, at our Sacrament, the 2nd Sabbath and 11th day, of June; and I am sorry that I cannot invite your husband to come along with you. I have had many an anxious thought about your difficult situation, but rejoice to hear of your devout and Christian behaviour therein.[27]

Troubled waters

For the next fifty years, life within both streams of the Secession proceeded relatively smoothly, but towards the end of the century they again found themselves in troubled waters. The question this time was the power and duty of the civil government in relation to matters of religion, and the result was that both Burghers and Antiburghers split into New Lichts and Auld Lichts. The former were increasingly suspicious of any interference by the state in spiritual matters: a 'new' light because it diverged from historical position of the Reformed church in Scotland. The Auld Lichts, on the other hand, continued to favour the old idea of a national establishment of religion.

The first body to let in the New Light was the Burghers, whose Associate Synod agreed in 1799 to allow divergent views on the question of the power of the state in relation to religion. Five years later, the General Associate Synod (Antiburgher) went even further, when it adopted a New Testimony which, among other things, categorically declared that the power of the state was limited to secular matters. Among both Burghers and Antiburghers, however, there was a dissenting minority, the most significant of these being the Antiburgher one, whose Auld Lichts separated and formed themselves into the Original Secession Church. Among these Antiburgher

---

26. Gib's conduct in relation to the excommunication of Erskine appears even more inexplicable in the light of a remarkable compliment he paid to him some time after his death. Having heard a colleague admit that he had never heard Erskine preach, he immediately rejoined, 'Well then, Sir, you have never heard the Gospel in its majesty' (*Life and Diary of the Rev. Ebenezer Erskine*, p. 482).

27. ibid., p. 448.

dissidents was the distinguished historian Thomas McCrie who, shortly afterwards (1807), published a *Statement* explaining their reason for constituting themselves a separate Presbytery and giving a cogent defence of the Auld Licht position with regard to the power of the civil magistrate respecting religion.[28]

The Secession was now split into four distinct denominations. There were Auld Licht Burghers and New Licht Burghers; and there were Auld Licht Antiburghers and New Licht Antiburghers. The list, and the very names, make it easy to view the Seceders with amusement, and it has to be admitted that with the presence of these four streams any 'map' of Scottish Presbyterian history suggests a nation given to fractiousness and division. We have to remember, however, that this situation obtained only for the brief period between 1804 and 1820. The vast majority of Seceders chose to accept the New Light, and in 1820 the two New Light bodies came together to form the curiously named United Secession Church. Nor did the process of reunification end there. In 1847 the Relief Church joined with the United Secession to form the United Presbyterian Church, a body with 518 congregations,[29] and some 150,000 communicants.[30]

The Secession was a body-blow to the National Church. The loss of a few ministers was hardly fatal, but these few commanded the loyalty of thousands of devout Christians; and the ministerial ranks were quickly strengthened. By 1742 the four had become twenty; two years later they had become thirty, though still not enough to supply their forty-six congregations; and the growth continued well into the nineteenth century until, as we have seen, there were over five hundred United Presbyterian congregations. Besides, there was extensive national coverage, as the Secession quickly spread through all the Lowlands, from Dunkeld to Cheviot, from St Andrews to Ayr, and from Angus to

---

28. Unfortunately, the title, which runs to some twenty lines, is extremely cumbersome. The short title would be, *Statement of the Difference between the Profession of the Reformed Church of Scotland, as Adopted by Seceders, and the Profession Contained in the New Testimony and Other Acts, lately Adopted by the General Associate Synod.* In 1871, when the Establishment Principle became a critical issue in union negotiations between the Free Church and the United Presbyterian Church, the *Statement* was republished with a Preface by Professor George Smeaton.

29. See the article 'Unions, Church in Scotland,' in *DSCHT*.

30. Andrew L. Drummond and James Bulloch, *The Church in Victorian Scotland 1843–1874* (Edinburgh: Saint Andrew Press, 1975), p. 43

Ross-shire. Later, their reach would also extend to the Orkneys and to the Western Isles.

By any standards this represented a serious haemorrhaging from the Established Church, and the beginning of a serious state of alienation between it and the Scottish people. But it wasn't merely a matter of numbers. The Secession radically altered the ecclesiastical landscape of Scotland. To Scottish theologians of the sixteenth and seventeenth centuries, the idea of 'true churches of Christ, side by side with one another, forming separate organisations, with separate governments' seemed utterly inadmissible.[31] The inadmissible had now become reality, with disastrous consequences not only for the Kirk but for Scottish Christianity. Not only were there now two or more congregations in almost every parish, but the sad truth was that they were not only 'side by side', living together in amicable coexistence: they were in competition. Anyone who was unhappy with their local minister or any aspect of life in their ancestral church, could now find a warm welcome in another; and churches would be happy to count themselves as 'growing' even when the growth consisted, not of 'brands plucked from the burning', but of transfers from other congregations. Besides, Erskine's legacy of bearing witness against defections could easily degenerate into sniping, and the targets were no longer confined to the lairds and their presentees. The revival in Cambuslang (1742–44), for example, was called into question by Ralph Erskine, and George Whitefield was barred from Secession pulpits because he was also prepared to preach in Established Church ones.[32] Once introduced, such sniping became endemic as each stream of Scottish Christianity sought to justify its separate existence by keeping alive the memory of ancient wrongs and the glaring shortcomings of their neighbours. And while the witness against defections in the Established Church might be eagerly listened to and readily believed, not everyone who left her joined the Seceders. Instead, they joined the ranks of the unchurched.

Sadly, Erskine gave little thought to the long-term and nationwide consequences of his action. Before God he had done his duty by testifying against the 1732 Act, and humanly speaking he had satisfied his conscience.

---

31. James Walker, *The Theology and Theologians of Scotland 1560–1750*, p. 97.

32. For relations between Whitefield and ministers of the Secession, see Donald Fraser, *The Life and Diary of the Reverend Ralph Erskine of Dunfermline* (Edinburgh: William Oliphant, 1834), pp. 286-344.

But why did the unity of the church not weigh heavily with him? Few men who start revolutions, even minor ones, are able to control them.

Yet not all is on the debit side as far as the Secession was concerned. By the mid-eighteenth century Moderatism had not only gained control of the General Assembly of the National Church: in partnership with heritors and landowners it had also gained control of many of Scotland's pulpits, and where that was the case, the message no longer focused on 'Jesus Christ and him crucified' (1 Cor. 2:2). Some truth there might be, but it steered well away from 'redemption by his blood'. Where there was a Seceder church, however, whether Burgher or Antiburgher, the gospel of St Paul, Augustine, Luther and the *Marrow* still sounded forth, still saved lost sheep, and still fed 'God's poor people'.

Thomas Carlyle's parents were members of the Burger congregation in Ecclefechan (near Lockerbie in Dumfriesshire), and his father, James Carlyle, was probably typical of his community in that he regarded poetry and fiction as not only idle, 'but false and criminal.'[33] Yet, however little the meeting-house contributed to the promotion of culture, 'a gospel was still preached there to the heart of a man, in the tones of a man.' Seceder preachers had little to say about secular affairs, and even seem to have carefully avoided using the pulpit to ventilate their views on patronage. Instead, they focused on 'the universal and weightier matters of the Law', and the result, Carlyle recalled, was that 'A man who awoke to the belief that he actually had a soul to be saved or lost was apt to be found among the Dissenting people, and to have given up attendance on the Kirk.'[34]

This situation was by no means confined to Ecclefechan. It was widespread throughout Scotland. Describing his experience as a journeyman mason at Niddry in the 1820s, Hugh Miller recalled that the working men of Edinburgh and its neighbourhood at this time, were in large part either non-religious, or included within the Independent or Secession pale. Then, referring to his own cohort, he wrote, 'All the religion of our party was to be found among its Seceders. Our other

---

33. Thomas Carlyle, *Reminiscences*, edited with an Introduction and Notes by K. J. Fielding and Ian Campbell (Oxford: Oxford University Press, 1997), p. 13. It's probably safe to say that a lack of interest in poetry and fiction was typical not only of Seceders but of working-class people generally.

34. ibid., p. 207.

workmen were really wild fellows, most of whom never entered a church,'[35] and even if they had, they would have heard no more than a 'respectable moral essay, and slept under it.' In many, though by no means all, parishes, the Seceders, still faithfully preaching the gospel of free grace, offered an alternative. This was not enough, however, to stem the haemorrhaging from the church. The Kirk made little attempt to recover those, especially from the humbler classes, whom it had lost in the two preceding generations, and the Seceders acquiesced in the prevailing view that religion was a matter of supply and demand. In Niddry, Miller noted, demand and supply were exactly balanced. There was no religious instruction, and no desire for it.

---

35. Hugh Millar, *My Schools and Schoolmasters* (Edinburgh: Nimmo, 1869), p. 322.

6

Theologians of the Secession

FROM THE VERY beginning, the Secession took seriously the importance of an educated ministry and, in line with this, one of the earliest acts of the Associate Presbytery was to appoint the Reverend William Wilson of Perth theological tutor to the young men who sought to serve in the Church's ministry. Of the original Seceders, Ebenezer Erskine and his nephew James Fisher were clearly first-rate theologians; and according to John Macleod,[1] Wilson was not a whit behind them. A Divinity Hall, meeting in Wilson's residence, was opened in Spring 1737, with six students, among them Adam Gib.[2] After the Breach of 1747, there were two Seceder Divinity Halls, Burger and Antiburger; the union in 1820 of the two New Licht streams of the Secession led to the establishment of the United Secession Divinity Hall; and when the Relief Church united with the United Secession Church in 1847, theological education became the responsibility of the United Presbyterian Divinity Hall: an arrangement which continued till the union between the United Presbyterian Church and the Free Church in 1900.

To begin with, each Hall had the services of only one professor who combined his duties as a theological tutor with those of a settled congregational pastorate, and this continued till 1807 when George Paxton was appointed Professor of Divinity in the General Associate Synod (Antiburger) and the synod, in making the appointment, insisted that he resign his charge (Kilmaurs and Stewarton, in Ayrshire), move to

---

1. John Macleod, *Scottish Theology,* p. 188.

2. For the story of theological education among the various branches of the Secession, see P. Landreth, *The United Presbyterian Theological Hall, in its Changes and Enlargements for One Hundred and Forty Years* (Edinburgh: William Oliphant, 1876).

Edinburgh, and devote himself full-time to his professorial duties. Behind this decision lay the conviction, based on experience, that 'the two offices, the pastoral and the professorial, were individually far too difficult and important to be held together by one man':[3] a view reinforced by the fact that all Paxton's predecessors were deemed to have died prematurely. At the same time, however, the synod recognised that it was important that those training men for the ministry should themselves have had previous experience of what the work of the ministry involved.

All students were expected to have had a university education prior to entering the Hall, and thanks to this were already able to read the Greek New Testament on sight. But the case with Hebrew was very different and the subject suffered the same fate among the Seceders as it did in other theological institutions, with the result that by the time they completed their studies many students had done little more than learn the alphabet. This was partly due to the naivety of the professors who, being pious souls themselves, never realised the power of indwelling sin in their students. Passages for translation were duly set, but when it came to checking whether the pious young men had done their homework, professors too often made the mistake of routinely calling on each student in the order in which he sat in class, with the result that students could calculate exactly which verse would fall to their lot, and could safely ignore all the others. How could such deceptions be practised by saintly divinity students![4]

But sometimes the artifices went beyond simply working out which verse would come up when it was your turn. Landreth tells the story of one student who carefully took up a position behind another who was liable to epileptic seizures, and when these occurred the man behind was only too willing to assist in carrying the sufferer to an adjoining room, where the patient's recovery 'was not held to be satisfactory until the last Hebrew verse for the day was read and parsed.'[5]

One day, however, the seating arrangements went askew, and this student, having calculated the progress of the lesson, quickly realised that, in place of the one verse he had prepared, another, and very difficult one, was coming his way. The situation was desperate. What was to be done?

---

3. Landreth, ibid., p. 140.

4. They could not have been practised in the class conducted by my late colleague, Professor John L. Mackay, a superb teacher of both Hebrew and Old Testament.

5. Landreth, ibid., p. 218.

The panic-stricken student suddenly stood up, sweeping coats and books from the bench, seized the epileptic student (at that moment perfectly well), and half-dragged, half carried him out of the room, taking care at the same time to push a hat over his brow to conceal the fact that his face showed no symptoms of a seizure. The victim's cries of surprise, anger and bewilderment were like enough to those that used to accompany his seizures but, struggle as he might, he was in powerful and desperate hands; and professor and fellow students alike were quick to applaud 'the prompt realisation and irresistible vigour with which the ready friend bore way the struggling man.'[6]

The aspiration of the Secession Divinity Halls was to provide the same level of education as was provided by the Divinity Faculties of the universities: a tall order when the whole burden fell on one professor. True, the education in view was an education aimed at equipping preachers, not academic theologians, but this was allied to the firm belief that preachers had to be theologians: hence the central place given to systematic theology; and, building on this, the Secession went on to produce, generation by generation, theologians who left a lasting footprint on the journey of Scottish theology. Among these, special mention must be made of Adam Gib, whose reputation as a domineering ecclesiastic must not be allowed to obscure the value of his theological contribution. His *Display of the Secession Testimony* shows a comprehensive grasp of the theology of the Reformation and offers a strong defence of the doctrine of the *Marrow*. It also provided a robust critique of Hypothetical Universalism when that issue raised its head among the Antiburghers following the publication of the second edition of Fraser of Brea's *Treatise on Justifying Faith* in 1749.[7] James Walker comments that Fraser's work quickly passed out of memory, but he also notes that the most important result of its publication was the theological discussions it brought forth from the pen of Adam Gib, 'the ablest and most important, I imagine, of their day.'[8]

---

6. Landreth, ibid., p. 218. He was himself an eyewitness of the event, but it should be noted that this, most emphatically, is not the way to give first-aid to someone who is having an epileptic seizure.

7. See Chapter 8 of this volume.

8. Walker, ibid., p. 83. Walker confesses (p. 116) that he had been 'strongly impressed by Gib'. However, although interest in Fraser's *Treatise* had waned by Walker's day, it was very much revived in the twentieth century (see, for example, Thomas F. Torrance, *Scottish Theology,* pp. 181-204).

John Brown of Haddington

Among other notable theologians of the Secession were John Dick, whose *Lectures on Theology* we have already noted;[9] and, at the end of the line, James Orr (1844–1913), a polymath who served first in the United Presbyterian College and, after 1900, in the United Free Church College, Glasgow. But perhaps the most remarkable feature of Secession theology was its succession of John Browns: three generations in all, grandfather, son and grandson, each making his own enduring contribution.

First there was John Brown of Haddington.[10] Born near Abernethy in Perthshire in 1722, he had lost both his parents by the time he was eleven years of age, but even while they were still alive he had little opportunity for education. Scotland's much-vaunted parish school system, so dependent on the support of the local heritor, was largely dysfunctional in Abernethy: having no permanent premises it had to rely on whatever empty shed it could find, and could guarantee a schoolmaster an annual salary of little more than five pounds. The result was that the school functioned only spasmodically and this, coupled with his parents' circumstances, meant that Brown completed very few terms in school. One of these, however (without his parents' knowledge), he devoted to the study of Latin: a reflection of the fact that at a very early age he already had a passion for learning languages. He continued to indulge this passion when, in his early teens, he worked perforce as a herd-boy. Helped by his minister, Alexander Moncrieff (who also served as Professor in the Secession's Divinity Hall), he resumed his study of Latin, and having achieved some proficiency in this ancient language he then proceeded to learning another: Greek. In this he had little help. While knowledge of Latin was fairly common, knowledge of Greek was not; and even had it been available, a herd-boy requesting help with the language of the New Testament would immediately be seen as having ideas far above his station. He had to work on his own, then, and it was a laborious process.

First, he had to learn the letters of the alphabet, and this he did by comparing the Greek names in the genealogies of Matthew and Luke with the corresponding English and Latin texts, confident that such

---

9. Volume 1, p. 390.

10. The most accessible biography is Robert Mackenzie, *John Brown of Haddington* (1918. Reprinted London: Banner of Truth, paperback, 1964). But see, too, David Wright's excellent article, 'Brown, John (of Haddington)' in *DSCHT*.

names as *David*, for example, were exact transcripts of the original. He then taught himself how to pronounce the letters by reading back into the Greek such English transliterations as *eloi, Siloam* and *Golgotha*; and from there he proceeded to reading the text.

By this time, he had saved enough money to buy a copy of the New Testament for himself, but the nearest place where he was likely to find such a thing was the university town of St Andrews, twenty-four miles away. Nothing daunted, he arranged for a friend to look after his sheep and set off, one evening in 1738, along the miles of the unknown road. Early the following morning, he found what he was looking for, but when the bookseller heard his request and looked at the youngster's bedraggled appearance, he was taken aback: 'What would you do wi' that book? You'll no can read it.'[11] At this point, one of the university professors happened to come in, overheard the conversation, asked the bookseller to bring in a copy of the New Testament, and announced, 'Boy' (Brown was then sixteen years of age), 'if you can read that book, you shall have it for nothing.' Read it he did, and 'by that afternoon he was back on duty on the hills of Abernethy, studying the New Testament the while in the midst of his flock.'[12]

But if his proficiency brought its rewards, it also brought its sorrows. To some, his knowledge of Greek was a miracle, and a sinister one. 'I'm sure the de'il has taught you some words,' said a companion. Brown took it as a joke, but it was no joke. The stigma of using the Black Arts was still a dangerous one to carry in eighteenth-century Scotland. Europe was only then beginning to emerge from that abhorrent era when theologians, monarchs and politicians of all shades regarded witchcraft as a crime deserving of death. Nothing can be said in mitigation of the horrors bred by such an attitude. Brown, however, was in no danger of being burned as a witch, though it was a close-run thing: the statutes which prescribed the death-penalty for those in league with the Devil and been repealed, but only in 1736, two years before Brown acquired his copy of the New Testament; and while the criminal law had changed, public attitudes hadn't. Even such a highly educated man as John Wesley, writing thirty years later, deplored the fact that accounts of witches and apparitions were increasingly dismissed as 'old wives' fables' (an unfortunate choice of words, since many

---

11. Mackenzie, *John Brown of Haddington*, p. 34.
12. ibid., p. 35.

of those condemned as witches had been precisely that: old wives). Giving up witchcraft, he declared, was in effect giving up the Bible.[13]

Brown's minister, Alexander Moncrieff, fully shared Wesley's attitude, and instead of defending his young parishioner let it be known that he believed the suspicions, and although the Kirk Session brought no formal accusation, they allowed the *fama* to cling to him. In the meantime, there was no prospect of Brown being admitted as a candidate for the ministry. Only in 1746 did the church at Abernethy agree to grant Brown a certificate of full church membership.

The following year, there occurred the Breach, and while Moncrieff sided with the Antiburghers, Brown remained loyal to Erskine and the Associate Synod, not because he was entirely happy with the terms of the Burgher Oath, but because he didn't think the issue warranted a rupture in the Church. Shortly afterwards, he was accepted as a student for the ministry and, without the normal preliminary requirement of a university course, was admitted to the Burgher Divinity Hall, where Ebenezer Erskine had replaced Alexander Moncrieff; and after three years' study under Erskine and his successor, James Fisher, Brown was inducted as Minister of Haddington's Burgher congregation in July 1751. Sixteen years later (1767) he succeeded John Swanston as the Associate Synod's Professor (James Fisher had died in 1763): a position he continued to occupy, along with the pastoral charge of Haddington, till his death in 1787.

As the sole professor he covered the whole curriculum: an arrangement which suited him perfectly since he was by temperament a polymath, aspiring, like a Renaissance man, to universal knowledge; and what he taught he published. Previous professors had made use of existing text-books such as Turretin's *Institutes* or the shorter *Theologiae Christianae Medulla* ('Marrow') of the Leiden Professor, Johannes Marckius. Brown, however, prepared his own system, which was published in 1782 with the title, *A Compendious View of Natural and Revealed Religion*. Earlier, in 1771, he had published a two-volume *General History of the Christian Church*.

But Brown's most significant contribution to the literature of Scottish Christianity lay elsewhere, first in his *Dictionary of the Holy Bible* (two volumes, 1769) but more especially in his *Self-Interpreting Bible* (two volumes, 1778), which came to occupy the same honoured place on the

---

13. Quoted in Mackenzie, ibid.., p. 39.

bookshelves of Scotland's popular piety as Boston's *Fourfold State* and
Bunyan's *Pilgrim's Progress*. According to Robert Mackenzie, it is difficult
to say how many editions were issued, but the British Museum listed
twenty-six.[14] Wright notes that it was repeatedly published in America,
with improvements well into the twentieth century by later editors. It
is clear, too, that its appeal was not confined to the unlearned. Charles
Simeon, a Fellow of King's College, Cambridge and from his pulpit at Holy
Trinity Church, an evangelical luminary in that city from 1782 to 1836,
bought a copy of the *Self-interpreting Bible* in March 1785, and from then
on it was his lifelong companion.[15] But then, at the other end of England's
social spectrum, when Brown's great-grandson found himself in 'a remote
hamlet among the hop-fields of Kent,' he was approached by a blacksmith's
wife who asked him if he was 'the son of the Self-interpreting Bible'.[16]

The phrase 'self-interpreting' reflects the fundamental principle of
Protestant hermeneutics, namely, that 'The infallible rule of interpretation
of scripture is the scripture itself; and therefore, when there is a question
about the true and full sense of any scripture … it must be searched and
known by other places that speak more clearly.'[17] In practice this meant that
in *The Self-interpreting Bible* every verse was illuminated by an induction
of references to parallel passages: the principle, in other words, that the
concordance is more useful than the lexicon.

---

14. Mackenzie, ibid., p. 185.

15. Mackenzie, 188. Cf. Handley C. G. Moule, *Charles Simeon* (1892. Reprinted
London: Inter-Varsity Fellowship, 1948), p. 27.

16. The great-grandson in question was Dr John Brown, M. D., son of John Brown
III, Minister of Broughton Place, Edinburgh. Brown was a distinguished essayist,
celebrated for his three-volume collection, *Horae Subsecivae,* and especially for his
essay, 'Rab and his Friends', a clear reflection of his love for dogs. The above story
occurs in his 'Letter to John Cairns', written in response to a request for information
from his father's biographer, and a gem in its own right. It occurs in the Second Series
of *Horae Subsecivae,* published in 1882. Rather confusingly, the spine-title is 'Rab and
his Friends'. The anecdote is related on page 66 of this volume. Dr Brown believed he
had in his possession the copy of the New Testament which the first John Brown had
bought in St Andrews.

He also records that when his great-grandfather was called to Haddington, one
man held out against the 'call'. One day they chanced to meet up, and the 'non-content'
expressed his mind plainly: 'Ye see, sir, I canna say what I dinna think, and I think ye're
ower young and inexperienced for this charge.' 'So I think too, David,' replied Brown,
'but it would never do for you and me to gang in the face o' the hale congregation!'
(ibid., p. 70).

17. The Westminster Confession of Faith, 1.9.

Brown's output as an author is a tribute to his unrelenting industry, but this had its downside. 'Rest he considered idleness'[18] and, for this, his students paid a heavy price. The professor was a 'bigot' on the subject of early-rising and regularly used to visit his students in their lodgings any time from six o'clock in the morning, and if he found them still in bed they were peremptorily rebuked as sluggards. But, as they did with their Hebrew, the students took their own measures. Some arranged with their landlady to alert them the moment she heard the dreaded step, whereupon they would leap from their bed to a table and chair where a theological tome lay conveniently open, presenting to their mentor's gaze the sight of a pious young man already hard at work (though still in his night-clothes). Other times the only remedy was to slip quickly under the bed, leaving their august visitor with the impression that they were 'out for an early walk – good lad!'[19]

John Brown of Whitburn

The second John Brown was John Brown of Whitburn. The eldest son of Brown of Haddington, he was ordained and inducted to the Burgher congregation of Whitburn in 1777, and there he remained till his death in 1832. On the face of things, it was a limited sphere, but, as Cairns points out in his *Life* of John Brown *tertius*, the Minister of Whitburn 'partook largely of the missionary impulse which had stirred the universal church'.[20] One manifestation of this was that he had a keen interest in the evangelisation of the Highlands: an interest stimulated by his contact with the drovers who passed through Whitburn on their way to the markets of the south. Brown was in the habit of offering tracts to everyone he met, but he was disturbed to find that few Highlanders could read them either in English or in Gaelic, and this prompted him to undertake repeated missionary journeys to the north and to organise numerous public appeals on behalf of spiritually neglected areas of the Gaidhealtachd. It also led him to take an active part in the movement which led to the formation of the Edinburgh Society for the Support of Gaelic Schools in 1810, with the Baptist, Christopher Anderson, as

---

18. Landreth, p. 170. 'He could study sixteen hours a day; but of course not a little of the labour performed at such an unduly protracted sitting must have been of inferior quality.'

19. Landreth, p. 173. Mackenzie, ibid., p. 143.

20. John Cairns, *Memoir of John Brown, D.D.* (Edinburgh: Edmonston and Douglas, 1860), p. 12.

its first secretary. He arranged, too, for the publication of a Gaelic translation of his father's Catechisms and of Boston's *Fourfold State* (1811), while at the same time serving as a Director of the London Missionary Society.

Unlike his father and son, Brown of Whitburn was never a theological professor, but he made an invaluable contribution to Scottish theology by publishing in 1817 his *Gospel Truth Accurately Stated and Illustrated*, widely regarded as the best succinct account of the *Marrow* controversy.[21] In his Preface, Brown acknowledges that 'many of the disputes which have agitated the Christian church have been so trifling in their subjects, and have been conducted in so improper a spirit, that it would be an advantage both to truth and charity, to bury them in perpetual oblivion.' The *Marrow* controversy, however, he views in a different light. Not only did it involve some of the most important principles of the Christian gospel, but 'there has seldom been displayed a more beautiful example of "earnestly contending for the faith" in the meek and humble spirit of the gospel, than in the conduct of the illustrious Boston, and his worthy associates.'[22]

There is little of Brown himself in *Gospel Truth*, but he does introduce the volume with an informative outline of the progress of legalistic preaching in the Church of Scotland in the decades leading up to the publication of the *Marrow*: a trend towards a 'refined arminianism' which he traces back to the prelates imposed on the Kirk by James VI and his son Charles, and which was already causing concern in the General Assembly as early as 1645. Apart from this, the Marrow Men are largely left to speak for themselves, *via* both biographical sketches of their leading figures and extracts from their writings, many of which would be hard to come by today. At the same time, however, he also recognises, as we have already, seen, that 'several of their opponents were also learned and worthy men'; and of these lives, too, he offers positive summaries.

He also notes that among the contemporaries of the Marrow Men there were some who were friends of the doctrine of grace but did not join the twelve Representers. Of special interest here is his sketch of Robert Riccaltoun. Riccaltoun is in many ways an obscure figure, but Brown speaks of him as a man whose 'genius' was such that he was able to read the Bible distinctly

---

21. Quotations from *Gospel Truth* in this chapter are from a reprint published by Pranava Books, India (no date).

22. But Brown also includes in a Preface the well-nigh mandatory disclaimer that he is not prepared to defend the *Marrow* as faultless.

before he was five years old. From there he proceeded *via* grammar school to Edinburgh University, but he never had a formal theological education, since in his early years he had no intention of becoming a minister and was set, instead, on life as a farmer. Privately, however, he studied the Scriptures assiduously, while at the same time immersing himself in standard works of Divinity, and when news of his abilities reached his local Presbytery (Jedburgh) 'they in a manner forced him upon trials'.[23] Brown comments that by this stage he was already an 'able divine, of the same sentiments as the Marrow-men.' He also informs us that it was while he was still a Probationer that Riccaltoun wrote *A Sober Enquiry*, which he calls 'a most judicious, moderate and masterly defence of the Marrow Men.' And while he is not definite, he does record that the authorship of *The Politick Disputant* was also commonly attributed to the same pen. This volume, too, he commends for its 'good sense and pointed wit'.[24]

Brown also hints, however, that Riccaltoun lived his life under a heavy cloud. He had allowed himself in his youth to stand surety for a large sum on behalf of one of his relatives, but the relative defaulted, leaving Riccaltoun in distressing circumstances. Yet he was in the habit of saying that this was the best dispensation that could have befallen to him: had he not been so borne down, he thought, he would have been very 'haughty and overbearing'. But whatever his distress, it did not interfere with his studious habits, and in this connection he seems to have had remarkable powers of concentration, so much so that while he was thinking or writing 'the various conversations of others gave him no disturbance'. Yet though studious, he was also sociable, happy in the company of young people, and a sincere friend, highly esteemed by such Marrow Men as Boston, Gabriel Wilson and Henry Davidson.

Of the high quality of Riccaltoun's work there can be no doubt, but its value is limited by its occasion and purpose. Had he written in a more serene environment he would not have been so quickly forgotten.

In another Appendix (II:VII), Brown draws attention to some 'modern' evangelical divines who taught the same doctrine as the Marrow Men.[25]

---

23. That is, trials for Licence as a Preacher of the Gospel, leading to his becoming a Probationer, and as such eligible to be called to serve as Minister of a congregation.

24. Brown, ibid., pp. 325-6.

25. By 'modern' he means contemporaries of the Marrow Men. He does not mean divines of his own generation: Willison had died in 1750. He appears to be referring to ministers who, though they had not joined the Secession, were nevertheless evangelical.

The first he mentions is John Willison, but he completely ignores the fact (of which he couldn't but have been aware) that Willison had voted against the Marrow Men in the General Assembly. Instead, he focuses on Willison's enthusiasm for the doctrine of an 'appropriating persuasion', a doctrine he shared with the Marrow Men, and which laid down that in true faith a sinner makes a special application of Christ and His promises to himself. 'Lord,' wrote Willison, 'I will not rest in a general belief and persuasion of the mercy of God in Christ, and of Christ's ability to save all that come unto him, but I will apply the blood and righteousness of Christ to myself in particular, and rest on him as one that loved me, and gave himself for me.'[26]

Brown quotes his father, Brown of Haddington, to similar effect: 'The more sinful and wretched I am, the more evident is my gospel right to receive the Redeemer who came to seek and save that which is lost'; and when he asks what it means to embrace Christ as He is offered in the gospel, the elder Brown answers, 'A particular persuasion that Christ in the promise is *mine*' (italics original). He does not accept, however, that this means that all believers are equally sensible of their embracing Christ: 'Sometimes Christ is embraced in the way of bold claiming of the promises, and sometimes in the way of desire, attended with much fear and doubting.'[27]

For the student, the supreme value of Brown's work is that it includes in one volume all the key documents of the *Marrow* controversy from the Assembly's Act of 1720 to the Representers' Protest of 17 May 1722. It also includes extracts from the works of such Marrow divines as Boston, Ebenezer Erskine and Gabriel Wilson. But before bringing his work to a conclusion, Brown offers a series of reflections on the whole controversy.[28] Among its lessons, he declares, is a warning that church courts should studiously avoid rash decisions, especially when these are driven by party interests. He clearly believes that this was at the root of the *Marrow* controversy. A few leading men condemned the *Marrow* and then, professing a regard to the honour of the Assembly, could not retreat. Then, in a footnote, he adds an observation made by an unnamed Marrow Man in the course of a sermon: 'When men, especially clergymen, who have all a tang of infallibility with them, have asserted anything amiss in

---

26. Quoted in Brown, ibid., p. 337. The source of the quotation was a sermon Willison preached on the words in Galatians 2:20, 'Who loved me, and gave himself for me.'

27. Brown, ibid., p. 348.

28. Brown, ibid., pp. 349-53.

doctrine, their pride will not allow them to retract. Truth itself must rather fall a sacrifice than that their reputation should sink.'[29]

On the other hand, Brown strongly believed that, however rash the decision of the 1720 Assembly, the providence of God was at work. While the leading men of the Church showed a spirit of great rancour and bitterness, the wrath of man worked to the praise of God, and the eventual outcome of the controversy was a wider diffusion of the *Marrow* and its doctrines. Ministers were led to search into divine truth with greater accuracy than ever, with the result that 'at no period of the Scottish church was evangelical knowledge so increased'. 'Prior to this controversy,' he concludes, 'much confusion of ideas respecting evangelical doctrine prevailed, and incautious expressions respecting them were found in many of the best writings, and the most serious pulpit discourses in this country. At that time, and by the means now mentioned, they were placed in a more clear, distinct and evangelical light, than perhaps they had ever been since the days of the apostles.'[30]

It is hard to imagine any such agitation as the *Marrow* controversy in Scotland today. Theological debate is a thing of the past, and we are proud that it is so: it was the hallmark of a bigoted and benighted age. But we should note the prominence of the phrase 'accurately stated' in the title to Brown's work. The Marrow Men were driven by the compelling certainty that every human being urgently needed the gospel of free grace, but it was a matter of equal urgency that this gospel be accurately stated, avoiding the peril of legalism on the one hand and antinomianism on the other. It had to be made clear to every sinner that the offer of Christ and His salvation was made to him simply as a sinner, and that it was his right to take Him as his own, however indefensible his previous life may have been. But it had to be proclaimed with equal accuracy that while salvation was pure divine gift, it meant salvation *from* sin, not salvation *in* sin. Grace transformed as well as forgave, ensuring that those to whom much was forgiven, would love much, and make the will of their heavenly Father the law and, indeed, the pleasure of their daily lives. It was for an accurate statement of this gospel that the Marrow Men strove, and the fact that it was banished from so many Scottish pulpits hurt them to the quick.

29. Brown, ibid., p. 350.
30. Brown, ibid., p. 353.

Uncle Ebenezer

Before taking our leave of Brown of Whitburn we should pause for a moment to take note of his brother Ebenezer, a remarkable man in his own right, though a very different personality.[31] Brown of Whitburn is described by the author of 'Rab and his Friends' as easy-going, full of love to all of God's creatures, and ready to share his gospel with every drover, servant-lass or wanderer he met; and when Sunday came he preached solid gospel sermons full of his own simplicity and love. 'Uncle Ebenezer,' as his great-nephew, the doctor, calls him, was a completely different character: a silent man, who shunned men, but who was 'great once a week':

> Six days he brooded over his message, was silent, withdrawn, self-involved, but the instant he was in the pulpit, up stood a son of thunder. Such a voice! Such a piercing eye! Such an inevitable forefinger, held out trembling with the terrors of the Lord; such a power of asking questions and letting them fall deep into the hearts of his hearers, and then answering them himself, with an 'Ah, sirs!' that thrilled and quivered from him to them.[32]

On one occasion, the celebrated Lord Brougham (Whig politician, law reformer and outstanding parliamentary orator) was among his hearers. He and a colleague happened to be on a professional visit near Inverkeithing, and on the Sabbath Brougham asked where they should go to church, whereupon their host offered to take them to 'a Seceder minister at Inverkeithing'. Brougham agreed, and having heard a description of 'the saintly old man', said they would like to be introduced to him. On arrival at church, their host left a message that 'some gentlemen' wished to see the minister. Back came the answer: that Maister Brown saw nobody before divine worship. The names of the illustrious gentlemen were then sent in, and back again came the answer, 'Mr Brown's compliments to Mr Stuart [their host], and he sees nobody before sermon.'

A few minutes later, out came the 'stooping shy old man', and passed by them on his way to the pulpit, unconscious of their presence. Brown preached a sermon full of fire and native force, the visitors came away greatly moved, and each immediately wrote to their friend Lord Jeffrey, eminent judge and literary critic, telling him not to lose a week in coming

---

31. All our information on Ebenezer Brown comes Dr John Brown's 'Letter to John Cairns' (*Horae Subsecivae*, Second Series, pp. 70-760.

32. ibid., p. 72.

to hear the greatest natural orator they had ever heard. Jeffrey came next Sunday, 'and often declared afterwards that he had never heard such words, or such a sacred, untaught gift of speech.'

Yet the word 'natural' must not betray us into thinking that Ebenezer's sermons were delivered without careful preparation. They were, indeed, punctuated by 'abrupt appeals and sudden starts', but, as we've already seen, he spent the week brooding over his message; and according to Dr Brown the sermons were 'carefully composed and written out'. But I would prefer to believe that the 'sudden starts' were what they seemed to be, rather than flashes of passion that came to him when writing, and were then delivered in such a manner as gave the impression that they were extemporaneous.

In his 'Letter to Dr Cairns' Dr Brown lets us know that Uncle Ebenezer, with all his mildness, was, like most of the Browns, stubborn to the point of obstinacy, and he relates a story which fully bears this out. But it also illustrates a more important truth. Every Tuesday, Ebenezer Brown conducted a service in North Queensferry, two miles from Inverkeithing. One such Tuesday happened to be a wild winter's day, the snow was drifting, and dangerous, and his family pled with him not to go. He smiled vaguely, but their pleas were in vain, and off he went, man and pony stumbling through the blinding snow. He was about halfway through his journey when the pony suddenly staggered and threw him. Both landed in a roadside ditch, and there he might have lain, and perished, had not some carters seen him fall. They were carrying a dubious cargo, casks of whisky, but they immediately rushed to help, and raised him up, 'with much commiseration and blunt speech: "Puir auld man, what brocht ye here in sic a day?"' They replaced his hat, cheered him up, knocked the balls of snow off the pony's feet, and stuffed them with grease. Then came the crowning kindness: one of the 'cordial ruffians' pierced a cask, brought Brown a horn of whisky, and said (speaking, no doubt, from experience), 'Tak that, it'll hearten ye.' Uncle Ebenezer took the horn, bowed to them, and said, 'Sirs, let us give thanks!'

> And there by the road-side, in the drift and storm, with these wild fellows, he asked a blessing on it, and on his kind deliverers, and took a tasting of the horn. The men cried like children. They lifted him on his pony, one going with him, and when the rest arrived in Inverkeithing, they repeated the story to everybody, breaking down in tears whenever they came to the blessing. 'And to think o' askin' a blessing on a tass o' whisky.'

At the next meeting of Presbytery, Brown, who seldom spoke, rose after the completion of ordinary business, and announced, 'I have something personal to myself to say. I have often said that real kindness belongs only to true Christians, but …' and then he proceeded to tell the story of the carters. He concluded, 'More true kindness I have never experienced than from these lads. They may have had the grace of God, I don't know; but I never mean to be so *positive* again in speaking of this matter.'[33] The 'ruffians' were in fact Good Samaritans.

John Brown of Broughton Place

Born in July 1784, John Brown III was the eldest son of John Brown of Whitburn. There is no record of what might be called a 'conversion experience' at any point in his life, but there were clear signs from an early age that grace was at work in his soul, and these signs were abundantly confirmed by his later life. From November 1797 to April 1800, he was a student at Edinburgh University, and from there he proceeded later that year to the Burgher Divinity Hall, then meeting in Selkirk under the oversight of George Lawson, the local Burgher Minister.[34]

Having completed his studies, Brown was ordained and inducted to the Burgher congregation of Biggar in 1806 and served there till he was called to Rose Street (Edinburgh) in 1822. In 1829, he was called to the city's Broughton Place congregation; then in 1834 he was appointed Professor of Exegetical Theology in the United Secession Divinity Hall.[35] This, as John Cairns points out, marked a moment of 'great originality'. No Scottish Divinity Hall had ever previously set apart a separate Professor of Exegetical Theology. What was not changed, however, was the arrangement whereby the work of a professor was combined with that of a congregational pastorate.

Today, John Brown of Broughton Place is mainly remembered as a leading Scottish advocate of Hypothetical Universalism and a central figure in the Atonement Controversy which rocked the United Secession Church between the years 1840 and 1845. This was, indeed, an important moment

---

33. Dr John Brown, ibid., pp. 74-75.

34. Lawson was remarkable both in gifts and personality. For a brief appreciation, see Cairns, *Life of John Brown*, pp. 32-38. A prolific author, his best-remembered work is his *Discourses on the Book of Esther* (Edinburgh: 1804).

35. The United Secession Church had been formed in 1820 by the union of the 'New Light' branches of the Burgher and Antiburgher traditions of the Secession.

in the history of Scottish Christianity, and it will be reviewed later. But this should not be allowed to eclipse the legacy of ground-breaking exegesis we have inherited from Brown's pen. When his *Expository Discourses on the First Epistle of the Apostle Peter* were published in 1848,[36] William Cunningham remarked that they 'formed a marked era in the history of scriptural interpretation in this country'.[37] In the following ten years, a succession of similar volumes followed, including expositions of the Epistle to the Galatians (1853), the First Chapter of 2 Peter (1856) and the Epistle to the Hebrews (published posthumously in 1862).[38]

When the first of these volumes was published, Brown was already sixty-four years of age, and behind them lay the riches gleaned in the course of many years' expository preaching, supplemented later by his academic lectures in the Divinity Hall. A passionate lover of books from early childhood, Brown brought to his work as commentator not only a thorough knowledge of the Classics but a love for literature in general. More important, however, he brought to it a comprehensive familiarity with the Christian exegetical tradition: the Greek and Latin Fathers, the Schoolmen, and the Protestant tradition in all its branches, including the Reformed, the Anglican, the Puritan, the Arminian and even the Socinian.[39] He had some knowledge, too, of the growing body of German biblical scholarship, but he was limited in this department by a lack of facility in the language.

One result of this comprehensive knowledge of the work of his predecessors was that, whenever he engaged with a particular biblical passage, Brown was familiar with almost all the interpretations ever imposed on them, and is sometimes inclined to spend an inordinate amount of time sifting through them. But the overall result of his breadth of scholarship was that he brought to the task of exegesis a rich store of

---

36. The original edition, published by Oliphant, was in three volumes. A two-volume edition was published by the Banner of Truth in 1975.

37. Quoted by Dr John Nicholls in his article 'Brown, John' in DSCHT.

38. Among Brown's other expository publications were *Discourses and Sayings of our Lord Jesus Christ, illustrated in a Series of Sayings* (three volumes, 1850); *An Exposition of our Lord's Intercessory Prayer*, a sequel to the former, also published in 1850; and *The Resurrection and the Life* (1851), an exposition of First Corinthians Fifteen.

39. From the age of fourteen, he was also a keen collector of editions of the Greek New Testament 'till ultimately the series embraced about a hundred – from Erasmus to Tischendorf – including some of the very rarest, and not less than fourteen before the Received or Elzevir text of 1624' (Cairns, ibid., p. 154).

biblical learning, and a deep-seated conviction that exegesis must be based on a sound philology, close attention to the rules of grammar, and sensitivity to the various cultures that prevailed in biblical times. He had a dread of exegesis that was more *impositio* than *expositio*: the Bible, he insisted, could not be understood theologically until it was first of all understood grammatically. In sum, he sought to instil in his students an 'exegetical conscience'.[40]

At the same time, however, he deplored any purely critical and coldly intellectual approach to Scripture. While he would have subscribed whole-heartedly to the doctrine that Scripture is the sole *principium cognoscendi* (the only source and norm of our knowledge of God) he viewed it primarily as a means of grace, and that is why his commentaries always retained the flavour of his pulpit expositions. His aim was to be at once 'exegetical, doctrinal and practical,' and in this respect his commentaries have their nearest peers in those of John Calvin and Robert Leighton.

1 Peter 3:18-19

Yet, determined as Brown was to read every commentary available on whatever passage he was studying, he was 'deaf to the charms of tradition, and could set aside the most venerable and time-hallowed misinterpretations without mercy.'[41] This becomes clear in the very first of his commentaries to be published: the one on First Peter, an epistle which presents the exegete with some of his most serious challenges. Of these, the most serious of all is the reference in 1 Peter 3:19 to Christ going to preach to the 'spirits in prison'. Brown doesn't shrink from the challenge, but in line with his underlying exegetical philosophy he refuses to treat the verse in isolation. Instead, he wants to clarify first of all what part it plays in the Apostle's overall argument, the reasons for his saying it, and the practical consequences that follow from it. Nor is he going to let himself be rushed. He cannot but know that the reader is impatient to get to the 'spirits in prison', but to arrive there he must first of all make his way through an extended exposition of verses 18-22 under the heading, 'The sufferings of Christ an Encouragement to Believers

---

40. Cairns, ibid., p. 158. Brown was a warm admirer of Thomas Chalmers. 'Dr. Chalmers,' he once remarked, 'has hit the true key-note, not, what *thinkest* thou? but what *readest* thou?' He added, however, 'Had he only himself been still more of an expositor, what weight it would have lent to his testimony' (Cairns, ibid.). For the most part, Chalmers was a topical, rather than an expository preacher.

41. Cairns, ibid., p. 157.

Suffering for his Cause.'[42] The bulk of the exposition is thus devoted to Christ's sufferings, but always in the context of the theme of the previous paragraph, where Peter commends 'suffering for righteousness's sake'. Then, drawing on the opening words of verse 18,[43] Brown gives a sixty-page overview of the sufferings of Christ as 'penal,' 'vicarious' and 'expiatory;' and only when he has completed this, does he turn to the statement that, 'Christ, having been put to death in the flesh but made alive in the spirit, went and preached to the spirits in prison.' This event, whatever its meaning, he argues, was a consequence of the Lord's atoning sufferings, and it served the same end, namely, to 'bring us to God' (1 Pet. 3:18). The 'spirits in prison' must not be detached from their context.

Brown quickly makes plain that he cannot accept what he calls 'the common Protestant interpretation',[44] namely, that through the Holy Spirit Christ inspired Noah as a preacher of righteousness to make known the will of God to the generation before the Flood. Against this exegesis he raises several intricate grammatical arguments, but he also raises a serious logical argument, describing it as unnatural to introduce into a discussion of the nature and design of the historical sufferings of Christ on Calvary the idea that, centuries before these sufferings, the Mediator had gone to preach to the doomed sinners of the days of Noah. Similarly, he argues, it is hard to see any link between this idea and the whole purpose of the paragraph, namely, to fortify persecuted believers by reminding them of the sufferings of Christ, so meekly borne.

Equally emphatically, however, Brown rejects the Roman Catholic understanding that between his death and resurrection Christ, in His disembodied state, went to Purgatory to release to Paradise those who had been 'sufficiently improved'[45] by their disciplinary sufferings; and no less emphatically does he reject the Universalist understanding that Christ went to Gehenna to offer the possibility of salvation to those who had died impenitent. He also cites several other variants on the theme that between His death and resurrection Christ went to the realm of the dead, but he decides, mercifully, that to deal particularly with every objection that might be raised against these 'would occupy a good deal of time, and I am afraid would afford little

---

42. Altogether the exposition covers pp. 123-233 of the Commentary.

43. 'For Christ also hath once suffered for sins, the just for the unjust, that he might bring us to God.'

44. John Brown, *Expository Discourses on the First Epistle of the Apostle Peter*, p. 195.

45. ibid., p. 199.

satisfaction and less edification to my hearers'.[46] He does, however, deliver a characteristic parting shot: 'No interpretation can be the right one, which does not correspond with the obvious construction of the passage, and with the avowed design of the writer'.[47] And as far as Brown was concerned, that design was clear: Peter was writing to encourage suffering Christians.

He then moves on to give his personal view of the passage, and at the heart of it lies the conviction that the phrase 'quickened by the Spirit' cannot be a reference to Jesus' resurrection.[48] Instead, he takes it to mean that Christ was 'quickened spiritually' or 'made spiritually alive'.[49] We have to remember that at this point Brown is still dealing with the consequences of Christ's vicarious sacrifice, and what he is saying here is that just as Christ's position as the vicarious sin-bearer meant that He had to die, so His patient endurance of His expiatory sufferings meant that He had to be rewarded; and His reward was to be made 'alive and powerful' in a sense and to a degree that He had not been alive and powerful before; and not only does the Saviour Himself enjoy this new life, but He is also able to communicate it to dead souls.

This clearly involves abandoning the common interpretations of the phrase, 'the spirits in prison'. Brown takes it to refer, not to some particular age or class of human beings, but to the whole human race, 'the slaves and captives of Satan, shackled with the fetters of sin':[50] the very people, he argues, that Jesus had in mind when, preaching in the synagogue in Nazareth, He described Himself as commissioned 'to proclaim liberty to the captives' (Luke 4:18). From this point of view, the spirits in prison in Noah's day, far from being a special case, were representative of men in all ages. We are all 'spirits in prison'.

---

46. ibid., p. 197.

47. ibid., p. 198.

48. Since the grammatically identical 'flesh' would then require us to translate the first phrase, 'being put to death *by* the flesh'. Christ was crucified *in* the flesh, not *by* the flesh.

49. The Greek reading is *zōopoiētheis de pneumati*. There is no preposition corresponding to the English 'by,' but *pneumati* is in the dative case, and this can indicate instrumentality or agency. More likely, however, it is a dative of reference, giving the sense 'with reference to the spirit', though the problem is further complicated by the fact that neither 'flesh' nor 'spirit' has a definite article. The generally preferred interpretation is that Christ was put to death with reference to His flesh (that is, underwent physical death), but was made alive with reference to His spirit. But this leaves us with the further question, Was the spirit/soul of Christ dead, and thus in need of being 'quickened'? As Brown pointed out (p. 195), the soul is not mortal.

50. ibid., p. 201.

But this, in turn, requires a re-interpretation of the reference to Christ preaching, and once more Brown strikes out boldly. It doesn't refer, he argues, to something the Saviour did bodily, but to something He did spiritually, through others, and most notably through His apostles, so powerfully anointed at Pentecost with the new life conferred on the Lord as a reward for His vicarious obedience and sacrifice. Whatever Paul did, for example, 'it was not he, but Christ by him'[51],

But this interpretation faces its own difficulties. When Peter speaks of Christ being 'quickened', the verb he uses is *zōopoieō*, and St. Paul uses a word from the same root when, in Ephesians 2:5, he describes believers as 'quickened together with Christ' (Eph. 2:5). But Paul is speaking of people who were dead in trespasses and sins (Eph. 2:1). They were spiritually dead until, by the grace of God, they underwent a spiritual resurrection (Eph. 2:6). It is impossible to think of Christ undergoing such a spiritual resurrection. He was spiritually alive during His *earthly* ministry, He had spiritual power during His *earthly* ministry, and when He described Himself as anointed to preach deliverance to the captives He was not referring to his post-Ascension work but to an *earthly* ministry that was already beginning (for example, liberating the diseased and the demonised).

Besides, if it is difficult to explain the sudden introduction of 'the days of Noah' into an account of the sufferings of Good Friday, it is surely no less difficult to account for these days being cited as a particularly striking instance of Christ's preaching. What the 'days of Noah' highlighted was not the life-giving power of the apostolic word, but the longsuffering of God, and His provision of a means of salvation, albeit only for a few (1 Pet. 3:20-21).

All in all, the words that Peter applies to some parts of Paul's epistles could equally well be applied to this passage in his own: it is 'hard to be understood,' and easily 'wrested', not only by the unlearned but by the learned. At no point in Scripture is greater humility required than here. This is not to say that the passage was unintelligible to the original readers, but they may well have had some background information or local context which is unavailable to us.[52] In the meantime we can only pray, *Da lucem, Domine.*

---

51. ibid., p. 204.

52. Cf. Paul's words in 2 Thessalonians 2:5, 'Do you not remember that while I was still with you I told you these things?' These 'things,' no longer available to us, might well hold the key to the identity of 'the man of lawlessness' (2 Thess. 2:3): another age-old challenge to the exegete.

Hebrews 2:9

Brown is often complimented for having 'rescued exegesis from undue subjection to formulated dogma',[53] and though this may be an exaggeration, it certainly reflects one of his main concerns.[54] It needs some qualification, however. It would be hard to find anywhere in his commentaries a statement incompatible with the Westminster Confession as he understood it. Admittedly, he does sometimes use some of the classic terminology of Hypothetical Universalism, as when he writes, for example, that 'no legal bar lies in the way of the emancipation of the spirits in prison, for the offered sacrifice has been accepted.'[55] But then, Brown did not believe that the doctrine of Hypothetical Universalism was contrary to the Confession. On the other hand, and to his credit, he is careful not to read it into New Testament passages which, on the face of things, seemed to lend it some support.

One such passage is Hebrews 2:9, which speaks of Christ tasting death 'for every man' (AV, ESV, 'for everyone'). Brown notes the three interpretations commonly offered: the Universalist, that Christ so died for all that all will finally be saved; the Hypothetical Universalist, that the death of Christ removed the obstacles to the salvation of sinners arising from the nature of a just and holy God; and the Particular Redemptionist, that Christ died only for those whom the Father had given Him.[56] Rightly interpreted, he declares, the passage 'furnishes no support to either of the first two theories mentioned. The universality here specified is plainly a limited universality.'[57] The Greek, he points out, does not specify 'every *man*,' or 'every human being': it merely says, 'every one (*pantos*).' You then have to ask, 'Every one of whom?' and when you look into the context you find a particular class of persons mentioned. For example, the passage specifies

---

53. John Macleod, *Scottish Theology*, p. 254. Cf. the comment of F. F. Bruce and M. D. Peat in their article, 'Exegesis, Biblical' in DSCHT: 'In his hands exegesis was less in bondage to dogmatic formulation than it had tended to be in his predecessors.'

54. Brown is one of many credited with the remark, 'This is truth, important truth, and truth taught elsewhere in Scripture, but not *the* truth taught in the text' (Cairns, ibid., p. 157).

55. *Expository Discourses on First Peter*, Vol. 2, p. 211.

56. *Hebrews*, pp. 101-02.

57. This was written in 1858. The Atonement Controversy had ended in May 1845, when the synod of the United Secession Church declared its 'undivided confidence' in Brown, despite his advocacy of Hypothetical Universalism.

the heirs of salvation, the many sons of God, the brethren of Christ, and 'those whom God had given him'. It was for every one of these that Jesus laid down His life.[58] No party-theological points are being scored here.

But Hebrews also contains a passage as challenging in its own way as 1 Peter 3:18-20. It occurs in Chapter Six, where the writer lays down that it is impossible to renew to repentance those who have fallen away from the faith (Heb. 6:4-6). In the early church, these verses had been used by such rigorist sects as the Montanists to support the view that those who sinned after baptism should never be restored to Communion, and this had led others to call in question the apostolic authorship of the epistle, which in turn had led to questions being raised as to its right to a place in the Canon. These questions did not trouble Brown;[59] he was keenly aware that the passage was a key weapon in the armoury of those who denied the doctrine of the perseverance of the saints, and this inevitably colours his exposition.

The first question to be addressed was the particular class of persons whom it is impossible to renew to repentance. Brown's position was that they were people who had made considerable progress in the Christian faith without ever fully embracing it, and who after a time had returned to their previous religion, whether Judaism or paganism. This is borne out, he argues, by the various experiences ascribed to them. They are described, for example, as those who had been 'once enlightened'.[60] Brown dismisses the idea that this is a reference to baptism, as if the sacrament itself brought illumination. But neither does he accept that it points to a life-changing inward spiritual illumination. Instead, he takes it to mean that they were people who were well informed about the principles of Christianity, and

---

58. *Expository Discourses*, p. 103.

59. In the *Prolegomena* to the Commentary, Brown has a brief discussion of the authorship of the epistle, and concludes, 'I am disposed to think that, though by no means absolutely certain, it is in a high degree probable, that this Epistle was written by the Apostle Paul.' Calvin, however, took a different view: 'I can adduce no reason to show that Paul was its author. The manner of teaching and the style sufficiently show that Paul was not the author, and the writer himself confesses in the second chapter that he was one of the disciples of the apostles, which is wholly different from the way in which Paul spoke of himself' (John Calvin, *The Epistle of Paul to the Hebrews and The First and Second Epistles of Peter*, tr. William B. Johnston; Grand Rapids: Eerdmans, 1963, p. 1). Most New Testament scholarship since Brown's day has been of the same view as Calvin.

60. The word rendered 'one' (*hapax*) points to the once-for-all-ness of this illumination. They could never undo it, or pretend that they had never received it. For them, life would never be the same again.

had moved from a position of complete ignorance of the new faith to a position where they were so impressed by it that they had renounced their old religious affiliation and publicly embraced the gospel.[61]

They are described, too, as having 'tasted the heavenly gift', which Brown takes to be a reference to the gospel, defined as the 'revelation of mercy through Christ'.[62] Not only had they been informed about this gospel: they had 'tasted' it in the sense that they had had personal experience of 'those pleasurable sensations of mind which the gospel, when understood, naturally produces.' They had enjoyed it, as someone enjoys a good meal. This is reminiscent of the stony-ground hearers who received the word with joy, but did not put down deep spiritual roots (Matt. 13:20).

But over and above enjoying the gospel, they had also been made 'partakers of the Holy Spirit', that is, they had shared in the miraculous gifts and operations of the Holy Spirit 'by which the primitive dispensation of Christianity was characterised': gifts, Brown notes, which were by no means confined to those who experienced real spiritual renewal.[63] He is reluctant, however, to rule out the possibility that this language may also mean that some people who are never converted may yet be 'the subjects of a divine influence'. He doesn't elaborate on this, but he does refer to such an influence as something we can 'resist', which suggests that what he has in mind is a strong drawing to Christ; and he warns that to reject Him in the face of such a drawing is the greatest of sins.[64] Similar 'alarms to the unconverted' are a staple feature of Brown's expositions.

Next, we are told, the apostates had tasted 'the good word of God', but at this point Brown is unusually obscure, to the extent that his exposition itself requires careful (and, perhaps, creative) exegesis. He rejects the common interpretation that the 'good word of God' was the gospel, but what he offers instead seems little different, namely, that the 'good word' was God's promise respecting the Messiah. This, he suggests, was 'that good thing'

---

61. Cf. Paul's understanding of his divine commission as one sent to 'open the eyes of the Gentiles, and to turn them from darkness to light' (Acts 26:18).

62. This understanding of the gift may reflect Brown's roots in the *Marrow* tradition, with its reference to the gospel as God's 'deed of gift and grant'.

63. ibid., p. 286.

64. In its chapter on Effectual Calling, the Westminster Confession (10:14) also refers to the fact that 'others not elected' may not only be called by the ministry of the word, but may also 'have some common operations of the Spirit'. Hebrews 6:4, 5 are appended as proof-texts.

spoken of by Jeremiah: the promise that God would raise up the Branch of righteousness who would execute judgement and righteousness in the land (Jer. 33:14-15). This had now proved to be a 'good word' because it had been fulfilled, and those who had fallen away had tasted that fulfilment. They had tasted the 'powers of the world to come' in the sense that, though apostates could never form a binding relationship with the Messiah, they had already enjoyed some of the advantages of the new dispensation, including the inherent power of the gospel to move heart and mind. 'The ancient economy,' Brown writes, 'was comparatively weak as well as unprofitable, but the new economy is powerful. It has everything that can enlighten, and convince, and alarm, and delight'.[65] Those who had fallen away, had tasted this 'power,'[66] and yet ultimately rejected the 'good word' that in Christ the Messianic age had come.

The most striking feature of the experiences listed in these verses is that none of them refers to a change of character. The people in view were intellectually well informed, they possessed gifts fitted to edify the church, and they had felt the power of the good Word of God. They were not, then, mere nominal professors, nor were they backslidden Christians. They were people who had been deeply exercised about Christianity, and drawn to it, but had fallen away. Brown criticises the AV rendering, 'if they fall away' and calls it 'scarcely a fair translation', as if the writer didn't mean to assert that such persons *could* fall away, but only that if they did (an impossible supposition) they could not be renewed again to repentance. The word in the original, he points out, is not 'if' but 'and', giving the clear message that such people *can* fall away, and that when they do, there is no hope of their spiritual recovery.

But Brown is also at pains to spell out what apostasy means: not merely an abandoning of the church, but 'a fall into an open, total, determined renunciation of all the constituent principles of Christianity, and a return to a false religion such as that of unbelieving Jews or heathens, or to determined infidelity and open godliness'.[67] Sadly, as Brown also points out, 'this miserable class of men is not extinct,' as witness the many spiritual companions of our youth who are now agnostics, or militant atheists, or converts to one or other of the world's many religions.

---

65. ibid., p. 288.

66. Cf. Romans 1:16, where Paul describes the gospel as 'the *power* of God unto salvation' (italics added).

67. ibid., p. 289.

Renewing them again to repentance

But what is meant by renewing them *again* to repentance? The people in question, says Brown, had already undergone a repentance, not in the sense of having been born again, but in the sense of having experienced a revolution in their attitude to Christianity; and when Hebrews speaks of the impossibility of a second repentance it is this sort of repentance he has in mind. The writer is not saying that they cannot be restored to a state of grace a second time: they had never been in a state of grace. The repentance he has in mind is a transition from a state of ignorance to a state of enlightenment. This transition can never be repeated: they have been enlightened once and for all; they can never again return to a state of ignorance; and now that they have rejected the light, they can never be re-enlightened. A man cannot be 'renewed' a second time from a state of ignorance of the 'good word of God' to a state of enlightenment.

But why is the 'renewal' of an apostate impossible: not just improbable, or very difficult, but impossible? Does it mean that it is impossible for God or impossible for man? Brown is not prepared to assert that it is impossible for God to renew the apostate, but it is impossible for man, and here Brown, as his wont, argues from the context. The whole object of the writer, he declares, is to explain to the original readers why he is not prepared to go over the fundamentals yet one more time, and the reason he gives is that 'it is impossible, by any renewed course of elementary instruction, to bring back such apostates to the acknowledgement of the truth'.[68] They had unlearned all they had learned, and there was no reason to believe that a restatement of what they had already learned would bring them back to the truth. On the other hand, there was every reason to believe that clarification of the higher branches of Christian truth ('strong meat', Chapter 5:14) would be of use to those who had 'held fast'. The writer is resolved, therefore, to concentrate on building up those who were steadfast in the faith, and on calling to repentance those who still remained in a state of utter ignorance.

This interpretation is supported by the verses (7 and 8) with which the section closes, where the writer justifies his approach by appealing to the example of a field which, being well-watered, brings forth the fruit required by the farmer; and another field, equally well-watered and well-tended, which brings forth only thorns and briers. No amount of labour can make

---

68. ibid., p. 293.

such a field productive and, by analogy, no amount of continued instruction in the fundamentals of the gospel can renew or recover the apostate. He already knows them, and has emphatically rejected them.

There remains the statement that apostates are crucifying Christ to themselves afresh and putting Him to an open shame (v. 6). Here again, Brown distances himself from the generally accepted exegesis that these words were intended to highlight the heinousness of apostasy and to account for its being (as was thought) unpardonable. Once again he invokes the context: the point of the passage was not to show the aggravated guilt of apostates, but to state plainly the hopelessness of trying to recover them. They were involving themselves in the guilt of the Crucifixion, endorsing the view of His accusers that Jesus was an impious imposter who richly deserved the ignominious death that He had died, and exposing Him to infamy as one whose faith they had tried and found wanting. In fact, 'They did more to dishonour Jesus Christ than His murderers. *They* never professed to acknowledge His divine mission, but these apostates *had* made such a profession – they had made a kind of trial of Christianity, and, after trial, rejected it.'

Before taking leave of this passage Brown pauses to warn against misapplying it. Aware of its appropriation by such disciplinary rigorists as the Montanists, and perhaps even by some in his own ecclesiastical circle, he avers that there is nothing here to warrant a church refusing to re-admit to Communion a person who has been guilty of open apostasy, but now makes a credible profession of repentance. Such a case is quite different from that of 'the open, determined apostate' who will never make such a profession of repentance and whom it is therefore impossible to reclaim.

Nor, he insists, should the passage present any discouragement to a person who had backslidden but is now convinced of his sin and guilt, and applies to God for pardon through Christ. Citing 1 John 1:7, he declares, 'This is exactly what he should do; and if he do it, he is sure of salvation.'[69] But he warns, too, against the misapprehension of the passage by 'sincere, but weak-minded Christians,' who fear that, having sinned after coming to a knowledge of the truth, there can be no mercy for them. The weak Christian is misreading his own mind if he attributes to himself the sin described in Hebrews Six, namely, 'a total and voluntary renunciation of Christ and His cause, and a joining with His enemies'.[70]

---

69. 'The blood of Jesus Christ his Son cleanseth us from all sin' (1 John 1:7).

70. ibid., p. 296.

And finally, he declares that there is nothing in the passage to invalidate the doctrine of the Perseverance of the Saints. Nothing is said of those described here but what is said of the stony-ground hearers (Mark 4:16-17), of those who are destitute of Christian love (1 Cor. 13:1-3), and of those whom Christ will at last disown as 'workers of iniquity' despite the splendour of their spiritual gifts (Matt. 7:22, 23). But at the same time Brown underlines the fact that it is the perseverance of *saints* that is certain, and he adds, 'Let us recollect that the perseverance of the saints referred to, is their perseverance not only in a safe state, but in a holy course of disposition and conduct. No saint behaving like a sinner can legitimately enjoy the comfort which the doctrine of perseverance is fitted and intended to communicate.'

2 Peter 1:20-21

The last commentary Brown published was *Parting Counsels: An Exposition of 2 Peter 1.*[71] The reference to *Parting Counsels* captured the Apostle's awareness that his own end was near (2 Pet. 1:14),[72] but it probably reflects, too, Brown's sense that this would be his own final work (he was now seventy-two years of age and died in 1758, two years after its publication). On the other hand, the fact that the commentary is limited to the first chapter was due, not to lack of time, but to the fact that 'he found himself labouring under such uncertainty in regard to much in the second and third chapters.'[73]

The first chapter presents, of course, its own challenges, but it also contains one of the key apostolic deliverances on the nature of Scripture: 'Knowing this first, that no prophecy of the scripture is of any private interpretation. For the prophecy came not in old time by the will of man: but holy men of God spake *as they were* moved by the Holy Ghost' (2 Peter 1:20-21, AV). Brown's exposition of these words enables us to see the overall doctrine of Scripture which underlies his exegesis of particular passages.

---

71. He did in fact also publish, a year later, an *Analytical Commentary on the Epistle of Paul to the Romans*, but its reduced scale reflected the fact that he no longer felt able to produce the 'grammatical, historical, and logical commentary' he had once intended (Cairns, ibid., p. 304).

72. 'Knowing that shortly I must put off this my tabernacle, even as our Lord Jesus Christ hath shewed me.'

73. Cairns, ibid., p. 300.

The passage is part of the argument used by the apostle to drive home the importance of taking heed to the 'word of prophecy', and Brown goes through the key phrases meticulously, beginning with the reference to 'private interpretation'.[74] Noting that the word *epilusis,* here translated 'interpretation', doesn't occur anywhere else in the New Testament, and only rarely in secular Greek, he proceeds to dismiss, with reasons, suggested meanings which he regards as unacceptable.

First among these is that what the apostle is saying is, that the prophets couldn't understand their own message. Brown concedes that to a certain extent this was true, and he draws support for this from 1 Peter 1:11, which tells us that the prophets were sometimes puzzled as to how or when their predictions would be fulfilled. But he doesn't concede that this was always true. In many cases the import of their message was perfectly clear to them,[75] though in many others 'there was far more in their prophecies than they were aware of.'

Secondly, he rejects the suggestion that the words mean that prophecy is not self-interpreting and that Scripture itself furnishes no means of clarifying the import of particular passages. Here again, Brown concedes that this may be true within certain limits, particularly in respect of unfulfilled prophecies, which are often obscure till they are explained by their fulfilment. At the same time, however, he remains loyal to both the vision of his grandfather and his *Self-interpreting Bible,* and to the Protestant doctrine of the perspicuity of Scripture (WC).[76] 'The Bible as a whole,' he writes, 'is a self-interpreting book,' and nothing is necessary to understand it but that it be read 'with a moderate degree of attention and intelligence'.[77] The light, he remarks, may be shining in a dark place, but the light itself is not a dim light.

---

74. Gk., *idias epiluseōs,* literally 'one's own explanation'. ESV, 'no prophecy of Scripture comes from one's own interpretation'.

75. For example, Jeremiah's prophecy with regard to the duration of the Exile: 'For thus says the LORD: When seventy years are completed for Babylon, I will visit you, and I will fulfil to you my promise and bring you back to this place' (Jer. 29:10, ESV).

76. As stated in, for example, the Westminster Confession, 1.9: 'The infallible rule of interpretation of scripture is the scripture itself; and therefore, when there is a question about the true and full sense of any scripture, it must be searched and known by other places that speak more clearly.'

77. This scarcely does justice to the important role of preachers and expositors such as Brown himself in opening up the Scriptures for the benefit of the people of God. It was to this, almost certainly, that the Westminster Confession was referring when it spoke of the

Thirdly, Brown rejects the idea that Peter's words are no more than a warning against people interpreting the Bible arbitrarily, that is, giving to a particular passage 'whatever sense may please their fancy, or seem to be necessary to support some particular dogma.' He recognises that this is a common fault, and insists that Scripture must be interpreted according to the general laws of interpretation. But why, he asks, would the apostle invoke a warning against arbitrary exegesis as a reason for giving heed to the prophetic word?

But most emphatically of all, Brown rejects the idea that 2 Peter 1:20-21 provided support for what was then the Roman Catholic practice of discouraging ordinary believers from studying the Bible for themselves: a position which rested on the dogma that the Church was the only authorised interpreter of Scripture, and which denied individuals the right to exercise their private judgement as to the meaning of the Bible, and especially their right to test the teaching of the Church in the light of Scripture. Peter's position, in Brown's view, is the exact opposite: 'Instead of referring his readers to any infallible human interpreter, the apostle calls them, each for himself, to take heed to the prophetic word, "as to a light shining in a dark place."'

Having rejected these views of the passage, Brown again strikes out on his own, declaring it impossible to arrive at a satisfactory understanding of the words so long as we take 'interpretation' to be the true meaning of *epilusis*. Instead, invoking the precedent of Calvin and others, he takes it to mean 'utterance', which yields the sense, 'No prophecy of Scripture is an utterance of the prophet's private opinion or an expression merely of what the prophet himself thought.'[78] And by way of further elucidation, he adds that biblical prophecies 'were not given forth in the exercise of the common

---

'unlearned' coming to a 'sufficient understanding' of Scripture through 'a due use of the ordinary means'. On the other hand, the 'learned' are themselves indebted to the labours of the generations of Christian scholars who have bequeathed to the church a priceless exegetical legacy.

78. It is doubtful if this understanding of *epilupsis* can claim the support of Calvin, who rejects a variant reading (*epēlusis,* meaning 'approach' or 'attack') and declares that he preferred the reading *epilupsis,* 'which means "interpretation".' However, his understanding of the apostle's point is the same as Brown's: 'Peter is saying that Scripture was not handed down from man or by human desire. Peter especially bids us trust the prophets as the undoubted oracles of God, because they did not give way to any private, human impulse.' (John Calvin, *The Epistle of Paul the Apostle to the Hebrews and the First and Second Epistles of St Peter,* p. 343). 'Interpretation' is still the standard translation of *epilupsis.*

faculties of human nature, or under any of the ordinary influences to which men are subjected.'

That this is the true import of St Peter's argument is confirmed by the words that follow: 'holy men of God spake as they were moved by the Holy Ghost.' Prophecy was not a matter of human *self*-disclosure, but of *divine* self-disclosure; nor was it a matter of human initiative, as if prophecy were a profession a man 'could adopt at pleasure', Instead, both the messenger and the message were a matter of the divine will. This didn't mean, however, that the prophets wrote either without or against their own volition. Brown recognises that both human will and human understanding were involved in their compositions, but it was human will and human understanding under the control of the divine will and the divine understanding. They wrote just what, and just as, God willed;[79]and they did so because they wrote as men 'moved' by the Holy Spirit. The term, as Brown notes, is a strong one, reminiscent of a vessel moved by a strong wind,[80] and the result is that the prophetic word is 'not so properly the word of the inspired man as of the inspiring Spirit'.[81] Moreover, as Brown is at pains to add, this is true of all the contents of the Bible: the precise point made by St Paul in 2 Timothy 3:16, though in different terms. Where Peter tells us that 'no prophecy was ever produced by the will of men', Paul, putting it positively, tells us that 'all scripture' (*pasa graphē*) was breathed out by God.

Yet this is not inconsistent with the fact that the Bible is also a human book: a point which Peter underlines by placing the word 'men' (*anthrōpoi*) in the position of emphasis at the end of the sentence, giving the literal reading, 'carried by the Holy Spirit spoke *men*.'[82] God did not override the

---

79. This is in marked contrast to the false prophets described by Jeremiah: 'They speak visions of their own minds, not from the mouth of the LORD' (Jer. 23:16).

80. The original term here is *pheromenoi*, meaning 'carried'. Cf. Warfield's comment: 'The term here used is a very specific one. It is not to be confounded with guiding, or directing, or controlling, or even leading in the full sense of that word. It goes beyond all such terms, in assigning the effect produced specifically to the active agent. What is "borne" is taken up by the "bearer," and conveyed by the "bearer's" power, not its own, to the "bearer's" goal, not its own' (from B. B. Warfield, 'The Biblical Idea of Inspiration' in Warfield, *The Inspiration and Authority of the Bible*; Philadelphia: Presbyterian and Reformed Publishing, 1948, p. 137).

81. *Expository Discourses*, p. 218.

82. Brown does not develop this point. Instead, he devotes a paragraph to clarifying the description of the prophets as '*holy* men of God'. Unfortunately, evidence for the word 'holy' (*hagioi*) at this point is slight, but Brown's work antedated the publication of Westcott and Hort's historic edition of the text of the New Testament, published in two volumes under the title, *The New Testament in Original Greek*, in 1881. Brown had died in 1858. Here he is following the Received Text.

prophets' human faculties, nor did He bypass them. Instead, He availed Himself of them, ensuring that 'no prophecy of the scripture' is devoid of the impress of its human author. The Bible is a book of dual authorship, written by human beings who were carried by the Spirit at every point in the work of composition. Such is the apostolic doctrine of Scripture, and it lies at the heart of any coherent doctrine of apostolic succession. Scripture was the apostolic Rule of Faith. Nothing that is contrary to Scripture, or lacks the support of Scripture, can claim to be apostolic.

These verses do indeed present a powerful argument for taking heed to the prophetic word, but they also lay the foundation for the single most important principle of Christian biblical hermeneutics: Scripture, as constituted by the breath of God, and written by men who were carried by the Holy Spirit, cannot contradict itself. All 'radical' biblical criticism proceeds from a denial of this principle.

Conclusion

It is hard to assess what impact Brown had on the future course of biblical exegesis in Scotland.[83] None of his students distinguished themselves in this field, although Dr John Eadie, who became his colleague when appointed Professor of Biblical Literature in the United Secession Divinity Hall in 1843, wrote notable commentaries on Paul's Epistles to the Ephesians, Colossians, Philippians, Galatians and Thessalonians; and it is a tribute to the high standard of these publications that he was called to serve on the company appointed in 1870 (following a resolution by the Convocation of Canterbury) for the revision of the English New Testament. Eadie, however, had been raised in the Relief Church and had pursued

---

83. We should also note that Brown was not the first distinguished Scottish commentator of the nineteenth century. As early as 1817 Robert Haldane had published a French edition of his *Commentary on Romans* and then, having worked on it for the next twenty years, an English edition appeared in 1834, fourteen years before Brown's *Exposition of 1 Peter*. The French edition reflected Haldane's more or less informal exposition of the epistle in his meetings with a group of Divinity students during a visit to Geneva in 1816 and relied on no other authorities than the original Hebrew and Greek versions of the Scripture, supplemented by modern versions in French, English, German and other European languages. In preparing the English version, however, Haldane read everything he could lay hands on. There are few signs of this research in the work itself, though Haldane does interact regularly with such scholars as Tholuck, Moses Stuart and MacKnight. The exegesis reflects an uncompromising commitment to Reformed Orthodoxy, but this commitment is always backed-up with coherent argument. This commentary, enthusiastically commended by such outstanding preachers as Thomas Chalmers and Dr Martyn Lloyd-Jones, was reprinted by the Banner of Truth in 1958.

his Divinity course at the University of Glasgow, and thus had not been exposed to Brown's influence.[84]

Looking beyond the Secession, other denominations were slow to follow the lead given by the United Secession Church in 1834 when it set up a Chair of Exegetical Theology. Only in 1857 did the Free Church act, appointing George Smeaton the first Professor of Exegesis at New College. However, although Smeaton's published works are thoroughly laced with exegesis, and though he was well acquainted with the work of German exegetes, he published no commentaries.

That same year, David Brown was appointed Professor of New Testament Exegesis at the Free Church College in Aberdeen, and although he published no stand-alone commentaries, he did make a significant contribution to 'Jamieson, Fausset and Brown': a six-volume, multi-author *Commentary, Critical, Experimental and Practical,* published between 1864 and 1870. Brown's colleagues in the venture were Robert Jamieson, a Church of Scotland minister serving the Glasgow parish of St Paul's, and Andrew R. Fausset, an Anglican priest and latterly Prebendary of York. Brown's was the most scholarly contribution,[85] covering the four Gospels and Acts-Romans, but while all three were competent scholars, the commentary is based on the Authorised Version rather than on the original. Still, as such sets go, this remains a valuable stand-by in a minister's library, especially on those books of the Bible where good commentaries are hard to come by.[86]

Before the appointment to their Exegetical Chairs of either Smeaton or Brown, Patrick Fairbairn had been appointed Professor of Divinity at the Free Church College in Aberdeen in 1853. Three years later he was transferred to the newly established Free Church College in Glasgow, initially as Professor of Theology and from 1857 as Principal. Fairbairn has been described as 'one of the first Scottish ministers to drink of the springs

---

84. Eadie is described by Landreth as much superior to Brown in his familiarity with German scholarship: 'To Dr. Eadie it was left to set the example of examining and expounding Scripture under the searching lights of German learning' (ibid., p. 294). It is symptomatic of changing theological winds in Scotland that Landreth can then write, 'British, compared with German, exegesis was a superficial and illiterate instrument of Bible interpretation' (ibid., p. 293).

85. Like Eadie, Brown served on the company for the revision of the English New Testament.

86. The six volumes were reprinted by Eerdmans in 1967.

of German theology', and as 'of such ample endowments that he could have made up a full theological faculty himself.'[87] His main interest, however, was in hermeneutics, and it was in this department that he produced the works for which he is best remembered: *The Typology of Scripture* (two volumes, 1845-47) and *The Interpretation of Prophecy* (1856).[88] But Fairbairn was also the author of two commentaries. The first of these was *Ezekiel and the Book of his Prophecy: An Exposition* (1851).[89] Any commentator on Ezekiel faces a formidable task, but this one is not only scholarly but readable (right through to the end!). This was followed, though only after an interval of twenty-three years, by *The Pastoral Epistles: The Greek Text and Translation, with Introduction, Expository Notes, and Dissertations*.[90] As the title indicates, this is a seriously scholarly work which not only offers a verse-by-verse commentary, but also devotes nineteen pages to a discussion of the authorship of these epistles, leading to the conclusion (p. 18) that it was 'infinitely more likely they should have proceeded from the hand of St. Paul, than from anyone falsely assuming his name.' The expository notes which follow are both thorough and stimulating.[91]

But none of these commentaries belongs to the same *genre* as those of John Brown, with their blend of exegesis, doctrine, practical theology and evangelistic application. By the time he died in 1858 the United Presbyterian Church had already begun to loosen itself from its confessional moorings and, prompted by such scholars as A. B. Davidson, Scottish biblical scholarship was increasingly coming under the influence of the radical Higher Criticism of Germany: an influence summed-up in George Adam's Smith's volume, *Modern Criticism and the Preaching of the Old Testament* (1901). Born and bred in the same country, reared in identical religious traditions, and their publications separated by a mere forty years, John Brown and George Adam Smith inhabited different intellectual universes.

---

87. Stewart Mechie, *Trinity College Glasgow* (Glasgow: Collins, 1956), p. 28.

88. A second edition of this work, published in 1865, was reprinted by the Banner of Truth (London, 1964). A two-volumes-in-one edition of *The Typology of Scripture* was published by Zondervan of Grand Rapids (no date).

89. A fourth edition of this work was published in 1876 by T & T Clark (Edinburgh).

90. Published Edinburgh: T & T Clark, 1874.

91. Fairbairn was a member of the company appointed to prepare a Revised Version of the English Old Testament, as was A. B. Davidson, Professor of Hebrew and Old Testament Exegesis at New College, Edinburgh. The Revised Version of the New Testament appeared in 1881; the completed Revised Bible in 1885.

7

James Fraser, Laird of Brea

JAMES FRASER OF Brae is an enigma. He lived in the seventeenth century, but it was in the eighteenth that his theology caused a stir; though he was never a Seceder, having died thirty-five years before the Secession, it was in that branch of the church that his work first provoked controversy; and having been ignored and neglected for two hundred years he suddenly became a theologian of interest in the twentieth century, hailed as a trail-blazer in the movement away from Westminster Calvinism to the evangelical faith of the early Reformers.

What is the story?

A revered field-preacher

James Fraser was born at Brae in the parish of Resolis in the Black Isle in July 1639 but, although well connected (his father was the brother of Lord Lovat), he had cast in his lot at an early age with 'God's poor people', had become one of the most revered of the field-preachers, and had borne his full share of the sufferings of the later Covenanters. Today, however, his fame rests on two volumes published long after his death in 1698.

The first of these was his *Memoirs*, first published in 1728.[1] They are carefully written, and Fraser clearly intended them for publication, but the friend to whom they were dedicated (the Reverend Thomas Ross, Minister of Kincardine in Ross-shire) and who, presumably, was charged with overseeing their publication, was in prison at the time. He died there, and

---

1. References to this work in this chapter are from *Memoirs of the Rev. James Fraser of Brea (Written by Himself), with Introductory Note by Rev. Alexander Whyte*; Edinburgh: The Religious Book and Tract Society, 1889. This edition also contains a Short Sketch of Fraser by Rev. Gustavus Aird, Creich.

the manuscript was lost. It was later recovered, however, and attested as genuine by several minsters who had known Fraser (and his handwriting) personally.

At one level, the *Memoirs* consist of a narrative account of the outward events of Fraser's life, culminating in his 'public sufferings' and concluding with his release from Newgate Prison towards the end of 1683. He lost his father when he was but ten years old and then inherited the Brae estate which, unfortunately, was heavily burdened with debt, not because of any profligacy on his father's part but because he had been too inclined to stand surety for others. The problem was exacerbated by the incompetence and dishonesty of those who administered the estate during Fraser's minority, with the result that it was a millstone round his neck for most of his life.

Recalling his childhood, he speaks of himself as 'a seeker' from an early age, but he also 'showed plainly that he had a will to do evil; for the seeds of wickedness did spring up, and appeared in many vicious, childish tricks.'[2] He qualifies this, however, by telling us that he learned well at school, 'though now and then I stayed away'. It is easy to understand why. The schoolmaster was of the kind who delighted in the 'scourging' of children, with the result that young Fraser was 'whipt' every day whether he deserved it or not; and so affected was he by this man's pedagogical methods that he sometimes took measures to shorten his own life, starving himself of food and deliberately exposing himself to extreme cold. He almost, he says, became his own murderer, but though he succeeded in making himself ill, he did not succeed in shortening his life.

From about the age of nine he began to experience what he called 'some common work of the Spirit'. He was seventeen, however, and already an Arts graduate of Aberdeen University, before he experienced what he described as his 'real and full conversion'; and following this, he changed his course of studies.[3] His original intention, in accordance with the expectations of his family, had been to study for the Law, but he had quickly lost his taste for it and had acquired, instead, a taste for the study of divinity, although at the time he did not yet see himself as called to the ministry. This study involved no formal tuition (Fraser never had any formal theological education), but it

---

2. *Memoirs*, p. 1. Further references in brackets in the text.

3. The timeline is hard to trace. He records that in 1661–62 he was in the South (Edinburgh) in connection with the business of the Brea estate and adds, 'I should have gone to the college, but I was otherwise taken up' (p. 99).

was certainly not superficial. His main interest was in writings on practical theology, but in the seventeenth century that had an entirely different connotation from what it has today, denoting, not 'how-to' courses on such subjects as counselling, leadership, missiology and church-planting, but the theology that addressed the spiritual challenges and temptations common to Christian discipleship.

Fraser's reading in this area included the works of Isaac Ambrose, Thomas Goodwin. Andrew Gray, Samuel Rutherford and 'most of all' Thomas Shepard's, *The Sound Believer.*[4] For the most part, however, his reading was related to his own personal struggles, and among the works he found helpful in this connection (apart from the Epistle to the Romans) were *Luther on Galatians*, Calvin's *Institutes* and the works of Bradwardine, Patrick Hamilton, George Wishart, John Knox and John Bradford. What is particularly interesting is that Fraser records that, many years before Thomas Boston stumbled on a copy of *The Marrow of Modern Divinity,* he himself was helped by 'that book' even more than he was by Luther and Calvin; and throughout his life Fraser's theology was aligned with that of the *Marrow*. What is scarcely less interesting is that he was also conversant with the writings of Richard Baxter, and 'abhorred' them because under the cover of opposing antinomianism he was 'a stated enemy to the grace of God' (p. 233).

In 1663 Fraser gave up attending on the ministry of the prelates and their curates, partly because he got no good from them, partly because he could not recognise prelacy as having authority from Scripture, and partly because the 'tenderest' of the godly were leaving them daily, and suffering for it (p. 114); and if they were suffering, he must suffer with them. From this point onwards he identified with the outed Covenanter ministers and their followers, and gradually began to exhort and to expound the Scriptures in private homes, as opportunity (and importunity) arose.

This inevitably raised the question whether he was called to the ministry, and he addressed it with what, as we shall see, was characteristic thoroughness. He was clear that no one could discharge the office aright without 'a sense of his divine call upon his spirit', but he was equally clear that the inclination might proceed only from his own fancy; and clear, too,

---

4. For a brief introduction to Shepard, see Alexander Whyte, *Thomas Shepard: Pilgrim Father and Founder of Harvard* (Edinburgh: Oliphant, Anderson and Ferrier, 1909).

that the call no longer comes as it came to prophets and apostles of old, through audible voices in an extraordinary manner (p. 230). He therefore set apart some solemn days on which, by prayer and fasting, he could seek light from the Lord. The outcome of these deliberations was that he was 'inclined to think' that God was indeed calling him.

Having reached this conclusion, Fraser proceeds to enumerate the grounds on which he based it. His starting point is that whatever gifts or talents a man possesses he is bound to use for God (1 Cor. 12:7), but to follow a particular calling the person must be fitted for this more than for anything else. 'Now,' he continues, 'I begin to see what is my talent; and truly there was no other thing I was more fitted for, or qualified, than serving God in the ministry' (p. 232). These qualifications included his natural endowments; the dealings of God with his spirit in the work of conversion; his great experience of the exceeding evil of his own heart; his conflicts with unbelief and legalism; his experience of great afflictions and the Lord's support under them; and the fact that his eyes had been opened to see the glorious mysteries of the covenant of grace.[5]

But still, he thought, gifts and the ability to preach are not a sufficient call to a man to be a minister, any more than the fact that a man has the natural gifts and ability for magistracy (politics) means that he is called to that office: 'some have gifts for divers offices, that yet are called but to one' (p. 234), and no man, however able or godly, is more warranted than another 'to exercise his talents in a public ministerial way until the Spirit determine his spirit' (p. 234). And this, he found, the Spirit did to him, persuading him to use his talents in this particular way, 'and [he] was at much pains with me till I should yield.'

There follows another rigorous and detailed account of the way the Spirit 'determined' his spirit: for example, by representing to his soul the beauty and glory of the office of the ministry; by drawing out and inclining his heart to this work;[6] by the fact that his heart was utterly averse to any

---

5. 'Truly, I had not been many days in Christ's school, judging the covenant of grace, when I thought I was come to a new world; my former life seemed a dark howling wilderness, and the life of grace I looked upon as the lightsome Canaan, the harbour of rest after my tossings' (ibid., p. 232).

6. 'Yea, I had marvellous delight in the exercise of any work belonging to the ministry, whether it was reading of theology, either practical or polemic, meditating upon or writing up my thoughts, studying or preaching of sermons. And, truly, parents send their children to these trades that they observe them to be most of themselves inclined to' (pp. 234-35).

other study or employment; by the benefit his soul received from preparing to minister: 'For it was by meditating upon subjects, and preaching of them, that I daily grew in grace and knowledge of Christ' (p. 235).

These issues seem to have been settled in his mind by the latter end of the year 1665, when 'the Lord put this call close to my door, told me I was to be his witness, to testify for him against the world, to do all the good I could to mankind wherever I was called; and that I should make this my only work, and be faithful, free, and full in it; that many things needed reformation, and that the Lord would employ me in it' (p. 236). How this was communicated to him, Fraser does not say, but despite its clarity it didn't evoke instant compliance. Instead, like Jonah, he fled from the work; and, again like Jonah, 'the Lord sent a storm of terrors after me, and I was casten into a sea and depth of hell many weeks.' Only seven years later, in 1672, did the event occur which is generally referred to as his ordination.

His ordination

The details of this event, however, are far from clear. We have two accounts of it, one in Fraser's own *Memoirs* and the other in the *Memoirs of Thomas Hog of Kiltearn*,[7] but neither account refers to it as an ordination. Hog's *Memoirs* refer to it as a licensing, the normal prelude to a presbyterian ordination, but Fraser merely records that after solemn trial of his gifts and conversation he was 'declaratively empowered' to exercise the office of the ministry and entrusted with the dispensation of the gospel (p. 236). There is no hint of any such ceremony as the laying on of hands, though this had been clearly prescribed by the *Second Book of Discipline*.[8] Nor does either account make any reference to a presbytery, though later historians refer to Fraser having been ordained by the Field Presbytery of Moray.[9] Fraser's account speaks only of 'the ministers and faithful servants of Jesus Christ' adding that, 'They were better judges than myself, and they found the Lord had called me' (p. 236). In Hog's *Memoirs* we read that he himself

---

7. *The Banished Minister; or, Scenes in the Life of Thomas Hog of Kiltearn (1654–1692)* (Edinburgh, 1756), p. 86. This is reproduced in *Memoirs of Mrs William Veitch, Mr Thomas Hog of Kiltearn, Mr Henry Erskine, and Mr John Carstairs* (Edinburgh: Free Church of Scotland, 1846). The relevant reference to Fraser of Brae is to be found on p. 108.

8. III:12 (see James Kirk (ed.), *The Second Book of Discipline* (Edinburgh: Saint Andrew Press, 1980), p. 180.

9. See, for example, M. Macdonald, *The Covenanters of Moray and Ross* (Second Edition, Inverness: Melven Brothers, 1892), p. 106.

was the prime mover behind the licensing, and there could have been no higher endorsement. Hog had been ordained and inducted to Kiltearn in 1654, when the controversy between protesters and resolutioners was still raging, but was deposed soon after the Restoration because, as a protester, he was under suspicion of being disaffected towards the reinstated monarch, Charles II, and was 'clear against hearing the curates' (p. 107); and a few years prior to the licensing of Fraser he had been imprisoned for 'keeping conventicles'.[10] It is not clear who the other ministers were, but they probably included John McKillican of Fodderty (who had himself been excluded from his charge in 1663) and Thomas Ross of Kincardine, who would later suffer two years imprisonment (1677–79) for preaching at 'house conventicles'. Ross' wife, Catherine Collace, appears to have been the source of the account of Fraser's licensing published in Hog's *Memoirs*, but she was mistaken in regarding this as the first nonconformist licensing. One of the forgotten names in the story of the Covenanters is that of Robert Gillespie, son of George Gillespie of Westminster Assembly fame. He was 'manumitted' by the informal presbytery shortly before Fraser, and was also the first to be imprisoned on the Bass for holding conventicles.[11] Clearly, extraordinary times called for extraordinary measures.

Apart from these narrative details, Fraser's licensing has two other remarkable features.

First, he was not being inducted to any particular charge. So far as it was an ordination at all, it was an ordination at large: a practice very much discouraged in Presbyterianism. But the times were unsettled, and all those involved in the licensing were themselves field-preachers, unattached to any particular charge. Besides, a normal parish ministry would have required collation by a bishop, and this was out of the question. Fraser could, however, conduct a ministry of private exhortation and 'transient occasional discourses' 'without breach of law' (or so he thought).

More important, however, was Fraser's own understanding of his call (p. 240). His commission, as he saw it, was indefinite rather than definite: not to preach to any particular flock but 'to preach in a vagrant manner, sometimes to one place, sometimes to another, here and there, up and down

---

10. Conventicles tended to be defined very loosely, and to refer to any religious meeting held at a location other than a parish church (Macdonald, ibid., p. 117).

11. ibid., pp.106-07.

the country, as I was called by the people, not staying a week in one place' (p. 240). Thus, although licensed by the Covenanters of Moray and Ross, much of his ministry was spent in the south, particularly in Edinburgh and the surrounding areas. 'I loved not fixed stipends and pulpits,' he wrote, 'while the Lord Jesus himself was unfixed; but thought it most kindly to follow the wandering ark and tabernacle' (p. 240).

The second intriguing feature of Fraser's licensing is that he did not see it as part of his call, but only as confirmation of his call. No act of man, he wrote, could give a call to a minister, 'for ordination by ministers, or election by the people, which are the two ways by which it is pretended this call is conveyed, is posterious to this call of God' (p. 230). In his own case, he had clearly not waited for either ordination or popular election before beginning his ministry. His warrant lay in the inner call of the Holy Spirit: the licensing merely confirmed it, and it would be further confirmed by the effects which followed his ministry: 'for by preaching and discharging my duty otherwise, I myself was watered, my gifts increased, more of the Lord's will was made known to me, and my labours were blessed to many, to whose heart and case the Lord made me many times to speak' (p. 237).

On the face of things, this looks like a clear departure from both the First and Second Books of Discipline, each of which stresses the importance of the call of the people.[12] We have to remember, however, that what is in mind here is a call to office in a particular congregation. This did not apply in Fraser's case, and he would certainly not have condoned the idea of ministers being intruded into their charges against the wishes of the people. On the other hand, the idea that one's own sense of call is the decisive factor and that one should follow it without regard to the will of the church, or even in defiance of that will, carries its own dangers, even when applied to such an itinerant ministry as Fraser exercised. When Paul and Barnabas set off on their first missionary journey, they did so as men commissioned by the church at Antioch, and to it they gave an account on their return (as they did, in another connection, to the church of Jerusalem, Acts 15:6-21). There is, of course, a real place for itinerant preachers and it is perfectly appropriate that they should have a wide area of discretion (and Fraser had the advantage, of course, that by the time of his licensing he was a man of independent means and in no need of financial support), but the itinerant is

---

12. See, for example, *The Second Book of Discipline*, III:6-9.

no more a freelancer than the pastor. He is a member of the body of Christ, he is no final judge of his own gifts, the gifts he has are for the benefit of the whole body, and he needs the church's counsels and prayers. He must also be aware of the damage he could do by wandering at will into another person's sphere of labour, ignorant of its peculiar circumstances and consequently liable to exacerbate its tensions. Indeed, one of the less welcome legacies of the Great Awakening was that it bequeathed to Western Christianity a culture of private spiritual enterprises, run on business lines, and leading to the huge (and lucrative) pseudo-ecclesiastical empires we see today.

There is no stereotypical call to the ministry any more than there can be a stereotypical pattern of conversion, and we can see this clearly if we compare Fraser's call with that of John Knox. Far from having a compelling sense of an inner call, Knox shrank from accepting the office of preacher even when it was pressed on him by the Castillians of St. Andrews;[13] and even those who had a real desire for the work have often been reluctant to volunteer and have waited for the church itself to take the initiative. We have also to factor in the case of such men as Thomas Chalmers, ordained while still unconverted, but called to a powerful evangelical ministry after later experiencing a great saving change. Nor should we overlook the fact, noted by Fraser (p. 229), that 'many are called of Christ who do not know it, but fear they are not,' do not respond to it, and live to regret it.

His public sufferings

By the time he has finished reflecting on his call to the ministry Fraser is close to the end of his narrative, even though his life still has twenty-seven years to run; and the one remaining chapter is headed, quite appropriately, 'Of my sufferings,' by which he means the public sufferings arising from his nonconformity and from his preaching without the bishop's authority (p. 267). He was not alone in these. By 1672, the number of dissenters was increasing, and these included not only the chief ministers, but also a large number of local gentry; and as the number of dissenters increased, so did the violence of the opposition. In 1674 Fraser was one of more than three hundred people who were 'intercommuned', that is, declared outlaws by royal writ. This was no small thing. Such writs were usually issued only

---

13. For the beginning of Knox's ministry, see D. Macleod, *Therefore the Truth I Speak: Scottish Theology 1500–1700*, p. 34.

against murderers and traitors, and they forbade any of His Majesty's subjects, on pain of death, to converse with the person named in the writ, to receive them into their homes, or to offer them any comfort.

The writ was unavailing, however, or, as Fraser puts it, it was 'powder without ball' (p. 270). In his own case, no one he cared for shunned his company. For two-and-a-half years, still intercommoned, he continued to preach, though fully aware that the bishops had him under constant surveillance, imagining him to be, as he says, 'of some parts, very active in preaching in the fields, and keeping up the Secession as they called it' (p. 271). Eventually, a price was put on his head, and in January 1677, while a guest in a home in Edinburgh, he was betrayed by a servant-maid and arrested by the Major of the city. This led to his first imprisonment on the Bass (January 1677 to July 1679), and his last months there must have been tense in the extreme. Archbishop Sharp had been assassinated on 3 May 1679, and the Covenanter forces had been crushed at Bothwell Bridge on 22 June. The prisoners on the Bass had good reason to fear the worst, but on 29 June 1679 the King ('out of what design I cannot tell,' comments Fraser) granted an Indulgence which included the command to set at liberty all the prisoners on the Bass who had been sentenced for mere nonconformity, and had not been accessories to 'the late rebellion'.[14]

But in early 1682 he was back in prison again. As he understood the terms of the release from the Bass, those who had been set at liberty were free to preach, but this was quickly modified to exclude meetings in the fields. He complied with this, and limited himself to house-conventicles. Even so, he was informed against, possibly on the slender pretext that if any of the hearers stepped outside, the house-conventicle was regarded as a field-meeting, 'and it was impossible for me to hinder or know when persons were without, and I thought it hard to shut doors upon them and had not freedom to do it' (p. 284). He was cited to appear before the

---

14. On 29 May 1679, the King's birthday, a body of radical Covenanters had ridden into Rutherglen, put out the celebratory bonfires, and forced the magistrates to accompany them to the Market Cross. There they read a manifesto denouncing the imposition of episcopacy, the outing of faithful presbyterian ministers, the Royal Supremacy over matters spiritual, and the illegal acts of the (Scottish) Privy Council. Armed rebellion was clearly in the air, and the battles of Drumclog (1 June) and Bothwell Bridge (22 June) followed soon afterwards (J. King Hewison, *The Covenanters: A History of the Church in Scotland from the Reformation to the Revolution;* 2 vols, Glasgow: John Smith and Son, 1908), Vol. 2, p. 292.

Privy Council, charged with preaching in the fields, preaching without authority, and venting principles that were 'pernicious, seditious, and rebellious'. He denied the charges, conducted himself astutely under cross-examination, and made such an impression that many of the councillors, he records, were much taken with his defence, and voted that he should be released. However, the matter being left to the bishops, he was sentenced to imprisonment in Blackness, to remain there till he had paid a fine of five thousand merks, and to give security either not to preach again or to go out of the kingdom. After a further six weeks' imprisonment in Edinburgh, he was taken to Blackness, where the young governor vented his spite by 'putting him into a gousty [sic], cold, wide, dark, filthy, smoky room, where I could not have lived six days, for smoke, darkness, melancholy, and cold' (p. 289). But relief came from an unexpected quarter: the governor's lady, a mere child fourteen years old, prevailed on him to change his room. Still, it was a 'sad place' where he could do nothing but pray for deliverance.

Unknown to him, however, his brother-in-law had petitioned the Privy Council on his behalf, craving that the fine be remitted, indicating that he was content to submit to the sentence of banishment, and requesting that he be sent at liberty. The request was granted, and after settling his affairs in Scotland he set off for London, arriving there on 16 June 1682.

But even in London he wasn't safe. Once there, he resumed preaching, mainly in private homes, but 1683 was the year of the Rye House plot,[15] and Crown agents were scouring the city looking for suspects. One of these agents chanced to visit a house in Cheapside where Fraser was transacting some business, recognised he was a stranger, decided he had some connection with the plot, and promptly detained him. Five or six hours later he was brought before a group of English Privy Councillors, including the King and his brother, James, Duke of York (the future King James II). He was asked what he knew of any plot, replied that he knew nothing, and was opposed to all violent attempts against His Majesty or his government. He was then asked whether he thought the killing of Archbishop Sharp was murder or not,[16] and replied that he had no connection with it, but was very grieved when he heard about it and would not justify it or have had a hand

---

15. This was a Whig conspiracy to kill both the King and the Prince of Wales, and put the Duke of Monmouth (the eldest illegitimate son of Charles II) on the throne. William Carstares was also arrested and tried on suspicion of being involved in the Plot.

16. Sharp had been assassinated in 1679.

in it for the whole world. However, being a doer of the law and not a judge of the law it was out of his sphere to judge whether it was murder or not: that belonged to His Majesty and his officers of justice, and as for his 'thoughts', he was not free to give an account of these to any human court. God alone was competent to judge these, and He had appointed a solemn court to be held for that purpose at the Last Day.

The interrogation then moved to the question of his attitude to the Solemn League and Covenant. Did he judge himself to be bound to it? 'I never took it,' he replied, 'nor was it ever tendered to me.'[17] He did, however, judge himself to be bound by what was of moral import in it and particularly to its 'two chief principles': 'reformation of our hearts and lives according to the Word of God' and the obligation to 'maintain and defend the king's just privileges, his person, and government' (p. 294).

The interrogation continued the following day, but this time it focused on the Oaths of Allegiance and Supremacy, and specifically on the Oxford Oath, which bound a man 'not to endeavour to make any alteration in the government either in state or church'. This Brae refused to do: apart from all else it would have bound him never to raise his voice against episcopacy.

For this he was sent to Newgate, and remained there for twenty-four weeks. Compared to the Bass and Blackness, life in the London prison was easy. He had one of the best rooms, large, clean and well-lit; the jailers were all very civil; he had comfortable fellowship with fellow-prisoners, 'and we wanted nothing, so that I could hardly call it suffering' (p. 296). His only serious grievance was that he had no privacy, 'for having a chamber-fellow with me, and all day oppressed with visitants, I could not in the twenty-four hours command one for myself.'

He was released promptly on the expiry of the twenty-four weeks. He took his leave of the Captain, thanking him for his civilities, and his account concludes with the grateful comment, 'My expenses in all not reaching above twenty pounds.'

These three imprisonments were all preceded by rigorous interrogations, though Brae was never subjected to torture: the authorities seemed to distinguish between those convicted only for nonconformity and those

---

17. The Solemn League and Covenant, a civil and religious league between the English and Scottish Parliaments (supported by the General Assembly of the Kirk), was signed in 1643. Brae was only four years old at the time.

charged with crimes that had anything of a political hue. In all these interrogations Fraser, aided by his knowledge of the law, comes across as an astute and quick-footed interviewee. He refused to answer questions on matters with which he was not charged, he limited himself to facts, and declined to divulge his thoughts and opinions, and he was consistently careful not to incriminate others. He never, for example, divulged the names of those who ordained him, despite repeated questioning. He was also careful not to condemn himself out of his own mouth; nor did he always feel himself surrounded by nothing but malice. Recalling his January 1677 interrogation, for example, he records that all the members of the committee were 'civil and sober persons' who would have been glad to deal with him leniently had they not been in such fear of the Archbishop, James Sharp, who, in a bitter invective, vehemently exaggerated his alleged crimes and portrayed him to the other councillors as a very 'odious and criminal person'.

Throughout these interrogations there was one point on which Brae was consistently clear: he was opposed to all violent attempts against His Majesty or government (p. 273) and even went so far as to say that he knew of no one, even among the most zealous asserters of the liberties of the people, who maintained that it was right to raise arms 'upon pretence of religion' (p. 273). This did not mean that armed resistance was never justified. It meant only that it was never justified in defence of religion.

Fraser made these remarks in the course of his interview prior to his first imprisonment on the Bass, and in the wake of the two major pitched battles of the Covenanting struggle: Drumclog on 1 June 1679 and Bothwell Bridge on 22 June that same year. By this time, repression had risen to new levels, and in response the practice had arisen, especially in the west, of carrying arms to the conventicles. It was one such armed (and large) conventicle that met at Drumclog, and when it was attacked by troops under the command of Graham of Claverhouse, the government forces suffered a heavy defeat. Encouraged by this success, the Covenanter forces then gathered in growing numbers at Bothwell Bridge, where they were routed by a ten-thousand strong detachment led by the Duke of Monmouth. Hundreds were killed, and over a thousand were taken prisoner and held under appalling conditions in Greyfriars churchyard. The ringleaders were executed, and those who refused to swear that they would never raise arms again were sentenced to transportation. Most of these died when the 'death-ship' carrying them to the West Indies foundered near the Orkneys in December 1679.[18]

Fraser had no sympathy with this recourse to the sword. He attributed it to 'some hot-heads' who thought, wrongly, that this was the way to deliver themselves from the hands of the oppressor, and he made his own position clear: 'I opposed rising in arms all I could, and preached against it, and exhorted them to patience and courageous using of the sword of the Spirit' (p. 254). He warned, too, that if they took to the sword, they would perish, whereas if they suffered patiently, God Himself would in some other way support and deliver them.

At the same time he recognised that there was great provocation: so great, indeed that he thought it was the design of government 'to stir us up that we might fall' (p. 255). But he noted, too, that amid the violent persecution the gospel prevailed more and more. Ministers still preached and laboured among the people, conventicles increased, many were converted, and the work of God did always prosper: 'until ... .'

'Until,' he adds, 'we destroyed ourselves,' first by needless divisions over the Indulgences,[19] and then 'by rash and unwarrantable taking up of arms unseasonably in the year 1679.' This is a clear reference to Bothwell Bridge, where, according to Fraser, great numbers of 'the dissenting party' gathered, but not in the Lord's strength, and by their divisions and ineptitudes ('follies') were made 'a prey to their enemies' (p. 255). The screw inevitably tightened, and men like Fraser and Hog, who now limited their preaching to house conventicles, found themselves charged as rebels and insurrectionists, potentially facing death-sentences as field-preachers, and ultimately sentenced to imprisonment on the Bass.

Surveying the Bass

Once on the Bass (a 'melancholy place', he calls it) Fraser surveyed the Rock with the professional eye of an estate-owner, and he has left us a

---

18. For an account of reprisals after the Battle of Bothwell Bridge, see James King Hewison, *The Covenanters: A History of the Church in Scotland from the Reformation to the Revolution*, Vol. 2, pp. 312-23.

19. The Indulgences were a series of royal decrees issued between 1669 and 1687 offering an amnesty to outed ministers on certain conditions. These Indulgences fractured Covenanter unity not only in the sense that some took advantage of them and some didn't, but also in the sense that serious tensions arose between the Indulged (who had 'failed in the day of trial') and the Non-indulged.

remarkably detailed description (pp. 275-77). Two miles north of the nearest point of land, he noted that it was three-quarters of a mile in circumference; the uppermost parts were covered with grass, but also hosted a herb-garden and some cherry trees; below the garden there was a chapel, but since no minister was provided to conduct divine service it was used as an ammunition store. He took particular note of the landing-places. Landing any where was both difficult and dangerous because of the violence of the swelling waves: sometimes so violent that they broke with a mighty force on the garrison walls six-hundred-and-twenty feet above sea level. There was but one place on the whole rock where you could land, and then only on a fair day and a full sea. If there were no full sea, you had to be craned up.

On the south side, where the rock fell away a little, there were several steps up to the governor's house, then several more steps leading up to a higher court which housed the prisoners and the soldiers, and then a path cut out of the rock and leading to the summit, where there was enough grass to feed twenty-four sheep, all of them 'very fat and good'. In these higher reaches there were several walks, sixty feet in length, where the prisoners sometimes entertained themselves. There was no well, the only water being provided by the rain and preserved in some hollow caverns dug out of the rock. Drinking-water had to be carried from the mainland by boat, and for this service the boatman had a salary of six pounds yearly, supplemented by whatever he received from the visitors he ferried across to see the prisoners. And finally, there were the several sorts of birds, particularly large numbers of solan-geese, 'whose young, well fledged, ready to fly, are taken, and so yield near one hundred pounds yearly'; but this, Fraser thought, was well below their real commercial potential. They might have yielded much more if they had been 'more carefully improved'.

At first glance, all this seems remote from Fraser's significance as a theologian, but when we look at his *Memoirs* we find him surveying his own mind with the same meticulous attention to detail as he applied to his survey of the Bass Rock (and presumably to his Brae estate). At first sight he is doing no more than complying with St Paul's injunction, 'Examine yourselves, whether ye be in the faith; prove your own selves' (2 Cor. 13:5), but we may also ask whether he is not also anticipating the course soon to be followed by Scottish philosophy from Frances Hutcheson to Thomas Reid. What distinguished this philosophy (known in its later phases as

'Scottish Realism')[20] was that it made the human mind itself an object of scientific observation. It assumed that the mind can know itself;[21] that by examination of our own consciousness we can discover what we perceive, know, believe, feel and desire; that we can identify which beliefs, if any, we hold intuitively; whether we are possessed of a moral sense; and what that moral sense commends as virtuous.

C. H. Spurgeon, in warmly commending Fraser's *Memoirs*, astutely notes that, 'As a record of human thought and emotion it is of great interest to the mental philosopher.'[22] But Fraser wasn't setting up as a mental philosopher or even, it has to be said, as an autobiographer. What makes his work 'exceedingly precious', as Spurgeon went on to note, is that it is 'a description of the experience of a deeply tried believer'. This is certainly what Fraser himself set out to do. He had derived great personal benefit from reading the records of other Christians' spiritual experiences, or, as John Henry Newman once put it, from tracing and studying 'the interior life of God's great saints',[23] and he was hopeful that the record of his own experiences would profit others. But in the Dedication to the *Memoirs*,[24] he also acknowledged the value to himself of 'a serious recalling to mind' of the Lord's dealings with him, even going so far as to declare that in nothing had he been 'more comforted and sanctified'.

His spiritual struggles

One of the most remarkable features of Fraser's *Memoirs* is his selection of what he deems worth recording. The modern reader would love to have detailed accounts of his sufferings. What did he have to endure as a field-preacher? What was daily life like on the Bass or in Blackness or Newgate? Who, apart from Hog and McKillican, were his fellow prisoners, what sort

---

20. For a brief survey, see Paul Helm, 'Scottish Realism,' in DSCHT.

21. An assumption shared by St Paul. Cf. 1 Corinthians 2:11: 'what man knoweth the spirit of a man, save the spirit of man which is in him?' The apostle goes on to add that, 'even so, the things of God knoweth no man, save the Spirit of God.' This divine self-knowledge is the presupposition of revelation, in which God shares with us a little of what He knows about Himself.

22. Quoted in Donald Beaton, *Noted Ministers of the Northern Highlands* (Inverness: Northern Counties Publishing Company, 1929), p. 36.

23. Quoted in Alexander Whyte, *James Fraser, Laird of Brea* (Edinburgh: Oliphant, Anderson and Ferrier, 1911), p. 9.

24. To Mr Thomas Ross, into whose keeping he had committed the manuscript.

of personalities were they, and how did they encourage each other or engage with the other prisoners? But in a volume of over three hundred pages, only a few are devoted to his 'public sufferings', and these few come towards the end. What we have, instead, is an intense and detailed account of his spiritual struggles, his decays and recoveries, his recurring episodes of 'dumpishness' and, above all, his doubts about his conversion, his personal interest in Christ and even about the existence of God.

These doubts were particularly intense in the three-year period following his conversion. In recollection, he viewed them as a deliberate strategy on the part of the Tempter, who, he noted, was continually making him 'raze the foundations' by proposing to him false marks of grace and sanctification, with the result that he didn't merely doubt his conversion, but firmly believed that he wasn't converted at all.

But apart from the Tempter's role, Fraser was also aware that there were serious 'objective grounds' for his doubts and he patiently describes no fewer than twenty of these (pp. 169-84). Many believers will have felt the force of some of them; poor Brae felt the force of all of them but, writing with the benefit of hindsight, he also answers them, giving us, in effect, a record of a sustained argument he had with himself.

The first reason for his lack of assurance was that he hadn't experienced such a deep work of preparation as he found described in theological treatises on the new birth. To this he replies that he had nevertheless been brought to see his lost natural condition as the greatest of all evils; he had made 'restless endeavours' to come out of it; and when he had discovered that in himself he was powerless to do so, 'the Lord did by a marvellous light discover the Lord Jesus to me as the Saviour of sinners and their full happiness; and my heart immediately closed with Him wholly and fully, which in its fruits hath continued to this day.'[25] But he also went on to observe that though the 'substantials of conversion' were the same in all cases, they were not all the same in 'circumstantials', and particularly in the length, measure and manner of conviction of sin. 'The question,' he added, 'is not so much how Christ came in, as *if* He be in. If ye find the fruits of holiness, it is well, though ye know not how they were sown or grown' (p. 170, italics added).

A second ground of his doubting his conversion was that he had only a rational, notional and natural knowledge of God, and that he was ignorant

---

25. *Memoirs*, p. 169. Clearly, Fraser was not plagued by doubts all his life.

of the glory of Christ as He really is. Here he finds comfort in the fact that he is not alone in this. All human knowledge of God is imperfect, and the most eminent saints have lamented their ignorance. 'This,' he comments, 'is a time of absence,' by which he means a time when we do not see God face to face. We have only a 'dark knowledge' of Him as One who is not present. Only in heaven will we know Christ as He is (and he wonders whether the sight we shall have of Him then will be specifically different from the sight we have of Him now). Nevertheless, he did find in himself the *effects* of real saving knowledge: he trusted Christ, he prized and esteemed Him, he longed for Him above all things, and he mourned for His absence as the greatest of all evils; but he adds, 'Our knowledge of God is better discovered in our obedience to Him than in our uptakings of Him.' 'The Lord,' he concludes, 'knows that it is the thing in the world I have most desired, to know God and to see His glory' (p. 172).

However, it wasn't only his dim apprehension of the glory of Christ that troubled him. He also had 'unkindly' conceptions of the Lord as a strange God rather than as a father, and friend and husband. This made it hard for him to trust Him with his whole heart, and this in turn made him fear that he lacked the spirit of adoption, and was therefore not a son of God, but a servant.

He admits that there had been grounds for this complaint in his past, but he tells himself that it is no longer the case. By serious meditation on Christ, and on His providence towards himself, he has come to see the Lord under the kindly notion of a Father, 'my best and nearest friend'. On the other hand, there was always the danger that those who had escaped from 'the spirit of bondage' would betake themselves to it again because, 'as no sin is perfectly healed in this life, so neither is the legal spirit of fear perfectly cast out' (p. 174).

A further factor contributing to his lack of assurance was a fear that he had never experienced the special love that God shows to His people. He had experienced only 'common mercies', nothing extraordinary. However, closer scrutiny showed that these 'common mercies' had special love and favour engraved on them. Besides, the blessings we meet with in this life are but the 'earnest' of the bargain: a part of what was promised, but also a pledge that the rest will follow;[26] and when it comes to an 'earnest', it is

---

26. The image of the 'earnest' (Gk. *arrabōn*) is taken from Ephesians 1:14, which portrays the Holy Spirit as the deposit, guaranteeing that the rest of the inheritance will follow.

equally secure whether it be little or much. The greatness of the estate is not to be measured by this first instalment, and 'we should judge of the Lord's love rather by His sanctifying influences, humbling and strengthening the heart, than by His ravishing enjoyments and consolations.'

Then, by way of further explanation, he adds, 'This is an evil time, a time of famine and beggary, in which it is good to be preserved from starving, and in which a little is worth twice as much as at another time.' The 'evil time' he is referring to is, of course, the time of the later Covenanters (1660 to 1688), and it was certainly an evil time in the sense that faithful preachers and their followers were under the lash. But then, an age which enjoyed the ministry of men such as William Guthrie, Donald Cargill, Alexander Peden, Alexander Shields, John Livingstone, John Welch of Irongray and Thomas Hog of Kiltearn, was hardly an age of spiritual famine. What Fraser's comment shows is the tendency of churchmen of all ages to bemoan their times, comparing them unfavourably to a glorious past while waiting for an even more glorious future. The danger is that, living in an age on which those who follow us may well look back with envy, we miss the best days of our lives waiting for them to happen.

The last ground of his doubting appears to have been prompted by the reference in Matthew 25:30 to the unprofitable servant who was cast into outer darkness. When Fraser compared his own service to that of former saints, he couldn't conceive how Christ could ever say to him, 'Well done, good and faithful servant' (Matt. 25:21). But then, he reasons with himself, heaven is not promised to some special measure of grace, but to grace simply. The Lord accepts widows' mites, cups of cold water, and faith as small as a mustard seed (Matt. 17:21); and so, Brea concludes, 'I do service, though I cannot weigh it by measure. Such is the condescendency and loveliness of Christ that He will crown those duties we are ashamed to own.' Just as parents are wonderfully pleased with the poorest and simplest actions of their children, so Christ is soon pleased, and his yoke is easy.

But the last word here must be that works, of whatever kind or measure, are not our title to glory. Heaven comes by blood, and here Fraser quotes Rutherford, 'No law music in heaven; no, but "worthy is the Lamb."' And this section of the *Memoirs* closes on this note:

> Look not to what thou hast done, but to what Christ has done; ye neither share in whole nor in part with Christ: good works are mentioned, not to purchase glory by, but to evidence an interest in Christ, and sincerity in grace; if there

be as much as will evidence sincerity, there is enough. The least gold is gold as well as the greatest piece (p. 183).

Atheistical doubts

But Fraser's doubts weren't confined to the question whether he was truly converted. Very shortly after his conversion he suffered a violent attack of atheistic doubts, though it is clear that this was not entirely a new thing. They had been there before, hissing like serpents, but had 'quieted': quieted, but not killed, and now they returned with a vengeance.

The description he gives of this episode in his life is far removed from the calm, logical summaries we have seen him give of the reasons for his decays, the steps of his recovery, and his call to the ministry. Here, he says, he was 'utterly jumbled', and the writing reflects that, flitting from aspect to aspect of the struggle. He was troubled by the fact that he could find no conclusive arguments for the truth of Scripture (p. 91); then he was troubled by the thought that he was an atheist; then he was terrified with a feeling of utter helplessness, because he was cut off from his usual supports. There was no God to turn to, and no Bible to yield him comfort: 'When the foundations are loosed, what means can I use? To whom shall I go when I doubt the being of God?' (p. 88). His melancholy thoughts then set him off in another direction, painting God to him as one terrible and fearful, one who had been watching over him all his life to do him evil; and this in turn stirred up the hatred and aversion to God that lay as scum in his heart. 'I was,' he wrote, 'a right representation of the damned in hell – tormented and hopeless, and raging against God and His providences' (p. 89). But in the next breath he would say, 'What a strange thing is this! thou thinkest there is no God, and yet art afraid of Him.' Then, looking back, he declares, 'The truth is, I did not positively believe that there is no God, but was afraid that I did not believe that there was one; and my fear of God did prove a God, and my belief of a deity.' Yet, a little earlier he had written that his soul abhorred God, and though he had never said it with his tongue, his heart wished that there were no God.

What of his recovery? One key factor was that amid all this turmoil he continued to read, pray and meditate, and this brought some healing, even though a cloud quickly came and overshadowed it. His doubts did not put an end to his religious exercises, and these, he thought, did him good, albeit insensibly. From a pastoral point of view this may be the best advice to give to someone who is going through a similar period of radical doubting. The Bible is its own best witness, but it doesn't bear that witness if we stop reading it.

Secondly, there was the impression made on him by 'T. H.', 'a godly and prudent man.' Fraser doesn't identify him, but he does speak of him as a minister (p. 93) and it is virtually certain that the reference is to Thomas Hog, who, he says, did him much good, not only by his company but especially by what he had to say about the nature of temptations and how the devil beats them into the soul violently by bold assertions, without reasons. T. H., he recalls, shed marvellous light on the Scriptures, bringing out their excellence: an excellence which was itself an evidence of Godhead.

But what he found most impressive about Hog was his personality. He had a cheerfulness which seemed to flow from a deep inner joy based on his faith in God. Fraser seems to have been unfortunate in his experience of professing Christians, at least during this period of violent attacks of doubt. They fell so far short of what they professed that their lives served only to confirm his atheism and to make him think 'a saint was but a fancy' (p. 92). In Hog, however, he saw a New Testament spirit, and was 'somewhat persuaded' by his holiness, his cheerfulness in God and his deep reach in spiritual mysteries, that there was a God, and that holiness was attainable: 'Such was the power of God in him, that with his seasonable discourse and prayer he would charm, and calm, and quiet my storms, even when I despaired of help and thought it impossible' (p. 92).

Yet it was shortly after a visit to Hog's house that matters came to a head. As he attempted to pray, his atheistical thoughts assaulted him with such violence that he was driven from his knees, unable to put four sentences together. He then sat on his knees and said to the Lord, 'If Thou be, Thou art Almighty, and canst reveal as much of Thyself as may convince me, and put away this storm, and convince me there is a God, and that Thy word is true; and if this very night Thou do, I will look upon it as a sufficient demonstration of Thy being.' After this, he sat passively by the fire, meditating on some rational arguments for the truth of the Scriptures, and not finding any 'but such as might be shifted' (p. 93).

At last, sitting pensively, he had his *eureka* moment: 'What a fool hast thou been!' he suddenly exclaimed, and thus began a dialogue with himself.

'Are you an atheist,' he asked, 'because you cannot prove there is a God? Or is there no God because you cannot demonstrably prove that there is? Or, because it is *possible* that honest men might lie, is it therefore *true* that the apostles lied? Have you ever seen an argument that demonstrated that there is no God, or that the Scriptures are false?'

Then, changing tack, he addresses the fallacy (under which he himself had clearly laboured) that a belief cannot be dismissed as untrue simply because objections can be raised against it. Even in the case of something that rested on the strongest evidential basis, might 'answers not be given against it, though undoubtedly true?'

But it wasn't reasoning alone that delivered him from the violent storm of doubts. It was, he says, the Lord shining upon it, 'and by the almighty power of Christ my clouds did fly away' (p. 94); and having reached this point, he proceeds, as was his wont, to ponder the lessons the experience had taught him.

For Fraser, this quest for certainty with regard to the existence of God was no mere intellectual matter. His relationship with God was the most important relationship in his life, and while it would have been devastating to discover that God didn't love him, it would have been utterly traumatic to find out that He didn't exist at all. It would have been a mega-bereavement. To many, it is a matter of utter indifference whether God is alive or dead, but not to Fraser. For him, it would have meant all the lights going out and the world being plunged into unbearable darkness: no duties, no hope, no help, no meaning. He needed Him, he wished Him to be there, and he would happily have admitted that there was a void in his heart that only God could fill.

On the other hand, his struggle wasn't a struggle to come to faith. He had already done that, and if St Paul is to be believed, it wasn't to be dated only from the moment of his conversion. According to the apostle, God has already introduced Himself to all human beings through the visible creation, and all of us are so constructed that we get the message loud and clear. His eternal power and divinity are not only clearly revealed, but clearly perceived (Rom. 1:20), and this is the seed from which all the world's religions grow. Now, in Fraser's case, this fundamental certainty was under attack; and it wasn't as if he himself had created the problem by his excessive introspection or by his need for an unattainable degree of certainty. It was satanic: 'Satan was let out upon me' (p. 87). This may be an unwelcome note to strike in modern ears, but it is a key element in the biblical world-view. Jesus' own temptations came from the Devil (Matt. 4:1); St Paul's thorn in the flesh was 'a messenger of Satan' (2 Cor. 12:7); and St Peter warns us that the Adversary, the great spiritual predator, is constantly on the prowl looking for Christians to destroy (1 Pet. 5:8). Fraser was convinced that it was from this source, from the gates of Pandemonium, that the barrage of doubts, questions and blasphemies was launched against him: a barrage tailored, no doubt, to his own temperament and cast of mind, but one which his mind by itself would never have launched.

But the barrage itself was not backed up with cogent reasons. Instead, the Tempter wisely limited himself to asking Fraser reasons for his own faith. This is a luxury that atheism (and its dominant modern form, secularism) always claims. It puts the burden of proof on theistic believers. They must demonstrate that God exists, and then all that is incumbent on atheists is to cross-examine and raise objections, while leaving no evidence in support of their view that the universe was its own creator; or, as Fraser saw so clearly, rather than argue from what is known to be true, they argue from what is possible.

Fraser acknowledged that rational evidence by itself could offer no unshakeable foundation for belief in the existence of God. Part of the problem here, especially in our post-Enlightenment world, is the insistence that 'rational' means a process of reasoning that sets aside all presuppositions. But this is itself a presupposition, and a vulnerable one. All human thinking has to begin with certain assumptions, whether it be that we can believe what we see, the authority of some inward moral sense or, most fundamentally, the competence of the mind itself.

It is the inability of philosophy to 'prove' such presuppositions that creates the illusion that 'rational proof' is impossible in such domains as theology, history, morals and aesthetics. Besides, unbelief is not merely a matter of the mind: it is also a matter of the will. This is why the New Testament often equates disbelief with disobedience. It is a refusal to be persuaded or even, as with the majority of Paul's hearers in Athens, a refusal to listen (Acts 17:22-33).

Yet, although he recognised the insufficiency of reason alone (as did Immanuel Kant), reasoning (or what he called 'passive meditation') did play a part in Fraser's recovery of faith: a reminder that a faith which did not begin with reasoning can nevertheless subsequently (*a posteriori*) find reasons to justify itself. This is what Anselm meant when he spoke of *fides quaerens intellectum*.[27] Faith seeks to understand itself and to assure itself that it is well-founded; and faith is not so proud as to refuse to stoop to repelling objections. Fraser was able to satisfy himself that atheism had never offered on its own behalf the 'demonstrative evidence' it demanded of theism; that the fact that objections may be raised against a certain position doesn't mean that the position is false; and that the fact of an alternative view being 'possible' doesn't necessarily mean that it is true.

But then, as in all other areas of human life, without the Lord evidence is in vain. The strongest evidence can leave us in the dark or, alternatively, leave us with nothing more than the faith of devils. There is an ungodly theism as well as an ungodly atheism. Fraser had come to the conclusion that his doubts were so violent that it would take a miracle to remove them, and so he prayed for one, including in his prayer the pledge that he would seek no other proof of a divine being than the removing of his doubts and fears. If the Lord did this, he would doubt no more (p. 91). God did hear, the violence ceased, peace descended, and peace, Fraser concluded, was 'a created thing of God'.

Microscopic introspection

J. Elder Cumming in his volume, *Holy Men of God from St. Augustine to Yesterday*,[28] devotes a chapter to Fraser of Brea and describes him as one who lived at a depth that few Christians have ever reached. But at the same time he is clearly uneasy about the kind of experience recorded in the *Memoirs*. What he sees there is a man dogged by a spirit of legalism, given to an excessive, microscopic examination of his own corrupt heart, and not only afflicted by doubts but inclined to cherish them as a mark of humility. He was a melancholy instance, comments Cumming, of those children of God who have deemed themselves under His ban and live their lives under

---

27. *Fides Quaerens Intellectum* (*Faith in Quest of Understanding*) was the original title of Anselm's book, *Proslogion*. Its seminal statement, as laid down in the first chapter, is, 'I do not seek to understand so that I may believe, but I believe so that I may understand.' Anselm's approach profoundly influenced Karl Barth (see his *Fides Quaerens Intellectum: Anselm's Proof of the Existence of God*; English translation by Ian W. Robertson, London: SCM Press, 1960).

28. London: Hodder and Stoughton, 1893. Cumming (1830–1909) was a Church of Scotland minister who served successively in the parishes of St John's (Perth), Newington (Edinburgh) and Sandyford (Glasgow).

a cloud that seldom lifts: 'It is a life to be read often in wonder, sometimes in awe, but not to be imitated.'[29]

But Cumming is not content with expressing reservations about the personal spirituality of Fraser. He takes a wider view, and sees 'the *perfervidum* of the national character' conspicuous throughout the *Memoirs*.[30] By 'the national character' he means the character of the Highland section of the Scottish nation, and particularly the piety characteristic of its Christian people: strength and intensity, continual self-questioning, an unwillingness to claim to be converted; the same array of doubts we find in Fraser, the same idea that doubt is the safest attitude, the same endless weighing of the evidence bearing on our own inward spiritual condition. These, he claimed, were still to be found among the Christian people of the Highlands, and this is due to Fraser's enduring influence.

Laying aside for the moment Cumming's comments on the religion of what he calls the 'North Country', is his portrait fair to Fraser? Was he really a religious neurotic? It is certainly not the case, as Cumming claims, that Brea's clouds never lifted and that he spent all his days under the shadow of melancholy (what Fraser himself called 'dumpishness'). The violent storms of doubts and fears were chiefly evident in the three years following his conversion in 1656, and he continued subject to alternating periods of spiritual depression and recovery until about 1665 (the year to which he assigns his 'last storm', p. 132).

To be fair to Fraser, however, we must remember that during these years his problems weren't entirely spiritual. He was also under considerable stress due to the sorry state of his Brae state: his creditors wouldn't pay, debtors pursued him at law, and at one point he faced the prospect of losing twenty thousand pounds (a huge sum in those days).

But even during those years there were periods when he felt refreshed, enjoyed fellowship with God, and experienced mighty gales of the Spirit. Nor were they years of stagnation and paralysis. In 1664, he made the decision to forsake the preaching of the curates and became increasingly involved in house-conventicles; by around 1665 he was already exhorting and instructing, and receiving encouraging feedback from 'professors' in the

---

29. ibid., p. 124.

30. ibid., p. 123.

South. At this time, too, he wrote his treatise against hearing the curates,[31] as well as several others which have, unfortunately, been lost; and when he came up for examination prior to his ordination in 1672 (aged thirty-three) he could describe his examiners as 'intimately and of a long time acquainted with me, having *frequently* preached in their hearing' (p. 236, italics added). In fact, the ordination itself was probably a deliberate move on the part of older ministers, keenly alert to presbyterian proprieties, to regularise a ministry which had been going on for several years, and with clear signs of divine blessing. Clearly, his 'dumpishness' did not lead to any abatement of his zeal.

The *Memoirs* conclude with his release from Newgate in 1684, but from 1665 we hear nothing of internal conflicts. Even in his periods of imprisonment (which are themselves alluded to only summarily) he shows no signs of morbid introspection or melancholy: indeed it was during the first of these, on the Bass Rock, that he wrote his *Treatise on Justifying Faith*: the lengthy, elaborate, scholarly and closely reasoned treatise on which his reputation as a theologian rests.[32]

Nor is it the case that it was his rigorous self-scrutiny that fuelled his doubts and fears. We must respect his own view that their real source lay outside of himself in satanic agency. After all, this was the experience of our Lord Himself. When Satan approached Him in the wilderness, the main point of his attack was to put a big 'If' against His sense of His divine sonship (Matt. 4:3); and later, it was a 'messenger of Satan' that buffeted St Paul (2 Cor. 12:7). Every Christian is subject to such attacks, without warning and without reasons, and once the seed of doubt is sown it can be enormously difficult to dislodge it.

Considered against this background, the truth is not that Fraser's introspection bred the doubts, but that his need to settle the issue, his need for certainty, led him, as he put it, to 'fall upon' an examination of his spiritual estate, assessing his condition by the rule of Scripture and the lives of the saints, 'and in the conclusion I found a marvellous light of God's

---

31. *The Lawfulness and Duty of Separation from Corrupt Ministers and Churches Explained and Vindicated.* This was not published, however, till 1744, when it served the purposes of the Seceders, who disapproved strongly of evangelicals who remained in the Establishment after the Secession.

32. James Fraser, *A Treatise on Justifying Faith* (Edinburgh: 1st edition 1722; 2nd edition with Appendix, 1749). The next chapter will look more closely at this volume and its significance.

Spirit through the Word, shining on my soul; and I found that according to the Scripture I was converted, and that the names, qualities, practices, and exercises of saints did agree with me' (p. 137). He records, too, that his survey of his spiritual estate showed that not only had he himself made many mistakes as to the nature of sanctification, but that most of the supposed marks of grace mentioned in books of Practical Divinity were unsound, and apt to mislead the reader; and this, clearly, had been a contributing factor to his own lack of assurance, particularly the stress that such books laid on the importance of a preparatory 'law-work'. He thereupon cast them aside, with the comment, 'Oh, what need is there of wisdom and light in the giving of marks! and what a great sin is it, either to speak or write of such marks at random!' (p. 137). Then, although admitting that Satan had made him 'pore excessively on evidences of grace' (p. 218) and occupy himself in continually laying the foundation 'and trying it, as thinking it never sure enough,' he clearly had no regrets about writing 'this Book of my Life, in which I found marvellous assistance, and found it a blessed mean to warm my heart with love to Christ, to see through many intricacies of my life which were before as a mist to me, and did tend much to my unsettling' (p. 149). Fraser needed certainty, because his relationship with God was the most important thing in his life, and his rigorous review of the workings of his own mind contributed to that certainty. However, his faith did not rest on the state of his own soul, but on the all-sufficiency of Christ.

Fraser and the national character

But what of Cumming's assertion that Fraser's struggles reflect the national character of the Scottish Highlander? Was he a typical Highlander, and do typical Highland Christians pass their days under a cloud of doubt and self-questioning, prohibited by the religious culture around them from enjoying an assurance of salvation?

Part of the problem here is that the difference between the Protestantism of the Highlands and the Protestantism of the Lowlands is too often greatly exaggerated. There was but one Scottish Reformation, initiated by Patrick Hamilton and consolidated under the leadership of John Knox in 1560. The Highlands had been affected by this movement from the beginning, particularly through the port of Cromarty, a convenient entry-point for Protestant literature from Germany; and after 1560, the Reformed Kirk quickly made its presence felt, not only on the eastern seaboards of Inverness-shire, Moray and Ross, but also in Argyll. As early as 1564, the General Assembly appointed Thomas Ross its Commissioner to Ross, charged with establishing and developing a work already begun. In 1567, John Carswell, originally Superintendent of Argyll but by this time Bishop of the Isles, published a Gaelic translation of Knox's *Book of Common Order*;[33] Calvin's *Catechism* was translated into Gaelic in 1631; the first fifty Psalms in 1659, with an appended translation of the Shorter Catechism;[34] and the Confession of Faith in 1725. It is safe to assume that, patchy as it was in those early days, particularly in the north-west, the Reformation in the south had its equivalent not only in those Highland communities which had already embraced the English language, but also in the Gaidhealtachd (that is, the Gaelic speaking communities of the Highlands).

But there were also other factors which should serve as a warning against the idea that Highland Protestantism developed separately from the south. Highland ministers had to undergo the same programme of university education as their counterparts in the south, many of them in Aberdeen; the powerful influence of Robert Bruce had imposed its stamp on the eastern counties before Fraser was born and, conversely, John Maclaurin (1694–1754), a Gaelic-speaking native of Argyll, would be a major influence in Glasgow at the very moment that Fraser's *Memoirs* went to press. A comparison of Boston's *Memoirs*, reflecting the religious life of the Borders, and Donald Sage's *Memorabilia Domestica*,[35] reflecting the religious life of the Highlands, makes plain that the same beliefs and practices (including the pattern of Communion Seasons) prevailed north and south. Even the practice of 'putting out the line', now so distinctive of Gaelic psalm-singing, was but a vastly-improved version of what was the custom in the churches of the south till the close of the eighteenth century.

Again, the experiences described in his *Memoirs* were by no means unique to Fraser nor peculiar to Highland Christians. In fact, they are already evident in Scripture itself. Psalm 88, for example, plumbs depths more profound than even Fraser ever reached: 'Thou hast laid me in the lowest pit, in darkness, in

33. *Foirm na n-Urrnuidhheadh.* According to Dr Donald Maclean, writing in 1912, only three copies of Carswell's book were then known to exist (*The Literature of the Scottish Gael*; Edinburgh: William Hodge and Company, 1912, p. 12).

34. The complete Psalter was translated in 1694.

35. Donald Sage, *Memorabilia Domestica; or Parish Life in the North of Scotland* (1889; 2nd edition, Wick: William Rae, 1899).

the deeps,' cries the psalmist in verse 6; and then in verses 14 and 16, he calls out, 'Lord, why castest thou off my soul? Why hidest thou thy face from me? Thy fierce wrath goeth over me; thy terrors have cut me off.'

This is never where a believer *should* be, but it is sometimes where he is. It is not merely a case of losing sight of the love of God: even the psalmist's faith in providence, and his hope of life after death, seem to have been lost. Stunned and stupefied with sorrow, as Calvin remarks, he is rendered unfit for the business of human life, the light of faith is extinguished in him, ill-advised words escape from his lips, and 'these lamentations at first sight would seem to indicate a state of mind in which sorrow without any consolation prevailed ... a sense of the divine anger must necessarily have agitated his mind with sore disquietude.'[36]

Besides, any biblical evaluation of religious experience must take account of Jesus' description of the 'blessed' as people who are poor in spirit, mourn, and are spiritually hungry (Matt. 5:3, 4, 6). These words do not point to the same levels of distress as are recorded in either Fraser's *Memoirs* or the eighty-eighth Psalm, but they do indicate that every believer, simply as a believer, has surveyed his own spiritual estate, faces the truth about himself, lives in the light of profound self-knowledge, and is led by that knowledge to be meek and merciful in relation to others; and we know from Romans Seven that the Apostle Paul, too, having surveyed the workings of his own mind, cried out in anguish, 'Wretched man that I am!' (Rom. 7:24). But then, like Fraser, he found relief and solace in the core gospel message, 'There is no condemnation for those who are in Christ Jesus' (Rom. 8:1). He would never have known the glory of that message had he not first known that he was a condemned and ruined sinner.

But what of believers of other climes and other ages? One thing that quickly strikes us is that the Protestants of the South of Scotland were no strangers to the doubts and fears experienced by the North-countryman, James Fraser. Robert Bruce experienced dreadful agonies of conscience, and even after he found peace he was still troubled by radical doubts; Samuel Rutherford lamented, 'I am put often to ask, if Christ and I did ever shake hands together in earnest';[37] and it is clear from their published sermons and

---

36. John Calvin, *Commentary on the Book of Psalms* (Edinburgh: Calvin Translation Society, 5 Vols., 1845–49), Vol. 3, pp. 415-16.

37. *Letters of Samuel Rutherford*, ed. Andrew A. Bonar (1891. Reprinted Edinburgh: Banner of Truth Trust, 1984), p. 315.

other writings that ministers in the Lowlands, no less than in the Highlands, were serving congregations where lack of assurance was an endemic problem. For example, the whole point of David Dickson's *Therapeutica Sacra* was to bring healing to those who were suffering from the spiritual disease of doubting whether they had been born again, and to do so by drawing them to faith in the divine covenants.[38] At the same time, Andrew Gray (1633–56), Minister of Glasgow's High Kirk, was preaching a series of three sermons on 'The Faith of Assurance' and tracing with the same thoroughness as Fraser the obstacles that lie in its way. He presses home the duty of seeking assurance, but at the same time warns that there are two great balances in which professed believers might weigh themselves. Some weigh themselves in the balances of deceit, approving themselves where Christ would never approve; others weigh themselves in 'the balances of the sanctuary' and thus are able, 'upon solid and most spiritual grounds,' to look Christ in the face and say, 'Thou art mine.'[39]

Another older contemporary of Fraser's was William Guthrie of Fenwick, born near Brechin in 1620, himself a sufferer for the Covenant, and celebrated as the author of the spiritual classic, *The Trial of a Saving Interest in Christ*, published around 1658 (the time of Fraser's conversion).[40] It is in two parts: Part I devoted to, 'The Trial [Test] of a Saving Interest in Christ'; Part II to, 'How to attain a Saving Interest in Christ'. It is not, like Fraser's *Memoirs*, autobiographical, but it describes the same spiritual landscape. In particular, it highlights the sort of questions that Scottish Christians, north and south, were asking in the mid-seventeenth century, and devotes almost two hundred tightly argued pages to discussing the mistakes people make regarding their interest, the marks of a saving change, and the evidences of

---

38. The English version of *Therapeutica Sacra* was first published in 1664. For relevant selections from this work, see *Select Practical Writings of David Dickson* (Edinburgh: Free Church of Scotland, 1845), pp. 198-299.

39. *The Works of the Reverend and Pious Andrew Gray* (Aberdeen: George King, 1839), p. 195. The three sermons on 'faith and assurance' occupy pp. 183-211. On the same page, however, Gray warns that there are some who are 'more desirous to know if they be in Christ, than indeed to be in him.'

40. For biographical information on Guthrie, see 'Memoirs of the Life and Character of Mr William Guthrie, Minister at Fenwick. By the Rev. William Dunlop, with Additions by the Rev. Robert Wodrow, and Rev. Robert Traill' in *Select Biographies,* ed. Rev. W. K. Tweedie (Edinburgh: Wodrow Society, 1847), Vol. 2, pp. 29-66. These 'Memoirs' formed part of the original Preface to *The Trial of a Saving Interest in Christ.* This classic was reprinted in 1951 by the Publications Committee of the Free Presbyterian Church under the title, *The Christian's Great Interest.*

a saved state. The section concludes with a memorable description of faith's view of Christ: 'now the heart is so enlarged for Him as that less cannot satisfy, and more is not desired.'[41]

It is a brilliant book,[42] as thorough in its own way as Fraser's, though without its atheistic doubts and its awareness of the demonic. This doesn't mean, however, that it unfailingly achieves the object Guthrie had in view, and it is one of the paradoxes of the spiritual life that the attempt to give reassurance sometimes succeeds only in creating doubt. I have a painful memory, going back some sixty years, of a moment when I recommended *The Christian's Great Interest* to a venerable mother-in-Israel, who at the time was under a spiritual cloud. 'Oh,' she said, 'it was that book that put me down in the first place.' Self-examination will not always produce the outcome we hope for.

But if Fraser had his peers in the South of Scotland he also had them further afield. Germany had its Martin Luther, and England had its John Bunyan and William Cowper, the latter crying, in one of his greatest hymns:

> Return, O holy Dove, return
> Sweet Messenger of rest!
> I hate the sins that made Thee mourn
> And drove Thee from my breast. [43]

Yet no one seriously suggests that the travails of Bunyan and Cowper are symptomatic of the 'national character' of the English; nor have people drawn great ethnological conclusions from the fact that Thomas Shepard (1605–49), although celebrated as a New England searcher of souls, was actually born near Northampton in Great Britain;[44] nor, yet again, have such conclusions been drawn from the fact that the English Puritan,

---

41. *The Christian's Great Interest*, p. 43.

42. The 'Memoirs' (p. 55) record an occasion when John Owen pulled out of his pocket 'a little gilded copy of this treatise,' described it as his *Vade mecum* which, along with his Greek Testament, he carried with him wherever he went, and declared, 'That author I take to have been one of the greatest divines that ever wrote. I have written several folios, but there is more divinity in it than in them all.'

43. From the hymn, 'O for a closer walk with God'. Cowper's friend and mentor, John Newton, was not a depressive, but he still put an 'if' into his best-known hymn, 'Glorious things of thee are spoken,' when he wrote, 'Saviour, *if* of Zion's city I, through grace, a member am' (italics added).

44. Shepherd (1605–49) was the author of such works as *The Sound Believer* and *The Parable of the Ten Virgins Opened and Applied*.

Richard Sibbes, felt called upon, 'at the desire and for the good of weaker Christians,' to publish in 1630 a series of sermons on *The Bruised Reed and the Smoking Flax;*[45] or that Jonathan Edwards, disturbed by some features of the Great Awakening, deemed it necessary to write a treatise *On the Distinguishing Marks of a Work of the Spirit of God* (1741).[46]

What made the searching, discriminatory preaching of such men as Sibbes, Gray and Edwards necessary? The answer is summed up in the title of another of Jonathan Edwards' works, 'Sinners in Zion Tenderly Warned.'[47] From the very beginning, the Church has contained members who were Christians in name only and who were thus in grave danger of being disowned by Christ at the Great Day.[48] There are those who regard their mere membership of the church as a guarantee of salvation; others who pride themselves on their (genuine) spiritual gifts; others who believe that their zealous theological orthodoxy will lead them safely home; and yet others who rest assured on the basis of a dramatic conversion experience, moments of spiritual ecstasy, or even close encounters, as they imagine them, with the flames of hell.

It was against this background that ministers saw it as their duty to warn people of the danger of self-delusion and to disabuse them of vain self-confidence. Here the instilling of self-doubt was the beginning of the road to recovery, and while the need for sounding the spiritual alarm is ever-present, it becomes especially urgent in some specific situations. For example, when, as was the case in seventeenth-century Scotland and England, there is a 'church by law established', every parishioner is easily

---

45. *Works of Richard Sibbes,* Vol. 1 (1862. Reprinted Edinburgh: Banner of Truth Trust, 1973), pp. 33-101. Sibbes' focus is on the question, How shall we know whether we are such as those that may expect mercy? 'Christ's course,' he says, 'is first to wound, then to heal. No sound, whole soul shall ever enter into heaven' (p. 46). Sibbes returned to the theme in his later (1635) treatise, *The Soul's Conflict With Itself,* where he writes, 'How many imagine their failings to be fallings, and their fallings to fallings away; infirmities to be presumptions; every sin against conscience, to be the sin against the Holy Ghost' (*Works,* Vol. 1, p. 137).

46. The most accessible edition is in *Select Works of Jonathan Edwards,* Volume 1 (London: Banner of Truth Trust, 1965), pp. 75-147.

47. *The Works of Jonathan Edwards* (2 Volumes 1834. Reprinted Edinburgh: Banner of Truth Trust, 1974), Vol. 2, pp. 201-06.

48. 'Many will say to me at that day, Lord, Lord, have we not prophesied in thy name? and in thy name have cast out devils? and in thy name done many wonderful works? And then will I profess unto them, I never knew you: depart from me, ye that work iniquity' (Matt. 7:22-23).

led to see himself as a Christian and to view admission to Communion and to the baptism of his children as his civil right. But at the other end of the spiritual spectrum, the same problem may present itself at times of revival such as the Great Awakening. At such times, whole communities may feel the power of the gospel, and many experience it savingly; but others become merely temporary believers, who in the excitement of the moment, immediately receive the Word with joy (Matt. 13:20), but fall away as soon as they are confronted with the cost of discipleship. Sometimes, too, there is an inner falling away while there is nothing outward to betray the lifelessness (or slumber) within; and while Reformed preachers were reluctant to rush in and weed out the tares, they felt it their duty to 'tenderly warn' all their hearers to engage in serious and regular self-examination.

This carries its own dangers. Congregations (and even whole traditions) may sometimes find themselves having to live on an unvarying diet of 'marks of grace': a diet which affords only occasional glimpses of the glories of the gospel. Nevertheless, the duty of self-examination is repeatedly urged by the apostles. St Paul, for example, prescribes it as an indispensable preparation every time we take Communion (1 Cor. 11:28), while St Peter counsels his readers to show diligence in making their 'calling and election sure' (2 Pet. 1:10).

Fraser of Brea's survey of his own soul was fully consonant with this advice, but unfortunately, as he later acknowledged, he set out armed with the wrong criteria such as, for example, that his conversion-experience must correspond to the conversion-narratives he heard around him, and that it was imperative to have a deep and dark preparatory law-work. He eventually disabused himself of such preconceptions, and found peace; but even so, the inspections continued, and as they continued they showed that his soul was carrying 'much dross' and that his spiritual life still had 'many cracks'.

What Fraser had to learn (and frequently to re-learn) was that it is only as sinners that we can enjoy the right to be called the children of God (1 John 3:1). We may, indeed, carry much dross, have many cracks, and bear the marks of many a defeat, and still be able to stand on the Rock singing the New Song (Ps. 40:2). But it is a song of mixed emotions or, as John Duncan put it, the song of a heart 'melting and breaking with a joyous grief and a grievous joy!' And sometimes, Duncan adds, as one putting his ear to it, 'it faltered and made wrong music; it jarred, and there was discord, and it grated on its own ear, and pained it. But if there was discord, it was removed by grace in atoning blood, and by the sweet accents of intercession; for it came up as music in Jehovah's ear, melody to the Lord.'[49]

How did Fraser learn to live with this on-going journey in self-knowledge? By returning time and again to the Covenant of Grace. At one point he writes, 'I have found much good,' he writes, 'by a long and serious study and pondering of the covenant of grace' (p. 206). At another, he records, 'Truly I had not been many days in Christ's school, judging the covenant of grace, when I thought I was come to a new world; my former life seemed a dark, howling wilderness, and the life of grace I looked upon as a lightsome Canaan, the harbour of rest after my tossings' (p. 232). Gazing into the covenant, he saw that Christ had stood for His people; that in Him God had taken all our obligations upon Himself; that the blessings of redemption were bestowed freely and unconditionally; that they were offered to men, not as in any way qualified or righteous, but simply as men and sinners. And he saw, too, that God's promises were the ground of faith, not the purchase of faith (p. 140). They were there before faith, as what faith believed in. It received; it didn't do, or earn. It simply took.

Reformed theology has often linked assurance to the so-called Practical Syllogism: 'All who believe in Christ are saved; I believe in Christ; therefore, I am saved.' Of these three propositions, by far the most important is the first, because it specifies the one indispensable object of our faith: Christ as Saviour. The belief that we ourselves are saved is not essential to salvation; the belief that all who believe in Christ are saved, absolutely is.

---

49. A. Moody Stuart, *Recollections of the Late John Duncan, LL.D.* (Edinburgh: Edmoston and Douglas, 1872), pp. 103-4.

8

Fraser of Brea and Hypothetical Universalism

IT WAS WHILE Fraser was a prisoner on the Bass Rock that he wrote his *Treatise of Justifying Faith*. That would have been between January 1677 and July 1679,[1] but it remained unpublished until 1728, twenty-nine years after his death; and twenty-one years later, another edition appeared, this time with an extensive 'Appendix concerning the Object of Christ's Death' (pp. 159-270).

Fraser tells us that when he wrote the *Treatise*, he had access to no books but the Bible, and this was certainly true while he was on the Bass. There are some signs, however, that afterwards, expecting to have the book published, he did consult some books. He was certainly well apprised of the views of other divines with regard to the extent of the atonement. He quotes (p. 162), for example, John Cameron's statement, 'Christ died for thee if you believe it';[2] and elsewhere he refers to such theologians as Paraeus, Preston, William Fennel and Macovius. However, the Cameron quotation is an easy dictum to remember, and there are no direct quotations from the others, only allusions. Nevertheless, it is entirely unwarranted to suggest, as Macdonald does, that the reason Fraser's utterances didn't always square with Calvinist orthodoxy was that he didn't have the benefit of a regular theological education.[3] Many of those who did enjoy such a benefit deviated

---

1. At the conclusion of the *Treatise*, Fraser writes '*FINIS*' and adds the date, 'Bass, July 9 1679.'

2. Latin, *Christus pro te mortuus est si is credas*.

3. M. Macdonald, *The Covenanters in Moray and Ross* (Inverness: Melven Brothers, 1892), p. 106.

even further from strictly Calvinistic lines, and all the signs are that, if self-taught, he was nevertheless an erudite scholar, and certainly fully able to set forth the views of others accurately, even when in no position to check their writings. And when it comes to setting forth his own views, whether right or wrong, he is able to assert confidently that he has not walked alone, or against the current of 'orthodox, godly, Protestant divines.' 'I affect not Singularity,' he wrote, 'but love to see the Footsteps of the Flock of Christ before me always.'[4]

The 1728 edition caused no stir, but when the second edition appeared in 1749 Adam Gib (and, presumably, others) quickly noted that the Appendix set forth what seemed to be the Arminian doctrine of Universal Redemption, though 'in somewhat of a new form'. This was something of a shock. Fraser was a man after the Seceders' own heart. He had been a notable field-preacher, a sufferer for the Covenant and, above all, a powerful advocate of secession from the ministry of the curates, especially in his work, *The Lawfulness and Duty of Separation from Corrupt Ministers and Churches Explained and Vindicated*. The Seceders clearly saw Fraser as a man of like spirit with themselves, and it was a shock to discover that he had had inclinations to Arminianism: so much of a shock, in fact, that Adam Gib resorted to casting serious doubt on Brea's authorship of the *Treatise*. 'None are known of,' he wrote, 'who can ascertain Fraser's involvement in that book.'[5]

The circumstances of its publication were certainly unusual.[6] Gib is very sceptical about the printer, referring to him dismissively as 'a pewterer in Edinburgh', and calling in question his claim that the *Treatise* was printed, without any alterations, from a copy prepared for the press by the author's own hand.[7] On the contrary, Gib argued, the printer could not but be aware that there was not one word of the alleged author's handwriting in the copy he had used because, far from printing from the author's original

---

4. *A Treatise of Justifying Faith* (Edinburgh, 1849). These remarks are from the Preface, though Fraser labels it a 'postscript' since he wrote it after he had finished the work. However, though it is placed at the beginning of the published volume, the pagination (pp. 337-38) follows that of its closing pages.

5. Gib, *A Display of the Secession Testimony*, Vol. 2, p. 131.

6. From an advertisement appended to the 1749 edition it looks as if the Appendix had at some point been published separately. The whole exercise, it has to be said, was very unprofessional.

7. See 'The Publisher to the Reader,' p. 9.

manuscript, he had worked only from a transcription of a copy which had been in the possession of George Mair, a colleague of Fraser's (and friend of Thomas Boston); and that copy of a copy had been transcribed by young relatives of Mair's while still schoolchildren.[8] Gib adds further that the printer had been approached by one of the copyists, who had asked that publication be delayed till the original manuscript (presumably the one which had been in Mair's possession) could be found, or at least until the copy of that copy could be revised. The world had no reason, then, Gib concluded, to take the printer's word even for the claim that the copy of the copy had been printed without alterations, especially in view of his evident enthusiasm for the 'singular doctrines' set forth in the volume.[9]

Gib makes a plausible case, especially against the idea that the text was printed without alterations. As we have already seen from Boston's experience with the first printing of *The Fourfold Estate* in 1720, it was no easy matter in those days to ensure a text went through the press in strict accordance with the author's manuscript. However, the case against the authenticity of the *Treatise of Justifying Faith* is far from proven. It may indeed be true that not a word of the printer's copy was in Fraser's own handwriting, but such an argument would tell equally forcefully against our New Testament documents, all of which are copies, not originals; and though at first sight the involvement of children might appear to compromise the process, children might well be the most reliable copyists, especially if working under the supervision of Mr Mair, Senior; and they were unlikely to meddle with the text for theological reasons. We also know from his own *Memoirs* that Fraser wrote such a treatise, and in the published version it concludes with a Postscript which fully accords with Fraser's personality. He asks to be excused for any weaknesses, infirmities and inaccuracies which may be found in the volume, and also for his lack of learning and pungency; it was written, he reminds his readers, at a time of 'manifold afflictions and temptations'.

---

8. In a footnote (p. 131) Gib adds, '*viz.,* By Mr. Thomas Mair, and one of his sisters; as he acknowledged to the writer of this account.' Thomas Mair was George Mair's son, and would be the catalyst for the controversy that later arose among the Antiburghers over the *Treatise.*

9. Gib is no doubt referring to the fact that in 'The Publisher to the Reader' there is a warm commendation of Fraser's view of the extent of Christ's death, 'a Subject that many have wandered in as in the dark' with the result that 'instead of laying a sure Foundation and Warrant for Faith' they 'have loosed all Grips for true and saving Faith to fix upon' (p. 6).

If this Postscript is a forgery, it is a very bold one; and while he craves to be excused for some defects in presentation, he makes no apology for the substance of the volume. Instead, he writes, 'Now blessed be the good Lord who of his Grace hath been pleased not only to put me out to begin this Work, but who hath been graciously pleased to stand by and assist his unworthy, poor Servant, and carry me along in this till I have finished the same ... may it be blessed for clearing of God's precious Truths, and for the Edification and building up of the souls of God's people in their most holy Faith.'

It is not at all impossible that the copy in George Mair's possession was in Fraser's own handwriting, that it had been prepared by him for publication, and that it had been entrusted to Mair for the very same reason as the *Memoirs* had been entrusted to Thomas Ross: namely, to see it through the press. But this raises its own problem, though one that tells rather in favour of, than against, the volume's authenticity. Why did his friend, George Mair (father of Thomas), not see to its publication? He clearly had not lost the manuscript. The most likely explanation is that he was uneasy about it, fearing both for Fraser's reputation and for the effects of putting his peculiar doctrines in the public domain; and there are signs that he would not have been alone in this. We learn from Robert Wodrow, writing in 1725, that the Reverend John Carstares (father of Principal Carstares) had exchanged several letters with Fraser on the subject of universal redemption.[10] In view of Carstares' close association with such representatives of Reformed Orthodoxy as James Durham,[11] it is highly likely that he was disturbed by Fraser's advocacy of a form of universal redemption. It is also possible that Fraser himself lost his enthusiasm for the volume. The *Memoirs* take us up to the years after his release from the Bass (and thus several years after the writing of the *Treatise*) but contain not a hint of the distinctive doctrines of the 'Appendix'. Indeed, on one key point, as we shall see, they contradict it.

---

10. Wodrow, *Analecta*, Vol. 3, p. 207.

11. In Durham's *Commentary upon the Book of the Revelation* (1658. Reprinted Pennsylvania: Old Paths Publications, 2000) there is an essay, 'Concerning the Extent of the Merit of Christ's Death, or, if it may be accounted a satisfaction for all men' (pp. 378-421). Durham's core thesis (p. 378) was that 'the death of Christ was not intended by Christ, nor accepted by God, as a price and satisfaction for the sins of all men, and for the procuring of Redemption for them, but only for some peculiarly chosen by God, and by his decree of Election separated from others.' The volume is introduced with an address 'To the Judicious and Christian Reader' from the pen of John Carstares.

At first, the Antiburghers took no action, Gib taking the view that 'no public hurt was like to follow therefrom among those under the inspection of the Associate Synod.'[12] The *Treatise* did, however, cause warm debate within the Reformed Presbyterian Church, one of whose ministers, James Hall, seems to have been actively promoting the book. When presbytery condemned it, Mr Hall, with the support of one other minister and some elders, set themselves up as a separate presbytery: a presbytery, Gib noted, 'wholly constituted on the ground of universal redemption.'[13]

This presbytery was soon dissolved, but Mr Hall took the further step of issuing a pamphlet vindicating its position on the extent of redemption, and at this point, Gib took alarm. The pamphlet, written in 'a plausible and deceitful strain', was inexpensive and easy to circulate, and he concluded that it posed a greater threat than the *Treatise* itself to the people 'under the inspection' of the General Associate Synod. The threat-level escalated when rumours began to circulate that Thomas Mair, now no longer a child, but an Antiburgher minister, was not only championing Fraser's *Treatise*, but had also spoken in favour of Hall's pamphlet.

Taken together, these developments, in Gib's judgement, posed an imminent risk of confusion and 'jumbling of people's judgements' in Secession congregations, and so, in December 1753, the Associate Synod met to address the problem. The following April it met again and adopted an Act which, although occasioned by Brea's book, made no direct reference to it, but styled itself, instead, *An Act containing an Assertion of some Gospel Truths, in opposition to Arminian errors upon the head of Universal Redemption*. At the heart of the Act lay an implicit rejection of Fraser's doctrine that Christ died for every man, but with different intentions for the elect and the reprobate: 'There is but one special redemption, by the death of Christ, for all the objects thereof,' declared the synod; 'he died *in one and the same respect* for all those for whom he *in any respect* died.'[14]

Thomas Mair distanced himself from this Act, remaining silent on some of its Articles, demurring from others and voting against the sixth (which laid down that the benefits purchased by Christ cannot be divided).[15] At

---

12. Gib, ibid., p. 133.
13. ibid., p. 135.
14. ibid., p. 139.
15. ibid., p. 140.

the following synod (August 1754), he gave in 'a paper of dissent', and there ensued a series of meetings in which, it has to be said, the synod showed remarkable patience, while Mair's attitude seems to have hardened. He refused to drop his opposition or withdraw his paper of dissent, and instead made plain his personal adherence to the double-reference theory of the Atonement, namely, 'That besides the special objective destination and intention of our Lord's death, respecting the elect, there was some kind of general or universal objective destination and intention thereof in the transaction of the New Covenant ... that in some sense Christ died for all mankind, or shed his blood for them – making a full payment of their debt, and a satisfaction to justice for their guilt.'[16] There came an inevitable parting of the ways, and Mair was deposed in April 1757. His congregation, however, remained loyal to him, and after his death in 1768 they joined the Associate (Burgher) Synod.

The *Treatise*

But what of the *Treatise*? First, we need to get our bearings. It is not in the first instance an argument for universal redemption, but an enquiry into the nature, and particularly the grounds, of faith: an enquiry which is in full accord with the preoccupations of the *Memoirs* and with Fraser's need to understand the workings of the human soul, particularly the workings of his own. Yet the volume as published suffers from a curious illogicality. The opening words are, 'Having spoken already of the Nature of Faith, it is fit that now some Things be spoken to the Grounds of believing.' But if these are the opening words, what can the 'already' refer to? Besides, the nature of faith is not discussed till we reach Chapter VIII (pp. 307-36). Either, then, the 'already' refers to an earlier work or the printer-publisher has mixed up the sheets. The latter is not at all unlikely.

When he does come to discuss the nature of faith, the treatment is brief, occupying only thirty pages (pp. 307-36), and in the published version these are placed after the Appendix. Taking his cue from Hebrews 11:1,[17] Fraser relates faith directly to the divine promises, and specifically to the promises of the New Covenant: promises which are made, not to sanctified persons, but to 'poor miserable woeful Sinners

---

16. ibid., p. 144.
17. 'Now faith is the substance of things hoped for, the evidence of things not seen.'

as such of Mankind'.[18] These promises, the Christian's *Magna Carta*, are the sinner's Title and Claim to all they stand in need of, and for the believer they constitute demonstrative evidence that their spiritual inheritance is secure, just as title-deeds are evidence that a property is yours. At the same time, Fraser does not appear to have regarded *fiducia* (trust) as itself of the essence of faith. The essence is assent or conviction, 'and resting on the Lord Christ is rather a Fruit of Faith than formally Faith itself' (p. 335).

Fraser also lingers over the idea of 'receiving' Christ (pp. 314-17). His fundamental point here is that we receive Him in His promise, that is, in His Word, which is the only place where the Lord makes Himself available for our faith to cling to. He then subjects this to a remarkably thorough, though brief, analysis, amounting to a description of the successive steps to faith. We receive Christ in the Word, he says, in a six-fold respect: we receive Him externally by the ear when listening to the Word; we receive Him when we understand the Word; we receive Him when we assent to the Word as truth; we receive Him when we not only believe it, but apply it to ourselves as a word which is spoken to us for our personal use; we receive Him when our hearts and affections clasp the promises as good news; and, finally, we 'receive' Him when we take the promises as held out to ourselves, and 'use' them for our own salvation. Thus, the poor sinner, at the hearing of these glad promises, and taking the Lord at His Word, steps forth from his sense of utter undone-ness, and declares, 'Lord, you are holden [bound], and I protest that it be so to me according to your Word'; and then, listening only to that Word, and renouncing all other defences, the soul is therewith quieted (p. 316).

Here, the *fiducial* element, the trust, is in the Word itself. We trust what it says.

The grounds of faith

The main concern of the *Treatise*, however, is not with the *nature* of faith, but with the *grounds* of faith, and even here the interest is carefully limited. Fraser's interest is not in the grounds of faith as discussed in formal Christian apologetics, covering such questions as the grounds of,

---

18. 'Christ,' he writes (pp. 325-26), 'is not an Enclosure or Piece of forbidden Ground, that only privileged Persons may repair unto, but he is a Way, a Highway, in which all may walk.'

for example, Christian theism. It is not man the sceptic he is addressing, but man the sinner; and, even more specifically, this man's question, 'What right do I have to believe that Christ is willing to be *my* Saviour?' Or, to rephrase it, 'Is it only those who are duly qualified who have a right to trust that Christ will save them?' He himself had once been trapped in this error, and he was clearly addressing others who might be similarly misled. He was certainly writing from experience when he warned against the idea that people have no right to believe in Christ until a sense of their own sin makes them miserable (p. 4). But he also warned against the opposite danger, characteristic of many legalists, of basing our assurance of salvation on having experienced just such a sense of misery.

No less serious, however, was the temptation to delay putting our faith in Christ till we experience the objective testimony of the Holy Spirit working mightily in our souls, and causing us to believe. The only objective testimony, Fraser argues, is what is given in the Scriptures, and these bind every human being, even before they are pressed home with power on the soul. To wait for the testimony of the Spirit *before* believing is to open the door 'for all Delusions and Enthusiasm': 'for if we be not obliged to close with Christ till the Spirit objectively tell us that our Sins are pardoned, that it is God's Will that we believe, then I see not but upon the same Account we may as well say what the Quakers and other Enthusiasts [say], that we are not to pray, read, hear, wait, give Alms, till stirred up thereunto by the Spirit; And then where are we?' (p. 9).

Then, with his familiar thoroughness, Fraser lists no fewer than six positive grounds of faith. Foremost among these is *the all-sufficiency of Christ*: such a sufficiency, Fraser declares, as answers all the soul's needs, and the needs of all souls: whether it be 'Darkness, Deadness, Guilt, Weakness, Sorrows or whatever it be … here is Meat for thy Hunger, Righteousness and Pardon for thy Sin and Guilt; he fulfilleth all the desires of thy Heart' (p. 53).

But Fraser also highlights in this connection *God's goodwill towards sinners*. Here he immediately acknowledges that this does not mean that God has decreed the salvation of every human being. Had that been the case, everyone would be obliged to believe that they are elect, which is a manifest untruth. Nevertheless, when Christ wept over Jerusalem (Luke 19:41-42), these were no crocodile tears, 'for this weeping and these Tears did really express the tender and compassionate Nature of Christ'

(p. 64); and though God has not predestined all men to salvation, yet (echoing 1 Tim. 2:4) there are four ways in which He may be said to will that all should be saved:

(1) By the will of His command. It is the duty of all to accept the salvation offered through Christ.

(2) By a will of complacency. Our salvation gives God pleasure.

(3) By placing within our reach the means necessary to lead us to salvation.

(4) By inviting and exhorting us to accept this salvation. When ministers, he adds, beseech us to be reconciled to God, 'Christ is in as good Earnest as they' (pp. 67-68), and when we come to Him he is 'as one that hath found great spoil' (p. 69).

This is well said, but it is interesting that in pressing home God's goodwill towards the human race Fraser does not at this point introduce the core idea of the Appendix, namely, that Christ died for all men. It would certainly have strengthened his case. Does this suggest that when he first drafted the *Treatise* he had not yet embraced the idea of universal redemption? Or does it suggest that when the first part was published in 1728 this idea was suppressed because those who oversaw the publication either feared for Fraser's reputation or shared the reservations expressed by such men as John Carstares?

Equally interesting is the fact that Fraser appears to stop short of saying that God's goodwill is extended to *all* sinners, and speaks instead of its being extended to all 'in the visible church' (p. 65). Such language is an acknowledgement of a clear difficulty. It is relatively easy to speak of God willing the salvation of those who enjoy the means of grace, and on whom He presses the promise of salvation. But what of the multitudes who never hear the gospel? Was the cross ordained as the means of salvation for them; and why, having ordained such an end, did God not ordain the means of accomplishing it? Many nations have set up iron gates to deny entry to the gospel. God has the key. Why does He not make these gates yield? And how earnestly do we ask Him to?

But Fraser's treatment of God's goodwill also raises another question. Why did he place at the very top of his treatment of this subject as bold a statement of the doctrine of predestination as any to be found among the advocates of the doctrine of limited atonement? 'God,' he writes, 'by the Will of his Decree wills not the Salvation of all Men, he doth not purpose to save all Men, for then should all be saved, yea God hath decreed that the most of Men shall be eternally damned and perish' (p. 62).[19] And why does he have to warn his readers that when he speaks of God's goodwill towards sinners, he cannot say to all, 'God has loved you with a special love and elected you to glory, therefore fear not' (p. 73).

Whence this compulsion to safeguard the doctrine of predestination? When St Paul declared in 1 Timothy 2:4 that God wills all men to be saved, he doesn't immediately add that this doesn't mean that all men are elect. The one thing that matters as we hear the gospel is the plain truth that here and now Christ is offering Himself to us as Saviour; and, linked to this, that the preacher's one duty is to plead with his hearers to accept this offer, and to give them a categorical assurance that if they do so they will be saved.

Christ's death for us a ground of believing

Having dealt with the third ground of faith, the sinner's right and title to all the benefits of the Covenant of Grace, Fraser then comes to the controversial heart of the *Treatise*, 'Christ's Death for us a Ground for our Believing.'[20] It is to this chapter that the Appendix belongs, not as an addendum to the book as a whole, and not even as a discussion of the extent of the atonement for its own sake, but as the foundation for the universal offer of the gospel, and in particular for the practice of pressing upon all, including reprobates, the duty of believing in Christ. Such a practice, argues the *Treatise,* is utterly unwarranted unless Christ died for all men.[21]

Here Fraser shows himself a forthright advocate, not of universal redemption in the Arminian sense, but of Hypothetical Universalism:

---

19. The final part of the assertion is unwarranted. There is no biblical ground for the belief that most men shall be eternally damned; and more cautious Reformed theologians would hesitate to speak of two symmetrical decrees, one consigning men to heaven, and a parallel one consigning others to hell. We should limit ourselves to the measured language of the Westminster Confession (3:7) which, while laying down that some were elected to eternal life, refrains from speaking of 'the rest of mankind' as elected to damnation, and instead refers to them as 'passed by'.

20. Chapter V (pp. 125-58). The Appendix occupies pp. 159-270.

21. Gib summarises the substance of the *Treatise* in an extended footnote (*Display of the Secession Testimony,* Vol. 2, pp. 132-35). His own view is uncompromising: 'In that book, and in a long Appendix to the fifth chapter of it – the Arminian point of universal Redemption is largely set forth; but in somewhat of a new form.'

an attempt to graft a firm belief in the universal reference of the death of Christ on to an equally firm belief in the doctrine of unconditional election. The argument begins (p. 182) by pointing out that we can hardly find fault with the expression, 'Christ died for every man,' 'seeing it is so frequently to be found in Scripture.'[22] No Reformed theologian has ever denied this. Instead, they have willingly acknowledged that some benefits have accrued to the whole human race from the death of Christ;[23] that His atonement is in itself sufficient to meet the needs of every sinner; that Christ and the benefits of His death are to be offered to all sinners; and that even the greatest of sinners should be assured that their sins can be cleansed by the blood of Christ (1 John 1:7).

But Fraser goes beyond this, though his statements are often clouded over with judicious qualifications. Sometimes we read that Christ died 'in some way' for all (p. 206); at other times that He died in such a way for every man that there is now no legal impediment to his liberation (p. 190). But on other occasions he is explicit. At one point (p. 176), for example, he writes that Christ purchased remission of sins 'absolutely' for all; at another he declares that 'the Doctrine of the universal Extent of Christ's Death doth yield a clear Ground and infallible Evidence for the strongest Faith, so as to remove all doubting' (p. 207); at yet another he states that by the satisfaction and death of Christ, the Law is satisfied for the Sinner, 'be what he will, and of Adam's posterity' (p. 190). Again, addressing the question, 'For whom did Christ satisfy?' he answers, 'He died for Mankind, for Adam, Eve and their posterity' (p. 269); and he quickly extends this to mean that He made atonement for the *nature* that he took on: 'Christ assumed or took on him our human Nature, and therefore satisfied *for all and every Individual of that Species*' (italics added); or, as he had put it earlier (p. 205), the merits of

---

22. See, for example, John 1:29, 'Behold the lamb of God, which taketh away the sin of the world'; Hebrews 2:9, 'that he by the grace of God should taste death for every man'; 1 John 2:2, 'And he is the propitiation for our sins; and not for ours only, but also for the sins of the whole world.'

23. Herman Witsius is typical when he writes, 'The suretiship and satisfaction of Christ have been an occasion of much good, even to the reprobate' (*The Economy of the Covenants between God and Man*, Vol. 1, p. 256). Cf. William Cunningham, *Historical Theology*, Vol. 2, p. 332: 'Important benefits have accrued to the whole human race from the death of Christ, and in these benefits those who are finally impenitent, and unbelieving partake.' Cunningham also stresses (p. 333) that these benefits were foreseen by God when He resolved to send His Son into the world and 'were contemplated or designed by him, as what men should design and enjoy.'

Christ extended to 'as many as the guilt of the First Adam did'; or, again, He bought the whole of mankind (p. 257f.), and this includes the heathen (presumably the unevangelised).

But the point that Fraser labours above all is that Christ died for the reprobate, which must mean, on his terms, for those who, according to God's decree, shall be eternally damned and perish. 'Christ,' he writes, 'may be said to die for all, and even for the reprobate' (p. 187): a conclusion which follows, in Fraser's view, from the specific unity of human nature as assumed by Christ. Every reprobate can claim to share in that nature, and so His death was sufficient to save them 'by an ordinate sufficiency' (p. 185: a phrase to which we shall return). By one indivisible action, and one infinite indivisible price, he satisfied for all men's sins: not for the elect apart, and the reprobate apart, but for both.

Yet, though Christ died in some sense for all, He did not die for all in the same way or for all men equally. This takes us back to Fraser's firm belief in a doctrine of symmetrical double predestination. Though Christ satisfied for the sins of all mankind, it was with different intentions for elect and reprobate (p. 222). Fraser's usual way of expressing this distinction is to speak on the one hand of a *common* redemption, embracing the whole world, including the reprobate; and on the other hand of a *special* redemption, embracing only the elect. The meaning of the former is clear: Christ's sacrifice effectually secured for the elect *all* the blessings of the New Covenant; not only the *accomplishment* of redemption, but the personal application of its blessings; not only forgiveness, but new birth, sanctification, perseverance and glory. For them, His satisfaction was sufficient in the truest sense: it purchased a complete salvation or, as Peter put it, he died to bring us to God: all the way (1 Pet. 3:18).

But what is meant by a *common* redemption, embracing all men and every man, yet carrying with it the very real possibility that many, despite being redeemed, will suffer eternal death for their sins? Part of the answer is that all men, including reprobates, have such an interest in Christ's death 'as that they enjoy many Privileges, Gifts and Mercies, which else they should never enjoy' (p. 186); and these include health, offers of peace, food, clothes, deliverances, external membership of the covenant, moral endowments, [spiritual] gifts and offices in the church. Even the fact that Judas was made an apostle was a privilege Christ purchased for him by His death. But over and above these, the death of Christ means that divine

Law now raises no objection to the redemption of any man; and it means, too, that all men now have a right to call on the services of Christ as their spiritual physician, just as everyone in the community has a right to the services of the local physician.

What this amounts to is that we owe to the death of Christ not only the blessings of redeeming grace, but also the blessings of common grace: a fact which, as we have seen, was emphasised as readily and as fully by believers in particular redemption as by believers in universal redemption. It may be argued, however, that when believers in particular redemption speak of such blessings flowing from the death of Christ to the whole human race, they mean that this happened only *per accidens*: it was an incidental consequence of His intention to save the elect, rather than an expression of divine goodwill towards all men and every man.

It is here that Fraser introduces the idea of an *ordained* sufficiency, and by this he certainly means that it was the deliberate intention and eternal counsel of God that, through the cross, blessings should fall on the evil as well as on the good; on the world, as well as on the church; and these blessings would be dispensed by the very same hands as were once nailed to the cross.

But 'ordinate [ordained] sufficiency', as used by Fraser, means more than this. He distinguishes it from the more traditional idea of an 'intrinsic sufficiency', which recognised that the sacrifice of Christ was of sufficient 'value' in itself to atone for the sins of all men and to redeem the whole world, *had that been God's intention*. 'Ordained sufficiency' means that it was God's intention that the ransom paid by Christ should be sufficient to cover the debt of every spiritual debtor: it was ordained to do so. It was paid in the name of every sinner.

But is this any more than playing with words? Fraser did not regard the sacrifice of Christ as divinely ordained to save the whole human race, and he concedes this explicitly: 'It never was Christ's intention to save Reprobates' (p. 262). The most that he and other Hypothetical Universalists can say is that the cross has removed all legal impediments to man's reconciliation with God; and with this, believers in limited atonement might well agree. Every human being may confidently plead before God the worth of the blood of His Son; or, in Old Testament terms, place his hands on the head of the sacrifice offered once for all on the cross of Calvary. But the removal of 'legal impediments' would not be a sufficient atonement. There is a second impediment: the bondage of the human will and, linked to that, humanity's constitutional unbelief. Unless this impediment is removed there can be no reconciliation with God because it leaves us incapable of accepting God's word of reconciliation (2 Cor. 5:19). Hypothetical Universalism offers only a conditional salvation, and the condition (faith in the Redeemer) is one which, left to ourselves, we cannot meet. We need a redemption that includes redemption from our moral and spiritual, as well as from our legal, bondage, and it is precisely such a redemption that is enshrined in the doctrine of definite atonement. Christ died not only to ensure that the whole world might be saved on condition that they would believe. He died to purchase for a multitude too numerous to count 'all things that pertain unto life and godliness' (2 Pet. 1:3): not only to expiate their guilt, but to sanctify them, and cleanse them (Eph. 5:26). United to Him, they would be raised from spiritual death and live a life sustained by the power of a risen Saviour.

The alternatives are clear: on the one hand a universal redemption which leaves the final choice with the human will; on the other, a particular redemption which ensured that the blood of Christ would not be shed in vain. This is the power of the cross: power to present the redeemed faultless before the presence of the Glory with exceeding joy (Jude 24); power to present the church in the presence of her Saviour holy and without blemish, without spot or wrinkle (Eph. 5: 27). This, a complete salvation, is what the cross accomplished, and it is this complete salvation which is to be put within the reach of every man and woman, every boy and girl, in the preaching of the gospel.

Hypothetical Universalism and the gospel offer

As we have seen, what prompted Fraser to write his *Treatise* was his concern to lay a secure foundation for this gospel offer. One element in this foundation was that Scripture made clear that the promises of the gospel were to be addressed not to men as 'holy', but to men as sinners. But then Fraser took a further step and argued that the only warrant for offering Christ to all was that He died for all; and then, beyond this, that the only warrant a sinner could have for embracing Christ was that since He died for all, 'he died for me.' Only on these terms can any human being be persuaded that he has a right to claim the promises of the New Covenant: only on these terms is it warranted to offer the benefits of the New Covenant to every human being, elect or reprobate; only on these could salvation be offered to a Judas or to a Cain. The only fit object for our faith, Fraser concludes, is the crucified Saviour held out to us in the gospel, but our faith acts rationally, and the only rational ground is that Christ died for all. Otherwise, how can the sinner know that Christ died for *him*? (p. 263)

This is a standard argument in the armoury of Hypothetical Universalists, and it cuts two ways. First, the fact that the call is universal must mean that the redemption is universal; secondly, if the redemption is not universal there is no warrant for making the call universal; or, more seriously, only a belief in universal redemption can inspire mission and evangelism.

But history teaches a different lesson. Belief in the doctrine of particular redemption did not deter Alexander Duff (or indeed A. A. Hodge)[24] from going as missionaries to India, or William Chalmers Burns from going to China, or Robert Murray M'Cheyne from working his heart out in Dundee or C. H. Spurgeon from electrifying London with his evangelistic messages or Thomas Chalmers from devoting his life to 'the Christian good of Scotland'.

What rational ground did such men (and the women who supported them) have for such zeal? Was it that they had solved the conundrum that though God sent them into the whole world He had not decreed the salvation of the whole world, but purposed only to gather His elect? Certainly not! Their commission was not to solve puzzles, but to obey their orders, and their obedience was not to be limited by their understanding. In the very highest sense, it was not theirs to reason why, or to be guaranteed a multitude of converts, before they slipped their moorings and sailed off into the unknown. Theirs was but to preach the gospel to every creature, and in this resolution they were strengthened by the example of the apostles, who, knowing full well that the Spirit blows only where He wishes (John 3:8), nevertheless dedicated themselves to 'warning *everyone* and teaching *everyone*' (Col. 1:28, italics added). Above all, they had the example (as well as the command) of the Lord Himself who, far from limiting His preaching to the elect, cast His seed on all sorts of soils, took the risk of His message being rejected, let Himself be seen weeping over Jerusalem, and loved the rich young man even though He knew it was easier for a camel to go through the eye of a needle than for a man of such wealth to enter the kingdom of God.

It was in obedience to such a commission, and fortified by such examples, that evangelists of Reformed persuasion spent themselves in the

---

24. A. A. Hodge, the author of such a robust statement of Reformed Orthodoxy as his *Outlines of Theology* (1860), served as a missionary in India from 1847 to 1850, when ill health forced him to return home.

effort to 'compel' men and women to enter the Kingdom. But they went forth, too, knowing that the blood of Christ was not only sufficient to wash away all the sins of all men, but that it had also secured for them, as preachers, the ministry of the Paraclete. They would not be going out alone, their effectiveness limited to what they could achieve by their own eloquence or power. He would go with them, He would be the pre-eminent witness for Christ, and His power would be the real measure of what was possible. And when, by His power, men and women turned to Christ, none would be turned away, but each would be joyfully welcomed, saved from a lost eternity, and live in and with Christ for ever and ever.

Adam Gib and particular redemption

To the list of those who were both zealous evangelical preachers *and* firm believers in particular redemption must be added the name of Adam Gib, the man who, above all others, had been disturbed by Fraser's 'Appendix'. When he was ordained as Minister of Edinburgh's first Secession church in 1741, he had to begin almost from nothing. By 1745, the congregation (meeting in Bristo Street) had grown to 1200,[25] and underlying this growth was a firm belief, shared by the whole Secession tradition, in the free offer of the gospel. This had been laid down explicitly in the Act of the General Associate Synod (1754) which had condemned the Arminian errors which Gib detected in the *Treatise*. 'There is,' said the Act, 'a *general*, free and unlimited *offer* of Christ, and salvation through him, by the gospel, unto sinners of mankind *as such*; with an interposal of divine authority in the gospel *call*, immediately requiring all the hearers thereof to receive and rest upon Christ alone for salvation, as he is freely offered to them in the gospel.'[26] This call, the Act further declares, rests on a threefold foundation: the intrinsic sufficiency of the sacrifice of Christ; the promise of eternal life through Him to 'sinners as such'; and Christ's relation as kinsman-redeemer to the whole human race.

This last point is developed further in Gib's account of the synod's 'Proceedings with Mr. Mair',[27] and specifically in his explanation of 'The True Ground of the Gospel Call'.[28] Gib acknowledges that Christ is kinsman-

---

25. For a brief overview of Gib's life and ministry, see 'Gib, Adam' in the *Dictionary of Scottish Church History and Theology*.

26. Gib, *A Display of the Secession Testimony*, Vol. 2, p. 140, italics original.

27. ibid., pp. 142-86.

28. ibid., pp. 152-67.

redeemer to the elect 'in a very special way', but the relationship is not confined to the elect. He is kinsman to mankind as such, and this relationship is totally independent of any divine intention with respect to the extent of the atonement. It arises, first of all, out of the constitution of our Lord's person; and, secondly, out of the nature of His mediatorial offices. With regard to the former, Christ, being God-man, is a redeemer in the human nature, 'and this relation can no more belong to the elect than to any other sinners in the same nature.'[29] He is kinsman to all men simply as such, without any distinction between elect and others, 'because the elect are no otherwise sinners, and no otherwise men, than what the rest of mankind are.' The call is to all humans as Christ's kinsmen, and in this respect the plight of fallen humanity, it is repeatedly stressed, is completely different from the plight of fallen angels. For them, no atonement, no kinsman-redeemer, was provided. For the human race there was, and all Christ's kinsmen are called to avail themselves of it, confident that His mediatorial work as prophet, priest and king is suitable and sufficient for every human being, simply as such. The mere fact of our being human beings qualifies us for calling on the services of Christ, the only Redeemer.

But what of Fraser's argument that 'ere faith can lay hold on Christ's blood for this End, namely, to be justified and saved thereby, the Sinner must of necessity see this Sacrifice offered up for him particularly, and close with Salvation through Christ's blood shed for *him*?' (p. 129, italics added). The first response to this, argues Gib, is that in terms of Hypothetical Universalism the only assurance a sinner can have as he hears the gospel is that Christ died for him *sufficiently*, but not *effectually*: that is, He deposited a ransom sufficient to secure his freedom, but not one *intended* (or ordained) to secure his freedom. He can know only that Christ died for him in the same sense as He died for Judas Iscariot.

Secondly, as Gib points out, the design of Hypothetical Universalism ('this new scheme,' as he called it) is to turn the eyes of the hearer away from the 'revealed things' and set them seeking a ground for faith in the secret decree of God.[30] At first sight, Gib's argument here seems inapposite, because what Fraser was saying was not that, before he can believe, a sinner must be assured that Christ died for him, but that he must be sure that He died for all men. However, the whole point of this argument from universal

---

29. ibid., p. 155.
30. *Display of the Secession Testimony,* Vol. 2, p. 280.

redemption is that it gives the hearer the warrant to believe that Christ died for *me*; and it is of this, says Fraser, that a sinner must be sure before he can believe.

But in what sense can he be sure? The message the hearer would take from a universal redemptionist sermon is, 'Christ died to save me,' but this is not what the preacher himself is sure of, and it is not how Fraser intended to be heard because when he says, 'Christ died for all men,' he almost invariably adds, 'Including the reprobate': in other words, 'Those who are never saved.' This leaves the anxious hearer impaled on the question, 'Am I elect or reprobate?' That is God's secret, and it is not made known to any individual *before* he believes, or before he comes to be in Christ, in whom alone we are chosen (Eph. 1:4).

But this doesn't mean that the sinner's initial act of faith is irrational because not grounded in any assured knowledge. He knows that, here and now, God is offering him salvation; and he knows that if he believes, he will have it. But he cannot know whether he is elect, and neither, says Gib, does he need to, because it is not our election that satisfies divine justice, but the vicarious obedience and sacrifice of Christ. 'In the case of a sinner's justification,' he writes, 'law and justice have no respect to God's sovereign counsel about what persons belong to the election of grace.'[31] Nor do they have any respect to the intended scope or extent of redemption. They look only to its intrinsic worth, 'the justice-satisfying and law-magnifying nature of this atonement and righteousness'; and in the same way, the eyes of faith must not be on election, or on the extent of redemption, but on 'the glorious person and offices of Christ, with his satisfaction and righteousness, as freely and equally set forth by the gospel unto all the hearers thereof, with absolute promises of justification and eternal life through Christ to mankind sinners as such.'[32]

In sum, the gospel-hearer has no interest in what is in God's secret book. What matters is the deed of gift and grant which is pressed upon him in the gospel, and to which he has a right and title, not because he is elect, but because he is both a human being and a sinner.

Gib also discusses the gospel offer in his discussion of the Covenant of Grace in a later volume, *Kaina kai Palaia*. It is largely extracted, as he

---

31. ibid., p. 141.
32. ibid., p. 142.

acknowledges, from the seventh article of the Antiburgher Synod's 'Act concerning Arminian Errors',[33] but it also contains additions and variations, and one of these deserves to be noticed. In the original Covenant between the Father and the Son, he writes, all the names of the elect were 'severally recorded therein, so that the promises, as there laid, are an expression of God's gracious purpose concerning each of them particularly, and them only'[34] (p. 258). It is far otherwise, however, in the public administration of the covenant through the preaching of the gospel. There, says Gib, the preacher brings forth an extract 'from that glorious original', but 'a blank is left where the names of the elect are recorded in the original'. Thus, the promises, as laid out in the gospel, have no regard to any as *elect:* they have a respect to them only as sinners of mankind. But these promises are there to be accepted and rested upon, and we are to do that by inserting our own names in the blank, 'by the hand of an applying faith, which all gospel hearers are equally and immediately warranted to do, by God's offer and call.' And the call to do so comes not from man, but from God.

Supported by other Protestant divines

Fraser was confident that his position on the extent of redemption was fully consistent with that of Protestant divines generally (pp. 251-53), and in his support he cites Luther and his followers, many Calvinists (but not Calvin), most of the professors of Saumur; and among approved British divines, John Preston. He even ventures to claim that his views were not contrary to 'the most approven and learned Writers of the Church of Scotland' (p. 251), including Samuel Rutherford and James Durham (though he admits, 'I have expressed myself variously from them on this Head').

He is certainly on safe ground with regard to the Magisterial Reformers, at least to the extent that neither Luther nor Calvin ever directly addressed the question of the extent of the Atonement, and thus never expressed any considered opinion on it.[35] On the other hand,

---

33. This Act was drafted by Gib himself.

34. Adam Gib, *Kaina kai Palaia: Sacred Contemplations in Three Parts* (Philadelphia, 1788), pp. 258-59.

35. But see Raymond Blacketer's article, 'Blaming Beza: The Development of Definite Atonement in the Reformed Tradition,' in David Gibson and Jonathan Gibson (eds.), *From Heaven He Came and Sought Her* (Wheaton: Crossway, 2013) pp. 139-41. Blacketer argues that other early Reformers such as Peter Martyr Vermigli (1499–1562) and Jerome Zanchi (1516–1590) shared Beza's belief in the doctrine of definite atonement.

while his views may have been consistent with those of such British divines as John Preston, they were certainly not consistent with those of John Owen, the most eminent of Puritan theologians.[36] And neither, despite Fraser's claims, were they consistent with those of such Scottish theologians as Rutherford and Durham.[37]

Fraser's true position is on that line of Hypothetical Universalism which can be clearly identified in European theology from the sixteenth century onwards. It was often labelled 'Amyraldianism', but Hypothetical Universalism antedates Amyraut (1596–1654), and Amyraldianism was but one expression of it. It was already expressed in Article XXXI of the *Articles of the Church of England* (1662), which laid down that, 'The offering of Christ once made is that perfect redemption, propitiation, and satisfaction for all the sins of the whole world, both original and actual'; it was defended by the Anglican delegation to the Synod of Dort, led by the distinguished Bishop of Salisbury, John Davenant; and it was introduced to Saumur only by Scotland's own John Cameron, who taught there from 1618 to 1621. Amyraut was a student at Saumur at the time, and was profoundly influenced by Cameron, who appears to have moved towards Hypothetical Universalism by way of reaction to Theodore Beza, under whom he had studied in Geneva.[38] Then, some twenty years after Amyraut, Richard Baxter set forth his own highly influential version of Hypothetical Universalism in the treatise, *Universal Redemption of Mankind by the Lord Jesus Christ.*[39]

---

36. See Owen's major treatise, *The Death of Death in the Death of Christ* in *The Works of John Owen* (16 Vols, London: Banner of Truth, 1965–68, Vol. 10, pp. 140-421). Adam Gib had this work republished in 1755 as an antidote to Brea's teaching.

37. In the course of his essay on the 'Extent of the Merit of Christ's Death,' Durham clearly expresses his disagreement with Amyraut's mentor, John Cameron (*Commentary upon the Book of the Revelation*, pp. 386, 389).

38. Amyraut propounded his views in his *Brief Traité de la Predestination et de ses Principales Dépendances* (1634). While a firm believer in predestination, Amyraut distinguished within it two decrees: a *conditional* decree 'to save all men through Jesus Christ, if they shall believe in him'; and an *unconditional* decree 'to give Faith unto some particular persons': in other words, to *apply* the redemption only to an elect chosen from among the redeemed. For a sympathetic discussion of Amyraut, see Brian G. Armstrong, *Calvinism and the Amyraut Heresy: Protestant Scholasticism and Humanism in Seventeenth-Century France* (Eugene, Oregon: Wipf & Stock, 2004). For modern statements of Amyraldianism, see Alan C. Clifford, *Atonement and Justification: English Evangelical Theology 1640–1790* (Oxford: Clarendon Press, 1990); and Alan C. Clifford (ed.), *Christ for the World: Affirming Amyraldianism* (Norwich: Charenton Reformed Publishing, 2007).

39. Published posthumously in 1694 but written sometime around 1656. There is also a succinct definition of Hypothetical Universalism in Baxter's, *The Saints Everlasting*

But although all these divines held to a doctrine of Hypothetical Universalism, there were significant differences between them. We have already noted Fraser's distaste for Baxter's theology, but this distaste was limited to his Neonomianism, according to which repentance and faith constituted a new 'evangelical obedience': a relaxation of the perfect obedience required in the Covenant of Works, but still a 'condition' to be met by all who sought peace with God, and from this point of view a new legalism.[40] On the other hand, Fraser agreed with Baxter in holding to a doctrine of universal redemption. Even here, however, there was a significant difference. Baxter was a post-redemptionist, that is, he placed the decree of election *after* the decree of redemption, so that, when Christ died, neither the Father in offering Him, nor He in offering Himself, made any difference between elect and reprobate; nor did he give satisfaction for the one sort rather than for another. He satisfied for the sins of all mankind, not only for some as elect 'or for one more than another, but equally for all.'[41] It follows from this that redemption and election are not of the same extent: 'not all [are] Elected that are Redeemed, but Redemption is universal.'[42] This leads to what is surely an extraordinary conclusion: the elect are chosen from among the redeemed, but many of the redeemed are reprobate, ordained to be ransomed by the blood of Christ, but also foreordained to suffer eternal wrath for their sins.

Fraser was not a post-redemptionist. Instead, he believed that the death of Christ was set in the context of God's eternal decree, but he followed Davenant (and Amyraut) in holding that in relation to the cross there were two divine wills, or, as he preferred, two 'divine intentions': the one to purchase a *common* redemption for all men, the other to purchase an *effectual* salvation for the elect. Yet neither of these implied a divine intention to save all men and every man; or, in the effectual sense, to redeem all men. On this last point all Hypothetical Universalists were agreed, and this means that in the final analysis no more are saved according to 'the new scheme' than

---

Rest, under the heading, 'The People of God Described' (Part I, Chapter VIII): 'He hath, according to the tenor of his covenant, procured salvation for all, if they will believe; but he hath procured for his chosen even this condition of believing.' See Richard Baxter, *The Saints' Everlasting Rest* (republished 1998 by Christian Focus Publications), p. 106.

40. Baxter, *The Universal Redemption of Mankind by the Lord Jesus Christ,* p. 37.

41. ibid., pp. 36-37.

42. ibid., p. 279.

are saved according to the doctrine of Beza and Owen. But then, neither does the Arminian form of the doctrine of universal redemption open the door to any wider hope. On all three understandings, all who believe are saved, and only those who believe are saved. What is compromised on both the Arminian and the Hypothetical Universalist scheme is the nature of the actual salvation secured by the cross of Calvary. Did it purchase the application of redemption as well as its accomplishment?

An 'ordinate' sufficiency

We cannot be sure that Fraser ever read John Davenant's *Dissertation on the Death of Christ*, but, whether directly or indirectly, he certainly borrowed one of the bishop's key concepts, the idea of an 'ordinate' or 'ordained' sufficiency, as distinct from a 'mere' or 'naked' sufficiency.[43] 'This,' writes Davenant, ' is understood when the thing that has respect to the ransom, or ransom-price, is not only equivalent to, or superior in value to the thing redeemed, but also is *ordained* for its redemption by some wish to offer, or actual offer.'[44]

To clarify his meaning, Davenant offers two illustrations. First, a man may be in debt for a sum of a thousand pounds, his brother has in his possession sufficient money to cover the debt, but if it is not paid up, the sufficiency avails nothing. The second illustration cites the example of a prince who has enough in his treasury to ransom ten citizens taken captive by an enemy, but unless the money is handed over as an 'ordained' or agreed ransom-price for these specific captives they remain in captivity, despite the prince having sufficient resources to secure their freedom.

Applied to the doctrine of the atonement, as understood by Hypothetical Universalists, this means that the death of Christ was not only sufficient to redeem every man, but that it was (divinely) *ordained* to redeem every man; the ransom was paid in *their* name, and it was accepted by God in their name. But the 'ordination' was not absolute: it was conditional. Salvation was promised to all, but only on condition of faith, and while the gift of

---

43. Davenant's *Dissertation* was first published in Latin in his *Exposition of the Epistle of St. Paul to the Colossians* (1627). An English translation of this work by Josiah Allport was published in two volumes in 1832. Allport's translation of the *Dissertation* was published separately by Quinta Press (Oswestry) in 2006, with an Introduction by Dr Alan C. Clifford. Quotations (and pagination) in this chapter are from this edition. Davenant's explanation of the distinction between an 'ordinate' and a 'naked' sufficiency covers pp. 71-102.

44. Davenant, *Dissertation*, p. 72.

faith would be conferred on those among the redeemed who were elect, it would not be conferred on all for whom Christ paid the ransom. Many spiritual captives would reject the proffered freedom, it was not part of the ordained sufficiency of the ransom to overcome such a rejection, and hence many of the redeemed would remain for ever in darkness and in the shadow of death.

This is not to be said lightly, nor is it enough, faced with such a solemn final outcome, simply to repeat the words, 'Even so, Father, for so it seemed good in your sight' (Matt. 11:26). It was certainly not the end of the matter for the One who first spoke to them: he went on to behold the city, and to weep over it (Luke 19:41).

Hypothetical Universalism and the Westminster Confession

Fraser was confident, as we have seen, that his doctrine did not contradict the position of the first Reformers nor that of the Articles of the Church of England. But was he also justified in claiming (p. 251) that it did not contradict the position of the Westminster Confession? He was certainly not the last to argue that, while the Confession expressly condemned Arminianism, it did not condemn Hypothetical Universalism. Professor A. F. Mitchell, editor (along with John Struthers) of the 1874 edition of the Minutes of the Westminster Assembly, was of the same opinion, though a shade more tentatively.[45] Richard Muller likewise concludes that on this issue, as on supralapsarianism, the Confession was drafted with a view to accommodating the 'variant Reformed views on the nature of the limitation of Christ's satisfaction to the elect'.[46] More recently, Lee Gatiss points in the same direction when he argues that on this issue the Confession was deliberately written 'with deceptive clarity' in order to accommodate 'shades of opinion within a generic Calvinism'.[47]

---

45. *Minutes of the Sessions of the Westminster Assembly of Divines*, ed. Alex. F. Mitchell and John Struthers (Edinburgh: Blackwood and Sons, 1874). The Introduction (pp. LV-LXI) is from the pen of Professor Mitchell. This edition of the Minutes has been superseded by Chad Van Dixhoorn (ed.), *The Minutes and Papers of the Westminster Assembly 1643–1652* (5 Vols., Oxford: Oxford University Press, 2012). Quotations from the Minutes are from this edition, with occasional modernisation of spelling.

46. Richard A. Muller, *Post-Reformation Reformed Dogmatics: The Rise and Development of Reformed Orthodoxy* (Grand Rapids: Baker Academic, Volume One, Second Edition, 2003), p. 76.

47. Lee Gatiss, *Cornerstones of Salvation: Foundations and Debates in the Reformed Tradition* (Welwyn Garden City: EP Books, 2017), pp. 139-58. Gatiss does comment,

The view that the Westminster Confession deliberately left the door open for Hypothetical Universalism is supported by two main arguments: (1) the presence of various shades of opinion on this question within the membership of the Assembly and (2) the ambiguity of the relevant statements in the Confession itself.

With regard to the first of these, it is certainly true that different opinions were represented in the Assembly, and these included several vocal advocates of Hypothetical Universalism such as Stephen Marshall, Lazarus Seaman and, above all, Edmund Calamy, all of whom played a prominent part in the key debate 'about the Redemption of the elect only' on October 22 and 23, 1645, and all of whom positioned themselves as successors to 'our divines in the Synod of Dort'.[48] In line with this, they distanced themselves (as Davenant had done) from Universalism in the Arminian sense. 'I am farre from universall redemption in the Arminian sense,' declared Calamy, and then made clear that what he did hold to was Hypothetical Universalism, according to which, 'Christ did pay a price for all, with absolute intention for the elect, conditional intention for the reprobate, in case [provided] they do believe.' He continued, 'Christ did not only dy sufficiently for all, but God did intend in giving of Christ, and Christ in giving himselfe did intend, to put all men in a state of salvation in case they do believe.'[49]

Later in the debate, Calamy invoked John 3:16, arguing that 'the world' in this passage is 'the world of elect and reprobate and not of elect only'; which may be true, but doesn't lead to the conclusion that Christ died

---

however, that, 'We cannot conclude with certainty that the Assembly, *qua* the Assembly, was aiming to be tolerant of diversity at this point' (p. 157).

For a critique of the views expressed by Mitchell *et al*, see B. B. Warfield, *The Westminster Assembly and its Work* (New York: Oxford University Press, 1931), pp. 138-44. Warfield concludes that the result of the debate in the Assembly was 'the definitive rejection of the Amyraldian views and the adoption of language which was precisely framed to exclude them' (p. 143). Warfield drew on arguments previously put forward by William Cunningham in *Historical Theology*, Vol. 2, pp. 326-31.

48. For the Minutes of this debate, see Van Dixhoorn, *Minutes and Papers of the Westminster Assembly*, Vol. 3, pp. 692-99. 'Our divines' refers to the Anglican delegates to the Synod of Dort, all committed to supporting Davenant in upholding the position of the Anglican Articles.

49. A condition, as Joshua Reynolds was quick to point out, 'that they cannot perform.' To Reynolds' charge that Calamy's opinion 'cannot be asserted by any that can say he is not of the Remonstrants' [Arminians'] opinion,' the latter replied that he did not, like the Arminians, believe that Christ's death put all men 'in an *equall* state of salvation' (italics added).

to redeem the reprobate. Then, moments later, he linked the doctrine of Hypothetical Universalism to the command to preach the gospel to every creature (Mark 16:15):[50] 'If the covenant of grace be to be preached to all, then Christ redeemed, in some sense, all – both elect and reprobate'; to which George Gillespie replied that this failed to distinguish between God's decretive will (*voluntas decreti*) and His preceptive will (*voluntas mandate*). The command is not a revelation of God's intention. God commands all men to believe, but He has not decreed that all should believe.

It is not necessary at this stage to make a theological evaluation of these statements. The question is whether the presence of such views in the Assembly requires us to revisit the Confession's statements on the extent of redemption. Were they so phrased that men like Calamy could have taken them as accommodating their point of view? Or were they intended to exclude the views of 'our divines at the Synod of Dort'? Mitchell, for example, argues that while the Hypothetical Universalists did not succeed in securing any positive endorsement of their opinions, it is just possible that the language of the Confession was so framed that they felt warranted to believe that it did not positively exclude them.

This cannot be dismissed out of hand, especially if we remember that the original reason for convening the Assembly was to prepare new Standards for the Church of England. Were men who were of the same mind as James Usher and John Davenant to be excluded? Over against this argument, however, we have to set the fact that at this stage it was not envisaged that the Church would require a strict form of subscription to the Confession. It never did become the Creed of the Church of England, of course, but even when it was formally adopted by the Church of Scotland on 27 August 1647 the General Assembly contented itself with recognising the Confession as 'most agreeable to the Word of God, and in nothing contrary to the received doctrine, worship, discipline, and government of this Kirk'.[51] The General Assembly prescribed no Formula of Subscription, nor was any such Formula envisaged in the Ordination Formula drafted by the Westminster divines.[52]

---

50. 'Go ye into all the world, and preach the gospel to every creature.'

51. Up to this point the doctrinal Standard of the Kirk had been the *Scots Confession*, which contained no deliverance on the extent of redemption. There was no occasion, therefore, for a 'contrary' position to be set forth by the Westminster Confession on this subject.

52. See James Cooper, *Confessions of Faith and Formulas of Subscription in the Reformed Churches of Great Britain and Ireland especially in the Church of Scotland*

In these circumstances, the Anglican Hypothetical Universalists would not have felt themselves excluded even by a more forthright statement on particular redemption, any more than believers in limited atonement had previously felt excluded by the Anglican Articles' apparent affirmation of Hypothetical Universalism.

But what of the actual language of the Confession? Are its statements on the extent of redemption clothed in 'deceptive clarity'? Do they attempt to secure unity at the price of deliberate ambiguity?

Fraser (p. 251) makes particular reference to the last paragraph of the eighth chapter and claims that it was not aimed at his position, but against Arminian universalism. It is in the following terms: 'To all those for whom Christ hath purchased redemption, he doth certainly and effectually apply and communicate the same.' On the face of things, this lays down clearly that the accomplishment and the application of redemption are of equal extent: it is applied to all for whom it was accomplished, and since it is clearly not applied to all (or even proclaimed to all), it was clearly not accomplished for all. If it had been, then all would have their hearts renewed, and their lives governed by Christ's Word and Spirit.

Fraser's reply is that it could never have been the mind of the Assembly that Christ applies the benefits of redemption to all for whom He died *sufficiently*. What they had in mind was that He applies them only to those for whom He died *effectually*, namely, the elect, whom He redeemed not with a 'common' redemption but with a 'special' redemption.[53] But if this had been the intention of the Assembly, it could easily have followed the precedent set by the Synod of Dort and inserted the word 'effectually' at this point.[54]

(Glasgow: Maclehose, 1907), p. 27. Only in 1711 did the General Assembly prescribe a Formula which required ordinands to 'sincerely own and believe the whole doctrine contained in the Confession of Faith'. This Formula is still in use in conservative presbyterian churches.

53. Gib, *Display of the Secession Testimony*, Vol. 2, p. 275: 'When our Confession teaches that Christ doth apply the benefits of his death unto all for whom he died, Mr. Fraser pretends that this is only meant of all for whom he died in a special way, as he did for the elect.'

54. According to the *Canons of the Synod of Dort* (Second Head, Article VIII), 'it was the will of God, that Christ by the blood of the cross, whereby he confirmed the new covenant, should *effectually* redeem out of every people, tribe, nation and language, all those, and those only, who were eternally chosen to salvation; [and] that he should confer upon them faith, which, together with all the other saving gifts of the Spirit, he purchased by his death.' It was the insertion of the word 'effectually' in this Article that satisfied the Anglican delegates that their position had been protected. Conversely, Westminster's failure

Instead, it simply states that Christ applies and communicates redemption to all those for whom he purchased it.

Fraser also suggests that this is the only Article in the Confession which can 'with any colour' be alleged against his position. But this is hardly the case. The statement from Chapter 8 which Fraser highlighted occurs in the context of the work of Christ as Mediator, but the same question is also addressed in the Confession's Chapter 3, 'Of God's Eternal Decree', where we read in the sixth paragraph, 'Neither are any other redeemed by Christ, effectually called, justified, adopted, sanctified and saved but the elect only.'[55] On the face of things, this sentence is making the same point as is made in Chapter 8, namely, that all who are redeemed, and only those who are redeemed, are effectually called, justified, *et cetera*. But this interpretation was questioned by A. F. Mitchell, who, in his Introduction to the *Minutes* of the Assembly, suggested (p. lvii), that believers in particular redemption 'unconsciously construed' these words as if they read, 'Neither are any other redeemed by Christ, *or* effectually called, *or* justified, *or* adopted, sanctified, *and* saved, but the elect only.'[56] But, taking the words simply as they stand, and without the 'unconscious construal', Hypothetical Universalists could readily have accepted them, taking the word 'redemption' to refer to the *accomplishment* of redemption and the following terms to its *application*, and taking the whole sentence to mean, that only the elect are redeemed *and* effectually called, justified, adopted, sanctified and saved. This would have allowed for the idea that all are redeemed, but only the elect come to enjoy the benefits of redemption.

But have we any right to isolate the word 'redeemed' in this way and to argue that while all the other terms in the sentence refer to the elect, the word 'redeemed' refers to all men, thus drawing the Confession uncomfortably close to the idea expressed in the second of the Arminian Articles, namely, that by His death on the cross Christ obtained redemption and the forgiveness of sins 'for all men and for every man'. What is the difference between 'redeemed' and 'obtained redemption'? At the most,

---

(refusal?) to follow the precedent set by Dort suggests that they had a less accommodating attitude towards Hypothetical Universalism.

55. Warfield (ibid., p. 138) describes this sentence 'one of the most deliberate findings of the Assembly'.

56. This 'unconscious construal' appears to be a slightly modified quotation from A. A. Hodge, *The Confession of Faith* (p. 72), reprinted by the Banner of Truth (London) in 1958, but first published in 1869, five years before Mitchell's *Minutes of the Westminster Assembly*.

the grammar merely allowed Hypothetical Universalists to put their own 'conscious construal' on the conclusion of the Assembly.[57]

A clear majority of the Westminster divines were firm believers in the doctrine of particular redemption. Why, then, did they speak of it in such muted tones that there is still room for debate as to what their statements on the subject meant? Why did they not speak with the clarity we see in, for example, the *Formula Consensus Helvetica* (1675), which declares unambiguously (Article XVI) that it cannot approve the doctrine of those 'who affirm that of His own intention, by His own counsel and that of the Father who sent Him, Christ died for all and each upon the impossible condition, provided they believe,' and then goes on to reject explicitly every detail in what Gib called 'the new scheme'.[58]

Several factors influenced the approach of the Assembly on this question, and they should influence our approach still. For one thing, this was a recondite matter, touching upon the sovereign will and secret intention of God, and therefore to be treated (if at all) only with reverence and trepidation. Besides, Scripture provided no express declaration on the issue; indeed, it never addressed the specific question whether it had been the eternal divine intention to redeem all men or to redeem only the elect. It was clear, too, that while the champions of Hypothetical Universalism denied the doctrine of limited atonement, they were fully committed to the doctrines of grace and firmly believed both that salvation was rooted in unconditional divine election and that faith itself was the gift of sovereign grace.

And, linked to these considerations was a clear recognition that, while Hypothetical Universalism was incoherent, there should be no rush to dub it a heresy. Men of the gifts, character and proven usefulness of Usher, Davenant, Amyraut, Calamy and Baxter were not to be put on a par with Arius, Pelagius, Socinus or even Arminius, and at no point in the course of the debates in the Assembly was it suggested that Hypothetical Universalists should be excluded from the ministry of the church.

---

57. George Gillespie famously observed at one point that if a certain word were left out 'every one may enjoy his own sense' (Mitchell, fn. 1, p, lv). But the remark was not made in connection with the debate on the extent of redemption. The subject under discussion at that point was whether they should speak of one 'decree' or of 'decrees' in the plural. The word 'one' was in fact omitted, and it may be argued that this conceded the principle of deliberate ambiguity. Both the Larger and the Shorter Catechisms, however, refer to 'decrees' in the plural.

58. For the text of the *Formula Consensus Helvetica*, see A. A Hodge, *Outlines of Theology* (New Edition, London: Thomas Nelson, 1880), pp. 656-63.

The Atonement Controversy in the United Secession Church 1841–1845

The stir caused by Fraser's *Treatise* was both very limited and very localised. For a brief moment it ruffled some feathers in the Reformed Presbyterian Church and among Gib's Antiburghers, but, rightly or wrongly, neither Brea nor his treatise would play any further part in the story of Scottish theology. Professor T. F. Torrance, naturally attracted to Fraser's universal redemption, claimed that the *Treatise* 'was to have a considerable influence in the varying course of Scottish theology, from the *Marrow* Controversy to the deposition of John McLeod Campbell,'[59] but there is no evidence for this: in fact, the *Marrow* controversy had been concluded before Fraser's 'Appendix' was even published. Nor is there any evidence for the idea that Fraser's advocacy of the universal offer of salvation to all people without discrimination 'was resented by the hyper-Calvinist establishment';[60] and there is even less for the claim that it was Fraser's *Treatise* that turned people's minds back to 'the primacy of the nature of God revealed in Jesus Christ and his infinite goodwill toward sinners, and thereby opened the door for the proclamation of the Gospel of free unconditional grace.' This whole portrayal is unfair to the long succession of Scottish preacher-theologians, from John Knox through the early Covenanters to the Marrow Men, who had placed the unconditional promises of God before all sinners 'of mankind lost', making no difference between elect and reprobate. It also ignores the powerful nationwide impact of Calvinist evangelism, not least in the great seventeenth-century revivals in Ayr and Irvine and the eighteenth-century revivals in Cambuslang and Kilsyth.[61]

The truth is that, revered as Fraser was for his personal godliness and as a witness for the Covenant, neither his preaching nor his writings had a national impact. Even when the United Secession Church was rocked

---

59. Thomas F. Torrance, *Scottish Theology*, p. 184. John McLeod Campbell was deposed from the ministry of the Church of Scotland in 1831, but he was not a Hypothetical Universalist. He taught a doctrine of universal pardon, though not universal salvation.

60. ibid., p. 202. The Establishment of the time was not hyper-Calvinist, and far from resenting the Treatise, Establishment figures don't seem even to have noticed it. Gib's was a lone voice.

61. It ignores, too, the Calvinist roots of the Great Awakening in North America under the leadership and preaching of Jonathan Edwards and George Whitefield. See Mark A. Noll, *The Rise of Evangelicalism: The Age of Edwards, Whitefield and the Wesleys* (Leicester: Inter-Varsity Press, 2004), pp. 63-126.

FROM THE MARROW MEN TO THE MODERATES

by the Atonement Controversy in the 1840s, Fraser's *Treatise* was never referred to, though *prima facie* it was directly relevant to the question at the heart of the debate.

The catalyst for this controversy was the appearance of the recently ordained James Morison before the Kilmarnock Presbytery of the United Secession Church in March 1841, charged with various errors.[62] One of these was that the object of saving faith was that Christ died for the sins of the whole world; another was that in the order of the divine decrees the decree to redeem the world came before the decree of election. This latter view, according to which the elect were chosen, not from among the fallen (the *massa corrupta*), but from among the redeemed, was closely associated with the Amyraldian form of Hypothetical Universalism.

Morison was suspended from the exercise of his ministerial functions by the presbytery and later deposed by the Synod of the United Secession Church, but the affair raised concerns as to what was being taught in the Divinity Hall, particularly by the two senior professors, John Brown and Robert Balmer. Morison was an outstanding student, he was known to be a favourite of Professor Brown's, he claimed that his doctrines were those he had learned from Professor Brown,[63] and when the synod voted to depose him, Brown dissented: a step which, Ian Hamilton suggests, 'allowed the suspicions of his antagonists to gain a degree of credibility.'[64]

Brown quickly felt forced to defend himself, beginning with his *Notes, Chiefly Historical, on the Question Respecting the Extent of the Reference of the Death of Christ* (Edinburgh, 1841). In these *Notes*, Brown referred for the first time to the distinction between the *general* and the *special* reference of the atonement. According to the former, the death

---

62. Shortly after completing his studies, Morison read Finney's *Lectures on the Revivals of Religion* and was profoundly influenced by them. He eventually moved beyond Amyraldianism, became an avowed Arminian, and in 1843 was one of the co-founders of the Evangelical Union, an association of Arminian Congregational Churches, often referred to as 'the Morisonians'. His mature views were set forth in *The Extent of the Atonement* (London: Hamilton, Adams and Co., 1882), which, in addition to advocating universal redemption, also propounded a doctrine of conditional election: specifically, a doctrine of election by faith.

63. Oliphant Smeaton, *Principal James Morison: The Man and his Work* (Edinburgh: Oliver and Boyd, 1901), p. 89.

64. Ian Hamilton, *The Erosion of Calvinist Orthodoxy: Seceders and Subscription in Scottish Presbyterianism* (Edinburgh: Rutherford House, 1990), p. 40. Hamilton further suggests that the controversy might not have happened had Brown not dissented from the synod's decision.

of Christ had reference to the whole human race, removing all the legal barriers that lay between any human being and reconciliation with God; according to the latter, the death of Christ had a peculiar reference to the elect, securing for them not only the removal of legal barriers, but all the benefits associated with eternal life. But Brown also argued that the sentiments of Cameron and Amyraut (which he considered to be his own) had become 'the common doctrine of most of the Reformed Churches, including the Church of England',[65] and, indeed, of the great body of Protestants in Europe, Britain and America. He also argued, quoting several passages from the Confession, that it admitted 'the larger interpretation': an argument he based not only on the careful phraseology of the Confession, but also on the unlikelihood that its framers could have meant to exclude from the ministry 'many of the best Christians and theologians who adorned that and the preceding age'.

The following year, as the controversy gathered momentum, Professor Balmer took steps to shore up and clarify his own case by republishing a classic statement of Hypothetical Universalism from the pen of a seventeenth-century English lay-theologian, Edward Polhill, whose *Works*, first issued in 1677, had included an essay, 'The Divine Will considered in its Eternal Decrees and Holy Execution of Them'. This essay addressed, among other things, the question, 'Whether Christ died for all men.'[66] Polhill answered in the affirmative, setting forth a doctrine of universal redemption very similar to Fraser of Brea's, and Balmer had this section of Polhill's work published under the title, *Essay on the Extent of the Death of Christ*, with a recommendatory Preface from his own pen. This included the statement, 'so far as the requisitions of law and justice are required, Christ has removed all the obstacles to the salvation of all'; and he added, 'a principle which lies at the basis of the preaching probably of every evangelical minister in Scotland.'[67]

The opposition to the professors was orchestrated by Dr Andrew Marshall, United Secession Minister at Kirkintilloch. Marshall has been

---

65. This is plausible, but not strictly true. The Hypothetical Universalism of Amyraut was not identical with that of Davenant, who believed that the decree of election came before the decree of redemption.

66. *The Works of Edward Polhill* (1677. Republished Morgan, PA: Soli Deo Publications, 1998), pp. 163-75.

67. Quoted in Hamilton, *The Erosion of Calvinist Orthodoxy*, p. 41.

described by Ian Hamilton as a 'polemical, theological, *provocateur*,'[68] and while he did make valid points against the position of Balmer and Brown, his language was often intemperate. This is particularly evident in the Appendix to his work, *The Catholic Doctrine of Redemption Vindicated*,[69] even though in the first instance this volume, as its sub-title indicates, was aimed, not at the two Secession professors but at the 'new theology' of Dr Ralph Wardlaw, a prominent and highly respected figure in the religious life of Scotland at the time. Brought up in the Burgher branch of the Secession, Wardlaw had early adopted Congregationalist views, and from 1803 till his death in 1853 served as the pastor of an Independent Church in Glasgow. In 1843, he published his *Discourses on the Nature and Extent of the Atonement of Christ*, propounding the doctrine of 'indefinite atonement or universal atonement, with gracious sovereignty in its effectual application.'[70] 'Christ,' he wrote, 'satisfied divine justice, or made atonement, for all mankind without exception, as well those who are not saved as those who are.' Like Amyraut, Wardlaw was a post-redemptionist, holding that the elect were chosen from among the redeemed (all men having been redeemed), but unlike Balfour and Brown he also rejected the idea of the death of Christ as a 'legal satisfaction to the law and justice of God on behalf of elect sinners' and adopted, instead, the governmental or rectoral theory of the atonement, which sees the death of Christ as the public vindication of the moral government of God, 'not binding God to pardon any, but rendering it honourable to his perfections and government, should he so will, to pardon all.'[71]

However, on the pretext that Balmer and Brown were 'coadjutors' with Wardlaw, Marshall introduces an Appendix focused on statements made by Balmer and Brown before a meeting of the United Secession Synod in 1843. These indicated, Marshall alleged, that they held a view of the

---

68. ibid., p. 54.

69. Andrew Marshall, *The Catholic Doctrine of Redemption Vindicated; or, Modern Views of the Atonement, Particularly Those of Dr. Wardlaw, Examined and Refuted*. The Appendix occupies pp. 229-51.

70. Wardlaw, *Discourses on the Nature and Extent of the Atonement of Christ* (Glasgow: Maclehose, 2nd edition, 1844), p. 67.

71. ibid., p. 74. For a brief discussion of Wardlaw's views, see Cunningham, *Historical Theology*, Vol. 2, pp. 358-70. Cunningham acknowledges (p. 358) that, despite his belief in a universal atonement, Wardlaw always 'asserted the substance of the scriptural doctrine of the atonement, as involving the ideas of substitution and satisfaction.'

atonement which would subvert the need for an atonement altogether:[72] the same view, he declares, as Dr Wardlaw, according to which the Saviour paid neither 'our debt of obedience nor our debt of suffering', but died only in the interests of public justice, and which allowed God to dispense pardon for Christ's sake only 'by suspending, and superseding, and overruling his law.'[73] This shifted the debate away from the extent of the atonement to the question of its nature, and attributed to Brown and Balmer a position which neither of them ever held. Like Fraser of Brea, they believed wholeheartedly that the death of Christ was a substitutionary expiatory sacrifice.

And then, never one to miss an opportunity to give colour to his case, Marshall introduces an observation the revered Dr John Dick had made to him about John Brown many years before.[74] Prior to his being called to Biggar in 1806, there was a prospect of Brown being called to a congregation in the neighbourhood of Glasgow, and the presbytery, in arranging the usual ordination trials, had prescribed a Latin dissertation on the question whether Christ had died for all human beings and for each individual human being.[75] Marshall recalled that at that point Brown had asked him to use his influence to get the subject changed and, looking back, he suspects that the reason for the request was that Brown was not keen to make full disclosure of his views before the presbytery.

Marshall later related the incident to Dr Dick, and their conversation provided a story in the genre, 'I always knew that man would be trouble.' 'I am sorry to hear it,' said the doctor (but with even more than his usual solemnity): 'hitherto we have been a united body – all, so far as I know, sound in the faith; but if individuals spring up among us, possessed of abilities as you say this young man is, and holding such opinions, who can tell what serious injury may soon be done to our church?'[76]

As he draws the Appendix to a close, Marshall's language appears to lose all sense of restraint. He accuses the two professors of dishonesty because, although they taught nothing contrary to the Church's Standards, they had not taught the full doctrine of these Standards, as they were appointed to

---

72. Marshall, *The Catholic Doctrine of Redemption Vindicated*, p. 233.

73. ibid., p. 246.

74. ibid., p. 248.

75. *An Christus pro omnibus et singulis mortuus sit?* This is the terminology used in the second of the Five Arminian Articles (1610).

76. Marshall, ibid., p. 249.

do, with the result that, for all the Church knew, 'a flood of Pelagianism has for years been issuing from our Divinity Halls, and overspreading the churches, without the Christian people being put on their guard.'[77] And not only was this Pelagianism flooding the churches at home: it might even be found that 'missionaries tinctured with Pelagian and other kindred heresies, have been going forth, for years past, to our several missionary stations, and that our people, in providing support for these missionaries, have been exerting themselves "to their power and beyond their power," not, as they supposed, in making known the doctrine of our Lord Jesus Christ, but in disseminating "another gospel."'

Conclusion and climax

The controversy reached its climax (and its conclusion) when Marshall presented a libel against Professor Brown at the July 1845 meeting of synod.[78] Among the charges was that Brown taught 'that Christ died not for the elect only, or made satisfaction for their sins only, but that he died for all men, and made atonement or satisfaction for the sins of all men.'[79] The professor was acquitted of this, as of all the other charges, but this did not mean that he was acquitted of holding a Hypothetical Universalist understanding of the extent of the atonement. He had never denied it. What the synod had decided was that Hypothetical Universalism was not a contradiction of the doctrinal Standards of Scottish Presbyterianism; and the decision was welcomed for two reasons.

First, Hypothetical Universalism appeared to provide a secure platform for the free and universal offer of the gospel. As Cairns pointed out, this didn't mean that the gospel would henceforth be preached more freely in the pulpits of the Church, 'for that was not possible.' But, he adds, 'relief was brought to many minds hampered and disturbed by the apparent inconsistency between a universal offer of salvation, and a limited atonement on which to rest it.'[80] It is tempting to reply that the inconsistency would have disturbed only those minds which are hampered by the reservation that a divine command is binding only if we

---

77. ibid., p. 250.

78. Professor Balmer had died on 1 July, 1844.

79. *Minutes of the United Associate Synod, July 1845.* Cf. Hamilton, *Erosion of Calvinist Orthodoxy*, p. 46.

80. Cairns, ibid., p. 255.

fully understand it. When Whitefield, Chalmers and Spurgeon heard the command, 'Go, teach!' they went.

Secondly, the decision of the synod was welcomed because, as Brown's biographer notes with satisfaction, it 'exerted a valuable influence in liberalising the tone of Scottish theology'.[81] Even he, however, could never have envisaged where the 'liberalising' would lead. The controversy made one thing clear: there was real confusion and uncertainty within the Secession with regard to both the doctrine of particular redemption and the Church's relation to its Confession. Some shared Brown's view that the doctrine of limited atonement was inconsistent with the universal offer of the gospel; others doubted whether it was actually a confessional doctrine at all; and others, while believing that it was, thought it dishonest to subscribe to it because it wasn't their own personal faith. At the same time doubts were raised as to whether any ordinand had studied the Confession with sufficient thoroughness to entitle him to declare with sincerity that he believed its whole doctrine; and doubts were expressed, too, about the length of the Confession. Was it not too long, and did it not include doctrines which were not fundamental, and to which the Church should not require subscription as a condition of entrance to her ministry? Then never far away, and frequently called upon, lay the argument that the status of the Confession threatened the place of Scripture as the only source and standard of Christian doctrine.

Yet there was a reluctance, for reasons of ecclesiastical politics, to abandon the Confession or even to modify its wording, and so attention focused instead on the terms of subscription, and particularly on the 1711 Formula, which required all the Church's office-bearers to affirm their personal belief in 'the whole doctrine' of the Confession.

Scarcely had the dust settled on the Atonement Controversy when a proposed union between the United Secession Church and the Relief Church concentrated men's minds on this issue, and when the discussions issued in the formation of the United Presbyterian Church in 1847, the union brought with it an alteration in the Formula of Subscription. The references to 'the whole doctrine', and to owning the Confession 'as the confession of my faith', were dropped, and a candidate would be required, instead, to affirm the Westminster Standards 'as an exhibition of the way in which you understand

---

81. ibid., p. 255.

the Holy Scriptures'.[82] This is a clear instance of studied ambiguity, capable of meaning exactly the same thing as the older Formula (in which case, why change it?), but capable, too, of meaning something much less rigorous, leading Taylor Innes to comment, 'The United Presbyterian Church has wholly abolished the Formula of Subscription.'[83]

But the decisive step in redefining the Secession's relation to the Confession was not taken till May 1879, when the Synod of the United Presbyterian Church passed, with little dissent, its Declaratory Act.[84] The opening paragraph contains a thinly-veiled assertion of universal redemption,[85] and the following paragraphs several less thinly-veiled criticisms of the Confession, implying that it is too muted in its testimony to 'the love of God to all mankind', and that its statements on the divine decrees, total depravity, the salvation of the unevangelised, and the destiny of those who die in infancy, were in serious need of more careful nuancing. These reservations and qualifications become irrelevant, however, when we reach the final paragraph of the Act, where it is made clear that no minister need feel bound to accept the Confession's position on these subjects, or, indeed on any other. Instead, the Act declares, 'liberty of opinion is allowed on such points *in the Standards*, not entering into the substance of the faith' (italics added). It then adds, as a disarming example of the points on which liberty of opinion would be

---

82. *Proceedings of the Synod of the United Presbyterian Church 1847–1856* (Edinburgh: 1856, p. 64.). See the discussion in Hamilton, *The Erosion of Calvinist Orthodoxy*, pp. 22-24.

83. Alexander Taylor Innes, *The Law of Creeds in Scotland: A Treatise on the Legal Relation of Churches in Scotland, Established and Not Established, to their Doctrinal Confessions* (Edinburgh: William Blackwood, 1867), p. 438. Innes did not disapprove of the change, since he regarded the Formula as 'the strictest, and, on Protestant principles, the most questionable part of the instruments of adherence to creed used by the Established and Free Churches.' It reflected, in his view, a move away from the older stress on uniformity to a greater stress on freedom of conscience (ibid., p. 247). An Appendix to Innes' volume (pp. 463-64) gives the full text of the Questions to be put to the various office-bearers in terms of the of the United Presbyterian Formula.

84. For the text of the Act, see *Proceedings of the Synod of the United Presbyterian Church 1877–79*, pp. 367-68. It is also reproduced in Hamilton, *The Erosion of Calvinist Orthodoxy*, pp. 192-93.

85. It highlights, as matters 'which have been and continue to be regarded by this Church as vital to the system of gospel truth', 'the love of God to all mankind, His gift of His Son to be the propitiation for the sins of the whole world, and the free offer of salvation to men without distinction on the ground of Christ's perfect sacrifice.' The insinuation is that these had somehow been compromised by the older Formula's commitment to the 'whole doctrine' of the Westminster Confession.

tolerated, the meaning of the 'six days' in the Mosaic account of creation: a subject on which Scottish Presbyterianism had never attempted to limit liberty of opinion. In practice, the Act would introduce liberty of opinion on virtually every point in 'the Standards', in effect evacuating them of all authority.

Other churches would soon follow the UP's example. To facilitate the Union, the Free Church adopted a similarly worded Declaratory Act on 26 May 1892,[86] and then in 1910 the Church of Scotland amended its Formula to read, 'I hereby subscribe to the Confession of Faith, declaring that I accept it as the Confession of this Church, and *that I believe the fundamental doctrines of the Christian Faith contained therein.*' In none of these formulas was 'the substance of the faith' defined.[87] What was clear, as James Cooper pointed out, was that the 'substance' was no longer the Confession itself, but 'something therein embodied';[88] and what that 'something' was, was itself a matter on which the churches allowed liberty of opinion, subject only to the discretion of a General Assembly.

Why was Fraser's *Treatise* ignored?

The seed from which these changes grew was the need of the Secession (and specifically the United Presbyterian Church) to accommodate the doctrine of universal redemption as espoused by Professors Balmer and Brown within the Subordinate Standards of Scottish Presbyterianism. Yet, although Fraser of Brea's *Treatise* was the only substantial Scottish treatment of the subject prior to 1847, no one drew on it, or even referred to it. Why was this?

---

86. For the text of this Act, see *Proceedings of the General Assembly of the Free Church of Scotland 1889–93*, pp. 418-19. It is reproduced in Alexander Stewart and J. Kennedy Cameron, *The Free Church of Scotland 1843–1910: A Vindication* (1910. Reprinted Edinburgh: Knox Press [Edinburgh], 1989), pp. 69-70). According to this Act (paragraph IV), 'diversity of opinion is recognised in this Church *on such points as do not enter into the substance of the Reformed Faith* therein set forth' (italics added). It was the passing of this Act that led to the Free Presbyterian secession of 1893 and, in 1900, to the refusal of the Free Church minority to enter into the Union with the United Presbyterian Church (to form the United Free Church).

87. It is noteworthy, however, that whereas the Free Church Act spoke of the substance of the *Reformed* faith, the United Presbyterian Act referred simply to the substance of 'the faith' and the Church of Scotland Act to the substance of the 'Christian' faith.

88. James Cooper, *Confessions of Faith and Formulas of Subscription in the Reformed Churches of Great Britain and Ireland Especially in the Church of Scotland* (Glasgow: James Maclehose, 1907), p. 72.

One obvious reason was that it would hardly have been wise for Balmer or Brown to identify with a work which the Secession had condemned so unambiguously in 1754. But there was a deeper reason. There was an element in Fraser's doctrine from which they recoiled: his doctrine of 'gospel wrath', closely linked to his insistence that Christ died for both elect and reprobate, but with different intentions. As far as the elect were concerned, all agreed that His intention was to secure for them the gift of eternal life. But with what intention did He die for the reprobate? Part of the answer was that He died in order that they should enjoy 'common' blessings. But there was a second intention, namely, that He died for them (and redeemed them) so that 'Reprobates, slighting the Offer of the Gospel and Salvation, might be made utterly inexcusable, and so liable to that sorer and greater Punishment which shall be inflicted on unbelievers.'[89]

The advantage of such a doctrine, from Fraser's point of view, was that it meant that Christ's death for reprobates was not inefficacious or in vain. It was a means of giving effect to the decree of reprobation according to which the Lord purposed to manifest on some, not only Law-Wrath, but Gospel-Wrath, but before they could be subject to this Gospel-Wrath it was necessary that Christ should die for them, that His blood be shed for them, and that salvation be offered to them through that blood; and necessary, too, that they should despise it and thus become fit objects of the sorer punishment appointed for reprobates (p. 255). He concludes, 'Therefore, as the Lord did decree to damn some for their Unbelief and Murder of the Son of God, necessary it was they should have an Offer of Salvation through his Blood.' This, argues Fraser, they could not have unless Christ had truly died for reprobates, but His intention in dying for them was not to save them, but 'that the eternal Design of making known Gospel-Wrath might take effect.'

These are painful sentiments to read, reflecting the dilemma faced by a man who has to explain why Christ died to redeem multitudes whom it was never His intention to save. What, then, was the point? The point, Fraser replied, was that the death of Christ put God in a position where He is justified in subjecting many of the human race to a more awful punishment than they would have been liable to if the incarnation and the cross had never taken place.

---

89. Fraser, *A Treatise of Justifying Faith*, p. 264.

Sadly, it was for this that Fraser was remembered, when he was remembered at all.[90] Yet we cannot be sure that this was his life-long personal belief. The *Treatise* was written while he was a prisoner on the Bass, and it may well be that his situation led his mind to dwell on the more dreadful aspects of religion. His *Memoirs*, however, were completed afterwards, and prepared by himself for the press, and in them he strikes a very different note and seems, indeed, to reject the idea of Gospel-Wrath. Taking his cue from the words of John 3:17,[91] he writes, 'It is with sinners that Christ has to do, and not to condemn them, but to give them life; and when they cannot come to Him for life, to seek them.' He then continues: 'Such is the nature of Christ, that He only came to show mercy … and it is as unreasonable to expect condemnation from Christ, as to expect cold water from fire; and, therefore, whosoever knows Him cannot but believe in Him. There is nothing in Christ but what is matter of joy and comfort. Shall I misdoubt Him, who is all mercy and no wrath, who came not at all to damn, whose offices and relations are all good?'[92]

Conclusion

Did Hypothetical Universalism represent, as Jonathan D. Moore suggests in the sub-title of his definitive study of its English variety, a 'softening' of Reformed theology?[93] We can well believe that this was part of the intention, at least in its later phases, though the primary aim always was to provide a secure foundation for the universal offer of salvation. But, supposing that men like Davenant, Preston and Fraser were concerned to soften the impact of such doctrines as predestination and reprobation, did Hypothetical Universalism really deliver such an object?

---

90. See, for example, John Macleod, *Scottish Theology*, pp. 183-84; and James Walker, *The Theology and Theologians of Scotland 1560–1750*, pp. 81-83. Both distance themselves from Brea's doctrine in no uncertain terms. 'How monstrous,' wrote Walker, 'the idea of the Father satisfied and the Saviour made the wrath-inflicter!'

91. 'God sent not his Son into the world to condemn the world; but that the world through him might be saved.'

92. Fraser, *Memoirs*, pp. 139-40. These were sentiments on which he drew for comfort at an earlier stage in his life, but he saw no reason to withdraw them when he finalised the draft of his *Memoirs*. It is doubtful if he ever finalised the draft of the *Treatise*, and even more doubtful that he finalised the draft of the *Appendix*.

93. Jonathan D. Moore, *English Hypothetical Universalism: John Preston and the Softening of Reformed Orthodoxy* (Grand Rapids: Eerdmans, 2007).

Superficially, perhaps, yes, because it allowed them to say that when they offered salvation through Christ to all their hearers, they were guilty of no deception: the ransom He had paid He had paid for all. But the hard questions still remained. There was no softening of the fact that salvation is a matter of sovereign grace; nor of the fact that God had not decreed the salvation of all men; nor of the fact that God does not bestow the gifts of faith and new birth even on all who hear His gospel; nor (and this is the hardest thing of all) that many are left, unsaved, on the broad road that leads to destruction. And while it might appear that on the Hypothetical Universalist understanding more were *redeemed* than were redeemed on the premise of particular redemption, not one more soul was actually *saved* on the one understanding than on the other.

Above all, Hypothetical Universalism offers no softening of the problem that confronts theism in all its forms: the problem of evil. Why did God permit sin, and why does He permit pain? That problem confronts us all, whether we are Universalists, Hypothetical Universalists, Calvinists, Arminians or Roman Catholics.

The business of theologians is not to soften or palliate the truth, but to find it, so far as it is within our reach. But sometimes it isn't, because God has kept it to Himself, at least in the meantime. Yet, although we cannot see all the details, God has shed upon our whole field of enquiry the light of the Cross: a light that reveals how passionately He cares for us and our world: a light in which we see Him inviting us with outstretched arms to embrace His love, assuring us that if we embrace it we will receive a complete salvation: transformation as well as forgiveness; body as well as soul; perseverance as well as conversion; glory as well as grace.

9

The Rise of the Moderates

THE FIRST USE of the word 'moderate' in a political/ecclesiastical sense can be traced back to a Proclamation of Toleration issued by James VII in February 1687. His Majesty's primary concern was to secure concessions for his Roman Catholic co-religionists, but to maintain credibility he had to extend the toleration to Quakers and some Presbyterians, and in this latter connection the Proclamation went on to declare, 'We allow and tolerate the *moderate* Presbyterians to meet in their private houses and there to hear all such ministers as either have or are willing to accept of our indulgence allanerly (only), and none other.' By his use of the word 'moderate' the King was distinguishing between those Presbyterians who were willing to be allowed to continue their ministry on the King's terms, and those, particularly the field-preachers, who were not. These got short shrift. Even the moderate Presbyterians were limited to meeting in their private homes and forbidden to build meeting-houses or even to meet in outhouses or barns. On the other hand, those who conducted field-conventicles or attended them or even connived at them were to be prosecuted 'according to the utmost severity of our laws'.[1] As defined by James, a 'moderate' was a Presbyterian who was prepared to exercise his ministry within the limits (and these were far from moderate) laid down by the Crown.

   William of Orange also urged moderation in his letter to the first General Assembly of his reign on 6 October 1690.[2] 'Moderation,' he wrote, 'is what

---

1.   William Croft Dickinson and Gordon Donaldson (Eds.), *A Source Book of Scottish History*, Vol. 3, p. 196.

2.   This was the first meeting of the Assembly since 1653. The General Assembly appointed for 20 July of that year had been dissolved on the orders of Oliver Cromwell,

religion enjoins, neighbouring churches expect of you, and we recommend to you. And we assure you of our constant favour and protection in your following of these methods, which shall be for the real advantage of true piety and the peace of our kingdoms.'[3] For William, moderation meant restraint and leniency in the treatment of episcopalian incumbents who, in the wake of the Revolution and the re-establishment of Presbyterianism, faced the prospect of being deprived of their livings. The King's own preference was for episcopacy, but he was also anxious about the effect the church settlement might have on public opinion in England, where Scotland's episcopalian clergy were being portrayed as the victims of a sustained campaign of persecution; and where, conversely, Presbyterians were being portrayed as intolerant fanatics determined to exact revenge for the sufferings of the previous thirty years.

When the General Assembly met on 17 October 1690, their formal reply to His Majesty's letter assured him that their management would be such as he had every right to expect, and would be marked by a calm and peaceable procedure. They would study the moderation he had recommended, convinced, as he was, that it was what religion enjoins, neighbouring churches justly expected, and what God expected from true disciples of Jesus Christ, who, though zealous against all corruptions in His church, was 'most gentle towards the persons of men'.[4]

But did their practice live up to their promise? The prevailing consensus among historians is that they did not and that, granted the nature of seventeenth-century Presbyterianism, moderation was hardly to be expected. After all, Presbyterianism was marked by a repressive puritanism, it was bound in the shackles of Calvinist orthodoxy, and it still harboured the theocratic dreams of the Solemn League and Covenant.[5] Above all, the sufferings of the later Covenanters had not cured them of their innate intolerance, and they were 'certain to demand retaliatory measures against the Episcopalians'.[6]

---

and its members ordered to quit the town. See the Editor's footnote, *Acts of the General Assembly of the Church of Scotland* (1843), p. 220.

3. *Acts of the General Assembly of the Church of Scotland*, p. 222.

4. ibid., p. 223.

5. T. M. Devine, *The Scottish Nation 1700–2000* (London: Penguin Press, 1999), pp. 64-65.

6. *Source Book of Scottish History*, Vol. 3, p. 211.

Anti-episcopal measures were certainly taken. In April 1689 Parliament decreed that all ministers must pray publicly for William and Mary as King and Queen of Scotland,[7] and by November one hundred and eighty-two members of the clergy had been deprived of their livings for refusing to do so. Later that same year, Parliament passed an Act abolishing prelacy, followed in June 1690 by another establishing presbyterian government.[8] This last Act also ratified the Confession of Faith as the public and avowed Confession of the Church of Scotland.[9] Two further Acts followed in 1693: one requiring ministers to take an Oath of Allegiance to their Majesties King William and Queen Mary, and another which required them to acknowledge William and Mary as not only *de facto* sovereigns but King and Queen *de jure*. It also required them to take an Oath of Assurance whereby they swore that they would 'defend and maintain their majesties' title and government against the late King James and his adherents'. Finally, in 1695, Parliament passed an Act in Favour of Presbyterian Clergy: an Act which opened the door for all former incumbents to remain in their charges, on condition that they took the Oaths of Allegiance and Assurance and complied with the related Acts. If they did so, they would 'enjoy his Majesty's protection' as to their respective kirks and benefices.

There is little evidence that these measures were driven by presbyterian malice.

Similar measures to safeguard the new order were put in place in England, where a number of High Church bishops refused to take the Oath to William and Mary, thus becoming 'non-jurors' and thereby giving up their power and their prospects for the sake of conscience. At the same time, the most zealous Scottish Presbyterians were of such strongly anti-Erastian sentiment that they were not at all happy to see the conditions of admission to the ministry dictated by the state; and those from a Cameronian background took it extremely ill that the National Covenant

---

7. As they had done for the Stuarts.

8. This same Parliament also restored to their parishes, whether they were vacant or not, the survivors among the ministers who had been ejected in 1662.

9. The Rescissory Act (March 1661) had annulled all the pro-presbyterian measures enacted by Parliament since 1633, among them the Act of February 1749 approving the Westminster Catechisms and Confession of Faith. This meant that the Scots Confession was once again the official Standard of the Church of Scotland.

of 1638 and the Solemn League and Covenant of 1643 were not endorsed as still binding on the Scottish nation. Clearly, Presbyterians, too, were having to make compromises; but they did make them, with the result that virtually the whole of Scotland south of the Tay acquiesced in the terms of the Revolution Settlement.

Still, there is a ready market for the portrayal of Presbyterians as men of violent intolerance and the episcopalians as the cultured and moderate victims of their vengeance. To say the least, however, this requires some qualification. The sixty old presbyterian ministers who had been ejected at the Restoration could certainly not have forgotten that episcopacy had been complicit in their sufferings: bishops and archbishops had regularly sat on the courts that had condemned them, and the 'curates' had gladly taken their vacant parishes and laid claim to their livings. Yet there was no policy of 'an eye for an eye, and a tooth for a tooth.' No post-Revolution episcopalian was ever summoned before a Court of High Commission; none was ever sentenced to imprisonment on the Bass Rock; none suffered torture by the thumbkins; none was banished; and none was sent to the scaffold. Instead, Presbyterians were content to celebrate the end of Stuart absolutism by doing no more than restoring to the Kirk the polity which had distinguished it in the days of Knox, Melville and Henderson, and of which she had been deprived at a stroke by a tyrannical monarchy *via* the Act Rescissory of 1661. They were not imposing Presbyterianism: they were restoring it as a polity in which they believed as an article of faith, which was dear to their hearts, and for which many had suffered not only the loss of their livings but imprisonment, torture and banishment.

Having said that, however, few will question Henry Moncrieff Wellwood's description of the views of late seventeenth-century Presbyterians as 'neither liberal nor enlightened', especially on such subjects as toleration.[10] But this, surely, was not a unique feature of Presbyterianism. It was a feature of the time. Neither divine-right Presbyterianism nor divine-right Episcopalianism nor divine-right Papalism was prepared to yield ground to its rivals. Each saw itself as possessing the truth; each saw error as potentially fatal to human souls; each thought that heresy should be weeded out; and each believed that blasphemy should be treated as a crime.

---

10. Sir Henry Moncrieff Wellwood, *Account of the Life and Writings of John Erskine, D. D.* (Edinburgh: Constable, 1818), p. 422. The comment appears in an Appendix (pp. 407-477) on the constitution and history of the Church of Scotland.

This mood was inevitably reflected in the Church Settlement of 1688–95, and we in the twenty-first century would certainly recoil from some of its provisions. Few would endorse the requirement that, not only ministers and elders, but all who held any office in university, college or school, should be required to subscribe to the Westminster Confession.[11] We are shocked that the civil power was sometimes called in to remove episcopal incumbents by force; saddened that the General Assembly, in its 1703 Address to the Queen, should entreat Her Majesty to ensure that all attempts by dissenters against the established government of this Church would be punished according to law;[12] taken aback that all magistrates and officers of justice should be urged by the same Assembly to give ready assistance in 'making the sentences and censures of Church judicatories effectual;'[13] and, above all, horrified that, by its silence and inaction, the Kirk was complicit in the execution of young Thomas Aikenhead for blasphemy in January 1697.

At the same time, however, the position of the episcopalians was far from straightforward. The 1695 Act in Favour of Presbyterian Clergy offered them a way back into the ministry, but the majority were not only episcopalians but Jacobites, seriously disaffected from the House of Orange and fiercely loyal to 'the King across the waters'; and even those who were not ardent supporters of the Stuarts still felt bound by their earlier oaths to pray for James VII and, by implication, forbidden to pray for William and Mary, or to recognise them as *de jure* sovereigns of the United Kingdom (a *sine qua non* of holding office in England as well as in Scotland). Others found it hard to renounce episcopacy and promise submission to presbyterian judicatories. And others, no doubt, found it hard to subscribe to the Westminster Confession (under episcopacy the creed of the Kirk had been the much briefer and less definite Scots Confession of 1560).

The net result of these factors was that, over and above the number of episcopalians who voluntarily demitted office, over six hundred were

---

11. But this should be seen in its historical context. South of the Border, the Test Act, originally passed in 1673, continued to exclude from public office all who did not take Communion in the Church of England, and the universities of Oxford and Cambridge barred dissenters (non-Anglicans) not only from teaching, but even from being admitted as students. Only in 1827 was the Test Act repealed, but even this did not bring immediate relief to dissenters, whether Protestant or Roman Catholic.

12. For 'dissenters' read episcopalians. Unlike England, there was no Protestant dissent in Scotland at the time.

13. *Acts of the General Assembly of the Church of Scotland*, pp. 322-23.

deprived of their livings between 1689 and the Jacobite Rebellion of 1715. By any standards, this represents a huge amount of suffering, involving the loss of home and stipend, and the disruption of family life.

There is little evidence, however, that the motive behind the deprivations was a desire for retaliation on the part of newly empowered Presbyterians, and particularly on the part of the Cameronians and other so-called Antediluvians. Quite apart from the fact that a 'mixed economy' of Presbyterians and episcopalians would have been unworkable, the truth is that the negotiation of the post–1689 Settlement was not in Presbyterian hands; nor, as we have seen, was the final arrangement entirely to their liking. The Settlement was in the hands of the Scottish Parliament, which did indeed contain one or two conviction-Presbyterians such as the Earl of Crawford, but was still largely composed of the same men as had acquiesced in both episcopacy and Stuart absolutism until fears for the Protestant succession rattled the London establishment and prompted its leaders to send for William of Orange. Only when they saw the boldness of their southern peers did Scotland's grandees fall in behind the drive towards constitutional monarchy. At the same time, they were confident that in re-establishing Presbyterianism they could count on popular support. As the Claim of Right (April 1689) had recognised, prelacy had long been 'a great and unsupportable grievance to the generalitie of this nation' while, at least south of the Tay (the only world any of them knew), Presbyterianism had long been received by general consent as the only government of Christ's church.

But even Parliament did not have sole discretion. There was also the position of the King: profoundly averse to any form of religious persecution, of episcopalian sympathies but well apprised of the popular aversion to bishops, yet deeply concerned that the sitting incumbents be treated with all possible leniency. It was he who called the first meeting of the General Assembly in October 1690: a prerogative William was not prepared to forego.[14] He shared to the full the Stuart and Cromwellian suspicion of large groups of his subjects gathering at times and places of their own choosing to discuss whatever questions took their fancy; and so, while he gave his consent to the Assembly meeting, he ensured that it was Parliament,

---

14. The Presbyterians had no option but to acquiesce in this, but it was a significant concession. The right to 'free assemblies' meeting when and where they wished, had been a key element feature in their earlier struggles.

not presbyteries, who chose the commissioners. Parliament, as might be expected, made 'a judicious selection' and the result was an Assembly described by Dunlop as 'remarkably moderate'.[15] Of the hundred-and-eighty members, sixty had been ordained under the old Presbyterian Order prior to the Restoration, and three were Cameronians. But there were no known 'wild Presbyterians' or 'High Flyers'. More significantly, there were no commissioners from north of the Tay, where episcopacy and Jacobitism went hand in hand.

It was to this Assembly that William addressed his letter urging moderation. However, the Assembly made no pronouncements regarding the terms to be offered to episcopalian clergy. The most important of these, the Proclamation appointing Prayers for William and Mary, the Act abolishing prelacy, and the Act establishing presbyterian government, had already been laid down by Parliament; and all subsequent arrangements would come from the same source.

Underlying all these anti-episcopal measures was the simple fact that the 'late conformists' were not only episcopalians but Jacobites; and if King William feared the Assemblies of the Kirk, he feared Jacobitism even more, and with good reason. He knew that, with the support of warlike and well-armed clans,[16] it posed a serious military threat, and the last thing he needed was to have these Jacobite sympathies inflamed by preachers hostile to the House of Orange, especially as he was fully aware that French armies stood poised across the Channel ready to give support to any rising. 'There seems to be little doubt,' wrote William Croft Dickinson and Gordon Donaldson, 'that the principal factor in moving William finally to acquiesce in the establishment of Presbyterianism was the incurable Jacobitism of the Scottish bishops and many of the clergy.'[17]

One result of this was that in many areas, especially north of the Tay, there was serious opposition from both high and low to the settlement

---

15. A. Ian Dunlop, *William Carstares and the Kirk by Law Established* (Edinburgh: Saint Andrew Press, 1967), p. 78. He suggests that this moderation was due to them having been warned that any robust action against episcopalians would have serious consequences for dissenters in England: a warning which implies, rightly or wrongly, that Anglicans were seen as inclined to take their own retaliatory action.

16. At the beginning of the eighteenth century, Highlanders formed an estimated third of the population of Scotland, and most of them, following the lead of their clan chiefs and the local gentry, were both Jacobites and loyal episcopalians.

17. *Source Book of Scottish History*, Vol. 3, p. 211.

of presbyterian ministers in vacant parishes. Landowners frequently preferred to prolong the vacancy rather than be parties to the induction of non-episcopalians.[18] Others vowed to prevent the installation of any such ministers, and warned that, even if they were inducted, they would receive no stipend or be allowed the use of manse or glebe. At the same time, many of the former incumbents, with the protection of the lairds, continued to exercise a clandestine ministry, performing baptisms, marriages and other ministerial duties,[19] and justifying their actions by assuring their followers that presbyterian orders were invalid (a position held by Anglicans down to the present day).

And at the popular level, too, resentment ran high with the result that presbyterian ministers were often 'rabbled' by angry protestors when they attempted to take up residence in their parishes. More remarkably still, certain clans, most notably the Macraes of Kintail, not content to prevent presbyterian settlements within their own bounds, made it their business to extend their activities further afield, provoking tumults at inductions as far distant as Dingwall and other towns in Easter Ross. But beyond these days lay what no one could then have foreseen: that by the end of the century evangelical Presbyterianism would flourish as the popular religion of those very Highland parishes which had so recently been strongholds of Jacobitism and episcopacy.

The emergence of the Moderate Party

Opinions will vary as to the degree to which the Revolution Settlement delivered the moderation that King William had called for. What is clear is that if there were 'wild Presbyterians' they certainly did not get things all their own way; and what is no less clear is that while there were moderate men (most notably William Carstares) at the heart of the Settlement there was as yet no Moderate Party.[20] This would emerge only in the 1750s, it

---

18. When the episcopal incumbent of Inverness died in 1691, the magistrates would not allow the charge to be declared vacant, and for the following ten years no presbyterian minister could be settled there. Fraser of Brea preached there for some time, but hopes that he might be admitted as Minister were frustrated. See Gustavus Aird's 'Sketch of Fraser' in *Memoirs of the Rev. James Fraser, of Brae* (1889), p. vi.

19. See John Macinnes, *The Evangelical Movement in the Highlands of Scotland 1688–1800* (Aberdeen: The University Press, 1951), pp. 31-32.

20. For Carstares' contribution to the Revolution Settlement, see A. Ian Dunlop, *William Carstares and the Church by Law Established*, pp. 77-79.

would operate very much in the manner of a modern political party, it would be a system of ecclesiastical management rather than a theological movement, and the label was not one coined by their opponents as a term of disparagement, but one 'the Moderates' chose for themselves, and in which they gloried.

The man chiefly responsible for the emergence of the party was William Robertson (1721–93), Minister successively of the parish of Gladsmuir in East Lothian and Old Greyfriars (Edinburgh), and Principal of Edinburgh University from 1762 till his death thirty years later.

At the heart of Robertson's policy was a determination to ensure that the Church complied with the Patronage Act of 1712 and that all its presbyteries obeyed to the letter the instructions laid down by the General Assembly in connection with the Act. As already noted, for many years after the passing of the Act there was no uniform or consistent policy when it came to filling vacancies. To begin with, many patrons, aware of the strength of popular feeling, demurred to the wishes of the people; but there was also a convention, to put it no more strongly, that if, after a lapse of six months, a patron had taken no steps to fill the vacancy, the right to present fell to the presbytery, leaving them with discretion as to the extent to which they would consult the members of the congregation. An Act of 1732, however, deprived them of this discretion,[21] laying down that only elders and heritors were to be consulted. All that was left to the people was the right to express disapproval of the nominee, but any such disapproval had to be accompanied with reasons, and it was entirely up to the Presbytery to judge whether these reasons had any cogency (which meant in practice whether they outweighed the opinions of the heritor and the elders; even the near-unanimous dissent of parishioners counted for little). The form of a Call was to be retained, but it was to be signed only by the heritors and the elders. The people were completely disenfranchised (as they were, of course, in parliamentary elections), and the Act was quickly followed by the Secession under Ebenezer Erskine in 1733.

In an attempt to stem the flow of Seceders, the Assembly of 1736 passed a mollifying *Act against Intruding of Ministers,* highlighting the fact that ever since the Reformation it had been a cherished principle of the Church

---

21. Act anent the Method of Planting Vacant Churches (*Acts of the General Assembly of the Church of Scotland,* pp. 620-21).

that no minister should be intruded into any parish contrary to the will of the congregation; and urging presbyteries to have due regard to this principle when filling vacancies. However, when the Act failed to win back the Seceders, it was forgotten,[22] and the 1732 Act began to be enforced with increasing rigour, despite the fact that a number of presbyteries still refused to induct the patron's nominee against the wishes of the people. To overcome this problem, the General Assembly resorted to the use of what came to be called 'riding committees', so called because they consisted of outsiders appointed by the General Assembly (or by a synod) to ride into a parish to induct a presentee over the heads of both presbytery and people.

William Robertson fully supported this policy of enforcement, and was himself a member of a riding committee commissioned to ensure that the patron's nominee was inducted to the parish of Torpichen despite the refusal of the presbytery of Linlithgow to comply with the instructions of the General Assembly. From the very beginning, his policy was governed by the clear and simple reasoning that patronage was the law of the land, law must be obeyed, and the Church must brook no defiance of the instructions given in the 1732 Act of Assembly. Behind this lay Robertson's firm belief in what he saw as a fundamental principle of Presbyterianism: the subordination of the 'lower' courts of the Church (Kirk sessions, presbyteries and synods) to the final authority of the General Assembly. If the Supreme Court could be defied with impunity, all order and discipline would collapse; and the impact would not be confined to the church. The right of private judgement would reign supreme, to the imperilment of the tranquillity and good order of society as a whole.

Matters came to a head in 1751 when the General Assembly ordered the presbytery of Stirling to induct the patron's nominee to the parish of Inverkeithing despite the objections of the people. The presbytery refused, and when the matter was reported to the Assembly, Robertson, making his maiden speech, called for 'a severe and exemplary sentence',[23] but, despite the fact that, according to his biographer, he argued his case

---

22. Facilitated, no doubt, by the fact that 'the will of the congregation' had never been carefully defined and could be reduced to 'the will of the heritors and the elders', the latter being regarded as laity (and, very often, heritors themselves).

23. Dugald Stewart, *Account of the Life and Writings of William Robertson* (Edinburgh, 1801. Republished Collingwood, Victoria: Trieste Publishing Company, 2017), pp. 13, 170. Stewart (1753–1828) was Professor of Moral Philosophy at Edinburgh University from 1785 to 1809.

'with extraordinary powers of persuasion and eloquence', he failed to convince the Assembly. In November 1751 the Commission of Assembly again ordered the presbytery to induct the presentee, but though the order was accompanied with the threat that, if they refused, the March (1752) Commission would pass a sentence of 'very high censure', they once again refused; and yet the Commission 'with a preposterous lenity, suffered their conduct to pass with impunity.'[24] Having failed at the Commission, however, Robertson succeeded two months later at the General Assembly of 1752.

The Inverkeithing case had two important outcomes. First, the deposition of Thomas Gillespie, Minister of Carnock in Fife. Gillespie was one of only six ministers who had defied the instruction of the Assembly,[25] but the Assembly seems to have decided to select one of their number as the subject of their 'very high censure', and the lot fell on Gillespie.[26] The procedure is recorded, (shamelessly, it has to be said), in the Minutes of the Assembly: 'Then, after prayer for light and direction to the Assembly in their procedure and decision of this matter, it was put to the vote which of the six brethren above mentioned shall be deposed, in pursuance of the resolution of yesterday; and the roll being called, and the votes marked, it was carried, Mr. Thomas Gillespie.' Wherever the Assembly's light came from, its eventual result was the formation of the Relief Church in 1761: another significant addition to the growing body of Seceders.[27]

The second outcome of the Inverkeithing case was the publication in the early spring of 'Reasons of Dissent' from the 'preposterous lenity' of the March 1752 Commission of Assembly. Although it was signed by Hugh Blair, Alexander Carlyle, John Home and other 'emerging Moderates', it is generally accepted as Robertson's work, and since the nineteenth century it has come to be known as 'the Manifesto of the Moderate Party'.[28]

---

24. Stewart, ibid., p. 170. Reflecting, no doubt, the sentiments of Robertson himself.

25. By failing to turn up at the prescribed time and place, and thus leaving the presbytery without a quorum.

26. See *Acts of the General Assembly of the Church of Scotland*, pp. 707-11.

27. Gillespie had been joined by Thomas Boston, the youngest son of Boston of Ettrick, who, after falling foul of patronage, had separated from the Church of Scotland in 1657. The third co-founder was Thomas Collier, minister of an Independent Church in Fife. By 1847 there were 136 Relief Churches.

28. For the text of the first two articles of the 'Reasons of Dissent', see Note K (pp. 282-89) in the Appendix to Stewart's *Life* of Robertson. This is supplemented (Note L,

At the heart of this policy lay the principle that the law of the land (in this case the Patronage Act of 1712) had to be obeyed, otherwise there could be no civil order; and it followed from this that there could be no civil order where people were free to decide for themselves whether or not the law should be obeyed. Anyone (for example, the ministers of an established church) who professes to respect the society he belongs to, enjoys its privileges, and accepts its emoluments, yet rejects its authority and refuses to obey its laws, 'manifestly acts both a disorderly and dishonest part.'[29]

Linked to this was the principle that there could be no society, least of all an ecclesiastical society, where there is no subordination. Presbyteries were subordinate to the General Assembly, and where the Assembly had laid down clear laws and given clear instructions, these must be obeyed. One of these laws, claimed Robertson, was the 1732 Act of the General Assembly, and this Act left presbyteries no discretion to reject a patron's nominee in deference to the wishes of the people. On the contrary, disobedience of the Supreme Judicatory of the Church deserved the highest censure. To act as the Commissions of Assembly had done in 1751, allowing defiance to go unpunished, was 'absolutely inconsistent with the nature and preservation of ecclesiastical society'.[30]

Stewart hailed the decision of the 1752 Assembly as 'the complete triumph of the principles for which Dr. Robertson and his friends had struggled'.[31] The more objective Ian D. L. Clark also highlights the importance of the episode which, he writes, 'was recognised by the Moderates themselves and their contemporaries as marking the decisive emergence of a new party within the Church with a consistent policy and increasingly elaborate organisation.'[32] The nature of this 'consistent policy' was now clear, and it had zero theological content. It meant only that the rights of patrons

---

pp. 289-93) by a summary of Dr Robertson's system of ecclesiastical policy from the pen of Dr George Hill, Principal of St Mary's College, University of St Andrews. Stewart describes the paper as 'the ground-work of the plan which he and his friends afterwards pursued'. Richard B. Sher refers to it as 'a major policy paper' (*Church and University in the Scottish Enlightenment: The Moderate Literati of Edinburgh*; Edinburgh: University Press, Classic Edition, 2015, p. 52).

29. Stewart, ibid., p. 234.

30. ibid., p. 285.

31. ibid., p. 171.

32. Ian D. L. Clark, 'From Protest to Reaction: the Moderate Regime in the Church of Scotland, 1752–1805' in *Scotland and the Age of Improvement* (ed. N. T. Phillipson and Rosalind Mitchison; Edinburgh: Edinburgh University Press, 1970), p. 206.

would be strictly enforced, that there would be no further need for riding committees, and every defiant would go the same way as Thomas Gillespie. This would be the creed of 'Principal Robertson's administration', and his biographer was fulsome in its praise, claiming that it not only produced in the ecclesiastical establishment 'a tranquillity unknown in former times', but that it had laid the issue of patronage to rest once and for all, with the result that 'The questions which were then agitated have long since ceased to be interesting.'[33] But while Robertson succeeded in imposing his policy on the Church till his sudden departure from the ecclesiastical scene in 1780, the questions which had 'long ceased to be interesting' would surface again with a new urgency eighty years later, leading to the Disruption of 1843. Robertson's arguments in favour of implicit compliance with either Acts of Parliament or Acts of the General Assembly would not stand the test of time.

For example, while it is true that the subordination of inferior courts to the superior is a fundamental principle of Presbyterianism, it is, to say the least, no more so than the right of the members of a congregation to choose their own ministers. In fact, this latter right was enshrined in both the First and Second Books of Discipline before the Church in Scotland even had such courts as presbyteries.

Robertson's defence of patronage on the grounds that all societies must abide by the laws laid down by their legislators, also lacks cogency in this connection. True though it is as a general principle, it doesn't follow that a secular parliament has legislative power over the internal affairs of the Christian church or, indeed, over the internal affairs of the local golf club. Within any given society, there are many other societies ranging from political parties to the Glasgow Gaelic Musical Association, each with a right to make its own rules and (crucially) to choose its own office-bearers. Presbyterianism has always claimed this right, and from this point of view, the 1712 Act of the Westminster Parliament was an indefensible power-grab. Dr Robertson and his friends ought to have known the official position of their Church on this question. After all, the Confession of Faith (30:1) explicitly declared that 'The Lord Jesus, as King and Head of his church, hath therein appointed a government in the hand of church-officers, *distinct from the civil magistrate*' (italics added). The Act of Patronage violated this distinction, imposing on the Church a law

---

33. Stewart, ibid., p. 13.

passed, not by her own Supreme Judicatory, but by a secular parliament profoundly hostile to Presbyterianism and determined to ensure that, despite the Articles of Union, the Church of Scotland would never be an independent, self-governing church.[34] As such, it was the greatest calamity ever to hit Scottish Christianity: a master-stroke of the Devil.

Then there was the glaring anomaly that while presbyteries were obliged, on pain of the severest censure, to ordain anyone presented by the patron, the General Assembly had protested every year 'for redress of the grievance of patronage'. Stewart appears to attribute the discontinuance of this practice to Robertson's influence, but it ceased only in 1784, four years after his retirement from ecclesiastical affairs. There is, surely, a blatant inconsistency in the fact that throughout 'Principal Robertson's administration' the Assembly annually described patronage as a 'grievance' while simultaneously dealing so harshly with churchmen who refused to be parties to it.

Finally, there was an argument which would run right down to the era of the Disruption: all the presentees had been duly licensed by the Church itself, and as such certified as appropriately educated and every way qualified to hold a pastoral charge. Besides, this argument continued, that judgement had been made by competent examiners appointed from the ranks of experienced ministers. Who were 'the people', then, to call in question such a man's qualifications?

But when the people expressed disapproval of a patron's nominee, they weren't questioning his formal qualifications or declaring that he wasn't fit to be a minister. They were saying only, 'This man should not be *my* minister. He is not the man to feed *my* soul.' And when a whole congregation, or a majority of it, spoke these same sentiments, the presbytery surely had every right to take cognisance of them, and to refuse to proceed to induct him to *this* particular parish.

This is a principle clearly applied in other walks of life. Someone may be fully qualified to serve as a Head Teacher, and yet not be suitable for a specific school; and a candidate may be in every way qualified to serve as a Member of Parliament and yet fail to convince electors that he or she would be the best MP for their particular constituency.[35] Secular governors

---

34. This was equally true of the Church of England, where the church is subject to the supreme governorship of the Crown-in-Parliament.

35. Hugh Miller, after the Reform Bill had significantly extended the franchise: the people fit to choose an MP, but not a minister.

can govern only with the consent of the people. The same is true of the governors of the church.

The invalidity of Robertson's arguments was recognised in 1874 when patronage, already abandoned by the Free Church and the various branches of the Secession, was abolished once and for all within the Church of Scotland. Today, the right of those in the pew to elect their own ministers (and all other office-bearers) is cherished throughout world Presbyterianism. But by the same token it is an emphatic rejection of the key policy of 'Principal Robertson's administration'. If he had devoted his undoubted talents to putting an end to patronage rather than to enforcing it, the history of Scottish Christianity would have been very different; and, we may suspect, much more glorious.

10

The Moderate Hegemony

WILLIAM ROBERTSON CONTROLLED the General Assembly of the Church of Scotland from 1752 until 1780, and his Moderate successors continued to exercise this hegemony until well into the nineteenth century. The achievement is all the more remarkable considering that at no point during these years could the Moderates be confident of securing a majority in the General Assembly.[1] Their rivals, by this time commonly referred to as 'the Popular Party', were still numerous, well organised, possessed of talented leaders such as John Erskine (Robertson's colleague at Old Greyfriars), and able on occasion to outvote the Moderates at both presbytery and Assembly level. Yet Robertson never lost control of the Assembly.

One reason for this was that as Principal of Edinburgh University,[2] he was *ex officio* a member of the General Assembly every year. This gave him a huge advantage over ordinary ministers, who could expect to be members only once in every three or four years: an arrangement which made it impossible for them, and still does, to introduce any serious proposal into the Assembly and see it through to completion. It also meant in Robertson's case that he had an unrivalled knowledge of the Assembly's procedures, close familiarity with its leading figures (including those on the Popular side), and an often decisive say in the appointment of key officials such as the Assembly Clerk, the Procurator, and even the Lord High Commissioner. Added to this was the fact that no one in the Popular Party could match him as a debater,

---

1. 'It cannot be stressed too strongly that the Moderates were a minority regime' (Ian D. L. Clark, 'From Protest to Reaction: The Moderate Regime in the Church of Scotland, 1752–1805,' p. 222).

2. He was appointed to this post in 1762 and retained it till his death in 1793.

especially as he added to his gifts a conciliatory and charming manner (which hid the steel beneath). He also appears to have had a clear sense of calling, having been led by the success of his efforts in the 1752 Assembly to believe that it was his duty to apply all his abilities to making sure that the Assembly adhered strictly to its rules and precedents; and, beyond that, to delivering the kind of Church he thought Scotland needed. This would be a Church whose pulpits would be occupied by men of polite learning and good taste, and in whose pews the social elite would not feel out of place.

But his success wasn't due only to his own personal abilities and to his annual performance on the floor of the Assembly. He was greatly helped by the composition of the Assembly itself. As Clark points out,[3] the government of the day always had a strong representation in the Assembly, including such figures as the Lord Advocate, the Solicitor General, and other officers of the Crown, all of whom shared Robertson's determination that the law of the land (specifically, the Patronage Act) must be strictly applied. Added to these was a galaxy of judges who sat in the Assembly as ruling elders and who, as the events leading up to the Disruption showed, were as a class jealous for the rights of patrons; and alongside them, in the same capacity, sat other senior members of the legal profession, most notably the members of the Faculty of Advocates.

All of these dignitaries were closely related to the landed class who viewed patronage as a property-right entitled to full legal protection; and over and above this, several of them were also outstanding orators. Henry Dundas (later Viscount Melville), for example, was Lord Advocate from 1775 to 1783, and the brilliance of his debating skills matched Robertson's own.

These powerful voices had a vested interest in standing behind Robertson; but behind him stood, too, the Moderate party-machine, deeply loyal to Robertson, fully committed to his policy, and kept in good working-order by the close circle of clerical friends who had put their names to his 'Reasons of Dissent' in 1751: Hugh Blair, John Home and, above all, Alexander ('Jupiter') Carlyle. Through assiduous canvassing, personal contacts, the free flow of information, and the offering of favours, they ensured that their 'interest' was well represented in every Assembly. They knew that Moderate clergy were not more numerous in the Church as a whole than evangelicals, but where they saw their opportunity was in the

---

3. Clark, ibid., p. 203.

election of elders, where they were able to exploit an anomaly that persists in Scottish Presbyterianism to the present day. When presbyteries appoint their ministerial commissioners to an Assembly, they are limited to those who are members of their own presbytery; and furthermore, they are usually appointed according to a recognised rota which ensures on the one hand that all have an opportunity, but on the other that ministers can expect to be members of Assembly only once in every three or four years.

The rules for elders were completely different, reflecting the fact that few, especially those from 'remote' rural presbyteries, could afford to take three weeks off work (and face the long journey to Edinburgh). Yet the regulations laid down that presbyteries had to return an equal number of ministers and elders. The problem was 'solved' by allowing presbyteries to nominate any elder from anywhere within the Church, and the Moderate managers took full advantage of this arrangement, 'offering' elders to presbytery clerks who were struggling to make up the numbers. The most glaring example of this was that for the ten years between 1775 and 1785, Dr Robertson's son, William, represented the Presbytery of Lewis, though 'represent' has to be the wrong word. He had never seen the island, and had no knowledge of either its clergy or its people. He was, however, guaranteed to vote in favour of the Moderate interest; and Edinburgh's legal profession provided an almost bottomless pool of such men. The Assembly was, after all, an ideal opportunity to make useful professional contacts.

Another factor which explains the Moderate ascendancy is that, by and large, it had good relations with government, and especially with the Whigs who dominated British politics from the accession of George I in 1714 until the 1780s. Robertson firmly believed that, in terms of the Establishment, Church and state formed an equal partnership, the former entitled to having its voice heard in the counsels of government, the latter benefiting from the Church's promotion of civil order. This 'equality' would ultimately prove a delusion, as those in power increasingly came to see the Church as an irrelevance, but in the short term it served Robertson well. He could expect to be consulted by the politicians of both London and Edinburgh. At the same time, he was conscious that patronage was largely in the hands of the Crown, and in particular in the hands of the Lord Advocate. In the final years of Robertson's involvement in Church affairs, the Lord Advocate was Henry Dundas, who could claim that he controlled the right of patronage to at least a third of the parishes of Scotland; and Dundas could generally, though not always, be relied on to exercise this control in favour of Moderates.

Over and above this, the Crown also had in its gift many military appointments of importance to the landed gentry, as well as such ecclesiastical 'honours' as Deaneries and Royal Chaplaincies: positions which carried no authority in themselves, but were cherished by aspiring clergy, and the Crown could usually (though, again, not invariably) be persuaded to award these to men who would serve 'the Moderate interest'. At the same time, however, the Moderates were not above using threats and warnings if they thought government was not paying their party the respect it deserved. On one occasion, as Clark records,[4] Robertson threatened to withdraw entirely from all Church business unless 'the ministry choose to bestow the marks of their countenance upon such clergymen as are friends to government and law' (meaning, of course, Moderates, whose influence he clearly saw as a decisive contribution to the stability of society). On another occasion his friend, Alexander Carlyle, warned that government policy had allowed 'a very great number of illiterate Fanaticks to slip in among us'; and later still, in 1793, Carlyle warned that if the Moderate clergy were not 'upheld' by government they faced the 'awful prospect' of the Assembly being filled with 'Burgh Elders raging with democratic zeal'.[5] It was a shrewd threat. Four years after the French Revolution, 'democratic zeal' would indeed have been an 'awful prospect' to Pitt the Younger and his government. On the other hand, the Moderates weren't being insincere. They dreaded any increase in people-power, and people-power was what the Popular Party represented, though not in political terms.

Inevitably, too, the Moderates at parish level courted the local land-owners,[6] many of them anglicised gentry aspiring to live lives marked by good taste, refined manners, and elegant living; and, conversely, inclined to judge potential presentees (normally young probationary ministers) on the extent to which they shared these values. They were also qualities which Robertson himself saw as essential in a parish minister, as he made clear in his contribution to the debate on the so-called Schism Overture in the General Assembly of 1766. The background to the debate was an Overture put to the

---

4. ibid., p. 219.

5. Clark, ibid., p. 219.

6. At this period the population of Scotland was still predominantly rural and agricultural. In 1750, for example, the population of Glasgow was a mere 32,000.

Assembly the previous year calling for an enquiry into the alarming number of defections from the Established Church.[7] The figures were certainly alarming. The defectors were said to number 100,000 people meeting in 120 new meeting-houses and receiving instruction from an ill-educated and disorderly ministry.[8] The sponsors of the Overture were mainly members of the Popular Party, and their argument was that the secessions were due to the high-handed manner in which the Moderates had imposed the law on patronage. The Overture failed to carry, however, largely due to a powerful speech by Robertson,[9] notable for an uncompromising defence of patronage: a defence which rested on the claim that it had led to a great improvement in the quality of Scotland's clergy, who were now as distinguished for their secular learning and polite manners as they had always been for their piety. 'The argument was a bold one,' writes Sher,[10] 'because it marked the first occasion on which the Moderates publicly asserted that patronage by an enlightened elite was the best means of filling parish vacancies.'

But does that not depend on the nature of the enlightenment? There is little evidence that the elite set much store by spiritual enlightenment, and it's doubtful if they would have taken it as a compliment had it been attributed to them. Patrons were certainly not going to be impressed by a man who might be tainted with the dreaded 'enthusiasm', and might even call them sinners.

The Moderate *literati*

Yet for all his success as leader of the Moderate Party, Robertson was more than an ecclesiastical manager, and far from content with whatever distinction might come to him as a mere presbyterian minister. We may indeed concede Dugald Stewart's claim that he performed the duties of his profession 'punctually',[11] but these were never the main preoccupation of his life, nor did he ever devote to them the whole of his strength.[12] It may be true, as Stewart also remarks, that 'his life was never wholly devoted

---

7. On this debate, Sher, *Church and University in the Scottish Enlightenment*, pp. 130-34.

8. Macinnes, *The Evangelical Movement in the Highlands of Scotland 1688 to 1800*, p. 83.

9. Supported by Henry Dundas.

10. Sher, ibid., p. 133.

11. Stewart, *Life and Writings of William Robertson*, p. 12.

12. Robertson combined with his ministry at Old Greyfriars (Edinburgh), the duties of Principal of Edinburgh University, Historiographer Royal for Scotland, and the labours of a prolific historian.

to the cultivation of letters',[13] but it is surely revealing that his biographer should deem it necessary to make such a disavowal; no less revealing that he devotes the bulk of the biography to an account of Robertson's writings; and more revealing still that none of these writings, with one very brief exception, is theological. They are ground-breaking histories, they formed the habitual preoccupation of his mind, they are his 'incomparable monuments', and it is as 'Robertson the historian' that posterity remembers him.[14] Literary distinction was his ambition, and this meant securing the admiration not only of his fellow countrymen but of the élite of London's literary establishment. The labour of composition was matched by anxiety about the reception his work would meet with.

But Robertson was not alone among eighteenth-century Scottish clergymen in harbouring such dreams. As we have seen, his 'Reasons for dissent ... .' were subscribed not only by himself but by his friends Alexander Carlyle, Hugh Blair and John Home, and together they soon emerged as a well-defined circle which came to be known as 'the Moderate literati', though it also included such sceptics as the economist Adam Smith and the philosopher David Hume. These figures were central to what later came to be labelled 'the Scottish Enlightenment'.[15] This was, of course, but one aspect of a wider European Enlightenment (otherwise known as the Age of Reason), stimulated by Descartes' attempt to achieve for philosophy the same certainty as is achievable in mathematics; Locke's rejection of the doctrine of innate ideas and his insistence that all knowledge was based on experience; and the claim of English deists and German rationalists that reason alone, without the aid of revelation, could provide an adequate basis for religion. Overall, the Enlightenment could be summed up in the principle, 'Dare to be wise' (Latin, *Sapere aude!*), which, being interpreted, means, 'Don't be dictated to by authority, think for yourself, and take nothing on trust.'

---

13. Stewart, ibid., p. 158.

14. Henry Moncrieff Wellwood, for example, describes him as one 'whose eminence as a historian has raised him above all his contemporaries' (*Account of the Life and Writings of John Erskine, D. D.*, p. 234). Erskine was colleague to Robertson at Old Greyfriars from 1767 to 1793.

15. Alexander Broadie points out that though the term, 'Scottish Enlightenment,' is in common use today, it was first used only in 1900, when William Robert Scott spoke of Francis Hutcheson as 'the prototype of the Scottish Enlightenment' (Alexander Broadie, Introduction to *The Cambridge Companion to the Scottish Enlightenment*, 2nd edition, eds. Alexander Broadie and Craig Smith; Cambridge: Cambridge University Press, 2019, p. 3).

It is hard to see any genetic connection between this phase of the Enlightenment and its Scottish expression which, despite a common presumption, was not deistical; neither, despite being very self-consciously tolerant, was it irreligious; and neither, yet again, was it a rejection of Christian orthodoxy. Robertson and his clerical friends never expressed any qualms about subscribing to the Westminster Confession, nor can they fairly be described as rationalists. In so far as the Moderate literati reflected on the relation between faith and reason they viewed them as partners, not as alternatives. The Scottish Enlightenment had passed its zenith before Immanuel Kant published his *Critique of Pure Reason* in 1781, arguing that reason, simply as such, could give no knowledge of the supersensuous world (including God, the soul, and life after death). Robertson, by contrast, accepted the value of natural theology. 'Careful observers,' he wrote, 'may often, by the light of reason, form probable conjectures with regard to the plan of God's Providence, and can discover a skilful hand, directing the revolutions of human affairs, and compassing the best ends, by the most effective and surprising means.' However, it is sacred history that draws aside the veil that covers the counsels of the Almighty and lays open His designs to the view of His creatures.[16] This is entirely consistent with the Westminster Confession's emphasis on both the reality and the insufficiency of the 'light of nature'; and the same position outcrops repeatedly in the sermons of Hugh Blair. For example, in his sermon, *On the Presence of God in a future State*, he writes that, 'It was consonant to the nature of man, to think that the Supreme Being was favourable to virtue' and would therefore lead 'good men' to a future state of life and happiness. He then adds, however, 'But what they indistinctly conceived, and could not with confidence rely upon, the doctrine of Christianity hath clearly explained and fully confirmed.'[17]

It is certainly not the case that the European Enlightenment struck Scotland like a bombshell in the 1750s. Thomas Halyburton, Professor of Divinity at St Andrews from 1710 to 1712, was already fully conversant

---

16. William Robertson, *The Situation of the World at the Time of Christ's Appearance: And its Connection with the Success of His Religion, Considered* (1755. 5th edition, Edinburgh: John Balfour, 1775), pp. 3-4. This sermon was preached at the Annual Meeting of the SPCK on Monday, 6 January 1755. It is the only sermon and, indeed, the only theological document, that Robertson ever chose to publish.

17. *Sermons by Hugh Blair, D. D.* (5 Vols, London, 1777–1801); Vol. 4 (1794), pp. 138-39.

with the literature of deism and was also already wrestling with the question of the grounds of Christian faith.[18] On the other hand, Moderates like Alexander Carlyle preferred to trace their genealogy back to Francis Hutcheson, Professor of Moral Philosophy at Glasgow from 1729 to 1746, whom the Moderates credited with having introduced new standards of learning, tolerance and taste into the ministry of Scotland. Hutcheson may well be regarded as the forerunner and prototype of the Scottish Enlightenment. Carlyle was one of Hutcheson's students, and he has left a vivid and engaging portrait of him as a lecturer who 'displayed a fervent and persuasive eloquence which was irresistible'.[19] But he also claimed that it was owing to Hutcheson and his successor, William Leechman,[20] that 'a new school was formed in the western provinces of Scotland, where the clergy till that period were narrow and bigoted, and had never ventured to range in their minds beyond the bounds of strict orthodoxy.'[21] The enlargement of mind they experienced under such professors 'soon gave them a turn for free enquiry, the result of which was candour and liberality of sentiment.'

This may have been due to the relative novelty of his subject-matter. The philosophical agenda, hitherto dominated by Aristotle, was now having to address the questions raised by John Locke, and Hutcheson's lectures thus drew presbyterian minds to such questions as the origin of our ideas of beauty and virtue; and not only to their origins, but to their nature.

---

18. See Thomas Halyburton, *Natural Religion Insufficient and Revealed Necessary to Man's Happiness in his Present State; or, A Rational Enquiry into the Principles of the Modern Deists* (Edinburgh, 1714); and *An Essay concerning the Nature of Faith; or the Ground on which Faith Assents to the Scriptures.* This treatise was likewise published in 1714 and seems to have been viewed as an appendix to the former. It was particularly focused on the views of John Locke. Both were covered by a 'An Epistle of Recommendation' signed by, among others, William Carstares, James Hadow (Halyburton's colleague at St Andrews) and William Hamilton (described by Henry Sefton in his *DSCHT* entry as 'a teacher of many Moderate divines'. The Recommendation describes Halyburton as abandoning the usual method of 'defensive' apologetics and 'carrying an offensive war into the enemy's territories'. The Preface to the original publication was written by James Hog, later a prominent Marrow Man, and the involvement of these varied divines shows that interest in deism among Scottish churchmen was by no means confined to Halyburton.

19. *The Autobiography of Alexander Carlyle of Inveresk 1722–1805*, ed. John Hill Burton (Edinburgh: T. N. Foulis, 1910), p. 78.

20. For a brief introduction to Leechman, see Christian Maurer, 'Early Enlightenment Shifts: Simson, Campbell, and Leechman' in David Ferguson and Mark W. Elliott, *The History of Scottish Theology, Volume II: The Early Enlightenment to the Late Victorian Era* (Oxford: Oxford University Press, 2019), pp. 50-52.

21. Carlyle, ibid., p. 94.

From this point of view, as David Daiches points out, while the Scottish Enlightenment in its heyday was centred in Edinburgh, 'it can be said to have begun in Glasgow with the publication of Francis Hutcheson's *Inquiry into the Originals of our Ideas of Beauty and Virtue* as early as 1724.'[22]

But Hutcheson's influence didn't derive only from his ideas. It was also a matter of his character and personality which, although he was never a Moderate in the party sense, provided, according to Richard Sher, 'a model for Moderate ministers to emulate,' particularly in his enthusiasm for learning, liberty and virtue.[23] However, while the Moderates may be defined by their adulation of Hutcheson, they may also be defined by their harsh criticism of men like Ebenezer Erskine,[24] who had different enthusiasms.

But whatever the impulses behind it, and whoever has the best title to be declared its prototype, there can be no doubt but that the era of the Moderate literati was a golden age in Scottish culture: an era which produced a remarkable flourishing of talent, covering a wide range of fields and bequeathing a legacy which still influences our lives today. Robertson gained world-wide eminence as a historian; David Hume still commands respect as one of the greatest of European philosophers; Adam Smith is still a powerful voice in economics; Hugh Blair pioneered the academic study of rhetoric and literary criticism; Adam Ferguson is widely regarded as the founder of sociology; John Home took Scottish drama to the London stage; and Colin Maclaurin, who carried forward the work of Sir Isaac Newton, was a world-ranking mathematician.

But the Scottish Enlightenment also made enduring contributions in more practical domains. James Watt harnessed the power of steam and put Britain at the forefront of the Industrial Revolution; James Hutton laid the foundations of modern geology; William Adam and his sons, Robert and James, introduced the neoclassical style of architecture; Professor Joseph Black, the doyen of Edinburgh University's Medical School, achieved international recognition for his discoveries in both physics and chemistry; and at the same time as these developments were taking place

---

22. David Daiches, 'The Scottish Enlightenment,' in David Daiches, Peter Jones and Jean Jones (eds.), *The Scottish Enlightenment 1730–1790: A Hotbed of Genius* (Edinburgh: The Saltire Society, 1996). p. 1.

23. Sher, ibid., p. 69.

24. And, by implication, of John Maclaurin, brother of the mathematician, Colin Maclaurin, who certainly cannot be dismissed as merely 'narrow and bigoted'. He could, however, be dismissed as an 'enthusiast' due to his support of the Cambuslang revival.

in the arts and sciences, the same enterprising mood was introducing radical improvements in agriculture, land-use and town-planning (work on building Edinburgh's New Town began in 1767).

The whole of Europe sat up and took notice. No longer were Scotland and its capital seen as barbarous extremities on the edge of Europe. Instead, Edinburgh came to be called the Athens of the North, and later historians have set it up as 'a hotbed of genius' and as 'a city that changed the world'. One English visitor reported, 'Here I stand at what is called the *Cross of Edinburgh*,[25] and can, in a few minutes, take fifty men of genius and learning by the hand.'[26] Even the cynical Voltaire declared, 'Today it is from Scotland that we get rules of taste in all the arts, from epic poetry to gardening.'[27]

Among the many remarkable features of this movement not the least is the fact that four of the 'men of learning and genius' named above (Robertson, Blair, Home and Ferguson)[28] were ordained ministers of the Church of Scotland and, far from being peripheral to the movement, they were central to it. They did not, however, operate a clerical closed-shop. Instead, as we have seen, the sceptics, Adam Smith and David Hume, were also part of their closely bonded circle; and Rev. Alexander Carlyle, though not himself one of the 'men of learning and genius', was nevertheless a key member of the group and, through his *Autobiography*, an invaluable chronicler of its activities, and particularly of its social life.[29]

---

25. Presumably near where the statue of David Hume stands today (though the great man is actually sitting).

26. Quoted in Daiches, ibid., p. 1.

27. Quoted in Sher, ibid., p. 3

28. Ferguson, a native of Perthshire, a Gaelic speaker, served for a period as Chaplain to the Black Watch but later decided that the ministry was not for him and took up an academic career as Professor, first, of Natural Philosophy and later of Moral Philosophy, at Edinburgh University. He also wrote (1783) a highly regarded *History of the Progress and Termination of the Roman Republic History*, which was unfortunately eclipsed by the publication seven years previously of the first volume of Gibbon's *Decline and Fall of the Roman Empire*. See further, 'Adam Ferguson' in James McCosh, *The Scottish Philosophy: Biographical, Expository, Critical, from Hutcheson to Hamilton* (London: Macmillan 1875), pp. 255-61.

29. Ian D. L. Clark describes the *Autobiography* as 'egregious' (outrageous'), p. 201, and suggests that it has been a tempting source for those who wanted to caricature the Moderates. It may be that Carlyle deliberately overdrew the picture, perhaps to show his contempt for the strictures of the 'narrow and bigoted'. But then, a complete lack of respect for the piety of the Popular Party was a key part of the image the Moderate literati wanted to project. Professor Ian Campbell describes Carlyle's work as 'an undoubted masterpiece of autobiography and literary memoir' (see 'Carlyle, Alexander,' in *DSCHT*).

Born in 1722, and known as 'Jupiter' Carlyle because of his august, Olympian appearance, he was Minister of Inveresk in the Presbytery of Dalkeith from 1748 till his death in 1805. He never aroused any suspicions of heresy, even less of dissoluteness, and less still of saintliness. He was very much a *bon viveur*, cultivating taste and refinement, and the company of the literati and the aristocracy.

He also had a clear delight in breaching the traditional code of clerical behaviour, and in this connection he was as capable of setting up his more timid Moderate friends as he was of expressing his contempt for the 'High Flyers'. He had known Robertson and Hugh Blair in his student days, and they remained close and lifelong friends, but at one point he takes delight in recalling how unhappy they were when visiting friends in the country in rainy weather.[30] They couldn't play cards because they were brought up at a time when it was a sin in the common people and a disgrace in a clergyman. Nor could they play golf or bowls. They were at a loose end, and Carlyle enjoys their discomfiture. But he boasts, too, that he himself had been the first minister to play cards and backgammon behind *unlocked* doors, 'and so relieved the clergy from ridicule on that side.' By the time they were sixty, however, both his reverend colleagues had learned to play whist: 'Robertson did very well – Blair never shone.'

While his natural circle was the literati of nearby Edinburgh, the *Autobiography* also abounds in references to dukes, lords and other members of the higher echelons of society. He is particularly honoured by his relationship with the Duke of Buccleuch, and gets very excited when in 1767 the young Duke and his Duchess come to take up residence at 'their palace at Dalkeith as their chief residence'. To make the distinguished couple feel more impressively the attachment of their 'vassals and tenants', Carlyle wrote a birthday-poem to the Duke, had it copied by another hand (it's not clear why), and had it dispatched to arrive on the day.

He also describes the birthday party, by all accounts something of a disappointment. There were about fifty ladies and gentlemen from the neighbourhood, but while 'the fare was sumptuous, the company was formal and dull.'[31] For this he blames Adam Smith, the only one present whom the Duke knew well but who, it seems, was 'but ill qualified to

---

30. Carlyle, ibid., p. 307.
31. ibid., p. 512.

promote the jollity of a birthday'. Had it not been for Carlyle himself, the event might have been very dull and might have been dissolved 'without even drinking the health of the day'.

On the other hand, there was the pleasure of seeing the Duchess, and if she ever read Carlyle's description of her, she would have been mightily pleased. She was extremely beautiful, her features being regular, her complexion good, her black eyes of an impressive lustre and her mouth, when she spoke, uncommonly graceful. You get the feeling that she is being judged according to the criteria of beauty laid down by Francis Hutcheson.

But this picture of Carlyle as a man with a penchant for the aristocracy is not the whole truth. It may be true, as Hill Burton suggested, that he was partial to the company of his superiors,[32] but they were his superiors only in the simplistic sense that they had land, and he didn't. In manners, taste and learning (and even influence) he was at least their equal. Nor did his links with the aristocracy mean that he neglected the needs of his humble parishioners. The inscription on his tombstone (written by his friend, Adam Ferguson) speaks of him as a willing guide to his people; and although at his first arrival in the parish he wasn't welcome (being the patron's choice, not the people's) he won them over, not least by using his standing among the aristocracy to plead his parishioners' cause. Their respect for him became obvious later when he was in trouble in the Church courts over his resolute defence of his friend and colleague, John Home, who had broken clerical convention by writing and producing a stage-play, *Douglas.* Carlyle's parishioners stood solidly behind him.

It would be a mistake, too, to assume that Carlyle sailed flamboyantly and nonchalantly through life. He had his full share of earthly sorrows. His four children, three boys and a girl, all predeceased him by thirty years: Sarah aged eight, Jenny six, Mary Roddam four, and last of all, in 1777, William aged four. 'It was the way of heaven,' he wrote, 'that I should lose them too soon.'[33]

We must also bear in mind that, to a much greater extent than the clerical 'men of learning and genius', Carlyle had a passion for the Church,

32. This remark occurs on page 569 in Hill Burton's Supplementary Chapter to his edition of Carlyle's *Autobiography* (pp. 563-603). Hereafter cited as 'Hill Burton'.
33. Carlyle, ibid., p. 552.

and not only for the institution but for the individuals who served it. He was painfully aware that many of her ministers were in dire straits, and aware, too, that the blame lay with the aristocracy who at the Reformation had grabbed for themselves the lands which had supported the mediaeval clergy and should, by right, have supported the new order of clergy as well.[34] The result was that the clergy had been 'allowed almost to starve', and 'on every application for redress, they [had] been scurvily treated.'[35]

Carlyle saw here a lack of gratitude, particularly on the part of the landed classes, for the contribution the Church had made to the stability of the country, and particularly for its support of the Hanoverian succession in the face of the Jacobite threat. But he saw, too, a threat to the quality of the ministry itself. The prospect of penury was not going to attract men with the sort of manners, taste and learning that Carlyle longed to see adorning the Kirk. The day might come, he warned, when the clergy were no longer a barrier against the radicalism that would sweep away the power of the landed class who now claimed as their own the resources which had been pledged to the support of the ministry.

These were the sentiments that prompted him in 1768 to give his whole-hearted support to those who were resisting proposals to have the widely unpopular window tax extended to the clergy, who were already struggling financially and were now liable to be hit particularly hard by a tax based on the number of windows in their residences (the base-line for the tax was five windows, which left many homes exempt, but few manses).[36] In 1767, the General Assembly had appointed a committee to address the issue, but the committee, as often happens, had done nothing, and Carlyle noted, 'I was obliged to stir myself about it.' This was no easy matter, however. The decision-makers were in London, and he had the full support of neither Robertson nor the successive Lord Advocates, all clearly averse to stirring

---

34. The new, Protestant order was not seen by Knox and his colleagues as a new church, discontinuous with the past, but as a re-formed church, which retained much of the theological legacy of the past (for example, the Ecumenical Creeds) and continued to use the vast majority of the pre-Reformation church buildings for public worship. The *First Book of Discipline* assumed that all the considerable assets of the mediaeval church would continue to be at the disposal of the new national religion, not only to provide for the maintenance of its ministry but also for the support of the poor and the provision of a national system of education.

35. Carlyle, ibid., pp. 527, 526.

36. ibid., p. 516.

themselves. It proved to be a tedious and tortuous affair, and was finally resolved to Carlyle's satisfaction only in 1782.

Driven by the same concerns, Carlyle also involved himself in a campaign for the augmentation of stipends.[37] Hill Burton (p. 587) describes this as a contest against the landed gentry, and this, too, was a protracted affair. A Tory government did in 1791 bring in a bill, but 'they found the country gentlemen of Scotland too strong for them', and the bill had to be abandoned. Only in 1810 did Parliament pass an Act declaring a minimum stipend of £150 a year. By this time, Carlyle was dead.

Unlike Robertson and Blair, Carlyle was not driven by ambition of literary fame, nor did he seek either popularity or preferment. Content with his parish he never sought presentation to an Edinburgh charge, nor did he covet the ecclesiastical 'honours' which attracted so many clergymen. The one prize he coveted, the Clerkship of the General Assembly, narrowly eluded him in 1789, not because of any personal failings, but because of a fear (probably justified) that such a strong personality would dominate the Assembly.

Taking an overall view of his life, Carlyle's ambition was not for himself, but for the Church, for which he longed to find 'a place along with rank, and wealth, and distinction of every kind.'[38] This lay behind everything he did. If he mingled with the aristocracy, it was to show them a class of clergymen of whom they need not be ashamed; if he sought to improve the lot of parish ministers it was to attract the 'right' sort of men into the profession; and if he worked tirelessly behind the scenes to guide patrons in their choice, presbytery clerks in their search for suitable elders, and the government in conferring honours on ministers sympathetic to 'Dr. Robertson's administration', it was to render the Established Church an institution which could command the respect of men of learning and genius, the support of men in power, and even the admiration of Europe.

Carlyle carried this agenda through to consummate success. Indeed, without him, there would never have been a Moderate ascendancy; and though he did not, like his friends, find a place in the hall of literary fame, Hill Burton is fully justified in claiming that, 'Scarcely a primate of the

---

37. Initially launched in 1788 by Sir Henry Moncrieff Wellwood, leader of the Popular Party, in a pamphlet entitled, *Sketch of a Plan for Augmenting the Livings of the Established Church of Scotland.*

38. Hill Burton, ibid., p. 603.

Church of England could overtop in social position and influence the Presbyterian minister of Inveresk.'[39]

The tragedy lies in the nature of the vision he entertained for the Church. Deeply ashamed of her past, and especially of her seventeenth-century past, he made his own vision plain, albeit unintentionally, in the Assembly of 1791, when he objected to the Church of Scotland being described as 'the poorest church in Christendom'.[40] On the contrary, he argued, she was rich in all the best goods a church could have, and he summed these up by declaring that there were few branches of literature in which the ministers of the Church had not excelled, and few subjects of fine writing in which they did not stand in the front rank. They had written the best histories, ancient and modern (Ferguson and Robertson); they had given the clearest delineation of the human understanding (Hutcheson and Thomas Reid); one of their number had written the best system of rhetoric and exemplified it by his own orations (Blair); another had written a tragedy which critical opinion had declared 'perfect' (Home). 'Let us not complain of poverty,' he concluded, 'for it is a splendid poverty indeed! It is *pauperitas fecunda virorum* (a poverty productive of heroes).'

All true, or at least plausible, and for a brief period the ministry of the Church of Scotland found itself the admiration of the world. But at what cost? The Church as described by Carlyle in this passage was a Church which the world admired because it reflected the world's own values: certainly not the sort of Church against which the gates of hell would bother to stir themselves. On the other hand, at this point the Minister of Inveresk reflected the values, not of the whole Church, but of one party within it.

This doesn't mean, however, that Carlyle lacked theological acumen, as he showed in a discussion of the Test Act in the General Assembly of 1791. There was a widespread sense of grievance since, in terms of the Act, no Scotsman could hold public office south of the Border unless he took Communion in the Church of England. Carlyle, however, championed the Act, and his argument seems at first sight an odd one. It deserved to be supported, he declared, as an expression of toleration towards the Church of England; and what this meant in practice was that no member of the Church of Scotland should have any qualms about taking Communion

39. ibid., p. 603.
40. ibid., pp. 588-89.

in the Church of England, as if it were a sin to give any countenance to episcopacy. 'He must be a very narrow Presbyterian indeed who, in the various circumstances in which he might be placed, could not take part in the worship of that Church.'[41] The Test Act, by allowing Scotsmen to hold office in England, had confirmed the Union, and if the two nations were one it would be a disgrace to the General Assembly to do anything that might seem to drive the two churches apart.

Though he doesn't say this, his clear meaning is that to refuse to take Communion according to the Anglican Order is to unchurch the Church of England, or at least to declare episcopacy, simply as such, a barrier to inter-Communion. Hill Burton contrasts this tolerant approach with the attitude that had prevailed among the presbyterian clergy Carlyle would have known in his younger days, when it was widely held that toleration of episcopacy was one of the great sins for which divine vengeance might fall on the nation. It is by no means clear, however, that Scotland's seventeenth-century theologians regarded the Anglican liturgy in this light; and although John Knox objected to the requirement that Communion be received kneeling, he did not, in his pre-Frankfurt days, distance himself from the Church of England; and far from denouncing the ministry of Archbishop Cranmer he paid a generous tribute to him and his fellow-martyrs, Bishops Latimer and Ridley, highlighting their 'lenity, sincere doctrine, pure life, godly conversation and discreet counsel.'[42] Besides, even the practice of kneeling at Communion, though lacking any warrant in the Last Supper, can bear a tolerable construction as a token of humility far removed from the Adoration of the Host. This is certainly how Cranmer intended it.[43]

On the other hand, a United Kingdom parliament dominated by Anglicans (including a powerful bench of bishops) could never have reciprocated Carlyle's tolerance and prescribed that Englishmen holding public office in Scotland should take Communion in the Church of

---

41. Hill Burton, ibid., p. 580.

42. Diarmaid McCulloch, *Thomas Cranmer: A Life* (New Haven and London: Yale University Press, 1996), p. 622.

43. The wording of the Order for the Administration of the Lord's Supper in the Book of Common Prayer is that communicants are to receive the holy Communion 'by one of the Ministers: both he and all the people kneeling *humbly upon their knees*' (italics added). During the kneeling, the minister is to say the words of the General Confession in the name of the people. The tone of the Confession is set by the opening words, 'We acknowledge and bewail our manifold sins and wickedness.'

Scotland. To give such countenance to Presbyterianism, and to recognise the validity of Presbyterian Orders, was unthinkable. So it remains, and all ecumenical discussion fails at the threshold because the very first thing Presbyterians must do is surrender their Presbyterianism in favour of divine right episcopacy.

The Poker Club

Carlyle was clearly gregarious, but he was not alone in this. It was true of the Moderate literati as a whole, and theirs was no casual socialising, but one that centred on well-organised clubs with clear constitutions, formal membership and firm rules. One early example of this was the Select Society.[44] The brain-child of the poet, Allan Ramsay, it first met on 22 May 1754, and the founder members included, besides Ramsay, David Hume, Adam Smith, John Home, Lord Kames (Henry Home) and Carlyle. Robertson was admitted to membership at the second meeting in June, the number eventually rose to one hundred and sixty, and it included, according to Stewart, 'all the intellectuals in Edinburgh and the area who were most distinguished by genius or by literary attainments.'[45] The meetings took place in the Advocates Library and for the fourteen clerical members they were an invaluable opportunity to move beyond their narrow ecclesiastical circle into secular society and the world of Scotland's ruling elite.

The express purpose of the Society was to help members improve their understanding of philosophical questions and to hone their skills in public speaking.[46] It certainly achieved this purpose, and men like Robertson benefited enormously from their participation in debates 'where the most splendid talents that ever adorned this country were roused to their best exertions by the liberal and ennobling discussions of literature and philosophy' which were the staple fare at meetings of the Select Society.[47] It is breathtaking to recall that in these meetings the brilliance of Hume the philosopher reacted regularly with that of Robertson the historian,

---

44. Jeffrey R. Smitten, *The Life of William Robertson: Minister, Historian, and Principal* (Edinburgh: University Press, 2017), pp. 164-65.

45. Stewart, ibid., p. 15.

46. Some members of the Society also formed a subsidiary Society for Promoting the Reading and Speaking of the English Language in Scotland. This reflects the determination of the literati to achieve a level of pronunciation and writing-style comparable to that of the London establishment.

47. Stewart, ibid., pp. 15-16.

Adam Smith the political economist, Lord Kames the jurist, Ferguson the sociologist, and Ramsay the poet. This cross-disciplinary collegiality was a key factor in the achievements of the Scottish Enlightenment.

The Select Society continued to meet until 1764, but that same year another club, the Poker, emerged, and took its place at the heart of the Edinburgh Enlightenment. It initially called itself 'the Militia Club', reflecting the fact that it had its roots in a campaign for a Scottish militia, now largely forgotten, but described by Richard Sher as 'one of the liveliest themes of Scottish history during the second half of the eighteenth century'.[48] It arose out of fears generated, north and south of the Border, by the Seven Years War (1756–63), when Britain and France fought for European supremacy. Britain's regular army was fighting on several fronts on the continent, leaving it short of reserves, and the homeland vulnerable to invasion. The Prime Minister, Pitt the Elder, recognised the danger, and Parliament passed the Militia Act in 1757.

The Moderati participated enthusiastically in the campaign for a militia, partly because of their experience when Edinburgh was occupied by the Jacobite army in 1745, partly because they had their fair share of what they saw as Scotland's traditional martial spirit, and partly because they saw a militia as 'a moral counterweight to the harmful consequences of prosperity'.[49] But when Parliament passed its 1757 Act, it excluded Scotland, presumably because memories of Scottish Jacobite 'militias' were still fresh in the memories of the British government, who seemed to hold the whole Scottish nation accountable for the 1745 Rising. At first, Scottish reaction to being excluded was muted, but in 1759 rumours of an imminent French invasion once again focused people's minds on Scotland's vulnerability, and from then on till the close of the Seven Years War (1763) the question of a militia continued to occupy the minds of many Scots. But lively as the agitation was, it produced no Scottish Militia Act.

When William Pitt secured the passing of the Militia Act, little did he know that a few years later it would provoke a group of Scottish presbyterian ministers into forming a poker club; and had he been told he would probably have been shocked to hear of clergymen being such enthusiastic gamblers. But truth it was, that Edinburgh's Moderate literati would not let

---

48. Sher, ibid., p. 215.
49. ibid., p. 220.

the matter of the militia rest, because they saw the attitude of government as a violation of the spirit of the Union and an insult to the traditions of Scotland; and so, in 1764 they formed the Poker Club. This, as we have seen, was not the original name, but as they cast about for something more cryptic (and that might keep people guessing as to what they were about), Adam Ferguson suggested 'Poker': 'an instrument,' as Hill Burton suggested, 'for stirring up the militia question.'[50] About half the members, including Carlyle, Robertson, Hume and Ferguson, had previously been members of the Select Society, and Carlyle is probably justified in recording that the club consisted of the literati of Edinburgh and its neighbourhood.[51] But they were also joined by 'a great many country gentlemen who, though not always resident in town, yet were zealous friends to a Scotch militia, and warm in their resentment on its being refused to us, and an invidious line drawn between Scotland and England.'

Clearly, Carlyle and his friends, despite their firm belief in the Union, were not averse to making their displeasure known to the government when they felt Scottish interests were jeopardised. Yet, despite the members' conviction that 'there could be no lasting security for the freedom and independence of these islands, but in the valour and patriotism of an armed people,'[52] there is little on record to show that the Poker spent much of its time stirring; and neither was it a mere continuation of the Select Society, which by this time had probably outlived its usefulness by raising the skills of its members to the levels they needed for their place in public life.

The Poker, despite its declared aim, was in effect a dining club, and Carlyle regales us with the details. They met in a pub, probably weekly, the 'establishment' was frugal and moderate, dinner was on the table at two o'clock, costing a shilling a head, the wine confined to sherry and claret, and the reckoning called at six o'clock. It is hard to avoid the impression of a sort of boyishness. Members were chosen by secret ballot, two blackballs excluding the candidate.[53] Besides a Preses (President) and a Secretary,

---

50. Hill Burton, ibid., p. 439.

51. Carlyle, ibid., p. 439.

52. Adam Ferguson, quoted in Sher, ibid., p. 232. The wording reflects the fact that part of the background to the agitation for a militia was a fear of a *standing* army and a preference for a *people's* army.

53. This does not indicate a link to free masonry. A form of secret ballot was widely used since the sixteenth century, and it frequently involved the use of white balls and black balls.

the Club also had an Assassin, 'chosen in a laughing humour' in case there was ever a deed for disciplinary action; and an Assistant Assassin, David Hume, chosen because his temperament would ensure that there would be no bloodshed.[54] There was never a hint of inebriety in any of the members, and everyone was content with the entertainment, as well as the company.

This latter remark goes some way towards explaining how a meal, especially a frugal one, could last for four hours. The conversation was such as might be expected in a club composed, as one member claimed, 'of the ablest men in Europe'. Another 'man of fashion and of the world,' whom Carlyle met by accident and invited to the Club, afterwards gave it an ironic endorsement. 'Doctor,' he said, 'I never was so much disappointed in all my life as at your club, for I expected to sit silent and listen to a parcel of pedants descanting on learned subjects out of range of my knowledge; but instead of that, I have met with an agreeable, polite and lively company of gentlemen, in whose conversation I have joined and partaken with the greatest delight.'[55] Members were expected to be learned, but they were not expected to display it. The skill of men like Adam Smith was to make the profound and complex accessible.

The Douglas affair

One of Carlyle's co-presbyters was his friend, John Home, Minister of the neighbouring East Lothian parish of Athelstaneford, to which he was presented in 1746. Like the other literati, Home cherished literary ambitions, but where Robertson sought fame as a historian, and Blair as a master of rhetoric, Home's thoughts took him in a direction no presbyterian divine had ever taken before: he became a playwright. His first work, *Agis*, was completed in 1747, and in the hope of having it produced at Drury Lane he took it to London and showed it to David Garrick, who, however, pronounced it unsuitable for the stage. He then set about writing a second play, *Douglas: a Tragedy*, finished it by the end of summer 1754, and circulated it among his Edinburgh friends. They were fulsome in their praise, suggested some corrections and improvements, and in February 1755 pronounced it 'completely ready' for the stage. But once again, Home

---

54. Carlyle, ibid., p. 441.
55. ibid., p. 444.

was rejected in London, even though it had been pronounced 'a perfect tragedy' by the best judges.[56]

It was then decided that they should seek to have it produced in Edinburgh, in the hope that if it succeeded there, Garrick could resist it no longer. The première took place on 14 December 1756 (both Carlyle and Robertson having taken part in the rehearsals), and Carlyle records that 'the play had an unbounded success for many nights in Edinburgh, and was attended by all the literati and most of the judges.'[57] Indeed, the whole town was 'in an uproar of exultation', proud that a Scotsman had written a tragedy of the first rate. One enthusiastic (and patriotic) member of the audience was even driven to cry out, 'Whaur's your Wullie Shakespeare noo!'[58] Some critics doubted whether the play had a moral (as would have been expected from a clergyman), but there could be no doubt about its impact on the 'passions', so important in the philosophy of Hutcheson and his disciples. It drew the audience into sympathy for the heroine and moved them profoundly, as she went from one extreme emotion to another. A year after the première, David Hume dedicated his *Four Dissertations* to John Home, and described *Douglas* as 'one of the most interesting and pathetic pieces that was ever exhibited on any theatre'.[59] He referred in particular

---

56. ibid., p. 317. The phrase was first used by David Hume, but Carlyle comments that 'he spoke only the sentiment of the whole republic of letters'.

57. ibid., p. 327.

58. Cf. Carlyle's retrospective comment (ibid., p. 341), 'This tragedy still maintains its ground, has been more frequently acted, and is more popular, than any tragedy in the English language.' Deidre Dawson, in her essay, 'Literature and Sentimentalism,' notes that 'Douglas was an immediate success, and more than 130 performances took place in London alone by the end of the century' (Alexander Broadie and Craig Smith, eds., *The Scottish Enlightenment*, p. 296). In 1950 it was performed at the Edinburgh International Festival, with Dame Sybil Thorndike in the role of the heroine, Lady Randolph.

59. Quoted in Dawson, ibid., p. 295. Later critics have been less enthusiastic. In the course of their tour to the Hebrides, James Boswell reminded Dr Johnson that he had once challenged the poet, Richard Sheridan, 'How came you, Sir, to give Home a gold medal for writing that foolish play?' The doctor followed this up by defying Sheridan to show him ten good lines in the whole play (James Boswell, *The Journey of a Tour to the Hebrides with Dr. Samuel Johnson*, ed. Ian MacGowan; Edinburgh: Canongate Books, 1996, p. 437). David Daiches (ibid., p. 16) describes the over-evaluation of *Douglas* as 'a symptom of the failure of the Scottish Enlightenment to cope adequately with works of the poetic imagination.' In similar vein, Richard Sher remarks (ibid., p. 16) that, 'Gone are the days when authors of studies of "second-rate" thinkers felt compelled to demonstrate the previously unappreciated brilliance of their subjects.' The more useful task now, he declares, is to explain how such rarely read and nearly forgotten works as Home's *Douglas*, Robertson's *History of Scotland,* and Blair's *Sermons* 'could have

to the audience's response: 'the unfeigned tears which flowed from every eye' were eloquent testimony to the 'unparalleled command' which Home seemed to have 'over every affection of the human breast'.

Such a compliment is easy to understand when we look at the nature of the play itself.[60] 'Douglas' isn't actually named as one of the *dramatis personae*: when the story begins he is already dead, having fallen in one of the regular battles between his family and the rival house of Percy. The real hero is Lady Randolph, Douglas' widow after a brief marriage, now caught in a second, but loveless, marriage, but still grieving for Douglas and for their child, who died in infancy. A member of the rival family, she had kept her marriage secret from her father, and on the night of her baby's birth her nurse had set off with the infant to take him to the safety of her own sister's home. It was a wild winter's night, and neither nurse nor child was ever seen again. They had perished in the River Carron's 'swelling flood'.

The first twist comes with the arrival in Act II of Young Norval, accompanied by Lord Randolph, whom he has just rescued from a band of would-be assassins (hired, it later transpires, by his Lordship's son, Glenalvon). The new arrival quickly introduces himself as a 'lowborn man', the son of a shepherd, unaccustomed to finding himself in such exalted company. Inevitably, however, things are not as they seem. A lowborn man he may seem to be, and 'of parentage obscure', but he disdains the shepherd's slothful life, desires to gain a name in arms, and has already given proof of his martial prowess. But this was not his only virtue. He is as wise as he is brave, and distinguished by a gallant modesty. Lady Randolph, hugely impressed, confides to her servant, Anna,

> *How blest the mother of young gallant Norval!*
> *She for a living husband bore her pains*
> *Whilst I to a dead husband bore a son*
> *And to the roaring waters gave my child.*

But the shrewd Anna has her own suspicions:

> *On him intent you gazed, with a look*
> *Much more delighted than your pensive eye*
> *Has deign'd on other objects to bestow.*

---

been among the most popular and influential writings in Great Britain and abroad two hundred years ago.'

60. For the text, see Gerald D. Parker (ed.), *John Home: Douglas* (Edinburgh: Oliver and Boyd, 1972). Page references (in brackets) are to this edition.

And Lady Randolph responds:

> *I thought that, had the son of Douglas liv'd*
> *He might have been like this young gallant stranger,*
> *And pair'd with him in features and in shape.*

Then in the search for the would-be assassins (Act III) they apprehend an old man who, on being searched, is found to be carrying jewels bearing the Douglas crest: the very jewels the nurse had been carrying the night she set off with the infant child. The old man recounts how on that wild night a basket had flowed down the river bearing a baby and the jewels. He had taken him home, he and his wife moved to another part of the country, they had raised the child as their own, and they had often observed that 'he bore himself, Not as the offspring of our cottage blood; For nature will break out.' 'My name,' he added, 'is Norval; and my name he bears'; at which point Lady Randolph breaks out,

> *'Tis he! 'tis he himself! O! sovereign mercy! 'Twas my child I saw!*

Shortly afterwards (Act IV), Lady Randolph finds herself alone with Norval and seizes the opportunity to tell him that he is not Old Norval's son, 'nor of a shepherd sprung,' but that he is 'the son of Douglas'. 'But does my mother live?' 'She lives,' she replies, 'but wastes her life in constant woe, weeping her husband slain, her infant lost.' 'Art thou my mother?' 'I am thy mother,' she replies, 'and the wife of Douglas.'

Had the play not been billed as a tragedy the audience would have been hoping at this point that they would all live happily ever after. But Lady Randolph has already (p. 59) sussed out Glenalvon, Lord Randolph's son (and her stepson):

> *But beware, my son*
> *Of yon Glenalvon; in his guilty breast*
> *Resides a villain's shrewdness.*

He resents the place Norval has won in Lady Randolph's heart and fears that her lands and her hereditary lordship may pass to 'A peasant's son, a wandering beggar-boy.' Old Norval, too, has his suspicions of Glenalvon, but for different reasons. He has overheard a conversation between Lord Randolph and Glenalvon, realised that they have discovered the secret of Young Norval's birth, and now seek his life. Then, having eavesdropped on the final meeting between Lady Randolph and her son, the pair wait till the Lady departs, whereupon Lord Randolph challenges Douglas to draw his sword. The younger man proves master, but in the very moment that he disarms Randolph he is stabbed in the back by Glenalvon and quickly expires.

Had Douglas (Young Norval) been the hero, the tragedy would have ended there, but he wasn't, and it didn't. It ends with the death of Lady Randolph. Her death is not shown on stage: she had exited shortly after Douglas' death, but Anna, who had followed her, witnessed her final moments (p. 74). She had run, like lightning, to the top of a precipice, and

> *Upon the brink she stood, and cast her eyes*
> *Down on the deep: then lifting up her eyes*
> *And her white hands to heaven, seeming to say*
> *Why am I forced to this?' she plunged herself*
> *Into the empty air.*

It is easy to understand how, with these emotions of life-long grief, rekindled hope, and final tragedy and despair, the tears flowed freely. The audience would also have been captivated by the play's underlying deference to the mediaeval code of chivalry with its emphasis on honour and individual military prowess: sentiments which had been rekindled, no doubt, by the debate over the need for a militia with its frequent allusions to 'Scotland's traditional martial spirit'. And, at a time when attention was being focused on the importance of speaking 'London English', Edinburgh's elite would have been impressed by the beauty of Home's Shakespearean blank-verse (even though it was still far removed from the daily speech of both the market-place and the Bench).

But the approval was not universal: 'The High-flying set were unanimous against it,' wrote Carlyle.[61] Suspicion of the theatre was not confined, however, to the Puritans and their successors. Alarmed by the political satire which had become characteristic of the stage,[62] and deeply resentful of its attacks upon both his Government and the Royal Family, the Prime Minister, Sir Robert Walpole, had passed the Licensing Act of 1737, which

---

61. Carlyle, ibid., p. 327.

62. And not only of the stage. Jonathan Swift's heavily satirical novel, *Gulliver's Travels*, had been published in 1726, and the tradition of satirical fiction continued with such novelists as Henry Fielding (1707–1754).

laid down that no play could be produced till it had been approved by the Lord Chamberlain (an official of the UK government), and even then only in licensed theatres. When *Douglas* was first produced in Edinburgh in 1756, there was no such theatre outside of London, and even London had only two, Covent Garden and Drury Lane.[63] It had become common, however, to get round these restrictions by advertising theatrical performances as 'concerts', and Edinburgh's political establishment, who shared the Moderates' aversion to what they saw as the bigotry of the 'unco guid', were happy to go down this route, although they took the further precaution of decreeing that the parts would be played by English actors; and of course, in line with the Moderates' social conservatism, the play, far from being satirical, was such that the most august judges were happy, as we have seen, to give it their seal of approval (and, presumably, to shed tears).

Yet there were, undeniably, deeper reasons for the opposition to the staging of the play.[64] There was a general feeling among religious people that the theatre corrupted morals, though it is hard to see how, in the absence of theatres, Edinburgh's churchgoers could have formed this judgement. It was thus assumed that Christians would never attend the performance of a stage-play, and shocking to learn that not only had some ministers patronised the theatre, but that one had even written and produced a play.

This attitude to the stage found articulate expression in John Witherspoon's *Serious Enquiry into the Nature and Effects of the Stage*, described by Sher as 'the best statement of the anti-theatre position'.[65]

---

63. Only in 1788 was a bill passed permitting local authorities to license theatres outside London.

64. Concern about the ethos of the stage had already been forcibly expressed in England by the High Anglican, Jeremy Collier, in *A Short Review of the Immorality and Profaneness of the English Stage* (1698). Collier objected not only to the blasphemy which he saw as characteristic of the theatre, but also to its depiction of women and of the clergy (see Isobel Grundy, 'Restoration and Eighteenth Century' in Pat Rogers, ed., *The Oxford Illustrated History of English Literature*; Oxford: Oxford University Press, 1987, p. 226).

65. Sher, ibid., p. 81. An American edition of the *Serious Enquiry* was published in 1812, along with *An Address by Several Ministers in New York, to their Christian Fellow-Citizens, Dissuading Them from Attending Theatrical Representations*. The background to this was the burning-down of a crowded theatre in Richmond, Virginia on the night of 26 December 1811. Seventy-five people perished in the flames: a judgement, according to the ministers, on 'an institution which is always, by us, esteemed pernicious to society.' However, such pronouncements on public calamities presuppose a degree of prophetic insight which ministers, as such, have no right to claim. Besides, churches as well as theatres, have been the scene of public calamities, as witness the Surrey Gardens Music Hall disaster of 19 October 1856. On that occasion, eight people were crushed to death

Witherspoon's approach is not overloaded with theology. His starting point is that there is no such thing as theatre in the abstract. There is only the theatre as it actually exists, and that means a theatre which seeks to deliver, not the improvement of moral standards, but entertainment and pleasure. As such, it has to appeal to the taste of the public: a public which has little relish for anything remotely spiritual. Instead, the demand is for the romantic (where love literally justifies all things), for the heroic (as embodied in the codes of mediaeval chivalry), for the escapist (represented by the amusing and the frivolous), and (at its worst) for the salacious.

This need to cater to public taste is reinforced by the need to cover the expenses involved in presenting stage-plays, particularly the cost involved in maintaining companies of actors. Witherspoon recognises that acting is a demanding art, and one at which no one can become expert unless they devote themselves to it as their main employment. When they do so, they naturally expect a fair wage; nor is it any secret that they expect a higher standard of living than is enjoyed by those they entertain. If you add to this the other costs of production, the theatre clearly has to be run at a profit, to achieve this it has to attract large audiences (in modern terms, each play has to succeed at the box-office), and it's hardly going to achieve this by presenting material which serious Christians would find edifying. This doesn't mean that there can be no such thing as drama which might have religious as well as artistic merit, but Witherspoon's point is that the theatre cannot survive commercially by providing a regular diet of the morally and spiritually uplifting. To succeed, it has to offer its audiences the entertaining, the titillating and the sensational.[66]

All Witherspoon's detailed criticism follow from this basic premise that the theatre has to be a commercial success, and that to achieve this it has to cater to the taste of a public which at its best cares little for piety and religion, and at its worst entertains itself by ridiculing it. This is why the stage presents as the norm a life in which Bible reading, prayer and church

---

when, shortly after C. H. Spurgeon began to preach, a mischievous member of the audience cried, 'Fire!' and panic ensued. Cf. Jesus' rebuke (Luke 13:4) to those who saw the fall of the Tower of Siloam as a judgement on the local population: 'those eighteen on whom the tower of Siloam fell and killed them: do you think that they were worse offenders than all the others who lived in Jerusalem?'

66. Of course, Christians could avoid these, and limit their theatre-going to such productions as *King Lear, Chariots of Fire,* and *The Cheviot, the Stag and the Black Black Oil.* But such productions represent only a tiny fraction of ordinary theatre-fare.

attendance have no part, especially in the lives of people of culture and good taste. Witherspoon even goes so far as to argue that in its concern to portray the lifestyle which prevails in polite society, it has to introduce its audiences to vices unknown even to the barbarians.[67] But even when it avoids such extremes, the 'virtues' it endorses are not such Christian virtues as humility, but pride, false honour, and revenge, 'that right hand of false greatness of mind.'[68] These may be the virtues of the well-bred man, but they reflect the maxims of secular society, not those of the gospel.

But while the theatre presents the well-bred man as a role-model, the clergyman, by contrast, is habitually presented on stage stripped of every virtue which should adorn his profession. If he appears to possess any degree of ability, 'hypocrisy is the leading part of his character. But for the most part, awkwardness, ignorance, dullness and pedantry are represented as inseparable from men of that function.'[69]

The great concern of *Douglas*, as a pathetic tragedy, was to arouse the passions, and for the stage the primary passion is love. Whether in the eighteenth century or in the twenty-first, it is of its fortunes that audiences demand to hear; and what, after all, could be more Christian than love? Witherspoon asserts, however, that on the stage love is stripped of its primary God-ward dimension, and the whole of virtue is confined to benevolence and the duties of social life. Even then, it is presented not in terms of self-denial, but as a passion which is not to be denied: 'this, which is the strongest passion, and the most dangerous in the human frame, and from which the greatest number of crimes, and crimes the most atrocious, sprung, was always encouraged upon the stage.'[70] This is *eros* as distinct from *agape*, and since audiences did not like love's labour to be lost, love literally justified all things. And with its converse, jealousy, it wrought, and still wreaks, havoc.

To Witherspoon, a Christian going to theatre is entering a world that is in its very nature spiritually toxic. We have to remember, however, the standpoint from which he is writing. He is looking at it from the point of view of someone for whom to live is Christ (Phil. 1:21) and who values every human pursuit according to the extent to which it helps them live to the

---

67. Witherspoon, *A Serious Enquiry*, p. 134.

68. ibid., p. 104.

69. ibid., p. 124.

70. ibid., p. 93.

glory of God. He is not denying that the theatre may civilise; he is denying that it sanctifies. It may contribute to the formation of a well-bred man: it does not contribute to the formation of saints. It may entertain, but it does not edify. On the contrary it distracts the Christian from their real priorities and fosters the very values and attitudes he is struggling to leave behind.

It follows from this that in Witherspoon's opinion acting is not a lawful profession for a Christian. One reason for this is that a career devoted to amusing and entertaining 'the idle part of mankind' (typically by 'foolish talk and crude joking,' Eph. 5:4) is tantamount to a prostitution of our rational powers. But Witherspoon also questions the effect on the players of the fact that most of the characters they have to represent are vicious, and that in order to play such parts effectively they have to spend their whole lives 'endeavouring to express the language and exhibit a perfect picture of the passions of vicious men. And can they do this so frequently without at last becoming what they are so often in appearance?'[71]

The argument is as old as Plato, and it appears particularly in his discussion of the education necessary for those who would one day be guardians, charged with directing all their energies to protecting the freedom of the state. This was the only role they were to play in real life, and they could never excel in it if they were also educated as versatile character actors. Instead, the characters on which they must model themselves from their earliest years must be 'men of courage, self-control, independence, and religious principle.'[72] They must no more act a mean part than do a mean action or any other kind of wrong, 'For we soon reap the fruits of literature in real life, and prolonged indulgence in any form of literature leaves its mark on the moral nature of a man, affecting not only the mind but physical poise and intonation.' It was indeed important that they be educated in 'suitable literature', but 'since we care for the moral welfare of our guardians', they would not be allowed to take the parts of women, or of slaves, or of bad or cowardly characters, or of madmen: 'We must recognise that there are men and women who are mad and bad, but we cannot have them represented in poetry or drama.'[73] Nor should the guardians play the roles of humble workmen such as smiths or craftsmen or oarsmen.

---

71. ibid., p. 109.

72. Plato, *The Republic*, trans. H. D. P. Lee (Harmondsworth: Penguin Books, 1955), p. 134.

73. ibid., p. 135. On Witherspoon's terms, this would mean that we couldn't have theatre at all since without both the mad and the bad, it would be totally lacking in

In sum, while a decent man would be willing to impersonate a good man and feel no shame at all, 'if he comes across an unworthy character, he will be ashamed to imitate it seriously. He has no practice in such representation and will not consent to model himself on characters which his judgement despises as lower than his own.'[74]

Whether in fact role-playing has such a decisive reflex effect on actors is a moot point, though we should certainly ponder how often audiences confuse the actor with the character he plays and love or hate the person because they love or hate his *persona* on stage. That is a tribute to how close the two can come to merging. And the number of 'stars' whose lives end in tragedy should certainly give us pause.

What is open to no doubt, however, is that in Witherspoon's day 'even those who are fondest of theatrical amusements do yet notwithstanding esteem the employment of players as a mean and sordid profession.'[75] This doesn't by itself prove anything. After all, many, then and now, regard the clerical profession as a mean one. But what is interesting is that even dramatists typically shared this attitude to actors, who reciprocated by calling the dramatists ungrateful employers. The writers particularly resented the fact that they received such a small return for their plays in comparison with the players: 'Puppets that speak from our mouths,' as one playwright called them.[76]

But even more telling is the fact that, not only in the ancient world, but in Elizabethan England (and in fact down to 1661) women were not allowed to act on stage. Instead, female roles were played by young boys: an arrangement which must surely have presented its own moral dangers. Today, there is no such ban, but any Christian woman contemplating a life on stage or screen has to reckon with the fact that so many productions would have to carry the warning, 'Strong language, nudity, and scenes of a

---

box-office appeal. From Plato's point of view, these roles could be played by lesser mortals who were not being educated as future guardians.

74.   ibid., p. 136. At this point Plato adds, 'except perhaps for the purposes of amusement.'

75.   This attitude prevailed well into the twentieth century. See, for example, Lawrence Olivier's comment, 'Even in my youth the actor was still on the fringe of society. He was to be patronised rather than accepted; he was an amusement, a plaything still looked upon as a rogue and a vagabond. Romantic, but not socially enticing' (Laurence Olivier, *On Acting*; London: Weidenfeld and Nicolson, 1986, p. 30).

76.   Cf. Witherspoon's comment, 'It is a thing impracticable to maintain a player at the same expense as you may maintain a peasant' (ibid., p. 41).

sexual nature.' Such considerations set a serious limit to a woman's progress in an acting career (and, indeed, to a Christian man's).

Critical appraisal of *Douglas*

Witherspoon made no attempt to offer a critical appraisal of *Douglas*.[77] His concern was with the theatre and with stage-plays in general rather than with one particular play, even though it was the public presentation of Home's work that had put theatre on the agenda.[78] But even had Witherspoon been of a mind to express an opinion on *Douglas* it would scarcely have been possible, since he had never read the play. This wasn't a case of typical clerical pontificating on something they had never seen or read: the text had not yet been published,[79] and this was in accordance with regular practice. In those days there was no copyright law to protect writers, and dramatists were naturally reluctant to furnish actors with their lines (and their livelihood) while receiving little reward for their own labour.[80] At the same time, and for the same reasons, the actors themselves were reluctant to see the text of their plays in general circulation. Once they had mastered a part and created a niche for it, they were far from keen to see it published for the benefit of their rivals. This outlook also prevailed among producers and theatre-owners, so that even if Witherspoon had wished to approach *Douglas* from the standpoint of a critic, it would have been impossible for him. The text had been circulated only within the limited circle of Home's Edinburgh friends. Witherspoon's criticisms of *Douglas* are thus aimed at the stage as such, and any criticism of *Douglas* is implicit rather than explicit, highlighting such factors as the stage's endorsement of a sub-Christian code of honour and its portrayal of love as the plaything of fate.

---

77. For a brief critical introduction, see Gerald D. Parker's edition of *Douglas*, pp. 1-9.

78. Sher, ibid., p. 337, notes that there has been little scholarship on Home's career as a dramatist. This is even more true of Witherspoon's response to Home's *Douglas*.

79. He refers to *Douglas* as 'the new tragedy lately introduced into our theatres' and notes that it has been commended as an attempt to make the stage more innocent and more useful, but adds, 'What this piece is in itself nobody can say with certainty till it has been published' (p. 128). Two editions, one in London and one in Edinburgh, were published in March 1758, but Witherspoon's pamphlet (128 pages) had been published in 1757.

80. Two of Shakespeare's plays, 'Venus and Adonis', and 'The Rape of Lucrece', were published in 1593 and 1594 respectively, but the First Folio, containing the collected edition of his works, appeared only in 1623, seven years after his death (*William Shakespeare: The Complete Works,* edited with an introduction and glossary by Peter Alexander; Glasgow: Collins, 1951, p. xxii).

Still, *Douglas* cannot escape being judged on literary and artistic grounds, if only because of the exaggerated praise heaped upon it by its first Edinburgh audience. What basis was there for the cry, 'Whaur's your Wullie Shakespeare noo?' or for David Hume's description of Home's work as 'one of the most interesting and pathetic pieces ever exhibited on any theatre'?[81] Is *Douglas* really worthy of being compared with the great Shakespearean tragedies, *Hamlet, Othello, Lear, Macbeth* and *Coriolanus*?

Any attempt to answer this has to recognise that Home's primary concern was to arouse the passions, and that even David Hume judged the play purely and simply on the basis of the audience's emotional reaction. They were in floods of tears over the life of grief to which fate had destined Lady Randolph. In 1758 Garrick agreed to present the play at Drury Lane for the same reasons. It would give his audience what it wanted, and it would give him an opportunity to show his own outstanding skills as a tragic actor.[82] But is its power to move an audience to tears the real criterion of tragedy, particularly great tragedy? And can we imagine the fate of Lady Randolph ever provoking the debates associated with such Shakespearean tragedies as *Othello* and *King Lear*: questions such as whether her tragedy was the result of some tragic flaw which left her unable to resist the forces that led inexorably to her destruction;[83] or whether her very virtue was the

---

81.   Quoted in Dawson, ibid., p. 295. Hume, who knew Paris well, even compared *Douglas* to Voltaire's tragedy *Mérope,* which, after its huge success in that city, was later translated into English and German.

82.   Charles Lamb, while admitting in his essay, 'On the Tragedies of Shakespeare,' that he never saw Garrick perform such heroic roles as Hamlet, expresses doubt whether it was ever his concern to represent the actual character of the *personae* he played: 'Those who tell me of him, speak of his eye, of the magic of his eye, and of his commanding voice: physical properties, vastly desirable in an actor, and without which he can never insinuate meaning into an auditory – but what have they to do with Hamlet? What have they to do with intellect?' (see Edmund M. Jones, ed., *English Critical Essays: Nineteenth Century;* London: Oxford University Press, p. 102). Lamb's core complaint is that in any on-stage portrayal the *mind* of the hero is always subordinated to the appearance of the actor. Cf. Laurence Olivier's admission that his ambition always was to lead his audience towards 'an appreciation of acting, so that they will come not only to see the play but to watch acting for acting's sake' (Olivier, ibid., p. 77). In line with this, when *Douglas* was performed at the Edinburgh Festival in 1950, the typical critic's comment was that it was 'a triumph for Dame Sybil [Thorndike]' who played the heroine, Lady Randolph (Gerald D. Parker, ibid., p. 9).

83.   According to A. C. Bradley this was for Shakespeare 'the fundamental tragic trait' to be found in all his tragic heroes: a total incapacity, in certain circumstances, of resisting 'a fatal tendency to identify the whole being with one interest, object, passion, or habit of mind' (A. C. Bradley, *Shakespearean Tragedy: Lectures on Hamlet, Otello, King Lear, Macbeth* (London: Macmillan 1957, p. 13).

cause of her undoing, while at the same time making us love the virtues not less, but more; or, regardless of his personal views, is the dramatist drawing us towards the conclusion that tragedy can never yield its innermost secrets?

'The plays of Shakespeare,' wrote Charles Lamb, 'are less calculated for performance on a stage than those of any other dramatist whatever.'[84] This may be disputed: Shakespeare certainly wrote them for the stage, and, after all, it was only by the performance, not by the writing, that he could make a living. But Lamb is making a serious point. The tragic force of Shakespearean tragedy lies not in the hero's outward fate but in the torment of his mind; that torment is expressed in the words of the text, whether they be dialogue or soliloquy; and, Lamb suggests, acting all too easily diverts attention from the words and torments of the character to the performance of the actor, whose primary concern is not to present the reasons behind the passions, but the passions themselves. Garrick, for example, had to simulate anger, grief and despair; and it is this simulation, culminating in the simulation of death, that moves the audience to tears, and to admiration for the actor. The audience will cry with him: but it is the performance, not the inner wrestlings of the hero, that has moved their passions.

Carlyle's position

Carlyle, having been deeply involved in the preparations, had, of course, gone to see the play. He did not, however, attend the first night, 'being well aware that all the fanatics would be on the watch, and make all the advantage they possibly could against me.'[85] His fears were well founded, and his position by no means secure. The Moderate ascendancy had scarcely begun, and, while they had succeeded in the General Assembly, they did not control the presbyteries, several of which had formally condemned the play, among them Glasgow, Edinburgh, and Dalkeith (Carlyle's own presbytery). Edinburgh, prompted by Patrick Cumin, Professor of Ecclesiastical History at the University, and Alexander Webster, a prominent member of the Popular Party, drafted an 'Admonition and Exhortation' condemning stage plays as illegal and 'prejudicial to the interests of Religion and Morality'.[86] It further directed that this Admonition be read from every pulpit within the

---

84. Lamb, ibid., p. 99.
85. Carlyle, ibid., p. 329.
86. Sher, ibid., p. 78.

presbytery; and then, to show diligence, the presbytery suspended for three weeks one of their number who had gone to see the play, Thomas Whyte, the Minister of Liberton. The comparatively lenient sentence was probably intended to show that they had given due weight to his plea that, 'though he attended, he concealed as well as he could, to avoid giving offence.'[87]

Not to be outdone, the Presbytery of Dalkeith cited Carlyle to answer for his conduct. His response was to 'endeavour to bring them over to my opinion', but instead he met only with 'contemptible dissimulation', which probably meant that, while they agreed with him in private, they could not stand by him in public. Realising that he had little support, he asked the presbytery to frame a libel, which they did, but with considerable embellishment of the facts. He was alleged, for example, to have been eating and drinking with some of the actors 'on the unlicensed stage; to have taken his seat in a disorderly manner; and to have forced some gentlemen to move out of their seats to make way for him and the ladies he was escorting.'

He resolved to stand firm, his first step being to challenge the relevance of the libel, arguing that he had committed no offence worthy of censure and had, at worst, been guilty only of a mere impropriety or indiscretion. In this, Carlyle was almost certainly correct. Since 1707, disciplinary processes in the Church of Scotland had been regulated by *The Form of Process,* and at its heart lay the principle that, 'Nothing ought to be admitted by any Church judicature as the ground of a process of censure, but what hath been declared censurable by the Word of God, or some act or universal custom of this National Church agreeable thereto.'[88] The *Form* then goes on to cite such offences as swearing, cursing, profaning the Lord's Day, drunkenness, fornication, adultery, but it says nothing of attending the theatre; and neither indeed, does Scripture or any of the constitutional documents of Presbyterianism. In fact, only once in the course of its history did the General Assembly make any official pronouncement on the subject of theatre, and that was in 1757, when it passed a 'Recommendation to Presbyteries' urging them to take care 'that none of the ministers of this Church do, upon any occasion, attend the theatre.' However, this is but a recommendation, and it passes no

---

87. Carlyle, ibid., footnote p. 330.

88. For the full document, see *The Practice of the Free Church of Scotland in her Several Courts* (1955 edition), pp. 180-97.

judgement on theatre as such, but bases itself entirely on the importance of 'regular and inoffensive behaviour on the part of ministers' and the need to 'preserve the purity and decorum of the ministerial character'.[89] Carlyle, inevitably, saw things differently. To have submitted tamely to the presbytery's views on Home's play would, he wrote, 'have stamped disgrace on the Church of Scotland, kept the younger clergy for half a century longer in the trammels of bigotry or hypocrisy, and debarred every generous spirit from entering into orders.'[90] Presbytery, however, found the libel relevant; Carlyle appealed to the synod, where he won his case, presbytery appealed to the Assembly, and the case was finally settled when the Assembly of 1757 agreed with the synod that the charges against Carlyle were 'not sufficiently clear and incontrovertible'.

Carlyle's case was helped by a speech by Robertson on his behalf, but Robertson's own involvement in the 'Douglas affair' was far from straightforward. While still a young man, his father had made him promise that he would never enter a theatre, and in his speech before synod in May 1757 he was able to declare, 'It gives me great pleasure to think I have kept that promise sacred.' He added, however, that he did not condemn members who patronised the theatre occasionally, 'without giving scandal to their people.'[91] But away from 'his people', and particularly on his visits to London, he was less scrupulous about the promise. On his first visit in February 1758 he met up, not only with familiar Edinburgh friends, but with key figures on the literary scene such as David Garrick and Tobias Smollett (with whom he smoked tobacco and drank punch for two days); and on this same visit he also had his first taste of the London theatre when he went to watch the first night of John Home's *Agis*.[92] Afterwards, in a letter to a family friend, Margaret Hepburn, he describes himself as still feeling 'all the surprise and wonder of a novice'. But, novice or not, he still offered perceptive comments, not least on Garrick, on whom he remarks, 'I had no conception of such admirable power of expressing the strong passions.' But he also adds (in line with Charles Lamb), 'I have been more moved by reading a good tragedy than I am by seeing it.'

---

89. *Acts of the General Assembly of the Church of Scotland*, p. 769.
90. Carlyle, ibid., p. 332,
91. Smitten, *The Life of William Robertson*, p. 9
92. For a description of this visit, see Smitten, ibid., pp. 113-14.

Conclusion

The '*Douglas* affair' is widely seen as a defining moment in the history of Scottish culture. It certainly did not mark the beginning of the Scottish theatre. Throughout the Middle Ages, in Scotland, as in the rest of Europe, plays and pageants depicting episodes from both the Old and the New Testament were regularly performed at the main Christian festivals;[93] in the lead-up to the Reformation David Lindsay's *Ane Satyre of the Three Estates,* dramatically highlighted the failures and corruptions of the clergy; by 1574 the General Assembly of the re-formed church was already warning against the temptations of the playhouse, but bands of English players still continued to visit Edinburgh well into the eighteenth century; Allan Ramsay's Edinburgh Playhouse had been opened in the 1730s but forced to close following protests by 'zealous presbyterians';[94] the Canongate Theatre (where *Douglas* would be premiered) was built in 1747 and fully operational the following year, albeit under the fiction that it was a concert-hall.

But if the *Douglas* affair did not mark the beginning of the Scottish theatre, it did signalise a revolution in the attitude of genteel society towards stage-plays and, to a lesser extent, towards actors. It now became respectable for members of the judiciary, the aristocracy and senior members of the government to patronise the theatre. Even more significantly, it became respectable for members of the clergy to attend the performance of stage-plays, and just how far this particular revolution went became evident in 1784 when the London actress, Sarah Siddons, celebrated for her performances in such tragic roles as Lady Macbeth, visited Edinburgh for the first time. Her visit coincided with the sittings of the General Assembly and, as Carlyle notes, 'that court was obliged to fix all its important business for the alternate days when she did not act, as all the younger members, clergy as well as laity, took their stations in the theatre on those days by three in the afternoon.'[95]

This titbit is recorded in virtually every history of the Moderates and every history of the Scottish Enlightenment, but neither the visit of Mrs Siddons nor the staging of *Douglas* marked the end of what is called

---

93. See Sarah M. Carpenter, 'The Bible in Mediaeval Verse and Drama' in David F. Wright, ed., *The Bible in Scottish Life and Literature* (Edinburgh: Saint Andrew Press, 1988), p. 67.

94. Sher, ibid., p. 76.

95. Carlyle, ibid., p. 339.

(usually contemptuously) 'Scottish Puritanism'. Nor did it mark a universal change in attitude among the Scottish clergy. Rightly or wrongly, there still remained hundreds of ministers who did not frequent the theatre, and hundreds of congregations where such a habit would have cost them the respect and goodwill of their people: a risk that even William Robertson was not prepared to take. After all, and as already noted, the Moderates (with whom most of the theatre going clergy identified) never represented a clear majority of Scotland's presbyterian ministry. Puritanism continued alive and well not only in the rapidly growing Secession tradition but, as the Disruption of 1843 clearly demonstrated, even within the Established Church itself.

Carlyle may have boasted that of the many exertions he and his friends had made for the credit and interest of the clergy of the Church of Scotland 'there was none more meritorious or of better effects' than his struggles on behalf of *Douglas*. Had ignorance, superstition and illiberal ideas continued to prevail, he wrote, 'a bar should have given check to the rising liberality of the young scholars, and prevented those of better birth or more ingenious minds from entering into the profession.' This was always the Moderate priority: not that Scotland's pulpits be occupied by men cast in the apostolic mould, determined to glory in nothing but the cross of Christ (Gal. 6:14), but that they be occupied by men of refinement and culture, acceptable to a pretentious aristocracy. In any case it is only theatre-goers who define culture and refinement in terms of a love for the theatre, as if such a love were sufficient by itself to drive out all coarseness and vulgarity. A glance at a daily newspaper is sufficient to dispel that illusion. Refinement may indeed be found among the celebrities of the entertainment and artistic world, but it can hardly be said to predominate. On the other hand, while Thomas Chalmers, Jonathan Edwards and C. H. Spurgeon never patronised the theatre, it is hard to accept the conclusion that they were therefore less educated, refined or cultured than their theatre-going counterparts.

To go or not to go? That remains a matter for the individual conscience, not for an ecclesiastical code of discipline. But here we face the same sort of dilemma as faced the believers who formed the first-century church in Corinth. Should they eat meat that had been offered to idols? The guidance laid down by St Paul still stands: whether you go, or don't go, do what glorifies God. In any specific situation, only the individual can make that decision.

11
Moderate Preaching: Hugh Blair

ROBERTSON'S CLOSE FRIEND, Hugh Blair, was the great grandson of Robert Blair (1593–1666), a distinguished contemporary of Alexander Henderson, Samuel Rutherford, David Dickson and James Durham (for whose *Treatise Concerning Scandal* he wrote the original Preface). Early in his career he served as a Regent at the University of Glasgow, but finding himself out of sympathy with the views of the principal, John Cameron (a firm supporter of the royal prerogative), he resigned and went to Ireland, where he became Minister of the parish of Bangor. He wasn't left long in peace, however. His presbyterian principles attracted the antagonism of the bishop, he was dismissed from his charge, and forced to return to Scotland, where he became, first, Minister of Ayr and then of St Andrews. Driven out of St Andrews by Archbishop Sharp, he ended his days as Minister of Aberdour. All the signs are that this Robert Blair was very much in the mould of those seventeenth-century Presbyterians whom the *literati* despised as crude and intolerant fanatics.[1]

The succeeding generations of Blairs were also a distinguished line, including among their number not only ministers of the gospel but a father and son, both called Robert, one of whom served as Solicitor General for Scotland and the other as Professor of Practical Astronomy at the University of Edinburgh. Hugh's father, John Blair, was a reputable merchant and magistrate in Edinburgh, though his fortune, like many others', suffered from his taking shares in what turned out to be the South Sea Bubble. Despite

---

1. For a full account of Robert Blair, see *The Life of Robert Blair, Minister of St Andrews, containing His Autobiography from 1593 to 1636, with Supplement and Continuation by his Son-in-Law, Mr William Row* (ed. Thomas M'Crie; Edinburgh: Wodrow Society, 1848).

this, he was still able to ensure that his son received a liberal education, first at Edinburgh's High School and then at the university, where he appears to have been a student for no fewer than eleven years, enrolling in 1730, aged only twelve, and continuing there until 1741. But while his biographer, John Hill, mentions his Professors of Latin, Greek, and Logic (Professors Adam Watt, Colin Drummond, and John Stevenson, respectively), there is no mention of his Professor of Divinity, and it is safe to assume that the tuition given in that department made little impression. He mainly distinguished himself in the Logic class.[2]

Licensed in October 1741, Blair's early preaching was regarded as sound and practical, but his language as somewhat flowery: a fault which was quickly corrected. In September 1742 he was ordained and inducted to the charge of Colessie in the Presbytery of Cupar, but the following year he was elected Second Minister of Edinburgh's Canongate Kirk. Hill records that this charge was filled by popular election, and he adds, innocently, that in order to secure the election 'no small effort was required.'[3] In fact, it took 'the most active exertions' on the part of Blair's canvassers, but the happy result was that out of two hundred and eighteen votes Blair secured one hundred and thirty-six.

After eleven years as Minister of the Canongate, Blair was called to Lady Yester's (another Edinburgh parish), his biographer noting that such was his professional merit that it 'could not stop at any point in the line of his preferment but the highest.'[4] But Lady Yester's proved not to be the highest point, and in 1758 he was translated to the High Church (St Giles), where it was 'his province to preach before the judges of the land, and to instruct the most learned and respectable audience which his country can present.'[5]

He would never relinquish this position, but beyond it there was a point which was higher still. At the time there was a growing interest in rhetoric and aesthetics among the *literati*. In 1848, Adam Smith, under the sponsorship of the Philosophical Society of Edinburgh, had delivered some public lectures on rhetoric and *Belles Lettres*;[6] in 1762, Henry Home (Lord

---

2. John Hill, *An Account of the Life and Writings of Hugh Blair* (Philadelphia, 1808), p. 16.
3. ibid., p. 20.
4. ibid., p. 21.
5. ibid., p. 22.
6. Smith was not satisfied with these, however, and destroyed the papers.

Kames) published his *Elements of Criticism,* and in 1776, Professor George Campbell of Aberdeen, his *Philosophy of Rhetoric.*

Blair ventured into this field in 1759, when he began to deliver a series of 'lectures on composition' at Edinburgh University. The following year he was appointed Professor of Rhetoric, and when a Regius Chair of Rhetoric and *Belles Lettres* was established in 1762, Blair was the first appointee. The two volumes of his *Lectures* in this department were not published till 1783 (after his retirement), and they form an interesting background to his *Sermons* (published in five volumes between 1777 and 1801). They discuss such questions as the principles of taste and the different kinds of beauty, but refrain from laying down abstract criteria, the only established law being that beauty is what the human species, in all ages and in all countries, has regarded as giving it the highest and the most extensive delight. The difference between beauty and deformity, he declares, is as immutable as that between truth and falsehood; to which it may be replied that, immutable they both may be, but truth (or at least veracity) is easier to establish than beauty, nor is it at all clear that there is a universal consensus as to what constitutes beauty. What have the Beatles in common with Mozart?

The most important part of the *Lectures* is Blair's treatment of the subject of style: a treatment which, in the opinion of his admiring biographer, is marked by 'almost every excellence that can belong to a didactic discourse'.[7] In particular, all ornament is studiously avoided: 'Perspicuity alone is courted.' At the same time, readers are treated to a discussion of the construction of sentences (drawing on Aristotle) and to an enquiry into the nature and use of such figures of speech as metaphor, hyperbole and apostrophe: familiar weapons in the armoury of the preacher (and, indeed, of the inspired writers of Scripture). This is followed by reflections on the nature of eloquence, in the course of which Blair comments on the requirements of the different forms of public speaking as represented respectively by Popular Assemblies (for example, parliaments), the Bar and the Pulpit. This includes a comparison of two celebrated classical orators, Demosthenes and Cicero, and here Blair shows a decided preference for the former on the grounds that in Cicero the art is all too obvious and draws attention to itself. It is marvellous, but intrusive. Even while speaking of the safety of the Republic, the Roman orator doesn't forget himself, whereas in

---

7. Hill, ibid., p. 54.

Demosthenes no studied ornament interrupts the energy of his thoughts.[8] He is thinking of what he wants to say, not of the words he should choose. Whether this is a fair comparison may be a moot point, but it is safe to say that it is a fair indication of the approach that Blair brought to his own lectures and sermons. The overriding concern was with lucidity, and there was a studied avoidance of obtrusive artistic embellishment.

Blair and Robertson were close friends,[9] equally committed to the values of the Enlightenment and the Moderate vision of the Church. Yet they were very different in gifts and personality. Blair admired Robertson's administrative abilities and his skill in managing the General Assembly, but he himself took little part in church affairs, and never spoke from the floor of the Assembly. He was, however, willing to give advice, though only in the background. The clearest example of this is that it was Blair who provided the first draft of the pastoral admonition which the General Assembly addressed to its people in 1799. It warned against two evils: first, the principles of anarchy and rebellion which had led 'the unhappy nation of the French' to slaughter their sovereign and overturn their government; and, secondly, the activities of the missionaries of the Society for Propagating the Gospel at Home.

This Society, founded by the brothers Robert and James Haldane, trained and deployed itinerant missionaries whom the admonition describes as 'a set of men whose proceedings threaten no small disorder to the country'. 'These men,' the admonition continues, 'are now traversing the whole country as evangelists without any sort of authority, without giving any public pledge for the soundness of their faith, or the correctness of their morals, and without those advantages of regular education, and of preparatory knowledge, which are regarded as indispensably necessary for the discharge of a gospel ministry by every branch of the Christian church.'[10]

The admonition is, indeed, characterised by what Hill calls 'a beautiful simplicity of style', but its contempt for the itinerant missionaries and its questioning of the patriotism of the Haldanes is seriously misplaced. The brothers were nephews of the distinguished Admiral Duncan, who had

---

8. Hill, ibid., p. 60.

9. So close, indeed, that neither of them ever published anything without first submitting it to the judgement of the other.

10. For the complete text of the admonition, see *Acts of the General Assembly of the Church of Scotland*, pp. 870-73.

defeated the Dutch fleet off Camperdown in October 1797; Robert had served with distinction as an officer in the Royal Navy, James had captained an East India merchantman, and each, had they so wished, could have retired into the comfort of their Airthrey Estate in Stirlingshire and the glamour of the London drawing-rooms. Instead, the estate had been sold, originally with a view to funding mission-work in India, but when this was frustrated by the East India Company and its powerful allies in Parliament, they had turned their attention to home missions; and while the itinerants did not have the advantage of a university education, they had undergone a period of rigorous training before being commissioned (and supported) as evangelists,[11] and going on to do sterling work in bringing the gospel to some of the most spiritually deprived areas of Scotland, including the northern and western Highlands. Their influence on the islands of Skye and Lewis was profound, and long-lasting.

But then, Blair is not to be blamed for the sentiments of the admonition, though he may well have agreed with them. The document is the voice of a General Assembly, still under the Moderate ascendancy and as little concerned to propagate the gospel at home as it was to propagate it in India. It was the failure of the national church to provide an evangelical witness in every corner of Scotland that stirred the souls of the Haldanes to the point where they could no longer sit back and do nothing. Blair, on the other hand, was driven by the ambition of literary fame: an ambition which, like Robertson, he achieved to the full and while, in public, he had a low-key attitude to his celebrity, it was plain to his inner circle that he valued the approbation of the world, and was flattered by the uncommon measure of it that came his way.[12] He had earned his fame by means which were entirely fair, and he had no desire to hide his satisfaction behind a cloak of affected modesty.

Blair's *Lectures on Belles Lettres,* delivered from his Chair at Edinburgh University, fitted naturally into this overall ambition. It is not so clear, however, that they fitted into his calling as a minister of the gospel. The

---

11. Both Robert and James Haldane were considerable scholars in their own right. Robert's classic *Exposition of the Epistle of Paul to the Romans,* first published in three volumes (1836–39) is still in print (1 vol., London: Banner of Truth. 1958), and highly regarded. James' many writings included a critique of Edward Irving's Christology (*Refutation of Edward Irving's Doctrine respecting the Person and Atonement of Christ;* Edinburgh: 1829) and an *Exposition of the Epistle to the Galatians* (Edinburgh: 1848).

12. Hill, ibid., p. 162.

preparation and delivery of such a course over so many years was inevitably time-consuming. Hill claims, indeed (p. 43), that in discharging the duties of both a clergyman and a professor he exhibited an uncommon zeal, and that due to his uncommon industry 'the labours of the pulpit never interfered with those of his academical chair.'[13] But this, surely, is a strange way of putting it. The real question is whether the duties of the chair interfered with the duties, not only of the pulpit but with his overall responsibilities as a parish minister. The apostolic injunction is not that a pastor/evangelist should put in a certain number of hours per week, but that he should give himself 'wholly' to reading the Scriptures, exhortation, and teaching (1 Tim. 4:15). This no pluralist can do. Besides, not content with lecturing on *Belles Lettres*, Blair also made time to publish (in 1763) *A Critical Dissertation on the Poems of Ossian the son of Fingal*. The *Dissertation* was widely praised for its display of critical acumen, but its defence of the authenticity of the poems failed to convince.[14]

But Blair's fame would rest neither on his *Dissertation* nor on his *Lectures*. Indeed, once the *Lectures* were published, he seems to have put them out of his mind, and to have turned the whole of his energy to the composition of his *Sermons*, 'upon the excellence of which it was his intention that his fame should rest';[15] and they did, indeed, achieve an astonishing popularity.[16]

What immediately strikes us about the *Sermons* is that even after two hundred years they are still an easy read: a clear tribute to Blair's mastery of style. The criteria he applied as a literary critic to the work of others he applied equally to what he wrote himself. The introduction immediately commands attention; the development of the theme is coherent and logical, prompting the reader to look forward to the next stage of the argument; the concluding peroration a suitably stirring climax. But while each sermon is a careful composition, there are few purple passages, few quotable quotes, and only limited, though effective use of illustrations and anecdotes. The

---

13. ibid., p. 43.

14. See Daiches, *The Scottish Enlightenment*, pp. 20-21; and cf. the entry 'Macpherson, James,' in Derick S. Thomson, Ed., *The Companion to Gaelic Scotland* (Oxford: Blackwell, 1983). Macpherson was himself the author of the Ossianic poems, but presented them as fragments from a remote Celtic past.

15. Hill, ibid., p. 178.

16. The *Sermons* were published in five volumes in London between 1777 and 1801 and, according to Richard Sher, were 'among the most popular English-language works of the late eighteenth and early nineteenth centuries' (Sher, ibid., p. 182).

sermons clearly succeed as literature, yet it appears that in delivering them from the pulpit Blair never read from a manuscript. Instead, he carefully memorised them.

It is clear, too, that Blair never forgot his audience, nor the range of human life represented by his St Giles congregation. It did indeed include the great, the good, and the successful, but Blair was also aware of the human suffering, failure, poverty and even viciousness to be found within the bounds of his parish.

It is easy to understand, then, why the published sermons were best-sellers, but no less easy to understand why, as they were delivered from the pulpit, the common people heard him gladly, and this leads to another striking feature of Blair's preaching: the topics covered. A high proportion of the *Sermons* deal with matters of common human preoccupation rather than with specifically Christian issues (as is the case, for example, with St Paul's Epistle to the Romans and the other New Testament documents). Among these are such topics as 'The Love of Praise,' 'Death,' 'The Improvement of Time,' 'The Duties Belonging to Middle Age,' 'On Envy,' 'On Idleness,' 'On Luxury and Licentiousness,' 'On Friendship,' and many others in the same vein.

The list clearly distinguishes Blair from the high-flyers, and the distinction is confirmed by the topics which are *not* covered, or which are at best muted. Picking up on this point, Stewart J. Brown comments, 'What was missing from Moderate sermons was much attention to such Reformed doctrines as unconditional election, limited atonement, and irresistible grace, as these were expressed in the Westminster Confession of Faith';[17] and Brown extends the list of omissions to include God's righteous anger, divine justice demanding Christ's sacrifice on the cross, and the need for salvation from eternal punishment. Moderate preachers did not deny these doctrines, but they tended to set them aside, or to view them as divine mysteries that were not appropriate to the pulpit.[18]

This certainly put clear blue water between Blair and his fellow Moderates on the one hand, and 'the crude and vulgar sermons' of men like Thomas

---

17. Brown, 'Moderate Theology and Preaching c. 1750–1800,' p. 77.

18. The idea that such mysteries should not be shared with ordinary believers was not one that the apostles subscribed to. Witness, for example, the Gospel of John and the Epistle to the Ephesians. On the other hand, we should note the Westminster Confession's warning (1:8) that the pulpit should handle these 'high mysteries' with special prudence and care.

Boston and Ebenezer Erskine on the other. Instead, aspiring to be seen as 'humane moralists', Blair and his colleagues placed the emphasis on 'the good heart and good works in a way that appealed to those philosophers of the Enlightenment who believed, following Francis Hutcheson, that man's innate moral sense would lead to an instinctive approval and pursuit of benevolence, and disapproval of its opposite.'[19]

Impressive though this sounds, however, it represents a radical departure from the biblical understanding of the norms which should govern relations between God and the human race. Gone is the idea of an objective revelation of the will of God such as we find in the Ten Commandments or the Sermon on the Mount. Instead, in typical Enlightenment fashion, the source of morality is found in something innate to man himself,[20] and at the same time the standard is relaxed. No longer is it the 'first and greatest commandment' that we should love the Lord our God with all our heart, soul, and mind (Matt. 22:37-8). Our innate moral sense prescribes only benevolence, or goodwill towards our fellow human beings; and in a further departure from the historic Christian point of view, it is assumed that such benevolence is well within our competence, despite all that the Bible and history tell us of the ravages of original sin: ravages such that our innate moral sense leads us to condone what God condemns and to condemn what He approves; ravages which resulted in the fact that 'the world knew not when he came, even God's eternal Son.'

And once it fell out of touch with Sinaitic law, Moderate theology quickly became reticent on other key elements of biblical faith and experience. Little is said of conviction of sin, the need for a new birth, or the necessity of conversion. Christianity is no longer seen as first and foremost a religion of redemption, nor the gospel as the message of God's remedy for the plight of man. Complacent in their pursuit of virtue and the practice of benevolence, men are no long crying, 'Lord, be merciful to me the sinner' (Luke 18:13). Christ is no longer pre-eminently the Saviour from sin. He is merely 'the pattern of the virtues', and Moderatism seems

---

19. David Daiches, 'The Scottish Enlightenment', p. 13. Cf. Brown, 'Moderate Theology and Preaching,' p. 77: 'Moderate emphasis was on the dispassionate, disciplined Christian life, and on the habitual practice of self-control and virtue within society.'

20. Blair did not, however, endorse Hutcheson unreservedly. It was calculated, he wrote, rather to please in theory than to assist in practice: 'Virtue is held forth in it as an object which we must admire and approve, rather than as a law for regulating our conduct.' Hill, ibid., p. 33.

to betray no awareness of the scale of the challenge that this 'pattern' poses to unregenerate humanity.

But the main casualty of the Hutchesonian revolution is the cross. Not that the Moderates ever publicly denied it, or the doctrine of the atonement that went along with it. In Blair's case, William M. Taylor calculated that of the ninety-one sermons that Blair published, in at least three or four of them 'we have such distinct and unqualified statements of the expiatory nature of the death of Christ as no Socinian could have made. But there is little allusion to that subject in the rest of the discourses.'[21] This is all the more remarkable in that from the beginning of the Reformed Church in Scotland the administration of the sacrament was always closely linked to the proclamation of the death of Christ. For example, *Knox's Liturgy* prescribed that during the distribution of the elements 'some place of the Scriptures is read, which doth lively set forth the death of Christ, to the intent that our eyes and senses may not only be occupied in these outward signs of bread and wine, which are called the visible word; but that our hearts and minds also may be fully fixed in the contemplation of the Lord's death, which is by this holy Sacrament represented.'[22] In later generations, the Eucharistic Sermon, preached before communicants took their place at the Table, characteristically focused on the same subject, as we can see, for example, in the Communion Sermons of Samuel Rutherford:[23] sermons which address such issues as Christ's being forsaken by the Father (pp. 123-24), and containing such sentiments as, 'What a sight is our Lord Jesus going out of the gates of Jerusalem, and his cross upon his back. He was even then bearing God's curse upon his back, and that was heavier than the cross' (p. 283).

But what is even more important is that Moderate reluctance to put the cross in the forefront of their message is totally inconsistent with the central place which the death of Christ occupies in the New Testament. Jesus Himself firmly underlined the redemptive purpose of His mission when He declared that He had come to give His life a ransom for many

---

21. William M. Taylor, *The Scottish Pulpit from the Reformation to the Present Day* (London: Charles Burnet, 1887), p. 148.

22. *The Liturgy of John Knox Received by the Church of Scotland in 1564* (Glasgow: University Press, 1886), p. 144.

23. *Fourteen Communion Sermons by the Rev. Samuel Rutherford*, with Preface and notes by Rev. Andrew Bonar (Glasgow: Charles Glass and Co., 1876).

(Mark 10:45); and He confirmed this at the Last Supper when He described the Cup as, 'my blood of the covenant which is poured out for many for the forgiveness of sins' (Matt. 26:28 ESV).

The same priority is given to the cross in the New Testament epistles, especially those of St Paul, who tells the Corinthians that in the very forefront of his message stood the proclamation that 'Christ died for our sins' (1 Cor. 15:3); and he steadfastly adhered to this despite the fact that the world's wisdom mocked his gospel as both foolish and offensive. Indeed, he summed up his ministry in one sentence, 'We preach Christ crucified' (1 Cor. 1:23); and in a memorable protest to the Galatians he averred, 'God forbid that I should glory save in the cross of our Lord Jesus Christ' (Gal. 6:14). The very topic the Moderates avoided for fear of offending 'men of taste', the apostles saw as the most important part of their message, and they preached it passionately and persistently, confident that it was the saving power of God (Rom. 1:16).

George Hill and the doctrine of vicarious punishment

Yet if Blair and his fellow Moderates bore only a muted witness to the cross, this doesn't reflect either denial of the doctrine of the atonement or lack of familiarity with it. In fact, one of the very best defences of the doctrine came from the pen of George Hill, who not only succeeded William Robertson as leader of the Moderate party, but also served as Professor of Divinity at the University of St Andrews (1788–1819). The lectures he delivered in that capacity were later published in three volumes, edited by his son.[24]

Hill begins his discussion of the atonement by striking an apologetic note: the first thing necessary for those who would defend the Catholic opinion is to show that it is neither irrational nor unjust (p. 435). No less striking, however, is the label he attaches to the doctrine he is setting out to defend. It is 'the Catholic opinion', and it quickly becomes evident that what he is referring to is the doctrine of vicarious satisfaction or penal

---

24. *Lectures in Divinity by the late George Hill, D.D.*; ed. Alexander Hill, 3 vols. (Edinburgh, Waugh and Innes, 1821). For his discussion of the Doctrine of the Atonement, see Vol. 2, pp. 435-551. While Thomas Chalmers was happy to commend the *Lectures* for their lucidity and to use them as a text-book, he did, however, lament the fact that 'though it be an evangelical system of truth which is ably and on the whole correctly expounded, the *sal evangelicum* is lacking: "We have the whole orthodoxy of the subject although not the feeling of it"' (Thomas Chalmers, *Institutes of Theology*, 2 Vols., Edinburgh: Thomas Constable, 1856), Vol. 2, p. 263.

substitution, but he views it, not as the opinion of some un-enlightened 'high-flyers', but as the catholic or universal doctrine generally held in the church since the days of the apostles, and incorporated not only in the Westminster Confession but in the creeds of all the established churches of Christendom. It is indeed the doctrine of the Church of Scotland, and clearly embodied in its Confession of Faith (8:5),[25] but it is no less the doctrine of the Church of England, as reflected in the second of the Anglican Articles, which declares that the Son of God 'truly suffered, was crucified, dead, and buried, to reconcile his Father to us, and to be a sacrifice, not only for original guilt, but also for all actual sins of men'; and, not content with inserting the doctrine in its Articles, the Church of England expressed it even more fully, Hill points out, in the Prayer of Consecration at the heart of its Order for Communion: 'Almighty God, our heavenly Father, who of thy tender mercy didst give thine only Son Jesus Christ to suffer death upon the Cross for our redemption; who made there, by his one oblation of himself once offered, a full, perfect, and sufficient sacrifice, oblation, and satisfaction, for the sins of the whole world.'[26] The same position is taken by all the Protestant confessions, and Hill might have added that it is also the doctrine of the Roman Catholic Church as enshrined in the *Catechism of the Council of Trent* which, in its discussion of the Fourth Article of the Creed, declares that in His passion Christ 'discharged the punishment due to our sins; and as no sacrifice more grateful and acceptable could have been offered to God, he reconciled us to the Father, appeased his wrath, and propitiated his justice.'[27]

It is completely misleading, then, to describe this as 'the penal theology of Calvinists'.[28] On the contrary, Hill claims (p. 432), all without exception who believe in the Trinity believe that the Eternal Son took human nature

for this purpose chiefly, that he might suffer for the sins of men; that the sorrows of his life, the agony of his last hours, and the bitterness of his death, were the punishment due to our transgression, which it pleased the Father to

25. Cf. the *Scots Confession*, Chapter IX.

26. *The Book of Common Prayer*, with an Introduction by Diarmaid MacCulloch (London: Everyman Publishers, 1999), p. 260.

27. *The Catechism of the Council of Trent: Published by Command of Pope Pius the Fifth*, tr. J. Donovan, 1829, p. 49.

28. Andrew Purves, 'New Trends: Erskine of Linlathen, Irving, and McLeod Campbell' in *The History of Scottish Theology*, ed. David Ferguson and Mark W. Elliott, Vol. II, p. 235.

lay upon him, and which he cheerfully undertook; and that the sins of those who repent and believe are forgiven upon account of this substitution of Jesus Christ in their stead, which is called vicarious suffering.

Thus, while it may be true that 'the Moderate conscience boggled at the substitutionary theory of the atonement,'[29] Hill's conscience did not. He defended it stoutly, fully aware of the formidable objections raised against it by Socinianism: so formidable, indeed, that to this day Liberal Protestantism contents itself with recycling them. But Hill was aware, too (p. 437), that these objections had called forth in defence of the doctrine 'some of the greatest masters of reason', and he instances two of these: the Anglican, Bishop Stillingfleet,[30] and the Dutch jurist, Hugo Grotius. Hill's own statement is heavily reliant on the latter's *Defence of the Catholic Faith concerning the Satisfaction of Christ, against Faustus Socinus* (1617).[31]

Socinianism, first propounded by the Italian Renaissance scholar, Faustus Socinus (1539–1604), was distinguished by two leading features: denial of the deity of Christ and denial of the doctrine of vicarious satisfaction. The latter, it argued, was a contradiction of all the moral attributes of the Deity: so much so that Socinians could not believe it even if it were taught in the Scriptures. It portrayed God as moved with fury at the insults to His Supreme Majesty; impatient to pour out that fury on some being, indifferent to whether he were innocent or not; appeased by finding an object for His vengeance in His own innocent Son; demanding a full equivalent for what men owe to Him, and finding it in the sufferings of His Son; transferring guilt (which is inherently personal and non-transferable) from the innocent to the guilty; and handing out rewards without regard to the character of those who receive them: in short, an inexorable being who did not remit any part of His rights.

That is the case for the prosecution. On the other hand, Hill concedes that the Socinian arguments have sometimes received countenance from the language of some over-zealous friends of the doctrine of penal substitution,

---

29. Ian D. L. Clark, 'From Protest to Reaction,' in N. T. Phillipson and Rosalind Aitchison, eds., *Essays in Scottish History in the Eighteenth Century* (Edinburgh: Edinburgh University Press, 1970), p. 209.

30. Edward Stillingfleet, *Six Sermons: with a discourse annexed concerning the true reason of the sufferings of Christ* (1669).

31. For a robust defence of the doctrine of Vicarious Satisfaction by a modern jurist, see William Lane Craig, *Atonement and the Death of Christ* (Waco, Texas: Baylor University Press, 2020).

whose loose and popular harangues were accommodated to prejudices which were inconsistent with truth and adverse to morality (p. 436). There is certainly some truth in this. In a climate where, for example, the idea of divine wrath is widely banished from the Christian pulpit, it is tempting to react not only by giving it undue emphasis, but to forget the difference between human fury and the calm, judicious anger of deity. One reflection of this is the current rush to defend and even to highlight the sentiment, 'the wrath of God was satisfied': a line not to be found in any Reformation creed, and one which conjures up, all too easily, the image of a parent who has lost his temper. God's anger is bounded by His justice, and it was this justice that was satisfied by the self-sacrifice of God's beloved Son (*Shorter Catechism*, Answer 25).

The temptation to major on shibboleths is always there, and if you know your audience is strong on divine wrath, it is tempting to lay it on thick. It is tempting, too, to seek to enhance the wonder of the cross by recycling such ideas as that one drop of Christ's blood would have been sufficient to atone for the sins of the world: a sentiment which immediately calls in question the justice of God. If one drop of the blood would have been enough, why did the Father command that Christ lay down His life (John 10:18)? Hill also questions the recurring use of the word 'infinite' in relation to the atonement in such phrases as the 'infinite gravity of sin,' the 'infinite majesty of Christ's person,' and the 'infinite value of his sufferings.' It is enough that Christ was enough, and did enough, which is, surely, what the concept of 'satisfaction' implies. More speculatively, Hill also cautions against the idea that atoning for human sin was the whole and sole purpose of the incarnation and death of the Son of God (p. 459). We mortals should not presume to know all the reasons why God did what He did: 'there may be in this transaction what the Scriptures call a manifold wisdom to us unsearchable; reasons founded upon relations to other parts of the universe, and upon the general plan of the divine government, which we have not at present the capacity of apprehending' (pp. 459-60).

Hill begins his attempt to show that the Catholic doctrine of the atonement is neither unjust nor irrational by clarifying the relationship in which sinners stand before God. We do not appear before Him simply as people who in a moment of petulance have insulted Him personally: if that were the case, an apology might suffice. Nor do we appear as mere debtors before a creditor; if that were the case, we might hope that, as sometimes happens in human affairs, the creditor might graciously cancel the debt. Nor, again, do we appear as creatures who have degraded ourselves by odious behaviour and thus compromised the Creator, who made us in His own image; if that were the case, repentance and amendment would suffice. Instead, we stand before Him as the Supreme Being, the Most High, whose laws we have violated; and although He, as the absolute Lord and Proprietor of all, has a right to dispose as He pleases of every part of His works and every one of His creatures, yet He does not exercise this absolute discretion in His government of His moral universe – His reasonable creatures. If He did, they would have no way of knowing what would please Him or what would offend Him. Instead, He has made known laws which make plain how He requires them to behave, and He has annexed to these laws clear sanctions which declare both the rewards of obedience and the penal consequences of defiance. Every human being knows that they are under these laws and subject to these sanctions (p. 442);[32] and all human beings know that when they speak of sin, this is what they mean: defiance of the law of God.

It is against this background that Hill develops his impeccably orthodox statement of the Catholic understanding of the cross, and we have no reason to believe that Blair ever rejected it. He writes, for example, that 'Insufficient though our own repentance be, to secure pardon from heaven, we are informed that an all-sufficient atonement has been made by Christ';[33] and he adds that in the light of this atonement, 'Neither the number nor the atrocity of offences excludes from forgiveness the penitent who returns to his duty. To all who come under this description, the offer of mercy extends without exception.'

The compassion of Christ

Yet, although the doctrine is not denied, it seldom outcrops in Blair's preaching; and when it does, it leaves us regretting that he did not take up the subject more frequently and treat it more thoroughly. He was certainly capable of it. There is an excellent sermon, for example 'On the Compassion of Christ' (Vol. 2, pp. 117-47).[34] Based on Hebrews 4:15, it was preached at

---

32. Cf. Romans 2:14-15, 'when Gentiles, who do not have the law, by nature do what the law requires, they show that the work of the law is written on their hearts.'

33. *Sermons*, Vol. 4, p. 100.

34. *Sermons*, Vol. 2, pp. 117-47.

a celebration of the sacrament of the Lord's Supper (the date is not given), it was probably the Action or Thanksgiving Sermon immediately prior to the distribution of the bread and wine, and in line with Scottish Reformed tradition it focuses on the person and work of Christ. Early in the sermon, Blair declares explicitly that the purpose of the Incarnation was that Christ, by suffering a painful and shameful death, should 'in that nature which had offended' offer 'a solemn expiation to God for human guilt' (Vol. 2, p. 119).[35] But he doesn't develop this, nor does he pause over the designation of Christ as the High Priest who 'passed through the heavens', carrying the blood of His self-sacrifice to make atonement in the Holy of Holies. Instead, he moves quickly to a different, but related theme, 'suggested in the text,' namely, that the purpose of the Incarnation was to supply the human race, struggling in a state of suffering and distress, with proper consolation and encouragement; and once he has committed himself to this theme, he develops it impressively.

This consolation, he declares, is linked to our having a clear grasp of two things. The first of these is the power of God, but although this divine attribute is indeed encouraging, it is not sufficient of itself to bring the consolation we need. We also need to know that the Mediator possesses the qualities of mercy and compassion: qualities which are highlighted in the description of Christ as one who was made 'in all things like his brethren' (Heb. 2:17), was tempted just like ourselves, and is able, as a result, to empathise with us in our weakness.

The sermon clearly touches on the common plight of suffering humanity, but the consolation is drawn from the highest flights of Christian theology, and above all from the fact that Jesus, God's own Son, had full experience of both the external and internal sorrows which are the lot of all men and women. 'Whatever,' he writes, 'is severe in the disregard of relations or the ingratitude of friends, in the scorn of the proud or the insults of the mean, in the virulence of reproach or the sharpness of pain, was undergone by Christ. Though his life was short, he familiarised himself in it with a wide

---

35. This same sentiment that the atoning sacrifice was offered in the same nature as had sinned is expressed by John Henry Newman in the hymn, 'Praise to the Holiest in the height':

> O wisest love! that flesh and blood,
> Which did in Adam fail,
> Should strive again against the foe,
> Should strive and should prevail.

compass of human woe; and there is almost no distressful situation to which we can be reduced, but what he has experienced before us' (*Sermons*, Vol. 2, p. 122). The eminence of His nature did not raise Him above the sensations of pain and grief. On the contrary, the sensibility of His nature was tender and exquisite, far removed from the impassivity of Stoicism: 'He affected none of that hard indifference in which some ancient philosophers vainly gloried. He felt as a man, and he sympathised with the feelings of others' (ibid., pp. 122-23).

But not only did Christ fully experience human distress and sorrow. His whole life was a severe trial of His constancy, with the result that He knows all the temptations and discouragements that virtue can suffer: 'Though he participated not of the corruption, yet he felt the weakness of human nature. He felt the strength of passion. He is no stranger to the disturbance and commotion which either the attacks of the world, or the powers of darkness, are able to raise within the breast of man.' But though the conflict was the same, the issue was different: 'We are often foiled; He always overcame.'

But was it necessary, asks Blair, for the Son of God to assume our nature in order to understand our infirmity and distress? As a divine person, was He not already perfectly acquainted with our frame before He descended to the earth? Could His experimental knowledge of human weakness increase the benevolence of a nature which was already perfect?

No, answers Blair, but Christ submitted to become acquainted with the feeling of our infirmities, not in order to understand us better, but to give us even greater confidence in the goodness which He already possessed. 'Distrust,' writes Blair, 'is a weakness incident to the miserable' (ibid., p. 128), and despite the many grounds afforded by Scripture for trust in God's goodness, the perfection of an Almighty Being is overwhelming to a timid human apprehension. This is why, in the Old Testament, the Supreme Being is often represented with the attributes of a man in order to accommodate Him to human capacity: 'The relentings of a friend, the pity of a parent, and the sighs of a mourner, are all ascribed to the Almighty.' But then, recalling the parameters of classical theism, to which, like all the Moderates, he subscribed, Blair quickly adds, 'We easily perceive such attributes to be no more than figures and allusions,' and they leave the mind in anxious uncertainty lest it err in its interpretation of these mere 'allegories' of mercy (ibid., p. 129).

But although the idea that such tender affections can be applied to God only by way of accommodation is supported by such eminent authorities as John Calvin,[36] we should not accept it uncritically. Scripture bears clear witness to the fact that God has a rich emotional life, even to the extent that it places compassion at the very heart of the divine name; and just how central such compassion was to God's self-revelation is made crystal clear in the seminal Old Testament passage, Exodus 33:17–34:9. Here, Moses has asked the LORD, Yahweh, to show him His 'glory', and the LORD replies by promising to make all His 'goodness' pass before him; and, as He does so, to proclaim His name. The passage contains three crucial synonyms: the LORD's name, the LORD's goodness, and the LORD's glory, but at the same time it is made clear that there are limits to what Moses is to be allowed to see. He will see God's back: he will not see His face, 'for man shall not see me and live.' Even in revelation the unveiling is only partial, and almost as if to make sure that Moses doesn't see too much, the LORD commands him to stand in a cleft of a nearby rock; and to make doubly, doubly sure the LORD will cover Moses' face with His hand. Only then will He allow the prophet to see His 'back', what has been called the 'after-glow' of His passing.

The fulfilling of this divine promise is recorded in Exodus 34:5-7, which relates that the LORD descended in the cloud, stood by Moses, and proclaimed His name. We are not told what Moses saw, only what he heard, namely the LORD proclaiming His own name, but that is surely sufficient. We no longer hear the voice of a mere human observer of the divine. Instead, we hear the voice of the divine describing Himself, and at the very heart of the self-description lies the emphasis, 'The LORD, the LORD, a God merciful and gracious.' We have to note at once that this implies no lessening of the majesty of deity. The one who is 'merciful and gracious' is *El*: the primary Semitic name for the Deity, derived from a root meaning 'power' and emphasising

---

36. See, for example, his comments on Hosea 11:8-9: 'God, we know, is subject to no passions; and we know that no change takes place in him. What then do these expressions mean, by which he appears to be changeable? Doubtless he accommodates himself to our ignorance, whenever he puts on a character foreign to himself.' Calvin extends this even to the divine anger: 'Why does Scripture say that God is angry? Even because we imagine him to be so according to the perception of the flesh' (Calvin, *A Commentary on the Twelve Minor Prophets. Volume 1, Hosea*; Edinburgh: Calvin Translation Society, 1846. Reprinted Edinburgh: Banner of Truth, pp. 401-02).

the transcendent otherness and sheer God-ness of God: what the Apostle Paul in Romans 1:20 refers to as His *theiotēs*. As Professor John L. Mackay pointed out, 'It is no sign of divine weakness that God is gracious.'[37] Nor is it a sign that He is indifferent to the gravity of sin. In this very same context, *El* makes it clear (v. 7) that He will by no means clear the guilty. But if we take the divine word as a whole, its purpose was to make plain the reputation by which God wished to be known; and, as Professor Mackay again points out, this revelation in Exodus 34:5-9 'became central to Israel's understanding of who God is and what he does;'[38] and just how central becomes clear in the fact that, not only is it quoted verbatim in Psalm 103:8, but that it is given further emphasis when the psalmist declares (v. 13 ESV), 'As a father shows compassion to his children, so the LORD shows compassion to those who fear him.'[39] Here again the divine pity is analogous to the human; or, conversely, human compassion is an image of the divine. That being the case, we should hesitate to speak of the reference to the divine compassion as mere baby-talk, where God stoops to accommodate His revelation to our human finitude. It is the divine compassion that is eternal and archetypal: ours is but a shadow of it.

The Hebrew word translated 'merciful' at this point by the ESV, and 'compassionate' by the NIV, is *rācham*, the adjectival form of the noun *rāhumim*, which in its singular form means 'womb.'[40] The Septuagint (Greek) equivalent is *oiktirmoi*, meaning compassion or pity. It occurs in several crucial New Testament passages, most notably in Colossians 3:12, where Paul writes, 'Put on then, as God's chosen ones, 'compassionate hearts,'

---

37. John L. Mackay, *Exodus* (Fearn: Christian Focus Publications, 2001), p. 563.

38. ibid., p. 562.

39. It is also quoted in such passages as Psalm 86:15, Psalm 145:8, and Joel 2:13. It clearly made a lasting impression on the faith of Israel.

40. Hence Professor Mackay's comment (ibid., p. 563), '"Compassionate" recalls a mother's love for her child, with a deep understanding of its weakness and need, keeping looking after it whatever its behaviour or thanklessness.' There is a close link between *rachumim* (mercies or compassions), and the singular, *rācham*, meaning 'womb'. For a fuller discussion of *rāhumim*, see the *New International Dictionary of Old Testament Theology and Exegesis*, ed. Willem A. Van Gemeren, Vol. 3, pp. 1093-95. There is a vivid illustration of its meaning in Genesis 43:30, where Joseph meets his brother, Benjamin, and, to avoid being seen overcome with emotion, rushes out to his own chamber to weep alone. In the New Testament the idea of being moved to feel pity or compassion is expressed by the word *splanchizomai*, linked to the noun *splancha* signifying such inward parts as heart, lungs and liver. This conserves the Old Testament idea that compassion is visceral. Cf. Hosea 11: 8, where God recoils from treating Israel as it deserves, and declares, 'My heart recoils within me; my compassion grows warm and tender.'

('clothe yourselves with compassion' NIV). Such compassion is one of the clear marks that we belong to the elect of God, but it is no less confirmation that the image of the Creator is being restored in us (v. 10). So central is this quality of *oiktirmos* to apostolic understanding of the nature of God that Paul can even refer to Him as 'the Father of compassions' (*oiktirmoi*, 2 Cor. 1:3, NIV), while in the same breath describing this pity or compassion as the source of the comfort with which God consoles us in every tribulation (v. 4). Then in Romans 12:1 Paul traces the whole divine plan of salvation back to this same pity or compassion, when, having completed his resumé of the gospel, he urges believers to respond by presenting themselves as living sacrifices. He has loved us, redeemed us, called us, justified us, adopted us, and given us His Spirit; and what moved Him to act in this way was His *oiktirmoi*: the divine pity. His heart was stirred by the pitiable plight of the human race, and it was stirred because that is His nature as divine. Where He sees distress, His instinct is to help, and it is this same instinct that He has implanted in His children, whose likeness to Him is shown forth by their compassion for all who are in any trouble.

The relief the gospel affords to the distressed

For another Communion sermon Blair chose as his text Matthew 11:28,[41] and took as his theme 'The Relief which the Gospel affords to the Distressed.'[42] This sermon, too, is richly evangelical. It clearly follows the contours of the text, addressing first of all the question, what is meant by the invitation, 'Come not me.' He notes in passing that theological writers have been 'involved in much needless mystery' over the import of this invitation, while the meaning is in itself plain and clear. The very metaphor, 'follow,' is a reminder that in the ancient world disciples flocked around their teachers, attending them wherever they went, in order both to testify their attachment and to imbibe more fully the teaching of their Master. By the same token, coming to Christ means resorting to Him as our declared Master, believing His teaching, obeying His instructions, and trusting His power to save: 'It imports that, feeling the corruptions of sin and the world, we follow that course of virtue and obedience which he points out to us.'[43]

---

41. 'Come unto me all ye that labour and are heavy laden, and I will give you rest.'

42. *Sermons*, Vol. 4, pp. 88-112.

43. *Sermons*, Vol. 4, p. 91.

There are two points here which are worth pausing over. One is the Moderate predilection for the word virtue (areté in Greek), a word which is rare in the New Testament but prominent in the pagan philosophers. Conversely, there appears to be a studied avoidance of such New Testament terms as sanctification, holiness and righteousness, presumably because they embarrassed the Enlightenment mind as savouring too much of the vulgar biblicism of the high-flyers. Yet the New Testament clearly defines the Christian as someone who hungers and thirsts after righteousness (Matt. 5:6) and lays down categorically that without holiness no one shall see the Lord (Heb. 12:14). This is not simply a question of words. Areté does not breathe the same atmosphere as 'holiness'. It carried with it the baggage of Stoicism and classical culture, with their emphasis on manliness, courage, self-reliance and dauntless endurance. Biblical holiness, by contrast, refers first and foremost to what the LORD, the God of Israel, is in His transcendent deity; and in redeemed men and women it shows itself first and foremost in the fear of the LORD, not caring for the views of 'religion's cultured despisers', but making it their priority to please God, their Maker, Redeemer and Heavenly Father.

Secondly, 'virtue' too easily lapses into the idea of 'common morality': a life-style defined by the mores or customs of the world; and in the Enlightenment context, following Hutcheson, the key element in this common morality was benevolence, defined as goodwill towards our fellow human beings. The moral man is a faithful husband, a loving father, an honest businessman, a loyal friend, and a patriotic citizen. Blair himself is aware both of the need for repentance and of the inadequacy of repentance, and aware, too, of the need for atonement, but these notes are seldom prominent in Moderate theology. We hear little of the apostolic message that 'all have sinned and come short of the glory of God' (Rom. 3:23), yet without it the gospel makes no sense. Nor do we hear of the apostle's anguished cry as he sees himself captive to the law of sin, 'Wretched man that I am! Who will deliver me from this body of death?' (Rom. 7:24), or of his confession that before he experienced the searching power of the Law he had no idea of the covetousness that lodged in his heart (Rom. 7:7). The charge that Anselm brought against his conversation-partner, Boso, when he suggested that a single act of repentance would be a sufficient atonement, could equally be brought against Moderate theology as a whole: 'You have not yet grasped the gravity of sin.'[44] Such topics as depravity, guilt,

---

44. Anselm, *Cur Deus Homo?*, Bk. I:5.

conviction of sin, and the need for a complete renovation of human nature (the new birth) were ignored as preoccupations of the previous, 'vulgar,' generation. Yet (and this cannot be said too often) without a sense of sin there can be no religion, and certainly no Christianity. Only the heart that cries, 'God, be merciful to me, a sinner!' (Luke 18:13) is going to seek rest in Christ. The road to spiritual recovery always begins with what Augustine calls 'anger against ourselves.'[45]

Following his clarification of the meaning of coming to Christ, Blair proceeds to address the question of those to whom the invitation is addressed, 'All who labour and are heavy laden.' This embraces all who feel distressed, and the distress may arise either from inward moral causes or from the calamities to which all human beings are liable in this life. A life devoted to pleasure and sin always brings ruin at last but, while it continues, it often blinds men to the destruction to which they're hastening. Circumstances arise, however, that disclose even to a vicious man the ruin which he is bringing on himself as an offender against God, and then the follies of past sins appear in a darker light as he considers himself under the judgement of a just God: 'What account shall he give of himself to his Maker? Self-condemned, polluted by so many crimes, how can he expect to find mercy in His sight? Hence an overwhelmed and dejected mind; hence dismal forebodings of punishment.' Such distresses may be dismissed by the giddy and the vain as confined to a tiny minority of people of distempered imagination, but to those (like ministers of religion), who see men and women in times of deep affliction, they are known to be far more frequent than is commonly assumed 'and throw over the human mind the blackest gloom of which it is susceptible.' Religious feelings, declares Blair, have a deep root in the nature of man. During the gay and active periods of life, they may be smothered, but with most men they are smothered rather than totally obliterated.[46]

---

45. Augustine, *Confessions*, IX:10.

46. Cf. Romans 1:32, which reminds us that even those who applaud men who excel in depravity, know that those who do such things are worthy of death. See, too, Calvin's comment (*Inst.* I:III, 2, 'One reads of no one who burst forth into bolder and more unbridled contempt of deity than Gaius Caligula; yet no one trembled more miserably when any sign of God's wrath manifested itself. He who is the boldest despiser of God is of all men the most startled at the rustle of a falling leaf.' According to a footnote inserted by Calvin's editor, John T. McNeill (Vol. 1, p. 45), Caligula, Roman Emperor from A.D. 37-41, was so terrified when it thundered that he would leap from his bed and hide under it.

But greater still is the number of those who experience much suffering and misery as a result of the calamities and evils of life. Blair avers that, on the whole, life offers more joy than grief, but while 'some trial is ordained for the sons of men,' the burden is not laid equally on all: there are always those on whom it falls with oppressive weight: 'Struggling with poverty, unable to support their families when they are languishing around them, they are at the same time obliged, under the forced appearance of cheerfulness, to hide from the world a broken heart;' and, not infrequently, borne down by the infirmities of a sickly body, left to drag out a painful existence without assistance or relief.

Blair had, no doubt, witnessed many such distressing scenes in the course of his own pastoral ministry, but he had also noted that even in the case of those regarded as prosperous men, many sorrows were to be found mixed with their pleasures. Even in a festive assembly, and amid so much affected gaiety, could we but look into the hearts of such apparently happy people, how often would we find them inwardly preyed upon by some tormenting suspicions, some anxious fears, some secret grief (*Sermons*, Vol. 4, p. 97). Many there are, he concludes, whose journey lies through a valley of tears; and many there are, too, for whom the journey through the valley is cheered by only transient glimpses of joy.

All this is a fair description of the plight of man, and as uncompromising a picture of human misery as could be painted by the most unsparing 'vulgar' evangelist; and fully in line, too, with the summary given by the Preacher, 'Vanity of vanities, all is vanity' (Eccles. 1:2). But to all these classes the Saviour extends the invitation, 'Come to me.' Not, cautions Blair, that Christ is always ready to accept the sort of piety which is merely the consequence of distress, or to welcome all those who are driven to Him by nothing but fear and danger, but His words make plain that every human heart which is softened by affliction is the object of His compassionate regard, and that if we apply to Him we shall be sure of meeting with a gracious reception.

Thirdly, Blair turns to the 'rest' which Jesus promises to those who turn to Him (pp. 98ff.). Retaining his previous sub-headings, he deals, first, with the relief offered to those whose distress arises from inward and moral causes, particularly those labouring under the sense of sin and guilt. As we have already noted, Blair declares that an all-sufficient atonement has already been made by Christ, and that on this basis the offer of forgiveness is extended 'to every penitent who returns to duty.' This last phrase might arouse a degree of unease: at first sight it jars with the key *Marrow* doctrine that the offer of mercy is extended to sinners as such, not only to those who 'now desire to become good and wise, and are determined for the future to keep a virtuous course' (p. 99). However, the core evangelical message is clear enough. Christ has brought with Him from heaven the olive branch: 'The atmosphere clears up on every side and is illuminated by cheering rays of divine mercy.' If we apply to Christ, we shall be sure of meeting with a gracious reception; and the reference to 'every penitent who returns to duty' goes no further than the Shorter Catechism, which includes in its definition of repentance (Answer 87) the statement that when the sinner turns to God he does so 'with full purpose of, and endeavour after, new obedience.'[47]

But what 'rest' does the religion of Christ offer to those whose distress arises, not from inward moral causes, but from the outward distresses to which human life is exposed? Blair notes at once that faith in Christ doesn't guarantee continuous and undisturbed prosperity. It does, however, mitigate the evils we are liable to, and supports us under them or, as the writer to the Hebrews puts it, He gives us grace to help in time of need (Heb. 4:16). At the same time, Blair is clearly conscious that in his mixed congregation there are many who, 'in the midst of health and affluence enjoy the various comforts of life' (p. 103), and he warns them against taking such comforts for granted. No one knows what vicissitudes may one day be their lot. But whether the distresses be present or future, 'the religion of Christ gives rest to the heart, by the fortitude which it inspires, and by the consolations which it effects' (p. 104). The believer has an almighty supporter: 'God is with him; Christ and the Holy Ghost are with him; and though he should be bereaved of earthly comfort, he can look up in heaven to a Friend who will never die' (p. 108).

But beyond these earthly consolations, there is the joyful prospect of a future state where believers enjoy eternal rest. This belief in an after-life where life's injustices are adjusted was one doctrine on which the Moderates never wavered. Let believers endure but for a little, and the 'virtuous' shall be assembled in those blissful regions prepared for them as their reward. This, declares Blair, 'is what all nations had eagerly longed for; what all philosophy had eagerly sought to discover; but what no research,

---

47. Cf. Proverbs 28:13: whoever confesses *and forsakes* his transgressions will obtain mercy.

no philosophy, were able to ascertain to mankind, till Christ brought the assurance of life and immortality from heaven; and conferred on his disciples this noble and inestimable gift' (p. 108). This clearly distances Blair from the deistic assertion of the sufficiency of general revelation.

At this point, Blair links his discourse to the administration of the sacrament. Here, he says, we join ourselves to Christ and His disciples, 'not in words and professions only, but in heart, and in truth' (p. 110). Let, then, those who labour under the sense of remembered follies and crimes come to Him with penitent dispositions, and they shall obtain pardon; 'and let those who labour under the suffering of present, or the apprehension of future sorrows, come unto Christ, and they shall receive consolation.' Nothing is said, however, to elucidate how the sacrament becomes effective as a means of grace, or to explain the 'conjunction' between Christ and the believing communicant.

Moderation

Finally, in the hope of getting some light on what Blair understood by the 'moderation' urged upon the Kirk by both James II and William of Orange, we turn to his sermon on this subject.[48] It is based on Philippians 4:5, 'Let your moderation be known to all men', and it quickly becomes clear that Blair has no intention of discussing moderation in the ecclesiastical sense. His whole focus falls on moderation in the life of the individual: a 'virtue' which consists, according to Blair, in the equal balance of the soul, especially 'such government of our passions and pleasures as shall prevent us from running into extremes of any kind, and shall produce a calm and temperate frame of mind' (Vol. 3, p. 243). Here he draws a helpful contrast between moderation and patience. Patience regulates the mind under the disagreeable incidents of life; moderation regulates it when circumstances are agreeable and promising; and having thus narrowed the field, he then highlights no fewer than five specific issues.

First, moderation in our *wishes*, especially our wishes with regard to the pleasures which we imagine the world capable of bestowing. These are the objects which warm the hearts of the young, animate the industry of the middle-aged, and frequently keep alive the passions of the old until the very close of life. There is nothing wrong, he notes, in wanting to enjoy a full

---

48. *Sermons*, Vol. 3, pp. 242-62.

measure of the comforts of life, but when such wishes are not 'tempered by reason' they can easily precipitate us into much extravagance and folly. Desires and wishes are the first springs of action, but when they become exorbitant the whole character is tainted, we feed our minds on plans of opulence and splendour far beyond our rank (*sic!*), and set our minds on high advancement and uncommon distinction, with the result that we become unhappy in our present station and unfit for the duties that belong to it.

There is a serious class element here. Blair knew his place. He was born into a culture of distinction and high achievement, and it was easy for him to keep his 'station in life'. Others, less privileged, should likewise keep theirs. But surely it is right that the slave should dream of freedom and of the advancement of his family?

Secondly, *moderation in our pursuits.* Here again the circumstances of our birth play a decisive role. Some men are formed by nature for rising into conspicuous situations in life, in following the impulse of their minds they are merely exerting the talents with which God has blessed them, and in doing so they can become instruments of much public good. Most men, however, are liable to overrate their own abilities and to imagine themselves equal to higher things than they were ever designed for by nature. He warns, therefore, that by aiming at a mark too high you may fall short of what is within your power (p. 250). One obligation, however, must be urged on all men alike, those of greatest abilities as well as those of no distinction. We must never transgress the bounds of moral duty: 'Amidst the warmth of pursuit, accustom yourselves to submit to the restraints which religion and virtue, which propriety and decency, which regard to reputation and character, impose' (p. 250). It is from a violent and impetuous spirit that all the evils spring which accompany ambition.

But Blair is hardly correct in suggesting that the level to which human beings may rise is limited only by talent. It is also a question of opportunity, as Thomas Gray reminds us in the course of his musings in a 'Country Churchyard':

> Full many a flower is born to blush unseen
> And waste its sweetness on the desert air ...
> Some mute, inglorious Milton here may rest,
> Some Cromwell guiltless of his country's blood.[49]

---

49. From Thomas Gray (1716–1771), 'Elegy Written in a Country Churchyard.'

In this respect all human beings are certainly not born equal. During the long reign of patriarchy, millions of women never achieved the level their talents deserved; and while some men are born with their feet already half-way up the ladder, millions of others are denied the basic educational opportunities which would have given stimulus and scope to their talents.

Thirdly, we must be moderate in our *expectations*. 'It was never,' writes Blair, 'granted to man on earth, to gratify all his hopes, or to persevere in one tract of uninterrupted prosperity' (p. 253). Yet we indulge in presumptuous expectations, and the natural consequence of these is an over-confident security, rashness of conduct, and a failure to take due precautions: 'The arrogant mind, and the proud hope, are equally contrary to religion and to prudence. The Almighty beholds with displeasure those who, intoxicated with prosperity, forget their dependence on that Supreme Power which raised them up.'[50]

Fourthly, we must be moderate in our *pleasures*. 'Every pleasure,' he writes, 'which is pursued to excess converts itself into poison' (p. 255). No sooner do we cross the line which temperance has drawn than pernicious effects begin to show themselves. Then, in a bold move, Blair invites his congregation to visit a cemetery, those 'monuments of death,' where they would behold graves peopled with the victims of intemperance: 'You would behold those chambers of darkness hung round, on every side, with the trophies of luxury, drunkenness, and sensuality. Where war or pestilence have slain their thousands, intemperate pleasure has slain its ten thousands.'

Finally, we are called upon to be moderate in our *passions*. This was a key element in the Stoicism which was never far away from the Enlightenment mind. Every passion, we are told, is a violent emotion of the mind,[51] and has an inherent tendency to run into excess. Indeed, nothing is more seducing than passion: when it grows and swells, it justifies itself, and this is true not only of those passions which are universally condemned, but of those which are deemed innocent: 'Every

---

50. This is one instance where there seems to be a studied avoidance of personal divine names, and a preference for the more impersonal and abstract names favoured by natural theology. This tendency reached its zenith in such twentieth-century divine names as 'the Ground of Being' and 'Ultimate Concern'.

51. Cf. Augustine: 'passion, a word derived from *pathos* (Gk.), signified a commotion of the mind contrary to reason' (*The City of God*, Bk. VIII, Chap. 17 [NPNF, Vol. II, p. 156]).

passion which has as its object any worldly good, is in hazard of attaching us too strongly, and transporting us beyond the bounds of reason, and rendering us negligent of duties which, as men or Christians, we are bound to perform' (p. 259).

Appeal to prudence and common sense

The striking thing about Blair's treatment of moderation is that his appeal throughout is to prudence and common sense. There is little biblical or theological underpinning, though he does note that the apostle reinforces his exhortation with the words, 'The Lord is at hand': 'Enlarged views of the destiny of man,' he writes, 'and of the place which he may hope to possess in an eternal world, naturally give birth to moderation of mind' (p. 262). But there is little close engagement with the apostle's text (Phil. 4:5). The word translated 'moderation' in the KJV is *epieikēs*, which the ESV translates as 'reasonableness'. It is less about controlling the passions or even controlling oneself, than about fairness and gentleness in human relationships: the opposite, as J. B. Lightfoot points out, to a spirit of contentiousness and self-seeking, and therefore often paired with such words as 'peaceful,' 'merciful,' 'compassionate,' and 'gentleness'.[52] It is applied to Christ Himself in 2 Corinthians 10:1, where the ESV translates it as 'gentleness' and where the original pairs it with meekness (Greek *praus*). In a civil context it is applied to fairness, or even leniency, in the administration of justice.

It is important to note that Philippians 4:5, like the epistle as a whole, is addressed, not to the sort of mixed audience Blair was addressing, but to 'the saints in Christ Jesus' (Phil. 1:1), and from this point of view *epieikēs* is rooted in grace, not in nature. It is part of the 'good work' (Phil. 1:6) which God has begun in believers, and as far as the Philippians are concerned it has a twofold application. First, it is addressed to them as a divided church, and constitutes a direct appeal for unity and mutual forbearance; and, secondly, it speaks to them as a Christian community faced with the opposition of a pagan world. Here it is a call, not only to be willing to submit to injustice, but to treat their unbelieving neighbours ('everyone') with fairness and graciousness.

---

52. J. B. Lightfoot, *Saint Paul's Epistle to the Philippians* (12th edition, London: Macmillan, 1900), p. 160.

It is fascinating to turn from Blair's sermon on 'Moderation' to another by W. G. T. Shedd on the same subject.[53] Shedd's text is Proverbs 16:32,[54] but he quickly places the concept of moderation within a comprehensive theological framework. In particular, he draws an intriguing contrast between the function of the Book of Proverbs in the Canon, and the function of the apostolic epistles. The latter set forth the great fundamental doctrines which lie at the heart of man's redemption; the former presents the lifestyle which it is incumbent on the redeemed to live: in other words, those principles of ethics and Christian prudence, which must always follow in the wake of evangelical religion.[55] These include some of the points already highlighted by Blair, such as the reforming of extravagance and the pruning down of luxuriance: and far from being secondary in importance to the core doctrines of redemption, the two, according to Shedd, form a coherent whole. Yet there is a clear order. The redemption (not the doctrine, merely, but the experience) precedes the lifestyle, and constitutes its indispensable dynamic.[56] More specifically, Christian moderation, like every other Christian grace, far from being within the compass of the natural man (1 Cor. 2:14), is impossible apart from the experience of the new birth. It is the fruit of the Spirit (Gal. 5:23).

This note is absent from Blair's sermon, and seldom featured in Moderate preaching as a whole. Instead, moderation is urged on the basis of common sense, and even as the key to prosperity and to good standing in the community; and just how weak such motives are, is clear from Blair's own description of self-indulgence as still so widely prevalent in his world. Only the divine power communicated through the gospel can produce the self-control, meekness and gentleness denoted by *epieikēs*; and in this life it is exhibited only imperfectly even in the lives of the saintliest.

---

53. William G. T. Shedd, *Sermons to the Spiritual Man* (1884. Reprinted London: Banner of Truth Trust, 1972), pp.19-33. When first published, Shedd was Professor at Union Theological Seminary, New York. A companion volume, *Sermons to the Natural Man* had been published in1871. Shedd was also the author of *Dogmatic Theology* (three vols, 1888–94), one of the finest, and certainly the best-written, systematic expositions of Reformed theology.

54. 'He that is slow to anger is better than the mighty; and he that ruleth his spirit than he that taketh a city.'

55. This is equally true of the other 'Wisdom' books of the Old Testament, such as Ecclesiastes and Job.

56. See further, John Murray, 'The Dynamic of the Biblical Ethic' in *Principles of Conduct: Aspects of Biblical Ethics* (London: Tyndale Press, 1957), pp. 202-28. The burden of Murray's argument is that believers are able to live out the biblical ethic because they have put off the old man and are new men, sharing in the resurrection life of Christ.

One clear implication of Shedd's observations is the need to reinstate the Book of Proverbs at the heart of Reformed piety. It may not contain the data we need to compile careful and minute statements of such doctrines as the Trinity and the Incarnation, or even of the New Birth or Justification, but the wise maxims and well-grounded ethics of Solomon will always follow up the evangelical truths and doctrines of the Apostle John and the Apostle Paul.[57]

Moderation and 'Moderatism'

Is there any discernible link between Blair's 'moderation' as a personal virtue and 'Moderatism' as a distinct movement within the Church? Blair and his colleagues were clearly determined to exclude from the life and witness of the Church anything that might offend the Enlightenment mind, and what that mind found most offensive was what it saw as the immoderate zeal which had characterised the 'vulgar' Presbyterianism of the seventeenth century: a zeal marked not only by bigotry and fanaticism, dogmatism and intolerance, but also by populist resistance to government, and the demand that the people be allowed to choose their own ministers. Religion, like the desire of pleasure, wealth and celebrity, should be kept under the control of reason.

It was a small step from this to suspicion of whatever smacked of 'enthusiasm', and this explains why the Moderates disapproved not only of the Covenanters but also of such revivals as took place in Cambuslang in 1742, the passionate preaching of men like George Whitefield, and the 'irregular' ministry of such itinerants as the Haldane missionaries. Preachers driven by a passion for the saving of souls, souls in anguish under conviction of sin, and earnest appeals to sinners in Sion, were a manifestation of the excess from which the Moderates shrank; or, to return to Augustine, the sign of a commotion of the mind beyond the control of reason.

But can Blair himself be accurately described as a 'Moderate' as that word is commonly understood? He certainly could not be embraced within common stereotypes of the class. He was not a deist; he had no reservations about the Confession of Faith; he was not negligent with regard to his ministerial duties; and he did not preach other men's sermons and pass

---

57. Shedd, ibid., p. 21.

them off as his own: a practice which was widespread and which had the advantage that such sermons were much more likely to suit the patron's cultured taste, while at the same time protecting the preacher from the charge of preaching 'vulgar' sermons.[58]

But there was another less flattering reason for the plagiarism: laziness. Many of the Moderates were reluctant preachers, and when forced to rely on their own resources the results were often ludicrous. Kenneth MacDonald recounts the story of one minister who did no more than regale his congregation with accounts of the battles of the kings of Israel and Judah, till he eventually came to the last, whereupon he went back to the beginning and started all over again.[59] At one period, however, he broke the sequence and embarked on a series of 'expositions' of the wars between the English and the French, only to be accused after one such sermon of having given false information. Forced to apologise, he did so profusely, telling his congregation, 'Don't believe a word of what I told you last Sabbath. It was all lies.'

In another instance, the minister had only one sermon, which he drew on whenever he couldn't get out of preaching. It was on Nicodemus, and eventually the congregation, weary of it, and exasperated that the clergyman should receive a comfortable stipend for so little effort, expostulated with him and extracted a promise that next Sabbath he would preach on a

---

58. As ministers lost their enthusiasm for preaching (or had nothing of their own to say), this practice became widely prevalent, and it wasn't confined to men of little ability. Even a man of the calibre of Thomas Reid descended to it. Reid (1710–1796) was the outstanding representative of what came to be known as the 'Scottish Philosophy' or 'Scottish Common Sense Realism,' which became widely influential on both sides of the Atlantic. Successively Professor of Philosophy at Aberdeen and Glasgow, he was compared in his lifetime to such figures as Descartes, Locke, and Leibniz, but he was also a Church of Scotland minister, having been ordained to the parish of New Machar in Aberdeen in 1737. But even though he had evangelical sympathies, he did not scruple to preach borrowed sermons, and on one occasion (McCosh, *The Scottish Philosophy,* p. 199) a lady in his congregation thanked him, in all sincerity, for preaching an excellent sermon by the Anglican, Archbishop Tillotson (a common source of plagiarised sermons). He vehemently denied that it was Tillotson's, but when he went to his bedroom later that evening he found a volume of the Archbishop's sermons on his bedside table, open at the page containing the very sermon he had preached. He was mortified: not, however, because he had been caught plagiarising, but by the fact that he was now presumed to have lied. The truth was that he had probably borrowed the sermon, not directly from Tillotson, but from some other collection where it featured without acknowledgement.

59. Kenneth MacDonald, *Social and Religious Life in the Highlands* (Edinburgh: Hunter, 1902), p. 77.

different text, which he duly did, announcing as his text the opening words of the Bible, 'In the beginning God created the heavens and the earth.' The audience sat up expectantly, only to hear the familiar words, 'We know next to nothing of this man, Nicodemus.'

As the modern media would say, it has not been possible to secure independent verification of such stories, and it would be unfair to tar all Moderates with the same brush. Hugh Blair was neither a reluctant preacher nor a plagiarist; and neither was he ever the butt of the sort of wit and sarcasm reflected in the countless anecdotes which circulated about the Moderate clergy, whose creed was once summarised in the following satirical lines:

> I do believe in stone and lime, a manse of large dimensions;
> Broad acres for a glebe and farm, *that* is my church extension;
> My folk may perish if they like, Christ's name I never mention;
> I take the stipend due by right, to men of good intention.[60]

In line with this, it was a common jibe that the minister was the best drinker, the best farmer, and the best dancer in the parish. But while the farm (the glebe) was taken seriously, the sacraments, and especially baptism, were not, as appeared in the story of the baptism of the infant John MacDonald. When he was born, his native parish of Reay was vacant, and his parents were obliged to apply to a neighbouring minister for the baptism of their child. They accordingly set off with the infant on a cold winter's day, only to discover on reaching the manse that the minister wasn't at home. He was out shooting, and wasn't expected home before sunset, leaving them with no option but to set off at once on the return journey. They hadn't gone far when the minister met them, and he quickly decided to administer the sacrament there and then: 'They were standing before a frozen pool, and after muttering a few words of prayer, the minister broke the ice with the butt end of his gun and, fetching water from the opening, sprinkled it on the face of the infant as he repeated the solemn words of consecration.'[61] But whatever the defects in the administration of the ordinance, they did not prevent the infant growing up to become the revered 'Apostle of the North.'

---

60. ibid., p. 77.

61. John Kennedy, *The Apostle of the North: the Life and Labours of the Rev. Dr. M'Donald* (London: Nelson and Sons, 1866), p. 23.

Kenneth MacDonald (p. 80) also relates the story of a conversation between two neighbours. 'What,' asked the one, 'did you think of our minister this evening? Is he not a grand dancer?' 'I think,' replied the other, 'that he was educated at the wrong end.' 'She evidently thought,' commented MacDonald, 'that his feet were better educated than his head or his heart, and that he was better qualified to dance a reel than to preach a sermon.' So much for the superior intellectual prowess of the patrons' nominees.

The very fact that such stories were recounted and perpetuated indicates the gulf that had developed between popular feeling and a large section of the clergy. But no such stories circulated in respect of Blair. Instead, he represented what Hugh Miller called 'Moderatism in its most respectable form.'[62] It had neither lived grossly, nor taught heresy. It had done no mischief – it had merely done nothing; and instead of perverting, it had only suppressed the truth, contenting itself with variations on the theme 'that it was well to be virtuous, not so well to be vicious; and that fanaticism was a great evil.' Such a man would cause no ripples, attempt no reforms, and disturb no conscience: 'the upper class deemed him a sensible man, and heard his sermon once a week; the lower had ceased attending church altogether.' And when his ministry ended, he would very likely be succeeded by an incumbent cast in the same mould as himself. Patronage guaranteed a Moderate succession, leading Miller to comment ironically that, 'It was impossible that a forced settlement could have taken place in the parish.' There wasn't enough religion in it to object to the patron's nominee, however little his enthusiasm for the gospel.

Yet the evangelicals were not entirely blameless. In the early days, at least, they had a strong presence in presbyteries, they repeatedly allowed unsuitable men to be recognised as candidates for the ministry and, later, to be licensed as preachers of the gospel. When they subsequently objected to a patron's nominee, the latter had a ready answer: the young man had clear credentials from the Church. How could the same Church now reject him as 'unsuitable'?[63]

---

62. Hugh Miller, 'Moderatism Popular, Where and Why,' in *The Headship of Christ and the Rights of the Christian People* (Fourth Edition, Edinburgh, William Nimmo, 1870), p. 242.

63. Cf. Bonhoeffer's comment with respect to the importance of doctrinal discipline: 'It is a matter of life and death for the Church that the utmost care be taken with regard to ordinations' (*The Cost of Discipleship*, tr. R. H. Fuller; London; SCM Press, 1959, p. 264).

Do style and good taste matter?

Before taking our leave of the Moderates, there remain two questions which deserve some brief reflection.

First, to what extent should Christian preachers pay attention to questions of style and good taste? To some degree this will depend on whether their sermons are intended to be read or to be delivered with more or less extempore freedom (bearing in mind that 'read' sermons are not essays, but oral discourses, and as such must retain the characteristics of the spoken rather than of the written word). But whatever the mode of delivery, there are, surely, two extremes to be avoided.

One is that substance and content are everything and that presentation doesn't matter. The only concern must be to give our hearers solid spiritual nourishment. On the face of things, this approach can claim the warrant of the Apostle Paul, who disclaimed any attempt to preach in the 'enticing words of human wisdom' (1 Cor. 1:17) or to adopt the rhetorical techniques of the 'super apostles' so admired by the Christians of Corinth. He chose, instead, to preach in words taught by the Holy Spirit (1 Cor. 2:13); and it is certainly preferable that we preach 'Christ crucified' with 'poor, lisping, stammering tongues' than that we preach our own wisdom in a style which will commend itself to literary critics. Besides, to be fair to Blair, he did studiously avoid decorative embellishments and purple passages, and warmly commended Demosthenes because his art never drew attention to itself.

On the other hand, however, the preacher is a persuader, and there is always a price to be paid for effective persuasion. We have to earn the right to be listened to, and, as Jesus Himself pointed out, that means that we have to be as wise as serpents as well as harmless as doves (Matt. 10:16). The fisher of men is not engaging in a hobby: He longs to see a spiritual harvest. Yes, like Jesus, we are addressing the common people, but the common people, especially in a world which provides universal education, are well familiar with their own vernacular and far from impressed by bad grammar and repeated mispronunciations; and quick, too, to spot a discourse which has cost the preacher little by way of preparation. Over and above this, they are also able to appreciate beauty of language and epigrammatic forms of expression, which is why poetry can flourish even in relatively uneducated societies. In line with this, Jesus Himself made every effort to capture and to hold the attention of His audience. His well-crafted parables caught the imagination, His one-liners achieved a proverbial status which endures to the present day and, while His theology soared far beyond that of His day, such discourses as the Sermon on the Mount and the great Intercessory Prayer (John 17) are marked by a clear order and careful arrangement. The apostolic epistles carefully link together the doctrinal and the practical; and while the Bible contains overall the greatest literature the world has ever seen, it also contains gems which stand out even against such a background: the creation narrative of Genesis 1, for example; the stories of Joseph and Ruth; Mark's account of Easter Morning (Mark 16:1-8); the hymn to love in First Corinthians 13.[64] In short, the Judaeo-Christian Scriptures abound in passages, and indeed whole books, distinguished by careful composition, meticulous word-selection, memorable metaphors, compelling narrative, and immense emotional force; and, taking our cue from the Apostle Paul, we have every reason to believe that all of these are excellences inherent in words taught by the Holy Spirit.

To a lesser, but still real extent, these characteristics have also featured in Christian preaching down the ages. Admittedly, most sermons (including, I am sure, 'the greatest sermon ever preached') have been irretrievably lost. They were not aimed at posterity, but at their own time and place. But a sufficient number have survived to enable us to see that such Fathers as Ambrose, Gregory of Nyssa, Augustine, and Chrysostom laboured in preparation; and the same was true of the Protestant pulpit. The Puritans were 'painful' (painstaking) preachers, and so too in their own very different ways were men like Robert Bruce, John Wesley, Jonathan Edwards, Thomas Chalmers, C. H. Spurgeon, J. C. Ryle; such outstanding moderns as John Stott and Dr Martyn Lloyd-Jones; and evangelists like John Macdonald (a poet as well as a preacher), D. L. Moody, and Billy Graham. None ever allowed the style to trump the message or deemed it their priority to make their sermons culturally palatable, but neither did they offer the Lord or their congregations what had cost them nothing. They veritably 'laboured' in the word and doctrine (1 Tim. 5:17).

---

64. Markus Bockmuehl suggests that even the order in which the New Testament Canon is arranged suggests careful deliberation on the part of the early Church. The books are arranged neither chronologically nor by author. Instead, the order keeps the books of the fourfold gospel together, it begins with the virgin birth, and it ends with the New Heaven and the New Earth (*Seeing the Word: Refocusing New Testament Study;* Grand Rapids: Baker, 2006, p. 111).

Blair, as we saw, made lucidity his priority, and we would do well to follow him. But this quality doesn't stand alone. The Cross will always give offence, but we have no right to add to it by confusing reliance on the Holy Spirit with a disregard for grammar, diction, and the accepted rules of composition and the principles of effective public speaking. We have to win the attention and interest of our hearers, and that means discourses marked by unity of theme, orderly development, and the most felicitous language within our compass. In the struggle towards such a standard each of us is hampered by our own personal limitations, but none of us should be ashamed to learn from those greatly used by God in the past, while making due allowance for the difference in time and place.

Moderatism and liberalism

Finally, what is the link, if any, between Moderatism and the liberalism which came to dominate Scottish Christianity in the late nineteenth century, and has continued to dominate it ever since? It is certainly true that in liberalism the Moderate coolness towards the confessional standards of the Kirk came to full fruition, leading to denial of such biblical miracles as the virgin birth and the resurrection of Christ. At the same time, belief in Jesus as God incarnate gave way to the view that He was no more than the ideal embodiment of Europe's bourgeois religion; and the idea that sin could be washed away by the blood of Christ's self-sacrifice was deplored as immoral and, indeed, disgusting. Such a repudiation of confessional orthodoxy went far beyond the mere 'moderation' of men like Robertson, Blair and Carlyle, and grew from a different stock. Instead of being rooted in a lack of enthusiasm for the popular religion, Scottish liberalism grew from the radically negative biblical criticism which was propounded by nineteenth-century German scholarship, and unquestioningly endorsed by Friedrich Schleiermacher (1768–1834), Albrecht Ritschl (1822–1889), and Adolph von Harnack (1851–1930), the leading architects of liberal Protestantism.[65] From the moment that such radical biblical criticism found a home in Scotland's theological colleges, her religion, firmly based on the principle of *sola scriptura*, was in mortal peril.

---

65. Karl Barth and neo-orthodoxy also exercised a significant influence on twentieth century Scottish Christianity but, although he distanced himself theologically from Schleiermacher and Harnack, Barth never questioned the school of biblical criticism which continued to dominate European theology. Neither did he have any sympathy with Reformed Confessionalism.

But it wasn't the Moderates who first introduced it to Scotland, but evangelicals such as A. B. Davidson, William Robertson Smith, and George Adam Smith, all of them ministers of the Free Church of Scotland. By the close of the century, their views had taken over all of Scotland's theological colleges and Divinity faculties, and from there they spread into the life-stream of every major denomination, with dire consequences for Presbyterian Confessionalism. This was not a case of one doctrine, or even a cluster of doctrines, becoming suspect in the light of 'the assured results of modern criticism'. It was a case of Scottish Christianity surrendering its Rule of Faith, and being left, without rudder or compass, to the mercy of the winds of theological and religious pluralism. What began with reservations about predestination would end with root-and-branch rejection of the ethics of Jesus, endorsement of same-sex marriage, and even denial of the binary distinction between a man and a woman.

Moderatism's only contribution to this was that it had sown the seeds of contempt for Scotland's native theology, leaving the field wide open to the allure of German scholarship. Whereas the Moderate *literati* had been obsessed with literary fame, nineteenth-century evangelicals came to be increasingly focused on academic promotion (a tendency stimulated by the need to staff the growing number of theological colleges), and time spent at a German university became an indispensable detail on the CV of ambitious young ministers. Eventually, many Scottish pulpits were left with nothing to preach but their doubts, and forced to justify their existence by majoring on 'youth work' and social compassion. Each of these is worthy of praise in its own right, but neither can compensate for the absence of the Cross-centred message of God's redeeming love. By the time a church's creed has shrunk to, 'Thou shalt have a food-bank,' it has lost its Christian savour.

Yet, like the poor, Moderatism, defined as a mood, is always with us, in evangelical denominations as well as liberal ones, and in ministers of evangelical conviction as well as in ministers who deplore what they dismiss as fundamentalism. By the time they leave their seminaries or theological colleges, the enthusiasm that originally fired many Divinity students has already begun to grow cold. In the case of others, the routine of parish ministry, coupled with the lack of 'success', quickly has the same effect. Every one of us knows the danger. The commitment, passion, and zeal have gone; preaching has lost its joy and biblical study its attraction, the great Christian doctrines have ceased to thrill, the Greek New Testament has been closed never to be opened again, and the thought of perishing souls has become less and less of a burden. Arrangements which are manifestly not working are left undisturbed: 'they'll see me out.' Instead of reaching out to the community, we offer the defence, 'Everyone knows where the church is, and they're all welcome.' What was once a sensitive social conscience has given way to the attitude described by the patriarch, Job, 'In the thought of one who is at ease, there is contempt for misfortune' (Job 12:5): the troubles of the poor are their own fault. And at the end, we are so weary of the work that retirement is taken at the first opportunity.

It is fair to say that 'moderation' in this sense is the greatest danger we face as ministers. But if there are many instances of pastor-preachers losing the zeal of their early years, there are also, thank God, instances of Moderates becoming enthusiasts. Here we have only to recall Thomas Chalmers. In his early years in the ministry, his mind was firmly set on distinction in the scientific and academic world, to the extent that in a pamphlet written in 1805 he boldly declared that one day a week was quite sufficient to perform the duties of a clergyman, leaving the other five days to be devoted to his favourite pursuit: in his case the study of mathematics.[66] But God intervened and filled his heart instead with a passion for 'the Christian good of Scotland': a passion with which he infected thousands of others.

But that is another story.

---

66. The pamphlet was 'resurrected' in the course of a General Assembly debate on pluralities twenty years later. Responding to the intervention, Chalmers declared, 'Alas! Sir, so I thought in my ignorance and pride.' His speech closed with a memorable peroration: 'Strangely blinded that I was! What, Sir, is the object of mathematical science? Magnitude and the proportions of magnitude. But, then, Sir, I had forgotten two magnitudes – I thought not of the littleness of time – I recklessly thought not of the greatness of eternity.' (William Hanna, *Memoirs of the Life and Writings of Thomas Chalmers, D.D. LL.D.,* 4 Vols, Edinburgh: Constable, 1851, Vol. 3, pp. 77-8. Cf. Vol. 1, pp. 91-4).

Bibliography

Armstrong, Brian G. *Calvinism and the Amyraut Heresy: Protestant Scholasticism and Humanism in Seventeenth-Century France* (Eugene, Oregon: Wipf & Stock, 2004).

Bavinck, Herman. *The Certainty of Faith* (1901. English translation, Potchefstroom: Institute for Reformational Studies, 1998).

Baxter, Richard. *Universal Redemption of Mankind, by the Lord Jesus Christ* (London: 1694).

Baxter, Richard. *Catholic Theologie: Plain, Pure, Peaceable, for Pacification of the Dogmatical Word-Warriors* (London: 1675).

Beaton, Donald. *Noted Ministers of the Northern Highlands* (Inverness: Northern Counties Publishing Company, 1929).

Beaton, Donald. 'The Marrow of Modern Divinity and the Marrow Controversy' (*Records of the Scottish Church History Society*, Vol. 1, 1926).

Blair, Hugh. *Sermons by Hugh Blair, D. D.* (5 Vols, London, 1777–1801).

Bonar, Horatius. *Catechisms of the Scottish Reformation* (London: Nisbet, 1866).

Boston, Thomas. *Human Nature in its Fourfold State,* (Banner of Truth Trust, London, 1964).

Boston, Thomas. *The Complete Works of the Late Rev. Thomas Boston, Ettrick*, 12 vols., ed. Samuel M'Millan (Aberdeen: 1848–52. Reprinted Stoke -on-Trent: Tentmaker Publications, 2002).

Boston, Thomas. *Memoirs of the Life, Times, and Writings of Thomas Boston of Ettrick. Written by Himself* (1776. New edition, Glasgow: John McNeilage, 1899).

Broadie, Alexander. Introduction to *The Cambridge Companion to the Scottish Enlightenment*, 2nd edition, eds. Alexander Broadie and Craig Smith (Cambridge: Cambridge University Press, 2019).

Brown, John. *An Apologetical Relation of the Particular Sufferings of the Faithful Ministers and Professors of the Church of Scotland since August 1660* (Rotterdam, 1665. Reprinted in *The Presbyterian's Armoury*, Edinburgh: Ogle and Oliver and Boyd, 1846).

Brown, John, of Wamphray. *The Life of Justification Opened* (Holland, 1695).

Brown, John, of Whitburn. *Gospel Truth Accurately Stated and Vindicated by the Reverend Messrs James Hog, Thomas Boston, Ebenezer and Ralph Erskine* (Edinburgh, 1817).

Buchanan, James. *The Doctrine of Justification: An Outline of its History in the Church and of its Exposition in Scripture* (1867. Reprinted London: Banner of Truth, 1961).

Cairns, John. *Memoir of John Brown, D.D.* (Edinburgh: Edmonston and Douglas, 1860).

The Autobiography of Alexander Carlyle of Inveresk 1722–1805, ed. John Hill Burton (Edinburgh: T. N. Foulis, 1910).

Carlyle, Thomas. *Reminiscences*, edited with an Introduction and Notes by K. J. Fielding and Ian Campbell (Oxford: Oxford University Press, 1997).

Chalmers, Thomas. *Institutes of Theology* (2 Vols., Edinburgh: Thomas Constable, 1856).

Clark, Ian D. L. 'From Protest to Reaction: the Moderate Regime in the Church of Scotland, 1752–1805' in *Scotland and the Age of Improvement* (ed. N. T. Phillipson and Rosalind Mitchison; Edinburgh: Edinburgh University Press, 1970).

Clifford, Alan C. *Atonement and Justification: English Evangelical Theology 1640–1790* (Oxford: Clarendon Press, 1990).

Clifford, Alan C. (ed.). *Christ for the World: Affirming Amyraldianism* (Norwich: Charenton Reformed Publishing, 2007).

Cooper, James. *Confessions of Faith and Formulas of Subscription in the Reformed Churches of Great Britain and Ireland especially in the Church of Scotland* (Glasgow: Maclehose, 1907).

Cumming, J. Elder. *Holy Men of God from St. Augustine to Yesterday* (London: Hodder and Stoughton, 1893).

Cunningham, William. *The Reformers and the Theology of the Reformation* (Edinburgh: T. and T. Clark, 1862).

Daiches, David. *God and the Poets: the Gifford Lectures, 1983* (Oxford: Clarendon Press, 1984).

Daiches, David. 'The Scottish Enlightenment,' in David Daiches, Peter Jones and Jean Jones (eds.). *The Scottish Enlightenment 1730–1790: A Hotbed of Genius* (Edinburgh: The Saltire Society, 1996).

Devine, T. M. *The Scottish Nation 1700–2000* (London: Penguin Press, 1999).

Dickinson, William Croft and Donaldson, Gordon (eds.). *A Source Book of Scottish History*, Vol. III (2nd. Edition, Edinburgh: Thomas Nelson, 1961).

Dickson, David. *Select Practical Writings of David Dickson* (Edinburgh: Free Church of Scotland, 1845).

Dictionary of Scottish Church History and Theology, Eds. Nigel M. De S. Cameron, David F. Wright, David C. Lachman, Donald E. Meek (T&T Clark, 1993).

Drummond, Andrew L. and Bulloch, James. *The Church in Victorian Scotland 1843–1874* (Edinburgh: Saint Andrew Press, 1975).

Dunlop, A. Ian. *William Carstares and the Kirk by Law Established* (Edinburgh: Saint Andrew Press, 1967).

Durham, James. *Commentary upon the Book of the Revelation* (1658. Reprinted Pennsylvania: Old Paths Publications, 2000).

Edwards, Jonathan. *The Works of Jonathan Edwards*, 2 vols. 1834 (Reprinted Edinburgh: Banner of Truth Trust, 1974).

Erskine, Ebenezer. *Sermons and Discourses upon the Most Important and Interesting Subjects* (4 Vols; Edinburgh: 1761).

Ferguson, David and Elliott, Mark W. *The History of Scottish Theology, Volumes I-III* (Oxford: Oxford University Press, 2019).

Ferguson, Sinclair B. *The Whole Christ: Legalism Antinomianism and Gospel Assurance – Why the Marrow Controversy Still Matters* (Wheaton: Crossway, 2016).

Fisher, Edward. *The Marrow of Modern Divinity* (London, 1645. Reprinted with Notes by the Rev. Thomas Boston, 1726).

_____. *The Marrow of Modern Divinity* (Geanies House, Ross-shire: Christian Focus Publications, 2009).

Fraser, Donald. *The Life and Diary of the Reverend Ebenezer Erskine of Stirling, Father of the Secession Church* (Edinburgh: William Oliphant, 1831).

Fraser, Donald. *The Life and Diary of the Reverend Ralph Erskine of Dunfermline* (Edinburgh: William Oliphant, 1834).

Fraser, James. *A Treatise on Justifying Faith* (Edinburgh: 1st edition 1722; 2nd edition with Appendix, 1749).

Fraser, James. *Memoirs of the Rev. James Fraser of Brea (Written by Himself), with Introductory Note by Rev. Alexander Whyte* (Edinburgh: The Religious Book and Tract Society, 1889).

Fraser, James. *The Lawfulness and Duty of Separation from Corrupt Ministers and Churches Explained and Vindicated* (Edinburgh, 1744).

Gattis, Lee. *Cornerstones of Salvation: Foundations and Debates in the Reformed Tradition* (Welwyn Garden City: EP Books, 2017).

Gib, Adam. *A Display of the Secession Testimony* (2 Vols, Edinburgh, 1774).

Gib, Adam. *Kaina ka Palaia: Sacred Contemplations in Three Parts* (Philadelphia, 1788).

Gibson, David and Gibson, Jonathan (eds.). *From Heaven He Came and Sought Her* (Wheaton: Crossway, 2013).

Gillespie, George. *A Treatise of Miscellany Questions* (1639. Reprinted in *The Presbyterian's Armoury;* 3 Vols., Edinburgh, 1846).

Gray, Andrew. *The Works of the Reverend and Pious Andrew Gray* (Aberdeen: George King, 1839).

Grundy, Isobel. 'Restoration and Eighteenth Century' in Pat Rogers, ed., *The Oxford Illustrated History of English Literature;* Oxford (Oxford University Press, 1987).

Hadow, James. *The Antinomianism of the Marrow of Modern Divinity Detected* (Edinburgh, 1721).

Halyburton, Thomas. *An Essay concerning the Nature of Faith; or the Ground on which Faith Assents to the Scriptures* (Edinburgh, 1714).

Halyburton, Thomas. *Natural Religion Insufficient and Revealed Necessary to Man's Happiness in his Present State; or, A Rational Enquiry into the Principles of the Modern Deists* (Edinburgh, 1714).

Halyburton, Thomas. *The Works of the Rev. Thomas Halyburton, with an Essay on his Life and Writings by the Rev. Robert Burns, Paisley* (Glasgow: Blackie and Son, 1833).

Hamilton, Ian. *The Erosion of Calvinist Orthodoxy: Seceders and Subscription in Scottish Presbyterianism* (Edinburgh: Rutherford House, 1990).

_____. *The Erosion of Calvinist Orthodoxy: Drifting from the Truth in confessional Scottish Churches* (Fearn, Ross-shire: Christian Focus Publications, 2010).

Hanna, William. *Memoirs of the Life and Writings of Thomas Chalmers* (4 Vols., Edinburgh: Thomas Constable, 1851–52).

Hewison, James King. *The Covenanters: A History of the Church in Scotland from the Reformation to the Revolution* (2 vols., Glasgow: John Smith, 1913).

Hog, Thomas. *The Banished Minister; or, Scenes in the Life of Thomas Hog of Kiltearn (1654–1692)* (Edinburgh, 1756).

Hogg, James. *The Private Memoirs and Confessions of a Justified Sinner* (1824. Reprinted Edinburgh: Canongate, 1994, with an Introduction and Notes by David Groves).

Innes, Alexander Taylor. *The Law of Creeds in Scotland: A Treatise on the Legal Relation of Churches in Scotland, Established and Not Established, to their Doctrinal Confessions* (Edinburgh: William Blackwood, 1867).

Kennedy, John. *The Days of the Fathers in Ross-shire* (1861. Reprinted Inverness: Christian Focus Publications, 1979).

Kirk, James (ed.). *The Second Book of Discipline* (Edinburgh: Saint Andrew Press, 1980).

Lachman, David C. *The Marrow Controversy: An Historical and Theological Analysis* (Edinburgh: Rutherford House, 1988).

Landreth, P. *The United Presbyterian Theological Hall, in its Changes and Enlargements for One Hundred and Forty Years* (Edinburgh: William Oliphant, 1876).

Macdonald, M. *The Covenanters in Moray and Ross* (Inverness: Melven Brothers, 1892).

MacEwen, A. R. *The Erskines* (Edinburgh: Oliphant, Anderson and Ferrier, 1900).

Macinnes, John. *The Evangelical Movement in the Highlands of Scotland 1688–1800* (Aberdeen: The University Press, 1951).

Mackenzie, Robert. *John Brown of Haddington* (1918. Reprinted London: Banner of Truth, 1964).

Maclean, Donald. *The Literature of the Scottish Gael* (Edinburgh: William Hodge and Company, 1912).

Macleod, Donald. 'Scottish Calvinism: A Dark, Repressive Force?' in the *Scottish Bulletin of Evangelical Theology,* Vol. 19, No. 2 (2001).

Macleod, John. *Scottish Theology in relation to Church History since the Reformation* (1943. Second edition 1946, reprinted Edinburgh: Banner of Truth Trust, 2015).

Macpherson, John. *The Doctrine of the Church in Scottish Theology* (Edinburgh: Macniven and Wallace, 1903).

Marshall, Andrew. *The Catholic Doctrine of Redemption Vindicated; or, Modern Views of the Atonement, Particularly Those of Dr. Wardlaw, Examined and Refuted* (Edinburgh: William Oliphant, 1844).

McCosh, James. *The Scottish Philosophy: Biographical, Expository, Critical, from Hutcheson to Hamilton* (London: Macmillan 1875).

McCulloch, Diarmaid. *Thomas Cranmer: A Life* (New Haven and London: Yale University Press, 1996).

McIntyre, D. M. 'First Strictures on *The Marrow of Modern Divinity*' (*Evangelical Quarterly*, 10 [1938].

M'Crie, Thomas. *Account of the Controversy respecting the Marrow of Modern Divinity*, Vol XXX, No. VIII (1831) to Vol. I, No. II (New Series, 1832).

Memoirs of Mrs William Veitch, Mr Thomas Hog of Kiltearn, Mr Henry Erskine, and Mr John Carstairs (Edinburgh: Free Church of Scotland, 1846).

Millar, Hugh. *My Schools and Schoolmasters* (Edinburgh: Nimmo, 1869).

Miller, Hugh. *The Headship of Christ and the Rights of the Christian People* (4th edition, Edinburgh: Nimmo, 1870).

Minutes of the Sessions of the Westminster Assembly of Divines, ed. Alex. F. Mitchell and John Struthers (Edinburgh: Blackwood and Sons, 1874).

Moore, Jonathan D. *English Hypothetical Universalism: John Preston and the Softening of Reformed Theology* (Grand Rapids: Eerdmans, 2007).

Morrison, John. *The Extent of the Atonement* (London: Hamilton, Adams and Co., 1882).

Muller, Richard A. *Post-Reformation Reformed Dogmatics: The Rise and Development of Reformed Orthodoxy* (Grand Rapids: Baker Academic, Volume One, Second Edition, 2003).

Murray, John. *Principles of Conduct* (London: Tyndale Press, 1957).

Murray, John. *The Epistle to the Romans: The English Text with Introduction, Exposition and Notes*, (Grand Rapids: Eerdmans, 1959).

Noll, Mark A. *The Rise of Evangelicalism: The Age of Edwards, Whitefield and the Wesleys* (Leicester: Inter-Varsity Press, 2004).

Owen, John. *The Works of John Owen* (16 Vols, London: Banner of Truth, 1965).

Parker, Gerald D. (ed.). *John Home: Douglas* (Edinburgh: Oliver and Boyd, 1972).

Polhill, Edward. *The Works of Edward Polhill* (1677. Republished Morgan, PA: Soli Deo Publications, 1998).

Riccaltoun, Robert. *A Sober Enquiry into the Grounds of the Present Differences in the Church of Scotland* (Edinburgh, 1723).

Robertson, William. *The Situation of the World at the Time of Christ's Appearance: And its Connection with the Success of His Religion, Considered* (1755. 5th edition, Edinburgh: John Balfour, 1775).

Rutherford, Samuel. *A Peaceable and Temperate Plea for Paul's Presbyterie in Scotland* (London, 1642).

Rutherford, Samuel. *A Survey of the Spiritual AntiChrist* (London 1648).

Rutherford, Samuel. *The Trial and Triumph of Faith* (1645. Reprinted Edinburgh: Free Church of Scotland, 1845).

Letters of Samuel Rutherford, ed. Andrew A. Bonar (1891. Reprinted Edinburgh: Banner of Truth Trust, 1984).

Ryken, Philip Graham. *Thomas Boston as Preacher of the Fourfold State* (Edinburgh: Rutherford House, 1999).

Sage, Donald. *Memorabilia Domestica; or Parish Life in the North of Scotland* (1889; 2nd edition, Wick: William Rae, 1899).

Sher, Richard B. *Church and University in the Scottish Enlightenment: The Moderate Literati of Edinburgh*; Edinburgh: University Press, Classic Edition, 2015.

Shields, Alexander. *A Hind Let Loose: an Historical Representation of the Testimonies of the Church of Scotland* (Utrecht: 1687).

Smeaton, Oliphant. *Principal James Morison: The Man and his Work* (Edinburgh: Oliver and Boyd, 1901).

Smitten, Jeffrey R. *The Life of William Robertson: Minister, Historian, and Principal* (Edinburgh: University Press, 2017).

Stewart, Alexander and J. Kennedy Cameron. *The Free Church of Scotland 1843–1910: A Vindication* (1910. Reprinted Edinburgh: Knox Press [Edinburgh], 1989).

Stewart, Dugald. *Account of the Life and Writings of William Robertson* (Edinburgh, 1801. Republished Collingwood, Victoria: Trieste Publishing Company, 2017).

Stuart, Moody A. *Recollections of the Late John Duncan, LL.D.* (Edinburgh: Edmoston and Douglas, 1872).

Torrance, Thomas F. *Scottish Theology from John Knox to John McLeod Campbell* (Edinburgh: T&T Clark, 1996).

Traill, Robert. *A Vindication of the Protestant Doctrine of Justification from the Unjust Charge of Antinomianism* (Edinburgh: Fleming, 1730).

Turretin, Francis. *Institutes of Elenctic Theology*, tr. George Musgrave Giger, ed. James T. Dennison, Jr., (Phillipsburg: P&R Publishing, 3 Vols, 1992–97).

Van Dixhoorn, Chad (ed.). *The Minutes and Papers of the Westminster Assembly 1643-1652* (5 Vols., Oxford: Oxford University Press, 2012).

Walker, James. *The Theology and Theologians of Scotland 1560–1750* (Second Edition revised, 1888. Reprinted Edinburgh: Knox Press [Edinburgh], 1982).

Wardlaw, Ralph. *Discourses on the Nature and Extent of the Atonement of Christ* (Glasgow: Maclehose, 2nd edition, 1844).

Wellwood, Sir Henry Moncrieff. *Account of the Life and Writings of John Erskine, D. D.* (Edinburgh: Constable, 1818).

Whyte, Alexander. *James Fraser, Laird of Brea* (Edinburgh: Oliphant, Anderson and Ferrier, 1911).

Witsius, Herman. *The Economy of the Covenants between God and Man* (2 Vols., tr. William Crookshank, 1822. Reprinted 1990 with *Introduction* by J. I. Packer; Escondido, California: The den Dulk Christian Foundation).

Wodrow, Robert. *The Correspondence of the Rev. Robert Wodrow*, Vol. 1, ed. Thomas M'Crie (Edinburgh: Wodrow Society, 1842).

Wright, David F. *What has Infant Baptism done to Baptism? An Enquiry at the End of Christendom* (Milton Keynes: Paternoster, 2005).

INDEX

Other books by Donald Macleod ...

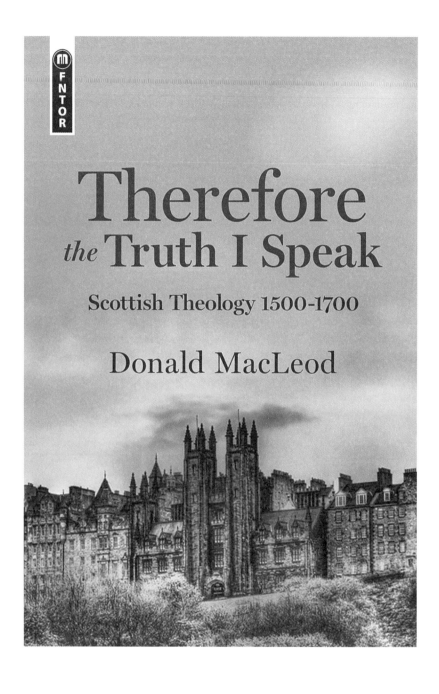

Therefore *the* **Truth I Speak**

Scottish Theology 1500-1700

Donald MacLeod

Therefore the Truth I Speak
Scottish Theology 1500 – 1700
Donald Macleod

- Historical theological study
- Foundation of reformed theology
- By one of Scotland's leading theologians

The Scottish church was forever altered by the arrival of the Reformation in the sixteenth century. Its legacy endured, and provoked a flurry of theological re–examinations which form the foundation for much of our modern understanding of Reformed Theology. In this informed and accessible historical study, Donald MacLeod, one of Scotland's current leading theologians, looks to the past to assess the impact of prominent theologians of the sixteenth and seventeenth centuries, always with an eye to demonstrating how their writings speak to contemporary challenges facing the Church today.

ISBN: 978-1-5271-0241-5

THE TRINITY AND THE
FELLOWSHIP OF GOD'S PEOPLE

30th
Anniversary Edition

Shared Life

Donald Macleod

Shared Life
The Trinity and the Fellowship of God's People
Donald Macleod

- 30th anniversary edition
- Faithful to Scripture
- One of Britain's most prominent theologians

Donald Macleod's faithful insight into what Scripture has to say about the Godhead is priceless, as relevant now as when it was first published. This 30th anniversary edition has been newly typeset and has a new cover, and will be an invaluable resource to a new generation of readers. Macleod argues that our understanding of the Trinity matters because 'it is the model for the way we should live, particularly in our relations with one another.' The relationship between Father, Son and Spirit is laid out in Scripture, and although fully grasping the concept of this divine mystery will always be beyond us, we can understand it better.

ISBN: 978-1-5271-1069-4

Christian Focus Publications

Our mission statement –

STAYING FAITHFUL

In dependence upon God we seek to impact the world through literature faithful to His infallible Word, the Bible. Our aim is to ensure that the Lord Jesus Christ is presented as the only hope to obtain forgiveness of sin, live a useful life and look forward to heaven with Him.

Our Books are published in four imprints:

CHRISTIAN
FOCUS

popular works including biographies, commentaries, basic doctrine and Christian living.

CHRISTIAN
HERITAGE

books representing some of the best material from the rich heritage of the church.

MENTOR

books written at a level suitable for Bible College and seminary students, pastors, and other serious readers. The imprint includes commentaries, doctrinal studies, examination of current issues and church history.

CF4•K

children's books for quality Bible teaching and for all age groups: Sunday school curriculum, puzzle and activity books; personal and family devotional titles, biographies and inspirational stories – Because you are never too young to know Jesus!

Christian Focus Publications Ltd,
Geanies House, Fearn, Ross-shire,
IV20 1TW, Scotland, United Kingdom.
www.christianfocus.com